RESEARCH IN EXPERIMENTAL ECONOMICS

Volume 1 • 1979

RESEARCH IN EXPERIMENTAL ECONOMICS

A Research Annual

Editor: VERNON L. SMITH
*College of Business and
Public Administration
University of Arizona*

VOLUME 1 • 1979

JAI PRESS INC.
Greenwich, Connecticut

Copyright © 1979 JAI PRESS INC.
165 West Putnam Avenue
Greenwich, Connecticut 06830
All rights reserved. No part of this publication may be reproduced, stored on a retrieval system, or transmitted in any form or by any means, electronic, mechanical, photocopying, filming, recording or otherwise without prior permission in writing from the publisher.

ISBN NUMBER: 0-89232-030-3

Manufactured in the United States of America

CONTENTS

AN EXPERIMENTAL ANALYSIS OF DECISION MAKING
PROCEDURES FOR DISCRETE PUBLIC GOODS: A CASE
STUDY OF A PROBLEM IN INSTITUTIONAL DESIGN
    John Ferejohn, Robert Forsythe and Roger Noll   1

INCENTIVE COMPATIBLE EXPERIMENTAL PROCESSES FOR
THE PROVISION OF PUBLIC GOODS
    Vernon L. Smith   59

VOLUNTEER ARTIFACTS IN EXPERIMENTS IN ECONOMICS:
SPECIFICATION OF THE PROBLEM AND SOME INITIAL DATA
FROM A SMALL-SCALE FIELD EXPERIMENT
    John H. Kagel, Raymond C. Battalio and James M. Walker   169

ON THE THEORY AND PRACTICE OF OBTAINING UNBIASED
AND EFFICIENT SAMPLES IN SOCIAL SURVEYS AND
EXPERIMENTS
    Carl Morris, Joseph P. Newhouse and Rae Archibald   199

LABOR SUPPLY BEHAVIOR OF ANIMAL WORKERS:
TOWARDS AN EXPERIMENTAL ANALYSIS
    Raymond C. Battalio, John H. Kagel and Leonard Green   231

INTERTEMPORAL COMPETITIVE EQUILIBRIUM: ON FURTHER
EXPERIMENTAL RESULTS
    Arlington W. Williams   255

SEALED-BID AUCTIONS: EXPERIMENTAL RESULTS AND
APPLICATIONS
    Meyer W. Belovicz   279

ON THE NUMBER OF TYPES OF MARKETS WITH TRADE IN
MONEY: THEORY AND POSSIBLE EXPERIMENTATION
    Martin Shubik   339

THE USE OF INDEPENDENTLY SCALED UTILITY FUNCTIONS
IN THE EXPERIMENTAL APPLICATIONS OF GAME THEORY
    Rudy V. Nydegger   361

AN EXPERIMENTAL ANALYSIS OF DECISION MAKING PROCEDURES FOR DISCRETE PUBLIC GOODS: A CASE STUDY OF A PROBLEM IN INSTITUTIONAL DESIGN

John Ferejohn, Robert Forsythe, and
Roger Noll, CALIFORNIA INSTITUTE OF TECHNOLOGY

I. INTRODUCTION

In the spring of 1974, the American network of noncommercial television stations used a decentralized market mechanism to acquire nearly half of the programs that were broadcast over the national network during the 1974–1975 television season. This mechanism, called the Station Program Cooperative (SPC), provides the motivation for the research reported in this paper. The SPC is a decentralized market mechanism for acquiring discrete public goods. A television program is a public good in the sense that its production costs and, for the most part, distribution costs are independent of the number of stations in the network that broadcast it. Programs are discrete public goods in that they are not offered in continuously variable amounts and qualities. Instead, prospective producers propose programs of a fixed duration, format, and composition that with few exceptions are either accepted or rejected as proposed to the network. Finally, individual stations can be excluded from participation in the network exhibition of a program, although the costs of enforcing exclusion might be quite high. To date, PBS has relied upon stations not to use programs that they had not participated in purchasing and has adopted no formal enforcement mechanism. The problem facing the member stations of the noncommercial network is to devise a "satisfactory" decision-making institution for selecting the programs to be distributed by the network.

The ultimate objective of the research reported in this paper is to provide normative judgments about alternative institutions that might be adopted by noncommercial television stations, or, indeed, by any other collectivity that sought to acquire discrete public goods when exclusion is possible. The method employed is to use the tools of theoretical and experimental microeconomics to design an institution that is regarded as workable and desirable by its users in practical applications.

The first step in attacking this problem is to specify as completely as possible the important technical features of the practical problem to be solved and the normative criteria that members of the collectivity would employ to evaluate a decision-making process. Section II contains a detailed discussion of the SPC that addresses these issues.

Another necessary part of the analysis is to develop candidate institutions that might be adopted by the collectivity. A natural place to start this analysis is to extract institutional designs from the existing theoretical literature on the public goods problem, especially the recent literature on decentralized, market-like mechanisms that avoid the free-rider problem. While this literature is helpful, most of the work to date has dealt with the problem of identifying efficient institutions for acquiring either a single discrete public good or a set of public goods from an activity with continuously variable inputs and output. Unfortunately, none of the solutions to the free-rider problem that have been proposed in the literature offers much guidance to the problem of devising an alternative to the SPC. Section III contains the reasons why this is so, as well as a summary of additional theoretical work that we have done on the problem of acquiring discrete public goods and a description of a decision-making procedure that is based on this work and therefore that for theoretical reasons appears to be a strong candidate as an alternative to the SPC.

Of course, theoretical arguments that abstract from information and transaction costs are insufficient as a basis for making a normative judgment about alternative institutions. Decentralized mechanisms for acquiring numerous public goods make nontrivial informational demands upon participants which can have an important effect on their performance. Section IV deals with the problem of designing small-group experiments to test the operational characteristics of the alternatives. Section V presents the results of these experiments.

The conclusions derived from the work reported here are presented in section VI. An important observation to be inferred from the experimental analysis is that a highly desirable characteristic of a decentralized decision-making procedure is to reduce relatively rapidly the complexity of the information faced by a participant. Because the SPC succeeds in rapidly shrinking the range of possible outcomes of the process as it progresses, it performs well in comparison with the alternatives even though it is known to contain design features that create important inefficiencies.

II. THE SPC

The participants in the SPC are approximately 150 managers of public television systems across the United States. Because some licensees operate several stations, these 150 managers make programming decisions for approximately 250 stations. The SPC is managed by the Public Broadcasting Service (PBS), which is the organization responsible for the technical management of the noncommercial television network and for scheduling the programs that are distributed over it.

Each noncommercial television licensee has several potential sources of programs. The most important source is PBS, which provides nearly all of the nationally distributed programs. PBS in turn acquires about half of its programs through the SPC, while the remaining programs are acquired through gifts from corporations and foundations or through grants from the Corporation for Public Broadcasting (CPB), a quasi-governmental organization that receives and disburses the annual federal appropriation for support of public broadcasting.

In addition to PBS, a station can acquire programs directly from producers, through regional networks, or from its own production facilities. Consequently, the SPC is one of several potential sources of programming, and a station can use programming funds that are not spent in the SPC in several other ways.

Except for an attempt to alter the system in 1976 that was quickly abandoned when it proved unsatisfactory, each SPC has followed essentially the same procedures. The station managers participate in a time-sharing, interactive computer system. In each round of the procedure, the center at PBS sends messages to participants about the identity and prices of the programs that remain in the market, and receives from each station a list of the programs that it wishes to purchase at the posted prices. A program is dropped when no station desires to purchase it at the last posted price (or when, with the handwriting on the wall, the producer withdraws the program). Each set of choices by the stations is used by the center to recalculate prices, and the procedure is repeated until a stable equilibrium is reached — that is, until so few changes occur in choices by stations that program prices are virtually constant in two consecutive rounds.

The mechanism for achieving a reduction in the number of programs remaining in the system is the formula for calculating the prices that each station faces for each program. Letting $i = 1, \ldots s$ index the stations and $j = 1, \ldots p$ index the programs, the price (q_{ij}) of a program j to a station i is:

$$q_{ij} = a_{ij} C_j \tag{1}$$

where C_j is the cost of the program to the network and a_{ij} is the tax share of station i for program j. The tax share is computed according to the following formula:

$$a_{ij} = \sum_{r=1}^{R} \left(\frac{b_r V_{ri}}{\sum_{k \in S_j} V_{rk}} \right) \tag{2}$$

where V_{ri} is the amount of some welfare measure possessed by station i, $r = 1, \ldots, R$ indexes the welfare measures entering the tax share computation, b_r is the weight accorded V_{ri} (with the sum of the b_r being unity), and S_j is the subset of the indices over stations that includes only stations that are participating in the purchase of program j. In the first round, S_j is assumed to contain 80 percent of all stations. In calculating a_{ij} in subsequent rounds, S_j contains station i and all other stations that in the proceding round included program j in the list of programs that they wished to purchase at the last posted prices.

In the first two markets (SPC I in 1974 and SPC II in 1975), two welfare measures were used in calculating the tax shares: the operating budget of the station and the population of the area served by the station. A weight of .8 was accorded to the budget, while population received a weight of .2. In SPC III and SPC IV, one welfare measure was used, the amount of the Community Service Grant awarded to the station. The legislation authorizing expenditures by CPB requires that a certain part of the money be passed through automatically to noncommercial stations. This fund is allocated among stations on the basis of the income of stations from sources other than the federal government, with a ceiling on the maximum grant. By using the amount of Community Service Grant received by a station, and before that the station's operating budget, the SPC has adopted what amounts to a tax system based upon ability to pay. Since both budgets and Community Service Grants are highly correlated with the population of the area served by a station, the formula also works toward equalizing the per capita tax shares of the areas served by public broadcasting.

A station is required to pay the price calculated in (1) and (2) only if the program is purchased and the station has listed the program among those that it wishes to receive. Otherwise, it neither pays for nor broadcasts the program, even if other stations eventually purchase it and it is included in the final network schedule.

The pricing mechanism used in the SPC has the property that the tax revenues raised cover the cost of a program if it is purchased. This is seen by summing the prices for program j over all stations. The q_{ij}'s corresponding to stations that do not list the program are zero. For the remaining stations, the sum of the a_{ij}'s reduces to unity because both the numerator and the denominator of the right side of (2) contain the sum of V_{ri}'s over S_j and because the b_r's sum to one. Hence the sum of the q_{ij}'s is simply unity times C_j.

Several other features of the SPC also are potentially important, and demonstrate the complexity and richness of the process. Access to the SPC market is controlled in two ways. First, program proposals must be sponsored, if not purchased, by a station or a producer that has formally been recognized by the member stations (such as Children's Television Workshop, the producer of *Sesame Street*). This amounts to a requirement that a producer find a station that is interested in a program before the program is accepted as a candidate for the SPC. Second, because the number of program proposals normally vastly exceeds the number of programs that are likely to be purchased, a pre-market voting mechanism is used to eliminate some proposals prior to the first market iteration. Over a period of a few months before the market starts, the center acts as a clearinghouse for information about program proposals. It publishes a catalogue that describes the format, talent, and producer involved in a program, and the cost, duration of an episode, and number of episodes of each proposal. It also organizes a meeting of station managers at which they can discuss program proposals with other stations and producers, and view pilots of the programs if they are available. At the end of this informational period, each station gives each program a score of 1 to 5 (5 best), and the programs with the highest scores are allowed to enter the market. This procedure normally reduces the number of proposals by about one half, leaving approximately 100 programs from which approximately 30 will be purchased.

After the SPC begins, the market iterations are divided into three categories. The first few iterations are called bidding rounds. During the bidding rounds stations are not committed to buy the programs that they include on their lists of acceptable programs, given current prices. By the same token, a program is not eliminated unless the producer withdraws it or only the producing station includes it on a purchase list.

After about five iterations, when the center decides that the obvious losers have been identified, the SPC enters elimination rounds. In these iterations, a station is committed to buy a program included in its purchase list if the price of the program does not increase for the next round and if some minimum proportion of the stations select it in that round. Thus, if enough stations vote for a program to cause it to cover costs at current prices the price in the next round will not go up, and the stations selecting the program in that round must select it again in all subsequent rounds if their numbers exceed some target. The target participation rate is successively lowered through the elimination rounds. This puts pressure on supporters of less popular (and therefore higher-priced) programs, for as the target falls the likelihood increases that the program will be declared purchased and their votes regarded as binding. As the elimination rounds proceed, a producer can guarantee the current price of his program to stations that select it by agreeing to make up the difference between production costs and revenues at current prices. Because a guarantee prevents prices from rising, stations selecting a program after a guarantee is announced are committed to buying the program. The price of a guaranteed program remains fixed at the guaranteed level until the number of stations selecting the program causes the revenues to exceed the production costs, at which time prices are lowered by reverting to the use of (1) and (2) to calculate prices.

At the end of the last elimination round, the SPC then moves to a third phase, called purchase rounds. In this phase, a program is declared purchased if its price does not increase for the next round, regardless of the number of stations selecting it. If a station adds a program to its purchase list that has already been purchased by the collectivity, the tax price of the station first goes to reduce the remaining amount of the producer guarantee, if any, and if no guarantee remains, is used to reduce the price of the program to all purchasers by recalculation of the tax prices from (1) and (2).

Table 1 summarizes the results of the first three SPC markets. The SPC converged in all three cases in about a dozen rounds. Table 2 shows the round-by-round results of the first three SPCs. The change in the number of stations selecting each program is used as a proxy for the directions of price changes. Although this estimate may be faulty when the stations that did not

Table 1. Capsulized Results of Three SPCs

	SPC I	SPC II	SPC III
Number of Program Proposals[a]	245	225	202
Number of Programs in Market	93	136	66
Number of Programs Purchased	25	38	28
Number of Rounds to Convergence	13	13	11
Number of Licensees Participating	151	153	155

[a]This number is approximate because program proposals are entered and withdrawn continuously over a period of several months.

Source: Records of SPC I, SPC II and SPC III maintained by the Public Broadcasting Service.

Table 2. Number of Programs in Market and Direction of Price Changes[a] by Round in SPC I, SPC II, and SPC III

	Round												
	1	2	3	4	5	6	7	8	9	10	11	12	13
SPC I													
# Programs in this round	93	87	73	44	40	28	26	25	25	25	25	25	25
# Dropped at End of Round	6	14	28	4	12	2	1	0	0	0	0	0	0
# Programs $\Delta q > 0$	89	59	38	26	15	3	0	0	0	0	0	0	0
# Programs $\Delta q = 0$	4	0	5	3	5	9	6	2	5	11	9	10	14
# Programs $\Delta q < 0$	0	19	30	15	20	16	20	23	20	14	16	15	11
SPC II													
# Programs in this Round	136	134	109	81	61	54	44	44	44	41	38	38	38
# Dropped at End of Round	2	25	28	20	7	10	0	0	3	3	0	0	0
# Programs $\Delta q > 0$	130	111	86	47	46	26	0	31	15	3	0	0	0
# Programs $\Delta q = 0$	1	3	4	8	1	6	1	6	9	13	6	14	21
# Programs $\Delta q < 0$	5	20	19	24	14	22	43	7	20	25	32	24	17
SPC III													
# Programs in this Round	66	57	43	39	34	33	31	30	28	28	28	—	—
# Dropped at End of Round	8	14	4	5	1	2	1	2	0	0	0	—	—
# Programs $\Delta q > 0$	57	33	19	11	7	0	5	2	0	0	[b]	—	—
# Programs $\Delta q = 0$	1	7	7	7	7	4	6	8	10	16	[b]	—	—
# Programs $\Delta q < 0$	8	17	17	21	20	29	20	20	18	12	[b]	—	—

[a]Changes in prices are estimated on the basis of the change in the number of stations selecting a program in the current and the preceeding round. The actual data might be marginally different because the actual price calculations depend upon the purchasing power, not the number, of stations that select a program. For round 1, the basis for calculating the change in prices was the difference in the number of stations picking the program in the first round and 80 percent of the total number of stations since the latter is used for calculating initial round 1 prices. The price changes refer to the effect of the current round selections on the prices of programs as posted for the next round.
[b]In SPC III, round 11 featured a "universal buy" option by which stations could receive all programs for a certain total payment. Several stations selected this option, thereby making it impossible to calculate individual program prices that would have resulted from this round.
Source: Records of SPC I, SPC II and SPC III maintained by the Public Broadcasting Service.

purchase a program in round (t−1) but did so in round t have a significantly different tax share than the stations that discontinue their purchases in round t, in practice this estimate is reasonably reliable.

As is apparent from Table 2, nearly all of the programs that are dropped are eliminated in the so-called bidding rounds when station messages are not binding and when the only mechanism for eliminating programs is loss of support owing to relative price changes. In all three SPCs, the final list of programs to be purchased was known no later than round 10, and the remaining rounds were purchase rounds in which all prices were nonincreasing. The impressive feature of the SPC is that it succeeds in selecting roughly thirty discrete public goods from about 100 proposals in approximately 12 iterations.

One factor that may contribute to the rapid convergence of the SPC is a practice of frequent interventions by the center to facilitate information flows among participants. The center actively encourages communications among member stations, indeed it even promotes the formation of cooperative groups. After some inconclusive experimenting in SPC I, the center assumed the role of facilitator for the formation of coalitions in SPC II. Called group purchases, the mechanism allows any group of three or more stations to form a coalition that through coordinated selections can lower the price of a particular program of the group's choice. The procedure is for a group of stations to propose a group purchase. The center, in coordination with the group, then works out an estimate of a realistic price reduction that might be accomplished through group action, usually setting a target percentage price reduction for the coalition to receive. There is no natural way to characterize this target since it is determined through direct negotiations among the center, the producer, and the stations that propose a group purchase. Then, the center polls the stations to determine how many would be willing to select the program in question if the price were reduced by the target amount. The center checks the responses to see whether the number of stations expressing a willingness to purchase the program is consistent with the target price. If so, the prices posted for the program in the next SPC iteration are the lowest target prices that appear feasible, rather than those based upon actual purchase lists in the preceding round.

The center has no mechanism for enforcing coalition agreements, nor does a coalition have access to information that would enable it to determine who its members are and whether they vote as promised in the next round. In SPC II, 15 group purchases were attempted after Round 5, the results of which are shown in Table 3.

Several features of Table 3 reveal interesting aspects of the behavior of the stations. First, for all programs that were eventually purchased, the number of positive responses to Question 1, which asked whether a station would be willing to buy the program at any price, was substantially lower than the

Analysis of Decision Making Procedures for Discrete Public Goods 9

Table 3. Results of Attempts at Group Purchases in SPC II Between Round 5 and Round 6

Program	# Stations Selecting Program			Change from Prices in Round 5 in.[a]		Target Price Change		# Stations Responding Yes		Price Changes Possible if Response Binding	
	Round 5	Round 6	Round 13	Round 6	Round 13	Q#2		Q#1	Q#2[b]	Q#1[a]	Q#2[c]
A	8	28	114	−71%	−93%	−93%		62	50	−87%	−85%
B	39	17	0	+131%	*	−67%		77	50	−49%	−11%
C	40	49	82	−18%	−51%	−25%		66	49	−39%	−24%
D	12	7	0	+71%	*	−75%		48	30	−75%	−38%
E	80	81	123	−1%	−35%	−20%		87	75	−8%	0%
F	41	35	120	+17%	−66%	−33%		65	53	−37%	−7%
G	26	19	0	+37%	*	−67%		48	36	−46%	−19%
H	31	27	0	+15%	*	−50%		51	39	−39%	−21%
I	40	44	127	−9%	−68%	−50%		81	70	−50%	−45%
J	14	7	0	+100%	*	−67%		49	27	−71%	−27%
K	30	22	0	+36%	*	−50%		68	56	−56%	−35%
L	24	20	73	+20%	−67%	−67%		37	35	−35%	−10%
M	39	42	106	−7%	−63%	−33%		51	49	−24%	−16%
N	36	31	109	+16%	−67%	−25%		58	51	−38%	−20%
O	32	28	49	+14%	−35%	−50%		41	39	−22%	−15%

[a] Price changes in these columns are estimates based on the percentage change in stations listing the program on their purchase lists.
[b] Question 1: "Are you interested in selecting [program title] at a price for your station that is lower than the present market price? Respond yes or no." Question 2: "Would you select [program title] at a price which is [target fraction] of the present market price? Respond yes or no."
[c] The calculations in this column are the actual price reductions, based upon the purchasing powers of the responding stations, that would have been possible according to formulas (1) and (2) in the text.
*Indicates that the program has been eliminated in an earlier round.
Source: Records of SPC II, Public Broadcasting Service.

ultimate number of stations that bought the program. Of course, 33 stations did not respond to the attempt at group purchases, but even if every non-respondent eventually purchased every program for which a group purchase was attempted, the sum of 33 and the number of positive responses to Question 1 is still less than the number eventually purchasing the program for all but two programs.

Second, only one program received as many votes in Round 6 as it received positive responses to Question 2, which asked whether stations were willing to pay a given target price for the program. On the other hand, this program was the only program for which the responses to Question 2 were sufficient to produce an estimated potential price reduction equal to the target value, assuming that everyone voted in Round 6 as they had responded to the poll.

Third, of the nine programs in Table 3 that were eventually purchased, the group purchase may have contributed to the survival of only two. Program A experienced a rather dramatic increase in support after the poll, and the poll results clearly signaled that the demand for the program might be elastic over a wide range of lower prices. Program C did not produce such dramatic results, but neither did it seek a large price reduction. In addition to being the only program that received enough support in the poll to support the price reduction hypothesized in Question 2, Program C was one of the least expensive programs in SPC II. Whereas the average program in the SPC cost in the range of $20,000 to $30,000 per hour (and the highest-quality programs cost on the order of $100,000 per hour), Program C cost approximately $6,000 per hour. In fact, the remarkable feature of Program C was that, in the final round of SPC II, nearly half of the stations still did not select the program, even though by that time its price to the average station was under $100 per program hour.

Obviously, the group purchase plan did not succeed in identifying and salvaging a significant number of programs that had elastic demand at current prices, although it may have brought a speedier demise to one or two programs that, on the basis of poll responses, were clearly destined to be losers—most notably, Program B, a relatively popular but expensive children's program that, according to the responses to Question 2, could not have come close to generating enough support to be purchased.

The failure of the group purchase mechanism is traceable to at least two possible sources. First, all 15 group purchase attempts were tried in the same round of the SPC. If the responses to each attempt were *ceteris paribus* responses, it is not surprising that programs did not receive as much support when reductions in the prices of all 15 were attempted as they received in the poll. Second, at the time the attempted group purchase was made, there were still 16 programs in the market that eventually were dropped. To the extent that programs in the group purchase attempt were substitutes for the programs that eventually were withdrawn, the ultimate support for the programs on the group purchase list could be expected to grow in later iterations. Third, because of the vast differences in the responses to Question 1 and the ultimate purchase decisions, it is possible that stations were playing strategic games in responding to the questions. Assuming that a station wanted, say, both Program D and Program E, it might have concluded that E would eventually succeed anyway but that D was in desperate trouble and voted for D but not E to do what it could to reduce the price differential between the two. A relatively large station, accounting for 2 or 3 percent of the total market, could by itself affect the difference in relative prices between these two programs by as much as 20 to 30 percent by its voting decision.

Another intervention by the center is the universal buy mechanism. All of the stations participating in the first three SPCs received matching grants for purchases of programs from a fund created by CPB and the Ford Foundation. A station received a discount on program prices, the discount being paid from the fund, up to a maximum amount for each station. This maximum was exhausted if a station purchased about 80 percent of the programs that were finally selected by the entire system.

The universal buy mechanism is offered before the last purchase round in the market. In SPC III, it allowed a station to receive all of the programs purchased in the SPC if it exhausts its matching grant fund. In SPC III, the first time the universal buy mechanism was attempted, 24 of the 155 participants already had exhausted their matching grant funds by the next to last round. When the universal buy offer was made, an additional 46 stations agreed to increase their spending up to the ceiling for the matching grants. Thus, 70 of the stations (slightly less than half) ended up buying all of the 28 programs purchased in SPC III. The additional funds collected from the universal buy were first passed on to stations that had spent more than their matching grant ceiling, then used to reduce producer guarantees that had not been eliminated in the purchase round. After eliminating all the excess of spending over matching grant ceilings and all remaining producer guarantees, approximately $15,000 was left, and this was placed into a contingency fund for special events programming that is maintained by PBS to finance coverage of fast-breaking program opportunities, primarily news events.

The universal buy option was the outgrowth of another intervention by the center after round 6 of SPC II called the benchmark target purchase. The purpose of this intervention was to try to encourage all stations to agree to buy all remaining programs in the market. At the end of Round 6, 44 programs were still in contention, and the votes of stations in Round 6 cumulated to a willingness to pay equaling 94 percent of the total costs of all the programs then in the market. The center informed the stations of this fact and proposed that stations that were spending significantly less than their ceiling for matching grants undertake a small increase in their total spending. In response to an inquiry from the center, 133 licensees expressed a willingness to spend at least their matching-grant ceiling, which was more than sufficient to generate enough revenue to buy all programs. On the basis of these encouraging results, the center reset the prices for each program to the lower price that was calculated on the basis of Round 6 purchase lists and the price that would have been obtained had the program received the votes of 80 percent of all stations. As is apparent from Table 2, this move to bring an immediate end to the SPC failed, as only 90 stations instead of 133 spent their matching-grant ceiling. Eventually six more programs were dropped which together accounted for 20 percent of the total costs of all programs still alive after Round 6.

The operation of the SPC is further complicated by the fact that the definition and costs of a program can change. Normally two or three rounds of the SPC are run over a few days, and then a hiatus of one to two weeks occurs during which time stations and producers can evaluate their positions. During these breaks, a producer has sufficient time to make a considered change in the nature of the program that has been proposed. For example, one producer in SPC II proposed two separate packages of movies. After three rounds, it was clear that the stations were unlikely to purchase both, so the producer created a new proposal that contained some of the movies from each prior proposal. This ploy almost, but not quite, succeeded. The two proposals received 30 and 33 votes, respectively, in Round 3 of SPC II. The combined offering received 51 votes in Round 4, rose to 85 votes in Round 7, but eventually died after Round 10, the last round in which programs were eliminated.

Six producers changed the number of episodes in their proposals with corresponding reductions in the cost per hour of programming. As shown in Table 4, two of the six attracted more votes in Round 4, but this is not a significant effect since 30 percent of all programs drew more votes in Round 4 than in Round 3. Nevertheless, the producer of Program A must have thought the strategy sound, for in SPC III the number of episodes was reduced from 13 to 7 during the market proceedings, and the program was purchased again by the system.

Another source of changes in program proposals during the operation of the SPC is an exogeneously determined change in the cost of a program proposal. A substantial part of the programming offered by PBS is paid for all or in part by grants from corporations and foundations. Producers with programs in the SPC are continually on the lookout for "angels" who will underwrite some of the costs of their programs. During the operation of the SPC, a producer may receive a grant, in which case the cost of the program to the SPC is immediately reduced by that amount. Of course, from (1), this immediately reduces the price of the program to each station.

Table 4. Changes in Program Proposals After Round 3 of SPC II

Program[a]	# of Episodes in Proposal[b]		# Stations Selecting Program	
	Round 3	Round 4	Round 3	Round 4
A*	26	13	26	21
N*	6	3	27	42
P	13	7	7	7
Q*	26	20	66	67
R	9	12	29	18
S	6	4	42	36

*Indicates a program that eventually was purchased.
[a] Programs A and N are the same as A and N in Table 3.
[b] Proposal R offered three more episodes at the same price. All others offered cost reductions for fewer episodes.
Sources: Records of SPC II, Public Broadcasting Service.

In SPC IV, still another complication was introduced, although only two programs took advantage of it. A producer could enter a program into the SPC with the price to each station fixed, rather than determined by the number of votes for the program. The prices had to be in the ratio of the "fair share" term in (1), but the questions of whether the program would be purchased and, if so, at what prices for participating stations took a different form.

The fixed-price mechanism is essentially the same as the pricing system for syndicated programming for commercial stations.[1] Syndicated commercial programming is national programming that is not offered over one of the three major commercial networks. Instead, the programs are sold on a station-by-station basis by an agent of the producer, either to independent stations or to network affiliates for use in time periods when the network does not supply programs or when the affiliate does not want to broadcast the network program. The price of syndicated program j to station i is usually calculated according to a formula of the form:

$$q_{ij} = c_j + a_j M_i \qquad (3)$$

where c_j and a_j are positive constants and M_i is a measure of the size of the market served by station i. In SPC IV, prices for fixed-price programs were set in the same manner, except that $c_j = 0$, M_i was equal to the Community Service Grant of the station, and a_j was calculated so that if the program received support from a target number of stations (to be negotiated between the producer and PBS, but normally in the range of 70 to 80 percent), it recovered its full costs. The producer also provided PBS with an "upset price" which is the minimum amount of revenue that the producer will accept for the program. The program is then purchased at the fixed price if the number of stations voting for it during an elimination or purchase round falls between the number required to generate the upset price and the target number. If more than the target number of stations desire the program, prices are reduced according to formulas (1) and (2) so that the producer can not earn excess profits.

The final complexity of the SPC is the possibility for late purchases. At any time after the SPC comes to an end, a station may purchase rights to whatever episodes remain to be broadcast of any program that was purchased by the SPC. Normally, the rights that are purchased by PBS are four showings in three years. Thus if a series is scheduled to run from October to March, a station, after seeing the reaction to the first few episodes in other cities, may buy the remaining first run rights plus all subsequent rerun rights to the program. Of course, the quality of a program is uncertain in the spring before it is produced, so stations have an incentive not to participate in the SPC if this option is available. Consequently, the center charges a premium for late purchases. The center first divides all programs into two classes: standard programs of lasting value and timely programs which can be expected to decline in value rapidly over time because of the nature of their content.

News and public affairs programs are in the latter category. The price for a late purchase is then governed by the last SPC market price of the program, the amount of programming remaining to be transmitted by the network, and the timeliness categorization. Table 5 shows the price structure for late purchases during the first release of a program; note particularly how the late purchase penalty rises with the amount of programing that has already been shown. In part this reflects the fact that a station that makes a

Table 5. Late Purchase Prices as Percent of SPC Price

Percent of First Release	Price as Percent of SPC Price	
Rights Remaining	Standard Program	Timely Program
91–100	105.0	105
81–90	95.0	95
71–80	92.5	85
61–70	90.0	75
51–60	87.5	65
41–50	85.0	55
31–40	82.5	45
21–30	80.0	35
11–20	77.5	25
0–10	75.0	15

Source: "SPC IV—Bulletin # 3," Public Broadcasting Service Memorandum, January 27, 1977.

late purchase can show prior episodes if they are broadcast later as reruns by the network, and in part this reflects the attempt to avoid the incentive to temper one's participation in the SPC for reasons of risk aversion. Tables similar to Table 5 are also available for purchases during subsequent releases. For standard programs, each release is assumed to account for 25 percent of the value of the program. Thus, second-release late purchase prices vary from 75 to 50 percent of the original price, depending on the proportion of second-release rights remaining.

As the preceding discussion makes clear, the SPC is an enormously complex mechanism. As a result, it is rather expensive to operate. Beginning with the review of program proposals in December of each year and concluding with the final purchase rounds in May or June, the process occupies a substantial amount of the time of center employees and managers of over 150 public broadcasting licensees for six months each year. Considering the costs of the computer system, the cost of the SPC in personnel and operating costs is probably in the range of one-half to one million dollars.[2] Considering that the total cost of all the programs purchased in the SPC runs between $15 and $20 million, the transactions costs of this market are around 5 percent.

Given the complexity and costliness of the SPC, a natural question is why the noncommercial television system continues to use it. The simple answer to the proposition is that the stations prefer the SPC to the alternatives that have thus far been conceived. Each year the question of whether to continue the SPC is discussed at the September meeting of station managers, and each year the SPC is renewed, usually with some minor alterations, by an overwhelming vote. In 1976, Profis (1977) found that of the 78 station managers who returned his questionnaire, 70 percent preferred retention of the SPC with no or minor modifications.

The deeper answer is that the alternatives have serious problems as well. One alternative is to use a syndication market, but this is undesirable for two reasons. First, the transactions costs are higher. With syndication, individual stations must still make complex decisions about which programs to purchase and agents normally extract fees of 10 to 15 percent of sales. Moreover, syndication sacrifices the advantages of networking. A network centralizes scheduling decisions, and thereby captures two kinds of scale economies: first, program promotions can be centralized since all stations have essentially the same program schedules, and second, only one central group needs to solve the scheduling problem, rather than each of the 150-odd station managers solving it independently. The last is not a trivial problem: some programs are more suitable for late audiences (mainly adults) than are others, and the audience rating of one program depends upon the type of programs that surround it in the schedule.

If syndication is inefficient, the other major alternative is to centralize programming decisions in the network, here PBS. The commercial networks make most of the programming decisions for their affiliates, and thereby avoid much of the costs of an SPC or syndication. Moreover, before SPC was introduced in 1974, public broadcasting had adopted the same model. When the federal government began providing financial support for public television programming in the late 1960s, CPB and the eastern regional network, centered in New York, operated very much like commercial networks. The centralized authorities made most of the decisions about which program proposals would receive financial support and which finished programs would be broadcast over the networks. The working model for American public television at the time was the most respected of noncommercial systems, the BBC in England.

The problem with a centralized network is twofold. First, and perhaps less importantly, it minimizes the extent to which differences in local tastes can be reflected in the programming that is offered on each station. Assuming that any network, commercial or noncommercial, is interested in achieving public popularity, centralized programming decisions reflect tastes near the mean of viewers for the nation as a whole. A decentralized system allows differences in programming by groups of stations from similar areas that differ in the tastes of their residents from the national mean. As remarked earlier, fewer than half of the noncommercial stations that belong to the national network broadcast all of the programs that are selected by the SPC; the mean number of programs purchased has run between 80 and 90 percent of the total programs that are purchased.

The second, probably more important, difficulty with centralized programming decisions is that they make the noncommercial system more vulnerable politically. The CPB Board of Directors is selected by the President of the United States, and the budget of CPB and PBS (including the grants that are passed through to the stations) is appropriated by Congress. It is natural to expect that these political leaders will be inclined to review the content of programming in making decisions about the management and financing of the system. This normal oversight function leads naturally to censorship. Politicians can be expected to take actions against controversial programming, especially if it criticizes the politicians or offends their personal tastes. In fact, this very meddling with the programming policies of the system during the early 1970s was responsible for the adoption of the SPC. Hartford Gunn, then the President of PBS, formally broke with the policies of CPB during this period and converted PBS from a largely technically oriented networking organization to a cooperative programming venture by the stations that actually was an alternative mechanism to CPB for acquiring programs. The particular issue that encouraged the stations to adopt a decentralized process was de-emphasis of news and public affairs programs by CPB, in response to expressions of dissatisfaction from the White House with the points of view being expressed by noncommercial newscasters.

Decentralized programming systems are less vulnerable to political control for two reasons. Most obviously, national politicians have no direct influence over the managerial decisions of local stations. Only coordinated actions by numerous state and local government officials could exercise the kind of influence at the local level that Congress and the President can exert at the national level. Moreover, a decentralized system provides no convenient political whipping boy. Whom can Congress or the President blame if a program is offensive—150 separate station managers? The Chairman of the Board of CPB or the President of PBS are not vulnerable, for they are only following the dictates of the stations.

The preceding discussion reveals the main purposes of the SPC—and the criteria that stations will use to judge a proposed alternative. First, the system should capture the benefits of political invulnerability that are possessed by a decentralized mechanism; therefore the place to look for alternatives is among the set of voting and market mechanisms. Second, the system should be designed with the problem of high transactions costs in mind. Because the time of station managers and computers is valuable, and because decentralized procedures for choosing from a large number of alternatives can be very time consuming, evaluation of alternative mechanisms must not ignore this important element of costs.

Also implicit in the design of the SPC are two important financial constraints. The center must not run a deficit, and the participating stations have binding maximum bounds on expenditures. An alternative procedure to the SPC must not run a deficit, and must guarantee nonbankruptcy of participants.

Subject to these caveats, the system seeks economic efficiency. Program managers, in discussing the operation of the SPC, clearly believe that it is not particularly efficient. They believe it to be biased against new program proposals and in favor of established programs, and they believe the system probably does not take great enough risks with innovative programming—although it is thought to be more risk taking than either the old centralized system or the commercial networks. Another efficiency-related concern expressed by some station managers is the possibility that the largest stations wield too great an influence on the outcome, although this seems dubious because no station accounts for more than a few percent of the purchasing power in the market.

These criteria boil down to the following technical requirements: nonbankruptcy, nondeficit of the center, rapidity of convergence, decentralized decisions, nonmanipulability, and Pareto efficiency. The remainder of the paper will discuss the properties of the SPC and its alternatives in these terms.

III. CHARACTERISTICS OF THE SPC

As mentioned in an earlier paper (1976), no systematic analysis and testing of the SPC was carried out prior to its installation. It therefore seems quite miraculous that the SPC not only has converged each time it has been employed but did so quite rapidly (in about 12 rounds), and that the final selections have been acceptable to the affiliated stations. Further, while the SPC generates incentives to misreveal preferences, successful insincere strategies seem to be quite difficult to locate and, as experimental results suggest, even more difficult to carry out.

How does the current SPC meet the criteria suggested in the previous section? For starters, it's easy to see that if a stationary point is reached both nondeficit and nonbankruptcy are satisfied. As to the remaining conditions, however, we show elsewhere (1977) that, under the hypothesis that stations exhibit Cournot behavior, the SPC has some shortcomings. First, a stationary point need not exist. Second, stationary points may or may not be Pareto optimal. Third, stationary points may exist but be impossible to reach from various initial prices. Fourth, stationary points may be unstable in the sense that small perturbations from the stationary prices may make the stationary point unreachable.

The SPC also is not incentive compatible in the following sense. In some cases, a station may have the incentive to purchase a program during the procedure even though its price exceeds the station's willingness to pay, given the information communicated by all other stations. In other words, dominant purchasing strategies generally do not exist in the procedure.

The SPC has some desirable properties as well as these deficiencies. First, in actual and experimental operation the SPC appears to terminate quite rapidly. As discussed above, the system has been modified in various ways that probably speed convergence. Although these modifications are not used in the experimental version, rapid termination still occurs.

Second, as pointed out above, participants have difficulty devising a successful strategy that entails misrevealing preferences. Station managers state that they could not see how they could significantly affect the operation of the procedure by their purchasing strategy. And, while a substantial amount of preference misrevelation was observed in the experiments, post-session discussions indicate that participants were not able to achieve desired effects from these actions and in fact usually achieved inferior allocations due to the use of devious strategies. If this result is general, as station managers gain experience in using the system they would probably learn to avoid the unsuccessful strategies that involve misrevelation.

Third, several program and station managers indicated in interviews that they thought the marketlike features of the SPC were highly desirable.

Analysis of Decision Making Procedures for Discrete Public Goods

They like the idea of making purchasing decisions at given prices and of only having to pay for programs actually purchased. Several respondents indicated that their stations serve peculiar types of audiences, that they found various programs to be valueless to them, and that they would therefore think it "unfair" to be required to pay for all programs.

Finally, it is generally believed that the decision task facing the station during the operation of the SPC is fairly easy to understand and that the stations are able to produce appropriate responses without difficulty.

Member stations report a number of dissatisfactions with the operation of the SPC. Perhaps the most frequently heard, both in interviews conducted for this study and in the studies by Profis (1977) and by Foote and Profis (1976) is that certain types of programs are disadvantaged. The usual categories mentioned are "innovative" programs, programs that are of high quality but very costly, and programs that were not purchased in the previous year.

The usual argument goes like this: In the first round of the procedure many new and/or innovative programs are put against a small list of old programs. For example, perhaps 20 in the latter category compete against 60 in the former. First-round purchases tend to spread widely over the new or innovative programs (for various reasons) while the older ones retain a stable core of loyal support. As a result, second-round prices on the new and innovative programs increase much more sharply than those on the old programs and, thus, stations switch support from new to old programs. This problem is directly linked to the fact that a station may only indicate its willingness to buy or not buy each program at a given set of prices. If a station is willing to pay some amount less than the current price, it has no normal way to communicate this information. Neither does a station which is willing to pay more than the current price have any way to signal the intensity of its preferences. Nor can a station indicate its next highest priorities at current prices should one of its current selections prove unviable. While the preceding constitutes only a story at this point, participants regard it as a potentially serious source of inefficiencies.

The data from SPC II and SPC III were examined for evidence of bias against new or innovative programs. The results are shown in Table 6. There were fewer than half as many programs in SPC III as in SPC II, and a much higher fraction of new programs were included in SPC II than were in SPC III. One would expect, therefore, that if the bias story is true fewer new programs would have been purchased in SPC II than in SPC III. The data in Table 6 do not support this expectation, although one other factor besides the number of programs in the market may account for the limited success of new programs in SPC III. The funds for matching grants fell from $10 million in SPC II to $5.5 million in SPC III. Because stations were spending more of their own money in SPC III, their behavior may have

Table 6. Success Rates of Old and New Programs in
SPC II and SPC III

	SPC II	SPC III
Number of Programs in Market:		
Total	136	66
Old[a]	20	29
New[b]	109	32
New 2nd Tries[c]	8	5
Number of Programs Purchased		
Total	38	28
Old	17	22
New	19	6
New 2nd Tries	2	0
Percent of Programs Purchased		
Total	28	42
Old	85	76
New	17	19
New 2nd Tries	25	0

[a] Programs purchased in previous SPC.
[b] New program proposals.
[c] Programs proposed in previous SPC but not purchased.

exhibited greater risk aversion. Thus, the field data are inconclusive on this point.

Apparently the major potential defects of the SPC may be grouped into two broad classes. First, coordination problems arise from the absence, in general, of dominant strategies in the SPC. Second, consistency problems arise because the price adjustments procedure may not lead to a stationary point. The next section investigates classes of institutions that are free of these deficiencies in hopes of uncovering procedures that may outperform the SPC.

IV. THE MODEL

While a considerable amount of recent research has addressed the problem of constructing decentralized decision-making institutions for efficient acquisition of public goods, none of the previously proposed mechanisms seems appropriate for the specific problem addressed here. The formal problem in institutional design that is suggested by the SPC is presented in this section as a prelude to discussing related research.

The procedure suggested in the literature can be described in the context of public television as follows. First, each station manager would communicate to the center exactly how much the station is willing to pay for each program. The center, using a rule which is public knowledge to each station manager, then determines which programs will be produced and calculates the amounts each station will be charged. These assessments are calculated on the basis of each station's budget, the production cost of each program, and the reported willingness to pay of all stations. The charge to a station need not equal the amount that it is willing to pay, and, in general, overcoming the free-rider problem requires that these two amounts are not the same.

Proceeding more formally, the following notation is employed:

S: the set of stations, $|S| = s$
P: the set of programs, $|P| = p$
$\Omega = \{0,1\}^p \times R_+^s$: the set of conceivable allocations
C_k: cost of program k
b_i: budget of station i
$\hat{\Omega} = \left\{ Z \in \Omega \mid \sum_{k=1}^{p} C_k Z_k + \sum_{k=p+1}^{p+s} Z_k \leq \sum_{i=1}^{s} b_i \right\}$: set of feasible allocations
m_i: message communicated by station i
$m^{(i)}$: (s-1)-tuple of messages communicated by all stations other than i.
$M^i(C_1, \ldots, C_p, b_1, \ldots, b_s, m^{(i)})$: Message space correspondence that gives the set of admissible messages by station i. For convenience we let $\bar{M}^i$ denote the range of $M^i(C_1, \ldots, C_p, b_1, \ldots, b_s,..)$
$\Gamma: \prod_{i=1}^{s} \bar{M}^i \to \hat{\Omega}$: a decision-making institution.

This formulation of the formal model already imposes certain requirements on the problem of institutional design. First, it requires that the set of admissible messages, M^i, depend at most on *observable* data (costs, budgets, and the messages of the other agents). Second, $F_k(m) \geq 0$ for $k = p+1, \ldots, p+s$, since the set of conceivable allocations restricts allocations of the private good to the nonnegative orthant. Finally,

$$\sum_{k=1}^{p} F_k(m) C_k \leq \sum_{i=1}^{s} b_i - \sum_{k=p+1}^{p+s} F_k(m).$$

Thus, if the quantity $b_i - F_{p+i}(m)$ is defined as the contribution of the ith station for the provision of a set of programs, the institution cannot run a deficit.

Each station is supposed to have a complete, transitive, reflexive preference relation, R_i, on Ω. The asymmetric part of R_i is denoted P_i and the symmetric part by I_i. Of particular interest is a special class of preferences, denoted by C. A preference relation R_i on Ω is in C if there is a vector $(V_1^i, V_2^i, \ldots, V_p^i)$ of nonnegative numbers such that for each $x, y \in \Omega$,

$xR_i y \rightleftarrows \sum_{j=1}^{p} x_j V_j^i + x_{p+i} \geq \sum_{j=1}^{p} y_j V_j^i + y_{p+i}$. The number V_j^i will be referred to as station i's true willingness to pay for program j.

Definition: F is nonstrategic $\rightleftarrows \forall i \in S \; \exists \; m_i \in M^i(C_1, \ldots, C_p, b_1, \ldots, b_s, m^{(i)})$ such that for each $m^{(i)} \in \bar{M}^{(i)}$, $F(m^{(i)}, m_i) R_i \; F(m^{(i)}, \bar{m}_i)$ for all $\bar{m}_i \in M^i(C_1, \ldots, C_p, b_1, \ldots, b_s, m^{(i)})$.

Thus F is nonstrategic just in the case in which each station has an admissible dominant strategy. If the dominant strategy for each agent is to express his true preference, the mechanism is said to be strongly individually incentive compatible (SIIC). Such may not be the case here, in as much as the SIIC strategy may be inadmissible [as in Green and Laffont (1976)].

Green and Laffont (1977b) have proved that if F chooses Pareto optimal allocations in the sense that for each m there is no $x \in \hat{\Omega}$ with the property that $xR_i F(m) \forall i \in S$ and $xP_j F(m)$ for at least one $j \in S$, then F is not nonstrategic. This difficulty arises from the fact that the usual definition of Pareto optimality requires that the mechanism exactly balance the budget (i.e. $\sum_{k=1}^{p} C_k F_k(m) = \sum_{i=1}^{s} (b_i - F_{p+i}(m))$), for each s-tuple of messages. In general, there is no such nonstrategic mechanism for allocating discrete public goods. The following analysis relaxes somewhat the efficiency requirement on decision-making institutions. The following definition is proposed:

Definition: x Pareto-dominates y if and only if
    (i) $x_k \neq y_k$ for some $k = 1, \ldots p$
    (ii) $xR_i y \forall i \in S$ and $xP_j y$ for some $j \in S$.

Thus one alternative Pareto dominates another whenever the first differs from the other in the list of programs chosen and the usual criterion of Pareto-domination holds. The set of maximal elements, $\bar{\Omega}$, of this binary relation on the set for which $F_{p+i}(m) \leq b_i$, for all $i \in S$, is called the *weak-efficiency* set and a decision-making institution is called *weakly efficient* if for all m, F(m) is in the weak-efficiency set.

The definition of efficiency is weakened here by requiring only that the center not run a deficit. The hope is that this provides an escape from the difficulties which arise from the need for balancing the budget. Indeed Green and Laffont (1976) have constructed a class of mechanisms that are weakly efficient and nonstrategic. In that paper, $p = 1$, and, as shown below, natural extensions of their procedures are unattractive.

The nondistributive requirement, $F_{p+i}(m) \leq b_i$ for all $i \in S$, has been added for the purposes of this application. For practical reasons, allocations must be ruled out in which a station may have more of the private good in the final allocation than it had initially; however, although they are not provided here, the proofs of Theorems 4 and 5 to follow depend upon this requirement. The implication of the nondistributive requirement of the above efficiency definition is that the usual criteria for Pareto efficiency become necessary, but not sufficient, conditions for weak efficiency. In particular, when the preferences of all stations are in the class C, each program j that is selected satisfies

$$\sum_{i=1}^{s} V_j^i > C_j.$$

Only allocation mechanisms which potentially satisfy this condition are considered, and they are defined as follows:

Definition: If $F_j(m) = 1 \Leftrightarrow \sum_i m_{ji} > C_j$, then F is called a *direct revelation mechanism*.

When speaking of these mechanisms the m_{ji} can be interpreted as a statement of the ith station's "willingness to pay" for program j.

Green and Laffont (1977a) have shown the nonexistence of weakly-efficient direct revelation SIIC mechanisms for discrete public goods when preferences are not separable. Due to this, attention will be restricted to cases in which the preferences of all stations are in the class C. Furthermore, one particular family of direct revelation mechanisms will be of particular interest, for reasons to be outlined below. Based upon the work of Groves (1973), this family will be called the Groves family (G-family) and is of the following form:

$M^i = \{m \in R^p | m \geq 0\}$
$F(m) = F_1(m)x \ldots x F_p(m)x(b_1 - t_1(m))x \ldots x(b_s - t_s(m))$
where

$$F_k(m) = \begin{cases} 1 \text{ if } \sum_{i=1}^{s} m_{ki} \geq C_k \\ 0 \text{ otherwise} \end{cases} \quad k \in P$$

and

$$t_i(m) = \sum_{k=1}^{p} F_k(m)[C_k - \sum_{j \neq i} m_{kj}] + h_i(m^{(i)}) \quad i \in S$$

where h_i is an arbitrary function.

The major theoretical results upon which the experimental research is based are as follows.

THEOREM 1: A direct revelation mechanism is SIIC if and only if it is a Groves mechanism.

PROOF: See Green and Laffont (1977a).

If the mechanism is required to satisfy nonbankruptcy ($t_i(m) \leq b_i$ for all m) and nondeficit, it is necessary to impose some constraint on the message space. To see this consider the case for which a station attaches a value (in terms of the private good) to the program which exceeds its budget. Since the liability of the station may never exceed its budget, it has an incentive to dramatically overstate its willingness to pay to insure that the program will be produced. Thus the message space must be constrained in a way that removes this difficulty.

THEOREM 2: Let $p = 1$. If $F(m)$ is a Groves mechanism and the message space is constrained such that $m_i \leq b_i$ for all $i \in S$, then each station has a dominant strategy given by $m_i = \min[v_i, b_i]$.

PROOF: See Green and Laffont (1976).

Green and Laffont then proceed to define Pareto satisfactory allocations under this message space constraint and establish that there exist some members of the Groves family which are Pareto satisfactory. When defining satisfactory states, they include the center in their lists of agents and define the utility of the center as its profit. Thus, many allocations which are not weakly efficient are Pareto satisfactory under their definition. As an extreme example, a mechanism which collects the budget of every station but does not produce any program is satisfactory but certainly not weakly efficient. This difficulty is addressed in the following result.

THEOREM 3: Let $p = 1$. If the message space is constrained such that $m_i \leq b_i$ for all $i \in S$, then there exist some members of the Groves family which are weakly-efficient.

PROOF: See Ferejohn, Forsythe and Noll (1977).

The reason that the Groves family must be restricted in Theorem 3 is that under the constraint $m_i \leq b_i$, some members fail to satisfy the non-bankruptcy and nondeficit criteria. Thus, only certain forms of the function $h_i(m^{(i)})$ are allowable. In particular, one allowable form to be used below is:

$$h_i(m^{(i)}) = \max[0, \sum_{j \neq i} m_j - (1 - \alpha^i)C]$$

where α^i is a constant defined for each station such that

$$\sum_i \alpha^i = 1.$$

An attempt to extend Theorem 3 to the case where $p \geq 2$ encounters a coordination problem. If a station's liability can not exceed its budget and the mechanism belongs to the G-family, the institution must be able to coordinate the desires of each station in such a way that the resulting allocation is in $\hat{\Omega}$. Unfortunately, this is not possible.

THEOREM 4: If $p \geq 2$ and $F(m)$ is a Groves mechanism, then F is not weakly efficient.

PROOF: See Ferejohn, Forsythe and Noll (1977).

This result raises the question whether any mechanism, not necessarily a direct revelation one, that is weakly efficient can be nonstrategic as well. The difficulty that arises here is that any rule that the center uses to resolve the coordination problem creates an incentive for strategic behavior on the part of the stations. The result may be summarized as:

THEOREM 5: If $p \geq 2$ and F is weakly efficient then F is not nonstrategic.

PROOF: See Ferejohn, Forsythe and Noll (1977).

The impossibility of creating an institution under which stations have dominant strategies forces examination of procedures and associated adjustment mechanisms that allow for some strategic behavior.

V. EXPERIMENTAL DESIGN

While the SPC mechanism is an iterative adjustment procedure that operates until it reaches a stable point, the mechanisms described in the previous section are static mappings from agents' messages to final allocations. This static property may not be objectionable when the agents have dominant strategies, but if dominant strategies do not exist such mechanisms must be implemented as adjustment procedures in order to enable the agents to locate equilibria.

Except for the work of Vernon Smith (1977), little attention has been given to the problem of constructing institutions for achieving "desirable" allocations with public goods in this fashion. It goes without saying that the theoretical analysis of adjustment versions of such institutions has not even begun. For this reason the application of the results reported in the previous section to the experimental institutions is provisional at best.

Two series of experiments were run: the first was a simplified version of the SPC, the second was a bidding procedure (B-procedure) similar to those proposed by Green and Laffont for discrete public goods. This mechanism was chosen to satisfy nonbankruptcy and nondeficit for all feasible messages, but as indicated above, if the number of discrete alternatives exceeds one, it is not nonstrategic. Nevertheless for a variety of preference distributions, dominant strategies do exist and weak efficiency will be satisfied.

The two experimental institutions are representatives from two broad classes of decision-making mechanisms. The SPC procedure is one in which the center sends price messages to the agents and the agents must respond in quantities. The B-procedure is one in which the center emits quantity information and the agents respond with internal prices. While in some settings this distinction might be inessential, here, because of the discreteness of the

Table 7. Values of Commodities to Agents (in dollars)

	Agent				
Commodity	1	2	3	4	5
A	3.00	1.80	2.40	1.20	4.80
B	1.20	3.60	6.00	1.80	3.00
C	4.80	8.40	6.60	2.40	5.40
D	3.60	6.00	3.60	3.00	7.20
E	1.20	5.40	3.60	4.20	1.80

quantity space, important differences separate these two classes. Most important is that under a B-procedure the agents have to be able to compute their willingnesses to pay for each commodity at each stage of the procedure without knowing the status of the other commodities. That is, agents are asked to give bids when they do not know for sure where they are in the commodity space. In the SPC this problem does not arise.

To minimize the effects of this problem, the environment of the experimental series was quite severely restricted. In particular, substitutes and complements were eliminated from the preferences of the agents by giving them linear monetary payoff schedules.

The preference distribution that was used throughout the two series is given in Table 7.

Table 8 lists the budgets of the agents, the program costs and the sharing rule (α_i) that were used in both experimental series. Notice that the budgets used in experiments SPC-1, SPC-2, and B-1 were different than those used in the remaining experiments. The change was made because the initial experiments apparently contained an artificially difficult coordination problem. The total group payoff in these experiments was maximized when

Table 8. Budgets, Costs Shares and Costs

	Agent				
	1	2	3	4	5
Budget (SPC–1 & 2, B–1)	3.00	7.50	9.00	4.50	6.00
Budget (SPC–3, 4, 5; B–2, 3, 4, 5, 6, 7, 8)	3.30	8.25	9.90	4.95	6.60
Share of cost (α_i)	.10	.25	.30	.15	.20

	Commodity				
	A	B	C	D	E
Cost	6.00	9.00	12.00	10.50	7.50

commodities C, D, and E were selected, and the costs of these commodities equalled the total budgets of all agents.

In the SPC procedure first round prices were based on the assumption that all agents were purchasing all commodities. These prices were the lowest prices that could be observed during the experiment. Once the initial purchase decisions were made by the agents, subsequent prices were calculated according to the following formula:

$$p_{ik}(t) = C_k \frac{\alpha_i}{\sum_{j \in S_k(t-1)} \alpha_j} \qquad i \in S, k \in P$$

where C_k is the cost of commodity k
 α_i is the basic cost share of agent i
and $S_k(t-1)$ is the set of agents purchasing the commodity during the period t–1.

These new prices were posted on the blackboard in front of the room and the agents were then asked to make new purchase decisions. This process continued until the experiment was terminated.

The termination condition for these experiments was that either (1) the same purchases were indicated by all agents for two consecutive rounds (after round 3) or (2) the round number exceeded some predetermined (secret) number (always 10).

In the B-experiments agents were asked to submit their initial bids under the hypothesis that, initially, none of the programs were to be purchased. Each agent's bid vector was required to be nonnegative and to sum to a total not greater than the agent's budget. Bid totals were posted on the blackboard at the conclusion of each round and the experimenter indicated changes in the list of provisional purchasing decisions. In B–1, B–2, B–3, and B–4 changes in the purchasing decisions were made subject to the restriction that at most *one* commodity could enter or leave the list each round. This restriction was placed on the mechanism so that when experiments are designed with preferences exhibiting complements or substitutes, agents could have a basis on which to formulate their willingness to pay; however, this restriction will cause high transactions costs in an environment like the SPC with scores of alternative commodities. In B–5, B–6, B–7, and B–8, no such restriction was employed. In all B-procedure experiments, termination occurred when (1) the round number exceeded some predetermined (secret) number (always ten) or (2) the same messages were sent by all agents for two consecutive rounds.

Agents were able to compute their tax liability according to a table provided to each of them at the beginning of the experiment. (See Appendix A–1 for a sample tax table.) The entries in this table were computed according to the following formula:

$$t_i(m(t)) = \min\left\{\sum_{k=1}^{p} Z_k(t)\left(C_k - \sum_{j \neq i} m_{kj}(t)\right) + \sum_{k=1}^{p} \max\left(\sum_{j \neq i} m_{kj}(t) - \sum_{j \neq i} \alpha_j C_k, 0\right), b_i\right\}$$

where C_k is the cost of commodity k,
α_i is the basic cost share of agent i,
$Z_k(t) = 1$ if commodity k was purchased in round t, and $Z_k(t) = 0$ otherwise,

$m_{kj}(t)$ is the bid of agent j for commodity k at round t. As remarked, this tax rule has the feature that nonbankruptcy and nondeficit are satisfied. It is not, however, nonstrategic because it may sometimes pay an agent to overreport his willingness to pay for a program.

The instructions that were used for experiments numbered SPC-2, 3, 4, and 5 and B-2, 3, 4, 5, 6, 7, and 8 are given in Appendix A–1. The instructions for the other experiments varied in fairly minor ways and are not given. These earlier experiments were pretests and, when more experiments are run, will be eliminated from the data base. For now, results from these runs are reported since they differ mostly in that the instructions were somewhat less clear than those used subsequently.

The subjects used in the experiments were mostly undergraduates at the California Institute of Technology and were sometimes known to each other. The experiments took place in two classrooms at Caltech. Communication of information labeled as private (preferences, tax tables) was successfully prohibited. Side payments were discouraged but no reference to their prohibition appeared on the instructions. Subjects were asked not to discuss the experiment with others, but this last request could not be enforced.

VI. RESULTS

The objective of this study is to find institutions that perform better than the SPC on various dimensions. For the current experiments attention will be focused on two criteria: efficiency and speed of termination. Since the incentive-compatibility properties of various decision-making institutions are sought primarily as a means of allowing the institution to achieve efficient allocations, also examined is the degree to which subjects truthfully report information concerning their valuations of the commodities.

While relatively few experiments were run, the results permit some preliminary comparisons between the institutions. Since the data are limited, the reporting of results will be quite informal and the additional graphic material is provided for easy reference in Appendix A–2.

A. Speed of Termination

Each of the five SPC experiments terminated before the artificial termination condition was imposed. An examination of Table 9 indicates that the pricing algorithm used in the SPC provides a powerful force in bringing the mechanism to rapid termination. These data (which parallel those reported in Table 2 on the actual SPC) indicate that the budget sets of the agents shrink during the operation of the system. Indeed, the budget set of agent number one in SPC-3 shrunk from 27 to 4 admissible purchase decisions from the initial round to the final round. This amount of shrinkage is typical for all agents.

While the B-procedure did not terminate by round ten in any of the eight experiments, it appeared to have settled down in five of the eight cases by the time that artificial termination was imposed.

There are several plausible reasons why natural termination might not have been observed. First, the set of admissible messages undergoes no shrinkage during the procedure. Second, the experimental institution in B–1, B–2, B–3, and B–4 allowed only one commodity to switch status at a time. This device introduced an incentive for players to game against the artificial termination rule, which evidently caused the very erratic bidding by

Table 9. Direction of Price Changes in SPC Experiments

	\multicolumn{8}{c}{Round}							
	1	2	3	4	5	6	7	8
SPC–1								
# $\Delta q > 0$	5	3	2	1	0	0		
# $\Delta q = 0$	0	1	2	2	3	5		
# $\Delta q < 0$	0	1	1	2	2	0		
SPC–2								
# $\Delta q > 0$	4	4	3	3	2	2		
# $\Delta q = 0$	1	0	0	0	2	2		
# $\Delta q < 0$	0	1	2	2	1	1		
SPC–3								
# $\Delta q > 0$	5	4	3	1				
# $\Delta q = 0$	0	1	1	4				
# $\Delta q < 0$	0	0	1	0				
SPC–4								
# $\Delta q > 0$	4	4	1	1				
# $\Delta q = 0$	1	1	3	3				
# $\Delta q < 0$	0	0	1	1				
SPC–5								
# $\Delta q > 0$	5	4	1	2	0	0	0	0
# $\Delta q = 0$	0	0	1	2	3	4	4	4
# $\Delta q < 0$	0	1	3	1	2	1	1	1

player five during B–3. Of course, the remaining B experiments failed to reach the termination condition either. Finally, unlike the Smith experiments there was no cost to failing to reach an equilibrium.

It appears that, unless the experimental B-institution is altered in some way, its speed of termination is slow compared to the experimental SPC mechanism. Nevertheless, if the B-institution were more efficient at the time of artificial termination than is the SPC mechanism at the time of natural termination, this would not be a problem.

B. Relative Efficiency

The relative efficiency of the two institutions is evaluated here in two different ways. The first is the ratio of actual to potential payout to subjects by the experimenter. The second is to determine whether an additional unilateral purchase or bidding decision could have been made in the final round that would have improved the payoff to each individual.

The maximum payoff total that subjects could achieve was $67.20 in SPC-1, SPC-2, and B–1 and $70.20 in the remaining experiments. The minimum was $30 in SPC-1, SPC-2 and B–1 and $33 in the rest, because all agents could choose to buy nothing and take home their initial budgets. The maximum is achieved when commodities, C, D, and E are purchased. The actual payouts given in the experiments are listed in Table 10, and show no clear superiority for either procedure.

The experimental record was examined to see if at the termination round a unilateral decision could have been made that would have improved everyone's payoff level. In B–1, had any of the agents bid one dollar less for C, E would have been purchased and everyone would have been better off. No such single decision was possible in B–2, B–4, B–5, or B–7. In B–3, if subject 4 had switched his $6.50 bid to commodity E everyone would have improved. Similarly in B–6 and B–8, changes in the last period bid by one agent would have improved everyone's payoff.

In the SPC experiments, agent one in SPC-2 could have increased everyone's payoff by purchasing commodity C. Similarly in SPC-3 agent 4 could

Table 10. Payoff Totals (in dollars)

	Experiment No.							
	1	2	3	4	5	6	7	8
SPC Experiments	54.35*	39.00*	54.95	61.55	61.55			
B Experiments	54.95*	57.80	45.85	56.80	67.45	30.15	68.15	45.60

*Indicates that budgets totalling $30 were used and maximum payout was $67.20. Otherwise, budgets totaled $33 and maximum payoffs were $70.20.

have improved everyone's payoff by purchasing commodity D in the final round. The remaining experiments actually ended in equilibrium so that no unilateral action could improve even an agent's own welfare.

These results indicate that neither procedure invariably terminated at an equilibrium and that Pareto improvements in outcomes were possible in the final round even when admissable strategies were constrained by the form of the institution and when termination occured naturally. The SPC system does seem to achieve a Nash point more often that the B-institution. It is not clear why the B-system is not achieving apparently reachable equilibria but one suspects that the agents may be attempting to take advantage of the strategic possibilities made available by the institution.

C. Choices of Strategies

The property of inducing truthful revelation of preferences is a desired characteristic of an institution primarily because it allows the attainment of efficient allocations. But, in expressing a concern about manipulability, station managers are obviously concerned about equity as well, perhaps because in a complex, decentralized institution like the SPC, successful manipulations are all but impossible to detect and compensate for. Both theoretical and experimental results indicate that neither procedure is free from strategic actions, although the SPC may perform a little better in this dimension.

For the SPC experiments, the optimal myopic (or Cournot) choice for each round was compared with the actual choice. Of the 165 choices made by subjects in the SPC experiments, 40 (or 24.2 percent) were inconsistent with the myopic rule. After the first two rounds (the procedures could not terminate until the third period), 19 of 115 (or 16.5 percent) were inconsistent with the myopic rule.

Examination of the round by round choices by the subjects revealed that strategic play did occur during these experiments. In SPC-1 and SPC-2 subject 5 purchased commodity A at a price of $6.00 several times, apparently in an attempt to lower the price of this commodity to others. Both attempts failed. On the other hand subject 5 during SPC-1 purchased commodity E during Rounds 3 and 4 even though the price of this commodity exceeded its value. Partly because of this behavior, subjects 1 and 3 purchased this commodity subsequently. This resulted in lowering the price of commodity E sufficiently to make it an attractive purchase for subject 5.

Evidently, then, there is some strategic behavior in the SPC experiments but its attractiveness to agents depends on their anticipation of non-Cournot behavior by the other agents. Thus nonmyopic actions occur but they are fairly infrequent and, apparently, usually unsuccessful in this institution. Obviously, more work has to be done to sustain (or undermine) this assertion.

Preliminary examination of the data from the B-experiments indicates that strategy choice is somewhat more difficult to understand. It is apparent that the Cournot hypothesis is not a good model of behavior in these experiments. In the Cournot model, if the sum of bids is near but not equal to the costs of the public good, bids will exhibit considerable round-by-round variability, but exactly the opposite phenomenon occurs. A satisfactory model of bidding behavior for this institution has not been unearthed, but research in this area is currently underway and results will be reported in subsequent papers.

While the strategic choice problem is more complex in the B institution than in the SPC, some strategic play clearly did occur. The usual pattern (see Figures A–2.2 through A–2.9) was for a subject to bid a large number for a commodity for several periods in order to ensure that it would be chosen by the group, and then reduce his bid gradually. A particularly clear example of this behavior was executed by subject 2 in B-3 in his bidding for commodity C during Rounds 3 through 10. Other examples are easily found.

Another pattern that occurred frequently was that certain subjects decided, after about Round 5, to hoard their budgets. This was probably due to the fact that the coordination difficulties involved in getting their peers to help finance a highly desired commodity appeared insuprable. In B-2, subject 3, whose budget was $9.90, spent no more than $4.00 during the final four rounds.

VII. DISCUSSION

This paper has sought to define a class of mechanisms that might operate successfully in an environment with discrete public goods. Two such institutions (the SPC and the B-institution) were isolated and experimental models of these mechanisms were constructed in order to attempt a comparative evaluation of their properties. While the preliminary results are not conclusive, the SPC thus far appears to be superior to the more theoretically attractive B-institution. Several modifications in the B-institution might improve its performance on various dimensions, and obviously versions of the SPC procedure that more faithfully capture the richness of its real-world counterpart may also perform better. Until new experimental series are obtained, it is impossible to conclude decisively that either institution (or any variant thereof) is inferior to the other.

This report is preliminary. Only a single bidding institution has been examined and compared with a simplified SPC, and only a few experiments have been carried out. Nevertheless, some interesting questions have been raised relating the design of allocative institutions.

1. Given the structure of any particular decision problem, how does one go about constructing the set of feasible institutions?

2. Given a class of feasible static institutions, how can adjustment versions of these institutions be designed without (unduly) impairing the desirable properties of the static mechanism?
3. What are the properties of the adjustment versions of these institutions?
4. How can one elicit design constraints from a diverse set of individuals?
5. How can the complexities of a real decision problem be condensed into a manageable theoretical and experimental problem while retaining enough of its features to support the qualitative conclusions of a comparative analysis of alternative institutions?
6. What are reasonable methods for judging the comparative performance of institutions in experimental settings?

Previous literature suggests some partial answers to some of these questions, but the primary value of this literature is to provide a source of suggestions about useful directions of inquiry. Detailed answers probably depend on the nature of the decision-making problem under study. As one might guess, all of these questions remain generally unanswered for the problem that motivated the study. Research on this particular case is continuing in the hope that it will provide more insight into these general questions concerning the practical problems of institutional design.

APPENDIX A1

Instructions for Experiments

AN EXPERIMENT IN GROUP DECISION MAKING—I

This is an experiment in the economics of group decision-making. The instructions are simple and if you follow them carefully and make good decisions you may earn a considerable amount of money which will be paid to you in cash at the end of the experiment.

You are a member of a group that must decide which of various commodities to purchase. You may purchase any of the commodities you desire. If you purchase a particular commodity, it has a certain *value* to you. If you turn to the last page of this handout you will see recorded there the *values* of each of the five commodities (A, B, C, D, E). This value is the amount the experimenter will pay you if you decide to purchase this commodity at the conclusion of the experiment. Each group member has a different set of values and these are to be considered private. You are asked not to reveal these numbers to anyone during the experiment.

The method by which the group will make its purchase decisions is as follows. There will be a sequence of periods. In each period you will be given a set of prices, one for each commodity. Also you are given a budget: an amount of money the experimenter has credited to you. Your budget is recorded on the last page of the handout. In each period you are asked to indicate which commodities you would purchase at the current prices. The amount which you may spend in each period must not exceed your budget. If the experiment is not terminated, you will proceed to the next period and the experimenter will give you a new price for each commodity. Your budget will remain unchanged and you will again be asked to indicate which commodities you wish to purchase.

The purchase decisions in each period determine the prices that the group members face in the following period. Each member may face different prices. Roughly speaking, the more other people purchase a particular commodity in a given round, the lower will be the price of that commodity to you in the following round. Similarly, your current purchase decisions affect the prices that the other members will face in the next round.

If you turn now to your record sheet you will see the initial round prices. The procedure begins when each group member indicates his purchase decisions given these prices. Once the experimenter has received all purchase decisions he will either terminate the system or announce a new set of prices for each member. In the latter case you should make new purchase decisions and resubmit these to the experimenter.

Termination

The experimenter may terminate the procedure at any time following the completion of Round 2. There are two conditions that will cause termination:
1. If all group members announce identical purchase decisions for two consecutive rounds.
2. If the experiment has not otherwise been terminated by Round 5, it will be after a predetermined number of rounds. This number is written on a paper in a sealed envelope in the front of the room.

Once the experiment is terminated, the amount the experimenter owes you is the amount of your unspent budget plus the value of each commodity you purchased in the last round. Your unspent budget is computed by subtracting the price for each commodity you purchased in the final round from your total budget. You should compute the amount which is owed to you by the experimenter and it will be paid to you in cash at the conclusion of the experiment. Feel free to earn as much cash as you can.

Are there any questions before we proceed with an example?

Suppose the values, prices and budget are as represented in Table 1.

Table 1. Trial Period, Budget = $2.00

Commodity	Value	Period 0 Price	Purchase
A	$1.00	$ .50	
B	3.00	6.00	
C	2.00	5.00	
D	1.50	4.00	
E	4.00	1.00	

Indicate what commodities you would purchase in the purchase column by writing an "X" in the row corresponding to the commodities you want. If this were the final round compute the amount the experimenter would owe you, given your purchase decisions.

AN EXPERIMENT IN GROUP DECISION MAKING—II

This is an experiment in the economics of group decision making. The instructions are simple and if you follow them carefully and make good decisions you may earn a considerable amount of money which will be paid to you in cash at the end of the experiment.

You are a member of a group that must decide which of various commodities to purchase. If a particular commodity is purchased by the group it has a certain *value* to you. If you turn to the last page of these instructions you will see recorded there the *values* of each of the five commodities (A, B, C, D, E).

This value is the amount the experimenter will pay you if this commodity is purchased at the conclusion of the experiment. Each group member may have a different set of values and these are to be considered private. You are asked not to reveal these numbers to anyone during the experiment.

The method by which the group will make its purchase decisions is as follows. There will be a sequence of periods. In each period you will be asked to communicate to the experimenter how much you would be willing to pay or "bid" in order to obtain each commodity. At the end of each period the experimenter will use the bids of the members to make up a provisional list of commodities to be purchased and a list which will give the total amount bid for each commodity by all members of the group. These lists will be posted on the blackboard in the front of the room. The experimenter will decide to purchase a commodity only when the total amount bid for that commodity at least covers the cost of providing it for the group. However, the status of only one commodity may change on the list of those which have been provisionally accepted from one round to the next. In other words the list of provisionally accepted commodities at the end of a round will either have one commodity added to the list provided at the end of the previous round or it will have one commodity deleted from that list. The experimenter will choose which commodity to add or delete in each period. On the last page of this handout you will find the cost of providing each of the five commodities to the group. Since these are the costs *to the group* this information is the same on each member's handout.

Bidding Rules

In your folder you will find a set of bidding forms. At the beginning of each period you will be asked to fill out one of these forms. The information which you must fill out on each form includes: your member number, the period number, and the amount you are willing to pay for each commodity. The bids which you submit must satisfy the following requirements:

1. Your bid on any commodity must be in multiples of quarters. For example, $.25, $1.50, $1.75, $3.25, or $6.00 are valid bids, but $.37, $1.61, $2.42, or $3.18 are not valid.
2. You are not permitted to bid a negative amount for any commodity, although you may bid zero.
3. In each period, the total amount which you may bid on all commodities must not exceed your allotted budget. You will find your budget is recorded on the last page of these instructions. This is the amount of money the experimenter has credited to you.

Here is an example of a list of bids which satisfy the above rules:

Commodity	Your Bid
A	$30.00
B	20.00
C	15.00
D	0.00
E	22.50

Budget = $100.00
Total Amount Bid $87.50

Computing Your Payoff

In order to determine the amount you must pay for the commodities you will need to use the information which the experimenter will provide for you at the end of each round. If you turn to page 38, you will find a tax table which will tell you what you must pay. The rows of the table correspond to the total amount bid for a commodity by all the *other* members of the group. You may compute this by subtracting your bid from the total amount bid for a commodity by all members of the group. You should recall that these totals will be posted on the blackboard in the front of the room at the end of each round. There are two columns for each commodity in the table, the left most one labeled "P" is to be used if the commodity is purchased and the right most column, labeled "NP" should be used if the commodity is not purchased. You may then compute your tax for each commodity by finding the appropriate entry in the table. If this number exceeds your budget you would be liable only for your budget. If it is less than your budget and, if the experiment terminates, then you would only have to pay the total tax. Each group member may have different tax table. The information on these tables is to be considered private and should not be revealed to anyone during the experiment.

Your payoff may be computed as follows. Consult your schedule of commodity values. Your payoff is the total value of the commodities purchased plus your unspent budget. Your unspent budget is the amount of your budget which remains after you pay your tax. If the system is terminated the experimenter will pay you this amount in cash. Otherwise he will ask you to submit new bids and will then issue new provisional purchase decisions and new bid totals. This process will continue until the termination condition is met.

Termination

The experimenter may terminate the procedure at any time following the completion of Round 2. There are two conditions that will cause termination:
1. If all group members submit identical bids for two consecutive periods

and the list of accepted commodities remains the same in both periods, or

2. If the experiment has not otherwise been terminated by the fifth period, it will be after a predetermined number of periods. This number is written on a paper in a sealed envelope in the front of the room.

Once the experiment is terminated, payoffs will be made. You should compute the amount which is owed to you by the experimenter and it will be paid to you in cash at the conclusion of the experiment. Feel free to earn as much cash as you can.

Are there any questions before we proceed with an example?

EXAMPLE: To assist you in computing your payoff we will work through an example together. Suppose that the following data is furnished to you at the conclusion of a period.

Commodities A, C and D are Purchased

Commodity	Value	Bid Totals	Your Bid
A	$5.00	$ 9.00	$3.00
B	2.00	4.00	0.00
C	6.00	15.00	2.00
D	3.00	12.00	4.00
E	2.50	4.00	1.00

Your Budget = $10.00

Using your tax schedule, compute your tax and your payoff if the system were to terminate at this stage. The experimenter will come around and check your work.

If there are no further questions we may begin. Please decide upon your initial bids and record them on your bidding form. Remember that these bids are *private* and should not be revealed to the other group members. Please pass these forms to the experimenter when you have recorded your bids.

SHARE OF COST FOR MEMBER

Commodities

	A		B		C		D		E	
	P	NP	P	NP	P	NP	P	NP	P	NP
0.	$6.00		$7.00		$12.00		$10.50		$7.50	
0.25	5.75		8.75		11.75		10.25		7.25	
0.50	5.50		8.50		11.50		10.00		7.00	
0.75	5.25		8.25		11.25		9.75		6.75	
1.00	5.00		8.00		11.00		9.50		6.50	
1.25	4.75		7.75		10.75		9.25		6.25	
1.50	4.50		7.50		10.50		9.00		6.00	
1.75	4.25		7.25		10.25		8.75		5.75	

Commodities

	A		B		C		D		E	
	P	NP	P	NP	P	NP	P	NP	P	NP
2.00	4.00		7.00		10.00		8.50		5.50	
2.25	3.75		6.75		9.75		8.25		5.25	
2.50	3.50		6.50		9.50		8.00		5.00	
2.75	3.25		6.25		9.25		7.75		4.75	
3.00	3.00		6.00		9.00		7.50		4.50	
3.25	2.75		5.75		8.75		7.25		4.25	
3.50	2.50		5.50		8.50		7.00		4.00	
3.75	2.25		5.25		8.25		6.75		3.75	
4.00	2.00		5.00		8.00		6.50		3.50	
4.25	1.75		4.75		7.75		6.25		3.25	
4.50	1.50		4.50		7.50		6.00		3.00	
4.75	1.25		4.25		7.25		5.75		2.75	
5.00	1.00		4.00		7.00		5.50		2.50	
5.25	.75		3.75		6.75		5.25		2.25	
5.50	.60	.10	3.50		6.50		5.00		2.00	
5.75	.60	.35	3.25		6.25		4.75		1.75	
6.00	.60		3.00		6.00		4.50		1.50	
6.25	.60		2.75		5.75		4.25		1.25	
6.50	.60		2.50		5.50		4.00		1.00	
6.75	.60		2.25		5.25		3.75		.75	
7.00	.60		2.00		5.00		3.50		.75	
7.25	.60		1.75		4.75		3.25		.75	
7.50	.60		1.50		4.50		3.00		.75	
7.75	.60		1.25		4.25		2.75		.75	
8.00	.60		1.00		4.00		2.50		.75	
8.25	.60		.90	.15	3.75		2.25		.75	
8.50	.60		.90	.40	3.50		2.00		.75	
8.75	.60		.90	.65	3.25		1.75		.75	
9.00	.60		.90		3.00		1.50		.75	
9.25	.60		.90		2.75		1.25		.75	
9.50	.60		.90		2.50		1.05	.05	.75	
9.75	.60		.90		2.25		1.05	.30	.75	
10.00	.60		.90		2.00		1.05	.55	.75	
10.25	.60		.90		1.75		1.05	.80	.75	
10.50	.60		.90		1.50		1.05		.75	
10.75	.60		.90		1.25		1.05		.75	
11.00	.60		.90		1.20	.20	1.05		.75	
11.25	.60		.90		1.20	.45	1.05		.75	
11.50	.60		.90		1.20	.70	1.05		.75	
11.75	.60		.90		1.20	.95	1.05		.75	
12.00	.60		.90		1.20		1.05		.75	

APPENDIX A2

Graphs Describing Experimental Results

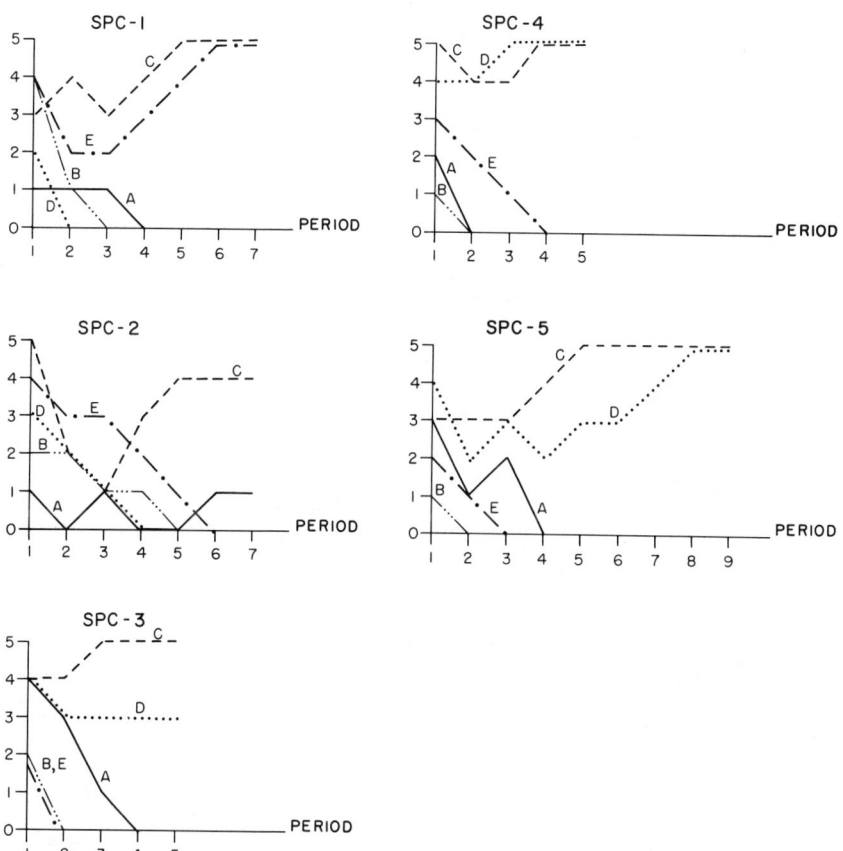

Figure A2.1. Number of Purchases Each Period

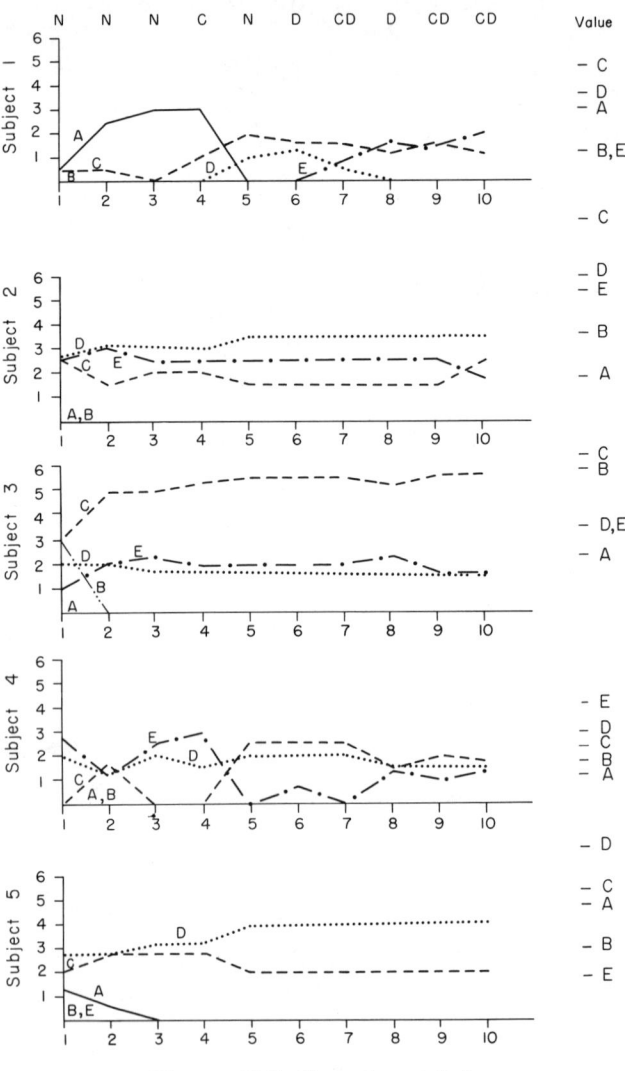

Figure A2.2. Experiment B-1

Analysis of Decision Making Procedures for Discrete Public Goods

Total Amount Bid by Period

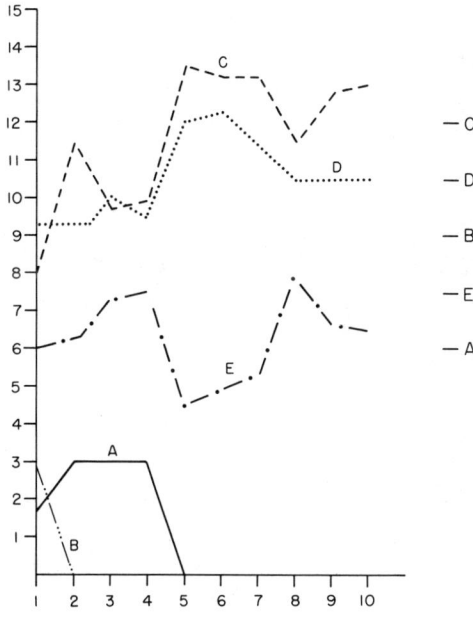

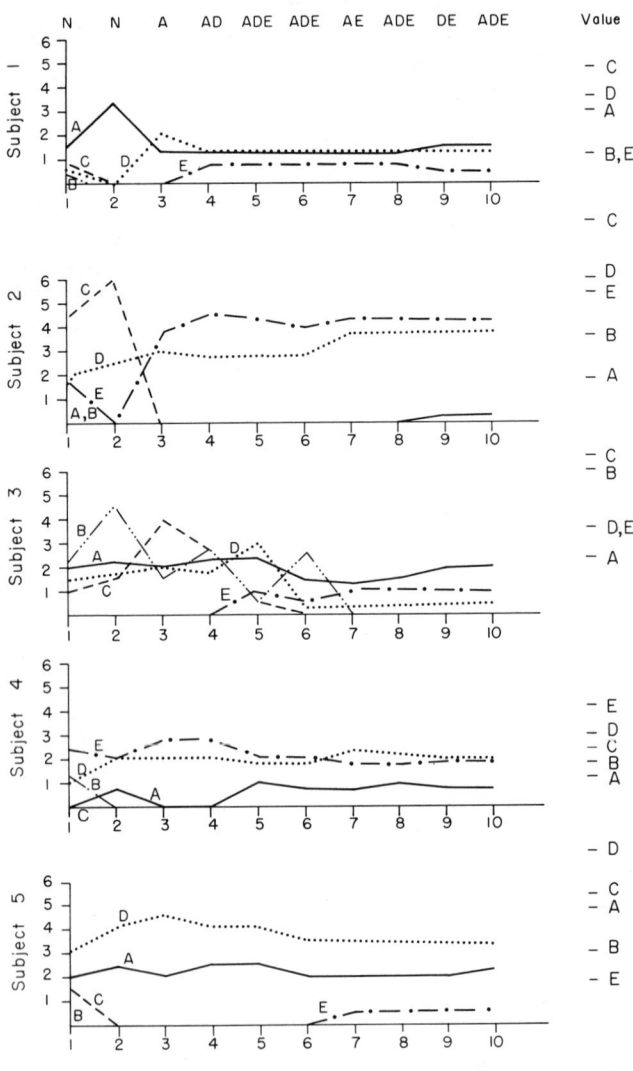

Figure A2.3. Experiment B-2

Analysis of Decision Making Procedures for Discrete Public Goods

Total Amount Bid by Period

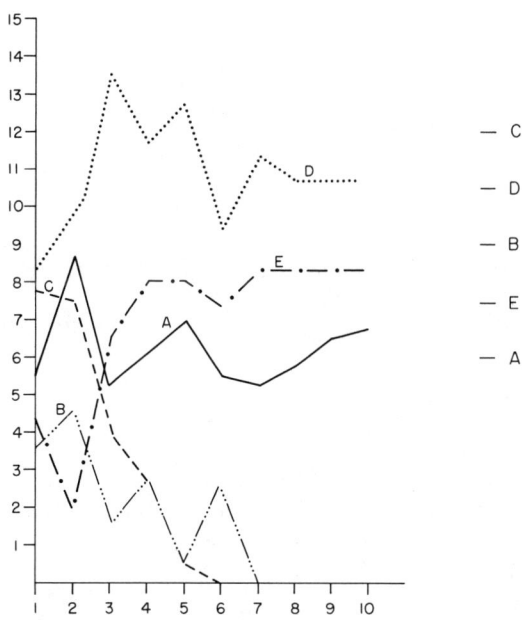

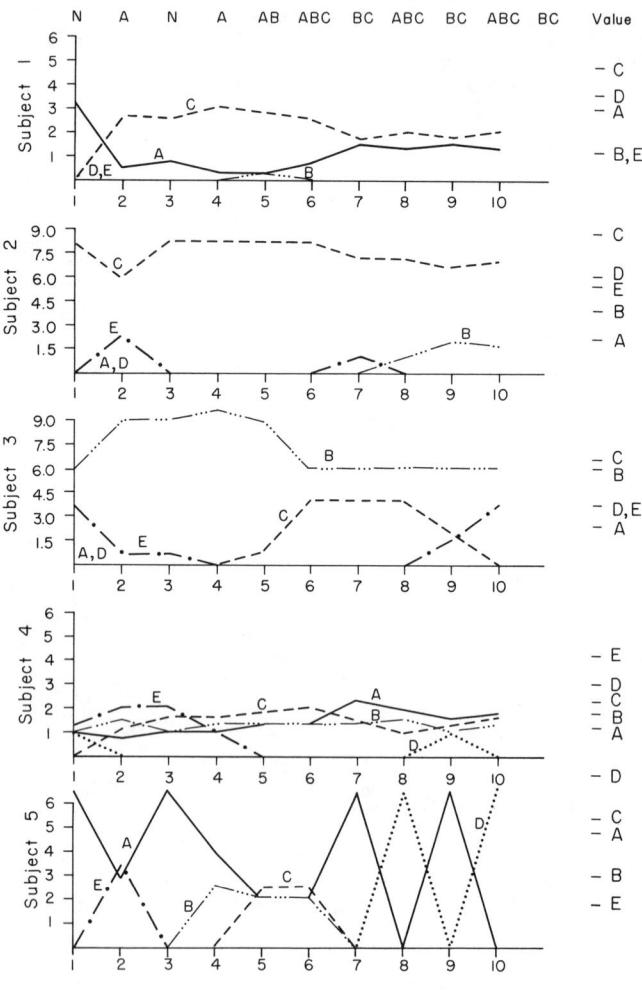

Figure A2.4. Experiment B-3

Total Amount Bid by Period

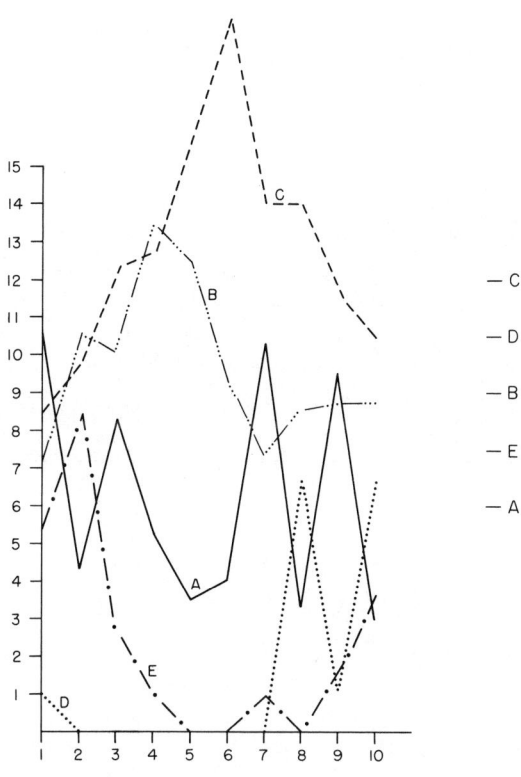

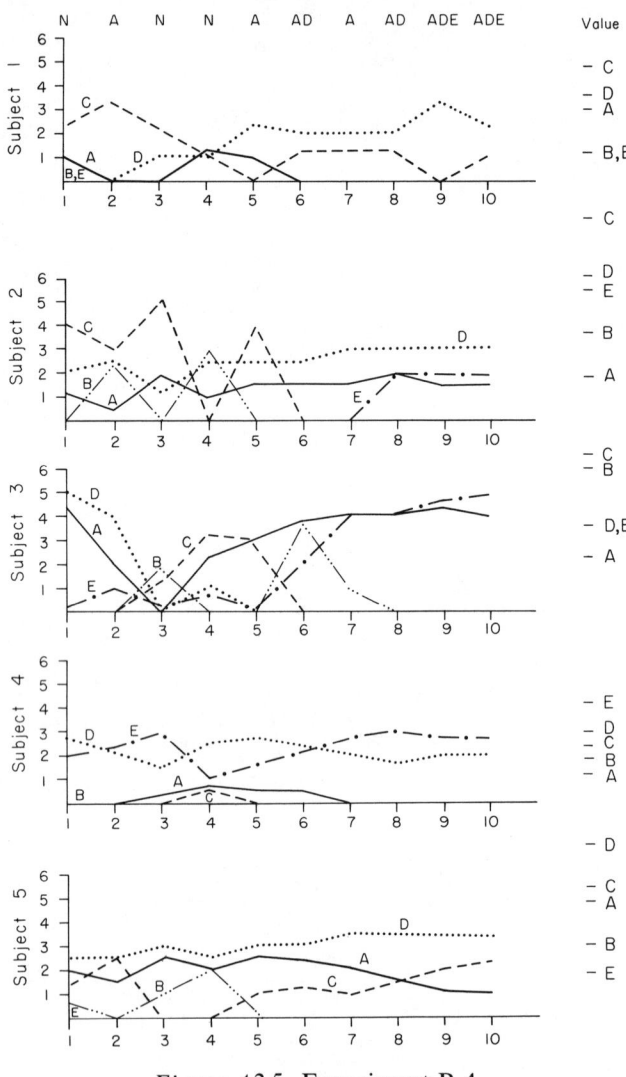

Figure A2.5. Experiment B-4

Total Amount Bid by Period

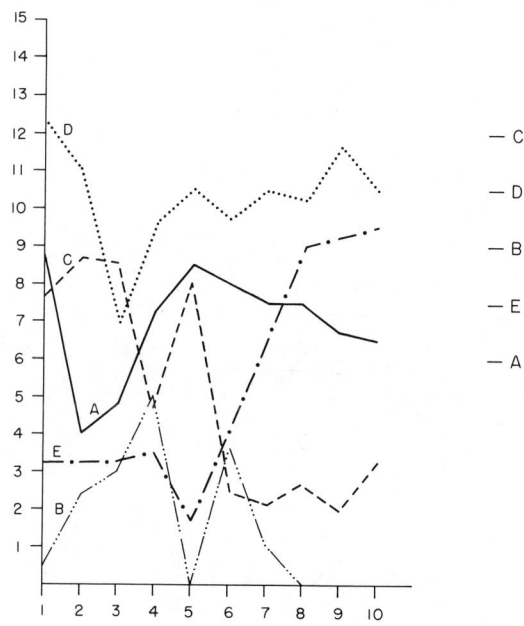

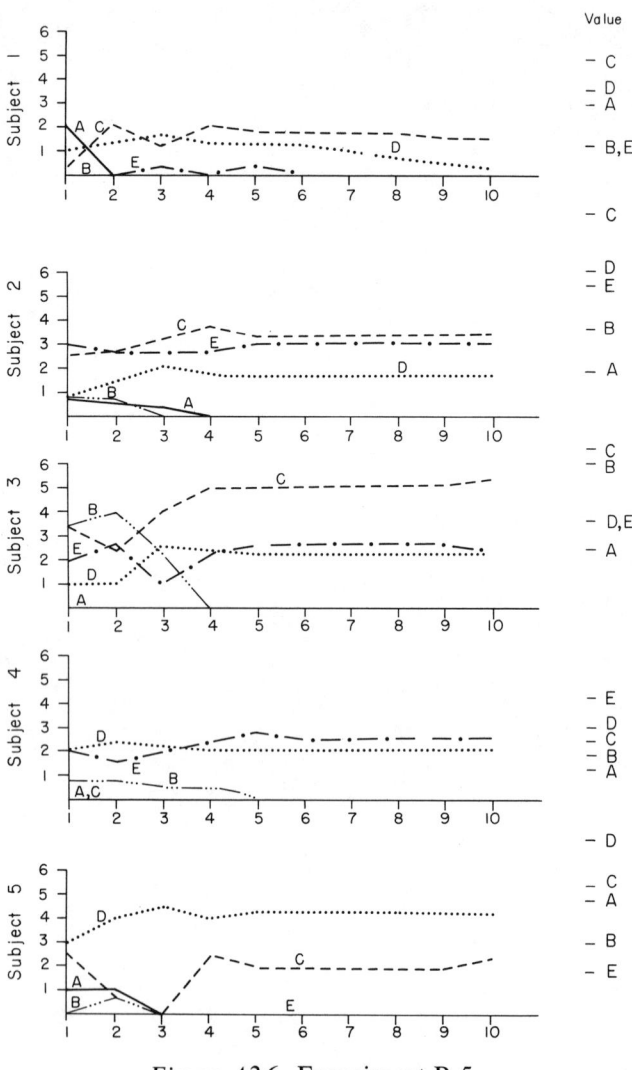

Figure A2.6. Experiment B-5

Total Amount Bid by Period

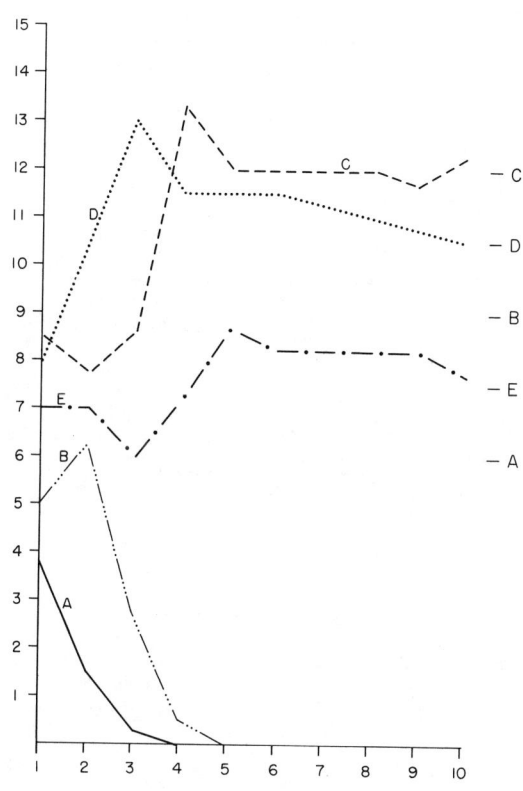

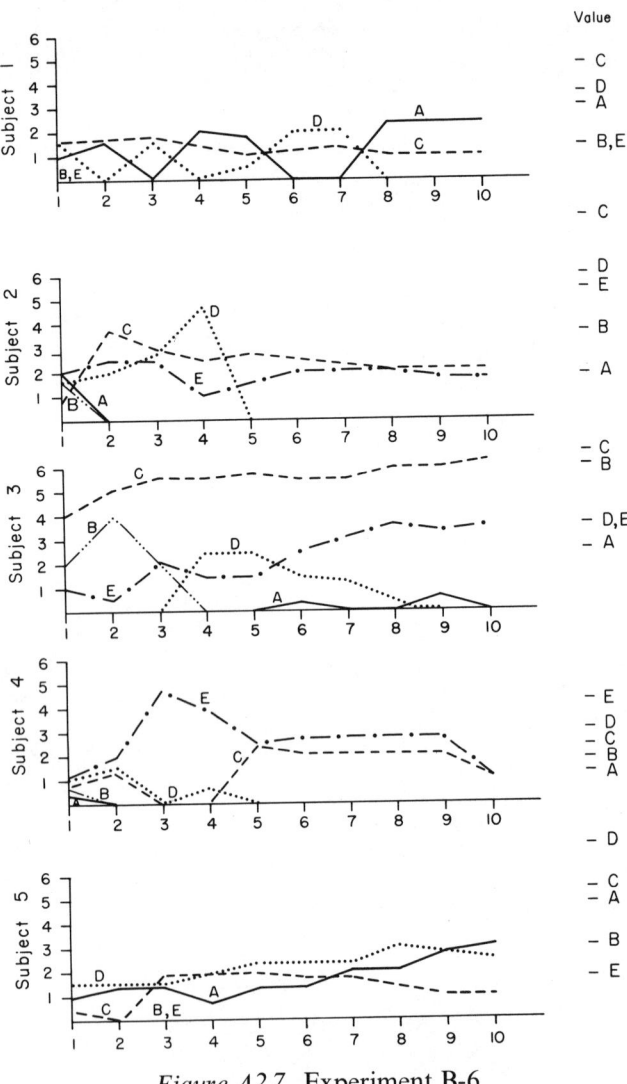

Figure A2.7. Experiment B-6

Total Amount Bid by Period

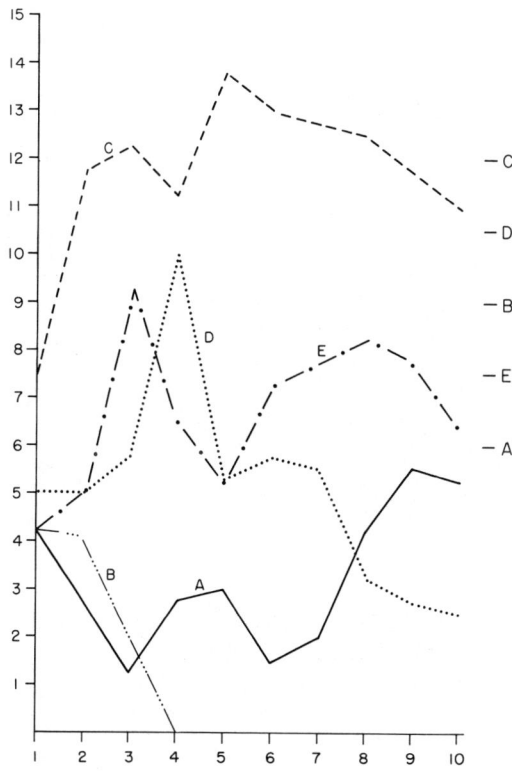

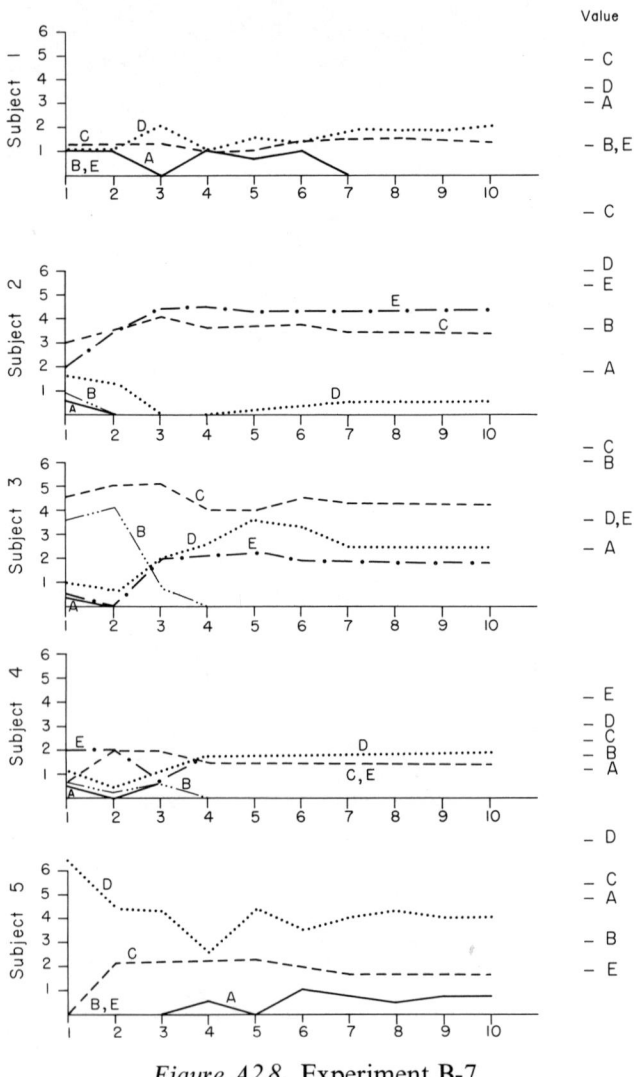

Figure A2.8. Experiment B-7

Total Amount Bid by Period

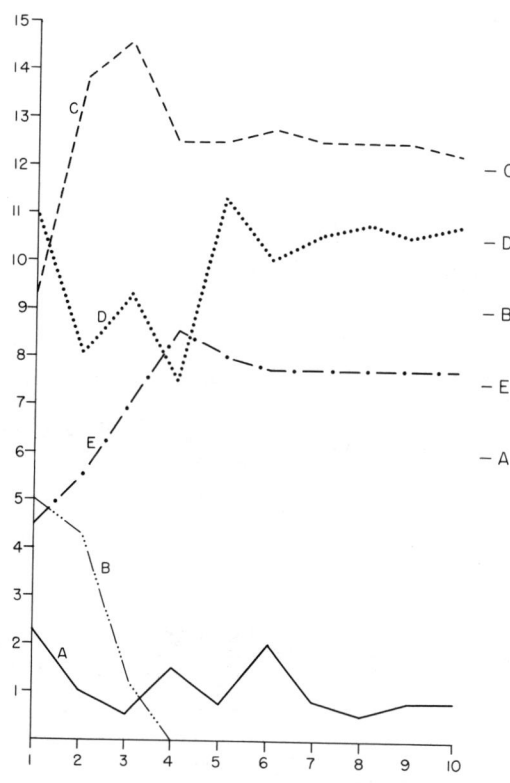

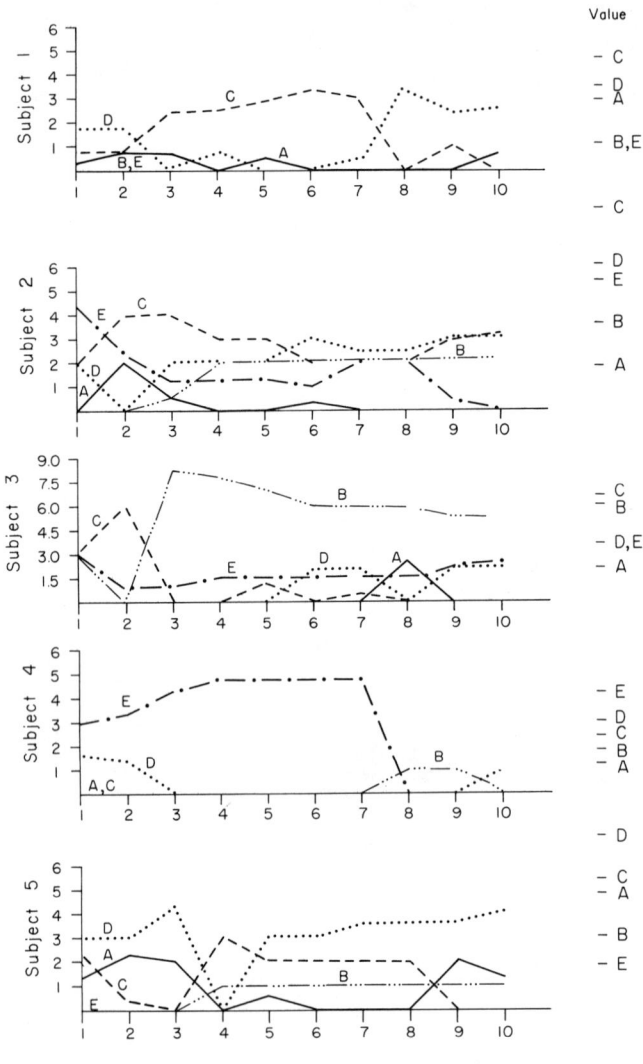

Figure A2.9. Experiment B-8

Analysis of Decision Making Procedures for Discrete Public Goods

Total Amount Bid by Period

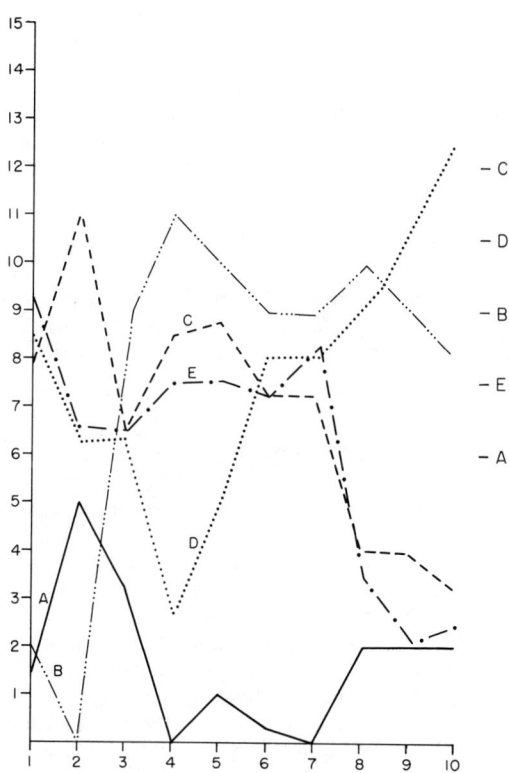

FOOTNOTES

The research reported here was supported by the National Science Foundation program of Research Applied to National Needs, grant No. APR76–01920. The authors gratefully acknowledge the advice and assistance provided by Richard Beatty and the cooperation of the Public Broadcasting Service during the execution of the research reported herein.

1. For a more complete discussion of syndication, see Noll, Peck, and McGowan (1973), especially chapter 3.
2. This is the estimate of Richard Beatty, who designed the SPC and operated it for the first three years. Details of his calculations, which are available on request, are based on several observed activities of the SPC. For example, each station manager attends at least one meeting lasting three days in which the SPC occupies nearly all the agenda of the meeting, reads all the material provided by the center about programs and the progress of the market, and devotes energies to deciding which programs to purchase. Although stations do not keep records of the way in which managers allocate their time, participation in all of these activities probably drains at least a month of the time of each manager. In addition, four PBS employees work full time on the SPC during its operations, and top management at PBS exercises continuing oversight of its progress. Computer terminals and telephone lines are required for all participants, complete catalogues are prepared before the initial selection takes place, and ten-minute pilots of all programs entering Round 1 of the market are transmitted over the national network to each station.

REFERENCES

Ferejohn, J. A. and Noll, R. (May 1976), "An Experimental Market for Public Goods: The PBS Station Program Cooperative," *American Economic Review* 66: 267–273.
———, Forsythe, R., and Noll, R. (June 1977), "Implementing Planning Procedures for the Provision of Discrete Public Goods," Social Science Working Paper No. 156, California Institute of Technology.
Foote, A. E. and Profis, V. S. (1976), "How Public Television Station Managers Feel about the Station Program Cooperative—A Study of Attitudes" (mimeographed), Athens, Ga.: School of Journalism, University of Georgia.
Green, J. and Laffont, J. J. (March 1977a), "Characterization of Satisfactory Mechanisms for the Revelation of Preferences for Public Goods," *Econometrica* 45: 427–38.
———(1977b), "Révélation des préférences pour les biens publics: Premiére partie, caractérisation des mécanismes satisfaisants," *Ecole Polytechnique*, C.P. No. A 1250176. Forthcoming in *Cahiers du Seminaire d'Econometrie*, C.N.R.S., Paris.
———(1976), "Satisfactory Mechanisms for Environments with Consumption Lower Bounds," *Harvard Institute for Economic Research*. D.P. No. 496.
Groves, T. (July 1973), "Incentives in Teams," *Econometrica* 41: 617–631.
Noll, R. G., Peck, M. J., and McGowan, J. J. (1973), *Economic Aspects of Television Regulation*, Washington, D.C.: Brookings Institution.
Profis, V. S. (1977), *The Present and Future of Public Broadcasting's Station Program Cooperative: A Survey of Station Managers*, Master of Arts dissertation, University of Georgia.
Smith, V. L. (1977), "Incentive Compatible Experimental Processes for the Provision of Public Goods," presented at the Conference on Experimental Economics, Tucson.

INCENTIVE COMPATIBLE EXPERIMENTAL PROCESSES FOR THE PROVISION OF PUBLIC GOODS

Vernon L. Smith, UNIVERSITY OF ARIZONA

After providing...[public expenditure]...theory with its... optimal conditions, I went on to demonstrate the fatal inability of any decentralized market or voting mechanism to attain or compute this optimum [Samuelson, (1955), p. 35].

...to say that market mechanisms are non-optimal, and that there are difficulties with most political decision processes, does not imply that we can never find new mechanisms of a better sort [Samuelson (1958), p. 334].

Providing the [public] expenditure in question holds out any prospect at all of creating utility exceeding costs, it will always be theoretically possible, and approximately so in practice, to find a distribution of costs such that all parties regard the expenditure as beneficial and may therefore approve it unanimously [Wicksell (1896), pp. 89–90].

How much of this [the principle of unanimity and voluntary consent in taxation]... may be of practical use in the near future, men of affairs may decide [Wicksell (1896), p. 73].

1. INTRODUCTION

The theory of public goods has, in the space of 20 years, revolutionized teaching and research in public finance, had a major impact on the content of microeconomic theory in general, and has provided, for many, the analytical foundation for an economic justification for the state. The most widely accepted proposition in contemporary public finance is the "fatal inability" of decentralized market or voting institutions to attain a Pareto-optimal allocation of resources when there are public goods. This proposition has been called into question by a series of important new contributions based on a variety of different behavioral assumptions. The first proposed mechanism for revealing marginal willingness to pay for public goods seems to be Earl Thompson's (1965) "D-Process," based on risk-averse behavior, in which demand is revealed by individual purchases of government-offered insurance against relatively unfavorable public outcomes. Two proposals based on minimax choice behavior are those of Drèze and Vallée Poussin (1971) and Malinvaud (1971). Contributions based on Nash equilibrium (or competitive) behavior, include the "demand revealing process" developed independently by Clarke (1971) and Groves (1969, 1973), analyzed further by Groves and Ledyard (1974, 1977) under the title of the "abstract" government (G*), and the simpler quadratic tax mechanism, or "optimal" government (O).

A remarkable precursor of Clarke, Groves and Groves-Ledyard is Vickrey's (1961) "counterspeculation" process, and the "second price" sealed bid auction developed to induce revelation of demand for private goods,[1] but having the essential behavioral features of the Clarke, Groves and Groves:Ledyard (G*) mechanisms. But, as indicated in Smith (1977), the most promising of these recent mechanisms appears to be the Groves-Ledyard (O) quadratic tax rule under which economic agents have a particularly simple maximum problem and are required only to communicate messages in Euclidean space. The "demand revealing" or G* process requires agents to communicate functions reporting marginal willingness to pay.

This study reports the results of 21 (exclusive of pilot experiments)[2] laboratory experiments using 118 subjects to test hypotheses about the performance characteristics of three different processes for the provision of public goods. The experimental methods are based on the use of nontrivial monetary rewards to induce controlled valuations on abstract goods or decisions (Smith, 1975). The treatment variable in these experiments is the public good cost allocation mechanism together with the supporting institution defining information transfer, agreement, and process outcome. The term "mechanism" will be used to denote a formal mathematical theory, while "process" will be used to denote a procedure for arriving at a collective decision. Thus, each of the three institutions of public choice to be studied are based on a mechanism of cost allocation and maximization, but we propose no adjustment mechanisms, i.e., formal dynamic theory, for these institutions. But the adjustment process for each institution is specified rather carefully to facilitate the possible articulation of formal adjustment mechanisms. For those interested in resource allocation adjustment mechanisms, but unfamiliar with laboratory experimental methods, it will become evident (cf. Hurwicz, 1973) that it is impossible to design a group decision experiment without designing an institution in all its structural detail (Shubik, 1974).

Section 2 and 3 discuss the Groves-Ledyard (G-L) tax rule and the experimental process using their mechanism. Since the G-L mechanism purports to solve the free-riding problem, it is necessary to design a control experimental process to establish that there is a problem to be solved. The scientific requirement must be to establish an evidential basis for free-riding that is comparable to the evidence supporting any proposed solution to the problem. The experimental control process is defined by a "Lindahl pricing procedure" in section 4 which attempts to reproduce the circumstances that scholars have in mind when discussing the free-rider phenomenon. Since such discussions do not typically involve the specification of a process, the control experiment is based on a process interpretation of public goods theory. Based largely on the Nash equilibrium properties of the G-L mechanism, section 5 offers some hypotheses concerning the comparative results to be expected from the Lindahl control and G-L research experiments. Section 6 presents the experimental designs and the results of four Lindahl and three G-L experiments. These results tend to support the hypothesis that the Lindahl process is not incentive compatible while the G-L process is. Section 7 replicates the G-L experiments with different design parameters.

Incentive incompatibility in the Lindahl mechanism is explained by the noncompetitive condition that each economic agent is placed in a position of exercising effective control over his own price. The G-L mechanism is incentive compatible because it removes such control over price from the individual. These considerations suggest still another mechanism, called the Auction Mechanism (section 8), in which each agent's share of cost is determined by the bids of the other agents. He may signal agreement only by matching his share of cost with his bid, and by matching the group's mean quantity proposal with his own proposal. This yields incentive compatibility, and has certain advantages such as simplicity and a balanced budget at all levels of the public good. Section 9 describes an experimental design and the results of 12 experiments based on the Auction Mechanism. These results tend to support the hypothesis that the Auction process leads to the Lindahl optimal provision of public goods.

This study suggests that the conventional wisdom, emphasizing the inevitability of the underprovision of public goods by decentralized institutions, is much too pessimistic. This conclusion receives evidential support in field and laboratory experiments reported by Bohm (1972), Ferejohn and Noll (1976) and Sherr and Babb (1975). Thus, Bohm reports that his experiments "indicate that the well-known risk for misrepresentation of preferences (for public goods)...may have been exaggerated" (Bohm, 1972, p. 111). Of course in field experiments it is not possible to know the Lindahl optimum. Only in laboratory environments, where Lindhal prices and quantities are well defined, can we make more percise judgments about the optimality characteristics of different processes.

What emerges from this paper, and finds support in the cited experimental studies, is that practical decentralized processes exist for the provision of public goods. Some of these processes lead to optimal or approximately optimal allocations. If there are a few such processes there must be thousands—some better, some worse, some cheaper, some dearer.

If these studies are corroborated by further investigation, the unanimity rule in public choice, endorsed in Wicksell (1896) and in the comprehensive work of Buchanan and Tullock (1962), will have empirical support far in excess of the weight of contemporary professional opinion.

2. THE G-L INCENTIVE COMPATIBLE TAX RULE

There are several possible forms for the G-L tax rule (Groves and Ledyard, 1974; 1977), and we shall use one of the simpler versions as a basis for the research (R) experiments to be reported here.

Consider a collective of I economic agents choosing a public good that can be produced in the amount X at constant unit cost q. Let $\Delta X_i = x_i \gtreqless 0$, be an increment to the quantity of the public good that is proposed by agent i, where $i = 1, 2, \ldots, I$, and $X = \sum_{i=1}^{I} x_i$ is defined as the group's proposed quantity of the public good. Also define $S_i = \sum_{j \neq i} x_j$ as the sum of the increments proposed by all members of the group except i. Then the G-L tax rule allocates to agent i a total tax cost, C_i, depending on his choice of x_i and conditional upon S_i, given by

$$C_i(x_i|S_i) = -\left(IS_i - \frac{q}{I}\right)(x_i + S_i) + \left(\frac{I-1}{2}\right)(x_i + S_i)^2 \quad (2.1)$$

The marginal tax to agent i is

$$C_i'(x_i|S_i) = -\left(IS_i - \frac{q}{I}\right) + (I-1)(x_i + S_i). \quad (2.2)$$

Since $X = x_i + S_i$, summing over the marginal tax levels of all I agents gives

$$\sum_{i=1}^{I} C_i'(x_i|S_i) = \sum_{i=1}^{I} \left[-I(X - x_i) + \frac{q}{I} + (I-1)X\right] \quad (2.3)$$
$$= -I^2 X + IX + q + I(I-1)X = q.$$

It follows that if agent i has a marginal willingness to pay for X given by $M_i(X)$, and if agent i chooses x_i^0 to maximize his net benefit, then $M_i(x_i^0 + S_i^0) = C_i'(x_i^0|S_i)$, and

$$\sum_{i=1}^{I} M_i(X^0) = q. \quad (2.4)$$

$X^0 = \sum_{i=1}^{I} x_i^0$ is the group's Pareto optimal amount of the public good. Under the G-L tax rule, if each agent maximizes his net benefit, then in equilibrium his marginal willingness to pay is revealed by his marginal tax level easily calculated from (2.2) for any given S_i.

It should be noted that this version of the G-L tax rule does not balance the budget for the public good for every X. That is,

$$\sum_{i=1}^{I} C_i(x_i|S_i) \neq qX,$$

for all X. Other versions of the G-L tax rule (Groves and Ledyard, 1977) guarantee a balanced budget for every $X \geq 0$.

3. AN EXPERIMENTAL ALLOCATION PROCESS BASED ON THE G-L TAX RULE

This section presents an experimental design in which the G-L tax rule is imbedded in one of numerous conceivable elementary adjustment processes for group choice of a public good.

Environment

The experimental environment specifies a very simple *technology:* An abstract public good can be produced at constant unit cost, q, only for integer values X, no larger than $\tilde{X}$, i.e., $0 \leq X \leq \tilde{X}$. Each experiment is conducted with a group of $I \geq 2$ subject agents. Utility is induced on units of the abstract public good by *privately* specifying functions $V_i(X)$, (increasing in X), and endowing subject i with the unabridged right to claim $V_i(X)$ dollars in U.S. currency net of his allocated share of the cost of the good, C_i, *if* the group agrees on the quantity X under the process stopping rules. If the group fails to reach agreement under the rules, each subject is to receive a "modest wage" small in comparison with the net dollar earnings, $v_i = V_i(X) - C_i(x_i | S_i)$.

Proposition 1. If each subject derives a strictly monotone increasing utility from U.S. currency, $U_i(v_i)$, and chooses x_i to maximize this utility of money, the reward rule $v_i = V_i(X) - C_i(x_i | S_i)$ induces the controlled marginal willingness to pay function $M_i = V_i'(X)$ on units of the abstract public good, which in turn implies a Lindahl group equilibrium.

Each i seeks to

$$\max_{x_i} U_i[V_i(x_i + S_i) - C_i(x_i | S_i)]$$

where $C_i(x_i | S_i)$ is given by (2.1). For U_i, V_i such that U_i is concave in x_i, it is necessary and sufficient for a maximum that

$$\{V_i'(x_i^0 + S_i) - C_i'(x_i^0 | S_i)\} U_i' = 0. \qquad (3.1)$$

But if $U_i' > 0$, (3.1) implies

$$V_i'(X) = C_i'(x_i^0 | S_i). \qquad (3.2)$$

Hence, $V_i'(X)$ is i's marginal willingness to pay for X. Since (3.1) and (3.2) must hold for all $i = 1, 2, \ldots, I$, then we have from (2.3) the *Lindahl equilibrium* $[X^0, V_1'(X^0), \ldots, V_I'(X^0)]$, such that

$$\sum_{i=1}^{I} V_i'(X^0) = q, \qquad (3.3)$$

for the experimental environment.

Adjustment Process

The experimental procedure (see the instructions in Appendix I) involves a dialogue between the subject agents and the experimenter in which the *language* consists of *private* messages (incremental proposals), $x_i(t) \gtreqless 0$, $i = 1, 2, \ldots, I$ chosen from the integers $\tilde{x}, \tilde{x}+1, \ldots, 0, 1, 2, \ldots, \tilde{X}$, and a *public* message (the group proposal), $X(t) = \sum_{i=1}^{I} x_i(t)$, on each "trial" $t = 1, 2, \ldots$

The process consists of the following iterative procedure:

(i) *Starting rule.* On trial t each subject independently, and privately,

chooses an integer $\tilde{x} \leq x_i(t) \leq \tilde{X}$, and records $x_i(t)$ on a prescribed record sheet. (Appendix I).
(ii) *Transition rules.*
  (ii.a) The experimenter records each $x_i(t)$, computes $X(t) = \sum_{i=1}^{I} x_i(t)$, and posts $X(t)$ on a blackboard, the posting to remain until the end of the process.
  (ii.b) Each subject records $X(t)$, then computes and records $S_i(t) = X(t) - x_i(t)$.
  (ii.c) Each subject determines his private net valuation of $[x_i(t), S_i(t)]$, from a pre-computed $(\tilde{X} - \tilde{x})^2$ table (Appendix I, Table 3) of the values
  $$v_i = \begin{cases} V_i(x_i + S_i) - C_i(x_i | S_i), & \text{if } 0 < x_i + S_i \leq \tilde{X} \\ 0, & \text{if } x_i + S_i \leq 0 \text{ or } x_i + S_i > \tilde{X} \end{cases}$$
  The resulting $v_i(t)$ is recorded on his record sheet. This completes trial t.
  (ii.d) Each subject then proceeds to trial $t + 1$ and chooses $x_i(t + 1)$ as in (i).
(iii) *Stopping rule.*
  (iii.a) The process stops on trial t^* if
  $$x_i(t^* - 2) = x_i(t^* - 1) = x_i(t^*), \forall i, \text{ and } t^* \leq T;$$
  (iii.b) Otherwise, the process stops on trial $t = T$.
(iv) *Outcome rule.* If the process stops by (iii.a) the group has reached *equilibrium* (agreement), and each subject is paid $v_i(t^*)$ in cash. Otherwie, he receives a small cash payment.

Discussion

Certain features of the above process deserve special emphasis:
(1) Each subject agent at all times is assured the right of privacy with respect to his total valuation, V_i, cost allocation, C_i, net valuation, v_i, incremental proposal, x_i, and the sum of all other such proposals, S_i. The only public information consists in the elements of the set $(I, q, X(1), X(2) \ldots X(t) \ldots)$. The publicity of such elements is *realizable* in any field application of the procedure. But the valuations $V_i(X)$ are subjective in field applications, and their publicity is therefore not credibly realizable, even if considered desirable.
(2) In addition to field realizability the condition of privacy in the laboratory experiments also has the important function of protecting the postulate of a neoclassical environment (no externalities in consumption). If agent i does not know V_j, C_j, or x_j for any $j \neq i$ then

the earnings and decisions of other agents cannot enter as arguments of i's utility function.[3] Thus, privacy helps to insure that U_i will depend predominantly on v_i only.

(3) The stopping rule requires every agent to send the same message on three successive trials. Hence agreement requires *unanimity* on any proposed X. Furthermore any agent who signals a desire to reach agreement by repeating his previous message may still veto the proposal by altering his subsequent message. This effectively precludes "accidental" agreement.

(4) The process has the desirable property that no transactions occur unless and until equilibrium obtains. This outcome rule is particularly important where, as in the case of public goods, the group decision pertains to the construction of durable capital. This is in accordance with one of the desiderata suggested by Hurwicz (1973, p. 26), but contrasts with the process examined by Drèze and de la Vallée Poussin (1971) which was an instantaneous utility criterion rather than a final-outcome utility criterion. The above outcome rule also contrasts with that of most of the experimental adjustment literature based on oral auction (Smith, 1964), sealed-bid auction (Smith, 1967), and posted-price (Williams, 1973; Plott and Smith, 1975) institutions of contract. In this literature, utility is derived from the flow of per period exchanges. Disequilibrium contracts are binding, and therefore agent "endowments" are altered by such contracts. But the final-outcome utility rule presents behavioral hazards in that it is pretty well established experimentally that the exchange of information under costless (no payoff) conditions differs from that under costly conditions. Strategic bluffing, inattentive decisions, and gaming utilities may make process convergence more difficult when utility is based on final outcomes instead of the flow of intermediate outcomes. But we have no choice except to confront these issues, since it is final-outcome utilities that are relevant to the public good decision.[4]

4. A CONTROL PROCESS BASED ON THE LINDAHL PRICING PROCEDURE

The control experiment is based on an interpretation of the "conventional" description of the free-riding problem in public good decisions (e.g., Samuelson, 1955). The alleged problem is that if each agent's allocation of cost for the public good is determined by his stated willingness to pay, then he will have an incentive to understate his willingness to pay thereby gaining an advantage by letting other members of the group carry a larger burden of the cost.

Environment

The technology and induced utility functions are the same as in the previous experimental process. However, agent i's share of unit cost is now determined by his bid for the marginal (proposed) unit of the public good. If his bid for unit X is $b_i(X)$, then his net reward is

$$v_i = V_i(X) - b_i(X)X,$$

if the group reaches agreement under the stopping rules, otherwise he receives a modest wage. The instructions (Appendix II) require the subjects to submit noncreasing lists of bids $b_i(1), b_i(2) \ldots b_i(\tilde{X})$ on each trial. Therefore (assuming differentiability), $b_i'(X) \leq 0$, for all i. The group proposal rule in the experiment is $X \geq 0$ such that $q = \sum_{k=1}^{I} b_k(X)$ (We ignore the trivial case in which $q > \sum_{k=1}^{I} b_k(0)$).

Proposition 2. If each subject derives a strictly monotone increasing utility from U.S. currency, $U_i(v_i)$, then maximizing this utility under the reward rule, $v_i = V_i(X) - b_i(X)X$ requires each subject's optimal bid function to be not greater than his marginal willingness to pay function, i.e., $b_i(X) \leq V_i'(X)$.

Agent i seeks to $\max_{b_i(X)} U_i[V_i(X) - b_i(X)X]$ subject to the group proposal rule that $q - \sum_{k=1}^{I} b_k(X) = 0, X \geq 0$. But since $q = b_i(X) + \sum_{j \neq i} b_j(X)$, this is equivalent to the problem

$$\max_X U_i\{V_i(X) - [q - \sum_{j \neq i} b_j(X)]X\}. \qquad (4.1)$$

If U_i concave in X, and $U_i' > 0$ it is necessary and sufficient for a maximum that

$$V_i' = q - \sum_{j \neq i} b_j(X) - X \sum_{j \neq i} b_j'(X). \qquad (4.2)$$

That is, through his choice of the bid function, $b_i(X)$, i implicitly chooses X so that his marginal willingness to pay equals his marginal net cost. His net total cost is the residual $[q - \sum_{j \neq i} b_j(X)]X$ left to be paid after netting out the contributions of all other agents $j \neq i$. Substituting from (4.2) into the group proposal rule,

$$b_i(X) = q - \sum_{j \neq i} b_j(X) = \qquad (4.3)$$

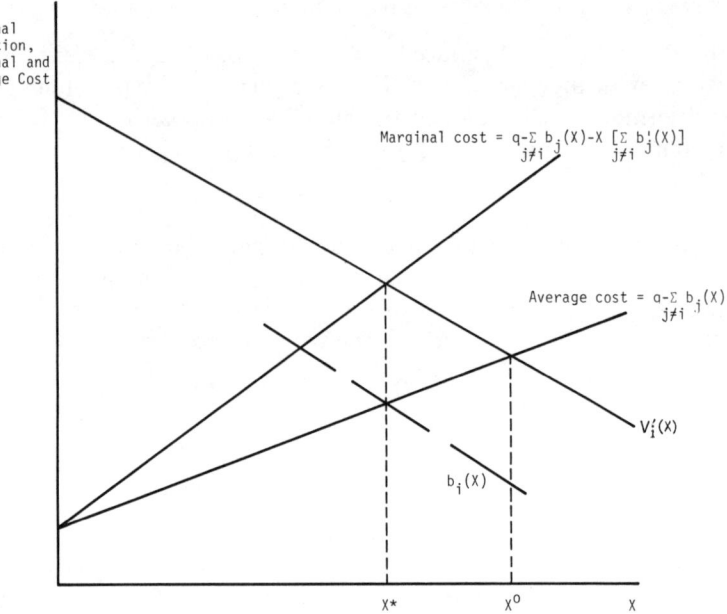

Figure 1.

$$V_i'(X) + X \sum_{j \neq i} b_j'(X) \begin{cases} < V_i'(X), X > 0, & \text{if } b_j'(X) < 0 \text{ for some } j. \\ = V_i'(X), X > 0, & \text{if } b_j'(X) = 0, \forall j \end{cases}$$

Consequently, if i believes that $b_j(X)$ will be decreasing for some j, and therefore $q - \sum_{j \neq i} b_j(X)$ will be increasing, he will bid less than $V_i'(X)$. This is because his net average unit cost, $q - \sum_{j \neq i} b_j(X) = b_i(X)$ is less than his net marginal cost, $q - \sum_{j \neq i} b_j(X) - \sum_{j \neq i} b_j'(X)$. If i believes that $b_j(X) \equiv b_j$ will be constant for every j, then his net average and marginal costs are the same, $q - \sum_{j \neq i} b_j$, and his optimal bid function is $V_i'(X)$. This property is exploited by the adjustment procedure to be discussed in section 8.[5]

But in the Lindahl procedure note that even if i is very optimistic about the bids to be submitted by $j \neq i$, and believes each will bid his marginal willingness to pay, then $b_j(X) \equiv V_j'(X)$. Therefore $b_j'(X) = V_j''(X) < 0$ and i will bid $b_i(X) < V_i'(X), X > 0$. Figure 1 illustrates the Free-Rider equilibrium quantity X^*, which is below the Lindahl equilibrium quantity, X^0.

Adjustment Process

The *language* of the Lindahl process consists of *private* bid messages $b_i(X, t), i = 1, 2, \ldots, I; X = 1, 2, \ldots \tilde{X}$, and a *public* message (the group proposal),

$\hat{X}(t)$ defined implicitly by

$$q \begin{cases} \leq \sum_{k=1}^{I} b_k(X,t), & X \leq \hat{X}(t) \\ > \sum_{k=1}^{I} b_k(X,t), & X > \hat{X}(t) \end{cases}$$

for each trial t. As in the research experiment, the process uses an iterative procedure as follows:

(i) *Starting rule.* On trial t, each subject independently and privately selects a vector of bids $[b_i(1,t), \ldots, b_i(\tilde{X},t)]$ that are written in non-increasing order on a bid submission form.

(ii) *Transition Rules*

(ii.a) The experimenter collects the bid forms, computes the sum

$$\sum_{k=1}^{I} b_k(X,t) \text{ for } X = 1, 2, \ldots, \tilde{X}$$

where $\hat{X}(t)$ is the largest integer X such that $\sum_{k=1}^{I} b_i(\hat{X}, t)$ is not larger than q. Then $\hat{X}(t)$ is posted on the blackboard where it remains until the end of the experiment.

(ii.b) Each subject records $\hat{X}(t)$ on a prescribed record sheet (Appendix II), determines $V_i(\hat{X}(t))$ from his valuation table, and enters this value on his record sheet.

(ii.c) The experimenter then privately communicates to each subject the subject's lowest accepted bid, $b_i(\hat{X}(t), t)$. In some experiments each subject obtained this from his own records.

(ii.d) Each subject then computes his share of facility cost $\hat{X}(t)b_i(\hat{X}(t), t)$, and subtracts it from gross value $V_i(\hat{X}(t))$ to determine net value, $\hat{v}_i = V_i(\hat{X}(t)) - \hat{X}(t) \cdot b_i(\hat{X}(t), t)$, and records it on his record sheets.

(ii.e) Each subject then proceeds to trial $t + 1$, choosing a new bid vector $[b_i(1, t+1), \ldots, b_i(\hat{X}(t+1), t+1)]$ as in (i).

(iii) *Stopping Rule*

(iii.a) The process stops if each subject's lowest accepted bid is the same on three succesive trials, i.e. on trial t^* if $b_i(\hat{X}(t^*-2), t^*-2) = b_i(\hat{X}(t^*-1), t^*-1) = b_i(\hat{X}(t^*), t^*)$, for all i where $t^* \leq T$;

(iii.b) Otherwise, the process stops on trial $t = T$.

(iv) *Outcome rule.* The subjects are paid $v_i(t^*)$ in cash if the process stops by (iii.a) otherwise a small cash payment for their time. In some variations this small payment was also added to $v_i(t^*)$.

Discussion

It is commonly asserted that the free rider problem is due to agents failing to report "truthfully" their marginal willingness to pay. But the issue is better stated as one in which the agent has a conflict of interest between *revealing* his marginal willingness to pay and enjoying a *low share* of the cost. It is unlikely that agent resolution of this conflict of interest will yield the same decision as would obtain in the absence of such a conflict. In the typical nonlaboratory group decision problem in which willingness to pay is subjectively and perhaps very vaguely defined, "truthfulness" (an objective concept) is not well defined.

It is because of these considerations that in the above interpretation of the Lindahl paradigm we do not request of subject-agents that they "truthfully" report their willingness to pay for successive units of X. We ask rather (in a more neutral manner) that they simply submit bids for successive units of the public good with the understanding that their private unit cost is determined by the lowest of their accepted bids. Some might think this is too bland a directive, and that subjects should be exhorted to be "very honest" and write down their "true" willingness to pay schedules. But this would be quite the wrong approach. To see why, suppose in the experimental situation that one could use such moral suasion to induce fairly consistent bid sequences at or near $V_i'(X)$. Such results would be nontransferable to field environments because in nonlaboratory environments we *cannot know* what are the "true" valuations. The proper approach, therefore, is to design a procedure, such as the one based on the G-L tax rule, that allegedly removes the conflict between the self-interest and the desired revelation. Then one designs a second "Lindahl" procedure, as outlined above, in which the alleged confict is given the opportunity to be expressed. Neither procedure should use forms of persuasion that could only have objective meaning in laboratory environments.

5. THEORY AND HYPOTHESES

The research experimental mechanism described above yields a static Lindahl equilibrium characterized by the important Nash property. It is this property that provides the motivation for our prediction of the experimental outcomes and the hypotheses to be tested. If we let $U_i[V_i(x_i|S_i)]$ be the utility derived by subject i when he chooses x_i given that all $j \neq i$ choose x_j, and let max $U_i[V_i(x_i|S_i)] = U_i[v_i(x_i^0|S_i^0)]$, for all i, $S_i^0 = \sum_{j \neq i} x_j^0$, then $(x_1^0, x_2^0, \ldots, x_1^0)$ is a Nash equilibrium: $U_i[V_i(x_i^0|S_i^0)] \geq U_i[V_i(x_i|S_i^0)]$, for all i, and all $x_i \neq x_i^0$ From Proposition 1, each i chooses x_i^0 so that his implicit bid is his marginal willingness to pay $V_i'(X^0)$, while from Proposition 2 we expect subjects in the Lindahl bid procedure to bid less

Incentive Compatible Experimental Processes 71

than $V'_i(X)$. We propose the following specific hypotheses for the first series of research (R1) experiments and a series of control experiments (C).

Hypothesis 1. In R1 experiments reaching equilibrium under the stopping rule (*iiia*) in section 3, the proposed quantities of the public good on the final trial will be distributed with mean X^0.

Hypothesis 2. In C experiments reaching equilibrium under the stopping rule (*iiia*) in section 4, the proposed quantity of the public good will be distributed with mean $< X^0$.

Hypothesis 3. Whether or not C experiments reach equilibrium, the C experiment bids for the marginal unit, X^0, of the public good will tend to be below the marginal willingness to pay for X^0, i.e. $b_i(X_0(t), t) < V'_i(X^0)$.

Hypothesis 4. Whether or not the C or R1 experiments reach equilibrium, the proposals, $X(t)$, in the R1 experiments will tend to exceed those in the C experiments, $\hat{X}(t)$.

6. EXPERIMENTS AND TESTS OF HYPOTHESES

Subjects and Design Parameters

Thirty-five subjects participated in two sets of experiments consisting of three R1 and four C experiments using five subjects in each experiment. No subject participated in more than one of the seven sessions. Volunteers were solicited for a "group decision making experiment in which participants will have an opportunity to receive payments in cash depending upon their decisions." The subjects were obtained from graduate or undergraduate economics classes at the University of Southern California, University of Arizona, Stanford University, and University of California (Berkeley).

The marginal valuation functions, $V'_i(X)$, for the C experiments are shown in Figure 2. The price of the public good is $q = \$45$ and the Lindahl equilibrium is $(X^0; V^i_1, V'_2, V'_3, V'_4, V'_5) = (5 \text{ or } 6; 3, 3, 8, 13, 18)$. For R1, Tables (1.1–1.4) in Appendix I exhibit the individual total and marginal valuation schedules $V_i(X)$, $V'_i(X)$. The form of the G-L tax rule used in the R1 experiments $(I = 5, q = 45)$ is $C_i(x_i | S_i) = -(5S_i - 9)(x_i + S_i) + 2(x_i + S_i)^2 + k_i(S_i)$ where

$$k_1(S_1) \equiv 2.5(S_1 - 1)S_1 - 3$$
$$k_2(S_2) \equiv 2.5(S_2 - 1)S_2 - 3$$
$$k_3(S_3) \equiv 2.5 S_3(S_3 + 1) - 3$$
$$k_4(S_4) \equiv 2.5 S_4(S_4 + 1) + 22$$
$$k_5(S_5) \equiv 2.5 S_5(S_5 + 1) + 42$$

The tabulations of $C_i(x_i | S_i)$ provided to the subjects are exhibited in Tables (2.1–2.4), Appendix I. These parameters of C_i produce a balanced budget for the public good at $X^0 = 6$. The resulting net valuations

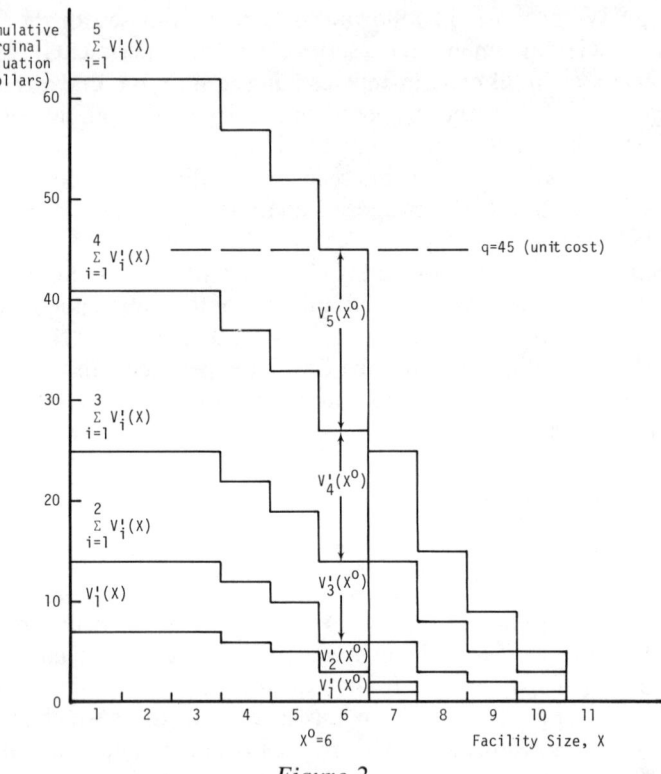

Figure 2.

$v_i = V_i(x_i + S_i) - C_i(x_i | S_i)$ are shown in Tables (3.1–3.4), Appendix I. A copy of the form used by each subject to record each decision and its consequence is also contained in Appendix I.

Appendix II contains the instructions and forms used in the C experiments including the bid submission form (Table 2), and the record form used by each subject to compute his net membership value on each trial.

The marginal valuation functions and Lindahl prices in Figure 2 were selected with two objectives. First, these design parameters correspond with a collective having very diverse preferences for a public good. Consequently, the Lindahl equilibrium is clearly distinct from an egalitarian equilibrium—such as an equal sharing of the cost burden. Second, it will be noted in Figure 2 that the marginal valuations are constant for $X \leq 3$, with $51 worth of consumer's surplus available at $X = 3$ (compared with $70 at the Lindahl equilibrium). It was thought that this design would, if anything, tend to favor the C experiments. With this experimental design, if free riding is not too extensive, there might appear to be a reasonable possibility that group agreement could occur for at least three units of the public good. Except for the values of $X \leq 4$ the marginal valuations used in R1 and C were the same, and the LE was the same.

Experimental Results, Discussion

Charts R1.1–R1.3 graph the sequence of choices, $x_i(t)$, for each subject, and the group proposal, $X(t)$, for the three G–L "treatment" experiments. Charts C.1–C.4 graph the sequence of lowest accepted bids, $b_i(\hat{X}(t), t)$ (or the first bid, on trials for which $\hat{X} = 0$), and the group proposal, $\hat{X}(t)$, for the four Lindahl control experiments. The numbers corresponding to selected observations represent trial earnings, $v_i(t)$, for each subject (or total group earnings, $\sum_{i=1}^{I} v_i(t)$, in bottom panel). For example, in Chart R1.1, trial 1, subject 1 chose $x_1(1) = 0$, with $S_1(1) = \sum_{j \neq i} x_j(1) = 2$, $v_1(1) = v_1(x_1(1)|S_1(1)) = -\$2$. In chart C.1, trial 1, the group proposal under the Lindahl procedure was $\hat{X}(1) = 2$, and the lowest accepted bid for subject 1 (his second bid) was $b_1(2(1), 1) = \$4$, with $v_1(1) = \$6$.

Experiments R1.1 and R1.3 reached the Lindahl quantity, $X(t^*) = X^\circ = 6$ under the stopping rules on trial $t^* = 16$, and R1.2 attained this quantity at $t^* = 29$. Two of the control experiments reached agreement: C.1 stopped on trial $t^* = 26$, with the null proposal $X(t^*) = 0$, and C.4 stopped on trial $t^* = 24$ with $\hat{X}(t^*) = 2$. Free riding was so extensive in C.1 that it was decided that if in C.2 and C.3 equilibrium did not obtain by trial 15, then on trial 16 a bid sequence identical with the marginal valuation schedule for each subject would be imposed privately. Following this the sequence of trials, with free choice of individual bids, would continue as before. This was accomplished by an announcement, following trial 15 in C.2 and C.3, that the experiment was being interrupted, and each member would be given a bid decision for trial 16. Each member was then approached independently and that member's sequence of marginal valuations was copied onto his or her bid form for trial 16. This procedure was used to provide a test of the *static stability* of the Lindahl equilibrium, if attained, although that equilibrium might be unattainable by the dynamic procedure. As evidenced in Charts C.2 and C.3, this Lindahl equilibrium was not stable as the subjects tended to lower their bids on trial 17 and thereafter. In both C.2 and C.3, four of the five subjects reduced their bids for the sixth unit.

Experiment C.2 was terminated on trial 21 by the unanimous consent of the somewhat frustrated subjects. In C.2, member 2 sent repeated cooperative signals (high bids) which seemed to have the primary effect of inviting others to free-ride. Experiment C.3 was terminated on trial 28 when it was indicated that not all bids would be repeated to yield equilibrium. Member 2 was unwilling to accept a zero imputation of the surplus, and reduced his bid from (7,7,7,6,5,3) on trial 27 to (7,7,6,0,0,0) on trial 28. However, member 3 did not alter his bids in spite of his zero imputation and indicated (after the experiment) willingness to receive nothing to assure better prospects of reward for the other subjects.

It was more difficult to maintain order in the C than in the R1 experiments as subjects in the former tended to express their frustration by breaking the silence rule. From postexperimental comments of the subjects it seemed apparent that they perceived the task of group agreement to be very difficult if not impossible in the C experiments.

Although in each R1 session group agreement produced the Lindahl quantity, only R1.2 resulted in Lindahl equilibrium (LE) incremental proposals (corresponding to implicit Lindahl prices) for every subject. In Chart R1.1, subject 5 was below his LE proposal by one unit, $x_5(t^*) = 2$ ($x_5^0 = 3$) and subject 2 was above his LE by one unit, $x_2(t^*) = 1(x_2^0 = 0)$. In R1.3, $x_2(t^*) = 1(x_2^0 = 0)$ and $x_4(t^*) = 1(x_4^0 = 2)$. In each case, of course, the low (high) member received a payoff greater (less) than his Lindahl surplus, or rent: In R1.1, $v_5(t^*) = \$22 > \$12 = v_5^0$, while in R1.3, $v_2(t^*) = \$12 < \$17 = v_2^0$. Two considerations make deviations from individual Lindahl (and therefore Nash) equilibria possible and perhaps likely: (*i*) The payoff structure provides limited rewards to game strategic behavior, i.e., if player i chooses $x_i < x_i^0$, and one or more players j make accommodating choices $x_j > x_j^0$, then i can gain at the "expense" (the game is nonzero sum) of j. (*ii*) There are subjective transactions costs inherent in the procedure (*any* procedure), and a risk of opportunity loss implicit in the stopping rule. Neither consideration can be illustrated better than in the play of subjects 2 and 5 in Chart R1.1. Only once, on trial 5, did subject 5 choose x_5 as high as his Lindahl (Nash) choice ($x_5^0 = 3$). Unable to turn a positive payoff on trials 7–10, the subject's proposal was lowered from 2 to -3 on trials 11–13. This "punishing" message produced zero or negative net benefits for all members, but subjects 1 and 3 increased their choices by 1 unit on trial 13, while subject 5 returned to his choice of $x_5 = 2$ on trial 14, yielding him \$22. Subject 2 (who had made the accommodation to 5's choice), when asked later why he or she did not lower from $x_2 = 1$ to 0, since it provided an increase in conditional payoff, replied, "Oh yes, but to change at that point would require us to continue at least three more trials, risking failure to agree, and the extra \$3 (from \$12 to \$15) wasn't worth it." There it is, the time cost of more trials, and the increased risk to group agreement when anyone changes his message—these may combine to make it entirely rational for a subject to accept an "unfavorable" deviation from his Nash choice.

Experimental Results, Tests of Hypotheses

Hypotheses 1 and 2 are not contradicted by the results summarized above and the charts; we shall consider them as tentatively confirmed. Hypothesis 3

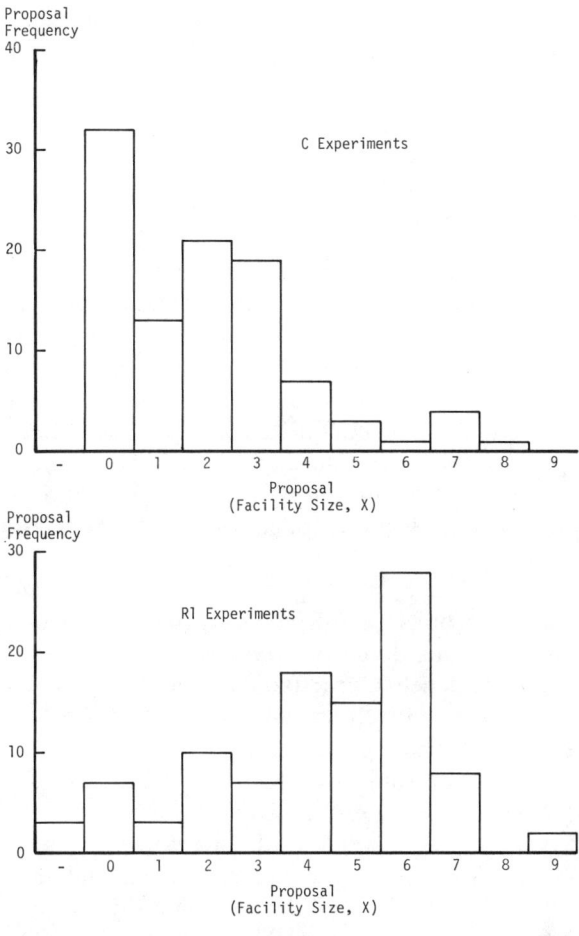

Figure 3.

is supported by the following calculation: Of the 495 total subject bids for the 6th unit in the four control experiments, 29 percent were equal to or larger, and 71 percent below, the Lindahl equilibrium prices (20 percent were zero). Using the binomial test, the null hypothesis that the probability of bids below the Lindahl prices is one half (and the probability of bids equal to or above the Lindahl prices is one half) is rejected at a significance level $p < .001$. Comparing the group proposals in the R1 and C experiments using the two-sample t–test, the null hypothesis that the proposals in C experiments exceed these in R1 experiments is rejected with $p < .001$. This calculation should be taken with the usual grain of salt as there is no a priori case for successive trial proposals to be statistically independent. Histograms of the distribution of proposals in the C and R1 experiments are shown in Figure 3. These data leave little doubt that the experimental results support hypothesis 4.

7. REPLICATION OF THE G-L EXPERIMENT WITH DIFFERENT PARAMETERS

The following unique features of the experimental design used in the R1 experiments suggest the need for further experiments to study the robustness of the G-L mechanism with respect to various parameter variations:

1. In R1 the experimental "joint facility" was a public good for every subject agent. However, the G-L mechanism can be applied to taste configurations in which the common outcome is a "bad" for some agents. If the public good harms an economic agent, the G-L tax rule allocates that agent a subsidy such that the person receives a net benefit depending upon the total surplus available from the public good, and the parameters of the tax rule.

2. The parameters I, $k_i(S_i)$, and q appearing in the tax allocation rule were chosen with the objective of balancing the budget at the LE and providing "reasonable" net dollar outcomes ($12 and $17) for the subjects. These choices resulted in net value (payoff) matrices $v_i(x_i, S_i)$ for each subject with the property that a relatively small number of row choices (x_i) provided some positive payoffs. Thus, in Appendix I, Tables 3.1–3.4, the choices $\langle -3, -2, -1, 0, 1, 2 \rangle$ for subjects 1 and 2, $\langle -2, -1, 0, 1, 2 \rangle$ for subject 3, and so forth, provide some positive payoffs.

3. The version of the G-L tax rule used in R1 does not balance the budget for every proposal. Consequently, there are strategies and group proposals that yield group payoffs in excess of the aggregate LE surplus. An example is represented by the play of experiment R1.1 which stopped with an aggregate surplus payment of $75.

Experimental Design

The first two of these features were eliminated in the design of a second research experiment (R2) based on the G-L mechanism. The design applies to a collective of I = 8 agents, with the joint facility a marginal "bad" at all levels of X for subject 1, and a "bad" in total at the LE quantity ($X^0 = 4$). Again, the budget was balanced only at the LE. The valuation and cost functions are the quadratics,

$$V_i(X) = (A_i - B_i X)X + \alpha_i, \tag{7.1}$$

$$C_i(X) = -(0.1 \, IS_i - q/I)X + (0.05)(I - 1)X^2 + K \tag{7.2}$$

Table 1. Parameter and Lindahl Equilibrium Values

Paramter Subject	A_i	B_i	α_i	x_i^0	v_i^0
1	−2.6	0	10	−4	$10
2	11.8	1.50	0	−1	24
3	11.8	1.50	0	−1	24
4	12.6	1.50	0	0	24
5	7.4	0.75	0	1	12
6	10.2	1.00	0	2	16
7	11.0	1.00	0	3	16
8	9.8	0.75	0	4	12
			Total	4	$138

where $I = 8$, $q = 8$, and $K = 5.6$. Table 1 lists the values of (A_i, B_i, α_i) and the equilibrium choices (x_i^0), and rents (v_i^0), by subject. The G-L tax rule allocates subject # 1 a subsidy such that his value net of the "disutility" of $X^0 = 4$ is $10. The design corresponds to a collective with quite diverse tastes and for which the cost of the public good is small in relation to its value. At the LE total cost, $qX^0 = 8 \cdot 4 = \$32$, total value is $170, and the net LE surplus is $138. For instructions, cost and valuation tables see Appendix III.

By comparison with R1, the net value matrices in R2 yield payoffs that are considerably less sensitive to deviations from the LE. Consequently, it is expected that the R2 experiments will exhibit greater deviations from this equilibrium than the R1 experiment.

Experimental Results

The trial sequence of choices, $x_i(t)$ for each subject, and the resulting group proposals, $X(t)$, are exhibited in Charts R2.1 and R2.2. Both experiments stopped under the agreement rule with the quantity proposal, 3. As expected, in comparison with the R1 experiments the relatively large surplus, and insensitivity of surplus imputations to individual choices, produces considerable deviation in equilibrium agreement choices from the LE values. No peculiarities seem to have arisen because the common outcome was a bad for one subject.

8. A DECENTRALIZED AUCTION PROCESS

Corollaries of the G-L and Lindahl Mechanisms

The unanimity feature of the stopping rule used in the above research and control experiments together with corollaries of the G-L and Lindahl cost allocation mechanisms may be combined to suggest a "new" adjustment procedure.

Consider the following bid interpretation of the G-L tax rule:

From (2.2) a maximizing agent choosing x_i^0, conditional on S_i, implicitly reveals the following bid message

$$b_i(x_i^0|S_i) = -\left(IS_i - \frac{q}{I}\right) + (I-1)(x_i^0 + S_i)$$

$$= Ix_i^0 - X + \frac{q}{I} \quad (8.1)$$

Given x_i^0, and the collective's proposal, X, we can always compute $b_i(x_i^0|S_i)$. Similarly, for all agents $j \neq i$, their bid message is $b_j(x_j^0|S_j)$. Summing over these bids, define

$$B_i = \sum_{j \neq i} b_j(x_j^0|S_j) = IS_i - (I-1)X + \left(\frac{I-1}{I}\right)q = -Ix_i^0 + X + \left(\frac{I-1}{I}\right)q \quad (8.2)$$

But rearranging (8.2),

$$Ix_i^0 - X + \frac{q}{I} = q - B_i,$$

and from (8.1) $b_i(x_i^0|S_i) = q - B_i$. Consequently, the G-L tax mechanism guides agent i to bid exactly the difference between public marginal cost and the sum of all other bids. The implicit private marginal cost to i is $q - B_i$, and his implicit cost allocation is $(q - B_i)(x_i + S_i)$. In effect, agent i has chosen x_i to maximize

$$U_i[V_i(x_i + S_i) - (q - B_i)(x_i + S_i)] \quad (8.3)$$

Under this interpretation (and nothing more is claimed for the above arithmetic) we have

Corollary 1. Maximizing (8.3) is equivalent to maximizing $U_i[V_i(x_i + S_i) - C_i(x_i|S_i)]$ in Proposition 1.

This corollary provides some additional insight into why the ingenious G-L tax rule is incentive compatible. The rule presents each agent with a "price", $q - B_i$, determined by the actions (bids) of all other agents, over which i has no "significant" control. (Since $B_i = \sum_{j \neq i} b_j(x_j|S_j)$, and x_i is a component of S_j, agent i may indirectly, but diffusely, have an effect on $q - B_i$). Agent i is then essentially in the position of an agent in any competitive market, and, from the experimental evidence, he responds in the expected manner.

This bid interpretation of the G-L tax rule is also suggested by the Lindahl cost allocation mechanism. In the proof and discussion of Proposition 2 we have already made note of the following special case:

Corollary 2. From (4.3) if agent i believes that $b_j(X) \equiv b_j$ will be constant for every j, then his net average and marginal costs are the same, $q - \sum_{j \neq i} b_j - B_i$, and his optimal bid function is $V'_i(X)$.

Hence, i's net reward is $v_i = V_i(X) - (q - B_i)X$ as in Corollary 1, and his competitive response in the Lindahl process would be to send the bid message $b_i(X) = V'_i(X)$.

An Alternative Decentralized Mechanism

Consider the following institution for collective public good decision:

(1) Let each agent i submit a bid and a proposed quantity (b_i, X_i) with the understanding that his share of unit cost is $(q - B_i)$, and his share of total cost is $(q - B_i)X_i$.

(2) Give each agent the right to veto or agree to the unit cost, $q - B_i$, allocated to him by all other agents. He signals agreement by choosing $b_i = q - B_i$ and a veto by choosing $b_i \neq q - B_i$. Also give each agent i the right to veto or signal agreement by choosing $X_i = \bar{X} = \sum_{k=1}^{I} X_k/I$ (agree), or $X_i \neq \bar{X}$ (veto).

(3) Group agreement prevails if and only if agreement is signaled by every agent $i = 1, 2, \ldots, I$, in which case $\bar{X}$ units of the public good are purchased, with each agent paying the unit cost share $q - B_i$.

Environment

In the experimental paradigm for this institution, member i receives net reward $v_i = V_i(X_i) - (q - B_i)X_i$, if the collective reaches agreement, and a small payment, v_0, otherwise.

Hence, utility is

$$u_i = \begin{cases} U_i[V_i(X_i) - (q - B_i)X_i], & \text{if } b_i = q - B_i, \text{ and } X_i = \bar{X} \text{ for all } i. \\ U_i[v_0], & \text{otherwise.} \end{cases} \quad (8.4)$$

Proposition 3. If $U'_i > 0$ and each subject i chooses (b_i, X_i) to maximize u_i in (8.4), this implies a Lindahl group equilibrium.

At a maximum for u_i,

$$[V'_i(X_i) - (q - B_i)]U'_i = 0, \quad (8.5a)$$

$$b_i = q - B_i, \quad (8.5b)$$

$$X_i = \bar{X}, \text{ for all i}. \quad (8.5c)$$

From (8.5a) and (8.5c) $X_1 = X_2 = \ldots = X_I = \bar{X}$, and $V_i'(\bar{X}) = q - B_i$.[6] Therefore from (8.5b) $q = \sum_{i=1}^{I} b_i = \sum_{i=1}^{I} V_i'(X^0)$, giving the LE.

In the sequel the mechanism defined by the institution (1)–(3) which leads to proposition 3 will be called the *auction mechanism*, or when combined with a dynamic procedure, an *auction* process. This identification is used because the mechanism can be interpreted (Smith, 1977) as a variation on the following well-known auction principle for markets in private goods (Vickrey, 1961; Smith, 1967): Each bidder in a market has an incentive to bid his marginal willingness to pay if his purchase cost is independent of his bid, and if his success in obtaining the good requires his bid to be not smaller than the cost. Thus, in the above public good auction mechanism any subject who bids less than his marginal willingness to pay increases the risk of excluding himself (along with the entire collective) from the benefits of the good.[7]

Adjustment Process

The *language* of the auction process consists of *private* messages ($b_i(t)$, $X_i(t)$), and the *public* messages $B(t) = \sum_{i=1}^{I} b_i(t)$, $\bar{X}(t) = \sum_{i=1}^{I} X_i(t)/I$ on each trial $t = 1, 2, \ldots$ The iterative procedure is as follows:

(i) *Starting rule.* On trial t, each subject independently and privately selects two integers ($b_i(t), X_i(t)$), each confined to specified intervals, and records these choices on a prescribed record sheet (Appendix IV).

(ii) *Transition rules.*

  (ii.a) The experimenter records each ($b_i(t), X_i(t)$), computes, then posts $B(t)$, and $\bar{X}(t)$ on a blackboard, the posting to remain until the end of the process.

  (ii.b) Each subject records $B(t)$, and $\bar{X}(t)$, then computes, and records, $B_i(t) = B(t) - b_i(t)$ and $q - B_i(t)$.

  (ii.c) Each subject determines his private net valuation of ($q - B_i(t), X_i(t)$) from a pre-computed table (Appendix IV, Tables 2.1–2.4) of the values $v_i = V_i(X_i) - (q - B_i)X_i$. The resulting $v_i(t)$ is recorded on his record sheet. This completes trial t.

  (ii.d) Each subject then proceeds to trial $t + 1$ and chooses ($b_i(t+1)$, $X_i(t+1)$) as in (i).

(iii) *Stopping rule.*

  (iii.a) The process stops on trial t^* if $b_i(t^* - 1) = q - B_i(t^* - 1) = b_i(t^*) = q - B_i(t^*)$, $X_i(t^*) = \bar{X}(t^*)$, for all i, and $t^* \leq T$;

  (iii.b) Otherwise the process stops on trial $t = T$.

(iv) *Outcome rule.* If the process stops by (iii.a) the group has reached *equilibrium* (agreement), and each subject is paid $v_i(t^*)$ in cash. Otherwise he receives a modest wage. In some experimental sessions this outcome was modified so that each i received $v_i(t^*) + \$2$ if (*iii.a*) occurs, otherwise $2.

DISCUSSION

In section 5 it was seen that the G-L mechanism yields Lindahl equilibria that are Nash equilibria. This same property characterizes the Auction mechanism. However, because of the discontinuity in (8.4) the Auction Mechanism provides multiple local Nash equilibria among which are to be found the Lindahl equilibria. From (8.4) if I agents choose *any* (b_i, X_i), $i = 1, 2, \ldots, I$ such that (1) $q = \sum_{k=1}^{I} b_k$, (2) $X_i \neq X^0$ and/or $b_i \neq V_i'(X^0)$ for some i, and (3) $V_i(X) - (q - B_i)X > v_0$ for all i, then unanimous agreement is individually rational, and the equilibrium is locally Nash stable. That is, if any agent deviated from (b_i, X_i) by choosing, say (b_i^0, X^0), where $b_i^0 = V_i'(X^0) \neq q - B_i$, then this constitutes a veto and the agent receives v_0 making him worse off. This is illustrated in Table 2a for a collective of $I = 2$ members with valuation schedules given by $V_3(X)$ and $V_4(X)$ in Figure 2, and with $q = 21$, $v_0 = 0$. The LE is given by $[X^0; V_3'(X^0), V_4'(X^0)] = [5 \text{ or } 6; 8, 13]$. Clearly, the set of choices ($b_3 = 8$, $X_3 = 5$; $b_4 = 13$, $X_4 = 5$) is a Nash equilibrium, but so also are all the choices with positive payoffs in Table 2a.

Table 2a. Auction Process Payoff Matrix

Table 2b. G–L Process Payoff Matrix

$x_3(t^*-1)$	$x_4(t^*-1)$ → $x_4(t^*)$ ↓ $x_3(t^*)$	3			4			5		
		2	3	4	3	4	5	4	5	6
1	0	0	0	0	0	0	0	0	0	0
	1	0	·/·	0	0	1/12	0	0	·/·	0
	2	0	0	0	0	0	0	0	0	0
2	1	0	0	0	0	0/0	0	0	0	0
	2	0	11/2	0	0/0	12/12	0/0	0	7/21	0
	3	0	0	0	0	0/0	0	0	0	0
3	2	0	0	0	0	0	0	0	0	0
	3	0	·/·	0	0	21/7	0	0	·/·	0
	4	0	0	0	0	0	0	0	0	0

It should be noted that the discontinuity in (8.4) is directly a consequence of the stopping rule requiring each i to avoid a veto by "matching" $b_i = q - B_i$, $X_i = \bar{X}$. The lesson here is that the *process* (complete with stopping rule) in which a mechanism is imbedded interacts with and alters the Nash equilibrium properties of the static payoff conditions of the mechanism. The same considerations apply to the G–L mechanism when we take account of a process stopping rule. For example suppose our stopping rule is that the choice of x_i must be repeated once, i.e., we stop on trial t^* where $x_i(t^*) = x_i(t^* - 1)$ for all i. Now consider the same illustration used in Table 2a. The choice $(x_3 = 2, x_4 = 4)$ is a static Nash equilibrium. But due to the stopping rule, the payoff matrix appears as in Table 2b, and this particular Nash equilibrium is achieved only if $(x_3 = 2, x_4 = 4)$ is repeated on the next trial. Hence, the G–L mechanism together with the stopping process also yields multiple local Nash equilibria among which are to be found the Lindahl equilibria.

9. AUCTION PROCESS; HYPOTHESES, EXPERIMENTS AND RESULTS

Hypotheses

The auction procedure of section 8 defines a new experimental research process (A). Since the auction process is incentive compatible, we expect it to yield quantities and cost shares corresponding to the LE. Specifically, we propose

Hypothesis 5. The sample quantities and prices determined by those A experiments reaching equilibrium under stopping rule (*iii.a*) in section 4, may be regarded as having been drawn from populations with means equal to the Lindahl equilibrium $[X^0; V'_1(X^0), \ldots, V'_1(X^0)]$.

Two groups of experiments (A2 and A3), which will be described in the next section, are identical in the structure (i.e., distribution) of member valuations and in the Lindahl optimal quantity of the public good, but in the second group I and q are each double their respective values in the first group. The variability of price and quantity outcomes is expected to increase with increased collective size since the maximum feasible surplus that can be captured by any one agent is increased.

Hypothesis 6. Replication of A experiments with the parameters I and q increased in the same proportion will increase the variance of equilibrium price-quantity outcomes.

Subjects and Experimental Design

Sixty-seven subjects participated in twelve different sessions within a design block of three series of auction process experiments (A1, A2, A3). Table 3 lists the design parameters, consisting of the LE prices, quantity,

Table 3. Auction Experimental Design Parameters

LE Prices, V'_i	Experiment A1	Experiment A2	Experiment A3
	Number of Subjects with LE Price V'_i		
−5	0	1	2
3	2	1	2
8	1	1	2
13	1	1	2
18	1	0	0
Number in Collective, I	5	4	8
LE Quantity, X^0	5 (or 6)	6 (or 7)	6 (or 7)
LE Total Surplus	$70	$69	$138
Public Good Price, q	$45	$19	$38
Number of Experimental Sessions	3	5	4
Total Subjects	15	20	32

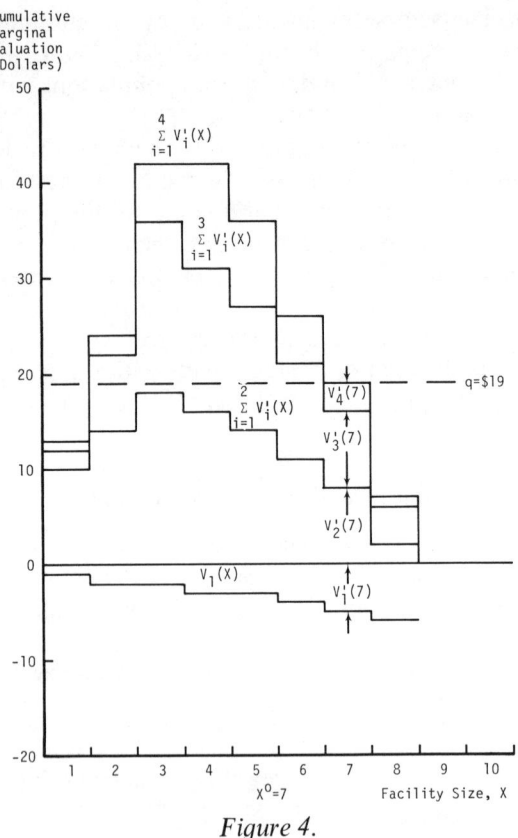

Figure 4.

and total surplus, the number of members in each collective, the price of the public good, and the number of experimental sessions and participating subjects for each set of design parameters. The marginal valuation functions, $V'_i(X)$, used in A1 are identical with those illustrated in Figure 2 for the C experiment. The A1 experiments are thus directly comparable to the R1 and C experiments.[8] Figure 4 illustrates the $V'_i(X)$ functions for the A2 experiments. Figure 4 also applies to the A3 experiments if each $V'_i(X)$ is vertically doubled, i.e., replaced with two identical $V'_i(X)$ functions. A3 differs from A2 only by the scale change from doubling the number of members with each configuration of tastes, $V'_i(X)$, and doubling the unit cost of the public good. This provides replication control over the effect of I on collective outcomes for the purpose of testing Hypothesis 6.

Experimental Results, Discussion

Charts A1.1–A1.3, A2.1–A2.5, and A3.1–A3.4 provide the sequence of bid-quantity choices $b_i(t)$, $X_i(t)$, and the resulting cost shares $q - B_i(t)$ and mean quantity proposals, $\bar{X}$, for all experimental sessions. The numbers corresponding to the last five cost share observations represent trial earnings, $v_i(t)$.

The following modifications were made in the transition rules, the stopping rules, and the outcome rule at various points in the chronological sequence in which these twelve experiments were performed:

(1) In the four experiments A1.1–A1.3, and A2.1, the group average proposal was not computed and made public until subject trial bids had converged nearly to their unit cost shares. In all subsequent experiments, average proposals were posted with the bid sums on every trial.

(2) In experiments A1.3, A2.1–A2.3, and A3.1–3.3 the stopping rule in the written instructions was supplemented by the verbal specification that the experiment would be terminated on trial 15 if by that trial the sum of the bids had not reached to within one dollar of the price, q. This instruction was introduced to discourage subjects from waiting until trial 20 or later to make realistic bids, causing coordination difficulties as trial 30 approached. This coordination difficulty first emerged in A1.2 which failed to reach stopping rule agreement when the bids overshot unit cost on trial 29. On trials 27 and 28 the bids were just one dollar below unit cost. On trial 29 three subjects attempted to make the agreeing bids, making it then impossible to satisfy the stopping rule before trial 30. Although the 15th-trial modification caused the bids to increase more rapidly, it did not solve all coordination problems. Thus, in experiment A2.1 all subjects repeated their bids, one dollar short of unit cost share, on trials 24–29, as each waited for another to increase his bid. Subject 3 at first raised his bid to $7 on trial 29 then changed it back to $6 fearful, as he indicated after the experiment, that another member would also raise causing an overshoot.[9] As a consequence of this experience the stopping rule was further modified to allow random choice among two or more subjects who, in attempting to produce agreement, cause an overshoot. But other, probably superior modifications might resolve these coordination difficulties among agreeing members. One possibility is to relax the lumpiness of the requirement that all bids be in whole dollar amounts, and give a bid rebate if the bid total exceeds cost.

(3) In experiments A2.4, A2.5 and A3.4, the outcome rule paid each subject an amount

(a) $v_i(t^*) + \$2$, if group agreement occurred
(b) $\$2$, otherwise.

Essentially, the purpose of the lump-sum payment, v_0, is to compensate for time and transactions cost which exist whether or not agreement occurs (Smith, 1975). If this sum is paid only as a small "consolation prize," and does not also supplement the Lindahl rents, a disincentive to agreement is provided any subject who finds, near the end of the trial sequence, that his choices have cornered him with a net value $v_i \leq v_0$.

The results of experiments A1.1–A1.3 demonstrate that the auction process possesses properties of incentive compatibility comparable to those in the G-L process for experiments R1.1–R1.3. Experiments A1.1 and A1.3 yielded stopping rule agreement at the LE quantity, 5, while the failure of A1.2 to produce agreement was influenced by coordination problems that can occur under the extremely exacting requirements of the stopping rule. On trials 26–30 in A1.2, subject choices are not in violation of incentive compatibility since the bids overshoot unit cost share on three of these trials. Table 5 compares final trial choices by subjects in the R1 and A1 experiments. The R1 session "prices" are the bids implicit in each subject's incremental proposal, x_i, given S_i computed using the $C'_i(x_i|S_i)$ applying to R1. It is clear that equilibrium quantities are as invariable in the Auction process as in the G–L process. The higher equilibrium quantity in the R1 experiments merely reflects the sharp Nash equilibrium and balanced budget at $X^0 = 6$, and is not significant. The Lindahl rents are the same at $X^0 = 5$ or 6 and the Auction process provides no incentive for collectives to choose the larger quantity.[10] In fact at the larger quantities individual earnings are more sensitive to unit cost shares, and it appears significant that (except for A2.5) the experimental groups for $I = 4$ and 5 always agreed on the smallest X that maximizes the total Lindahl rent available.

The more rapid convergence of the R1 experiments may be of significance although the sample is much too small to be sure. The lower dimensionality of the choice space in the G-L process may favor convergence. At this stage

Table 4. Equilibrium Price-Quantity Outcomes, Experiments A2 and A3

		A2 Sessions, Prices						A3 Session, Prices			
Subject	$V'_i(7)$	A2.1	A2.2	A2.3	A2.4	A2.5	$V'_i(7)$	A3.1	A3.2	A3.3	A3.4
1	−5	−5	−6	−6	−4	−6	−5	−4		−4	−3
2	13	13	12	14+	13	14	13	14		13+	14
3	8	7+	8	7	7	6	−5	−6	no	−5	−3
4	3	4	5	4	3	5	13	13	agree-	10	14
5							3	1	ment	4	4
6							8	9		5	8
7							3	0		5	2
8							8	11		10	2
Equilibrium Quantity		6	6	6	6	7		6	7	6	7
Final trial	t*	29	26	29	19	15		28		29	16

+Simulated bid increase by subject chosen at random among those demonstrating willingness to increase.

one can only speculate on the dynamic behavioral differences between the two processes. Hypotheses concerning such detail must be sharply enough fomulated to allow the appropriate testing experiments to be designed.

Selected results of the A2 and A3 experimental sessions are summarized in Table 4. Briefly, the following characteristics of the results of these experiments may be noted:

(1) In most of the A2 and A3 sessions the collective attained a stable equilibrium quantity proposal before the bids and cost shares reached agreement (A2.2, A2.3, A2.4, A3.1, A3.2, A3.3, A3.4). It was easier to agree on the quantity that maximized the total surplus to be divided, than on the cost shares that determine the distribution of that surplus. The Auction process provides motivation for efficiency in the sense of the Lindahl optimal quantity.

(2) Although the A2 collectives largely agree on the smallest quantity that maximizes total surplus, the A3 collectives do not. Perhaps the greater adjustment freedom provided by an increase in the size of the collective from 4 to 8 generates less member resistance to agreeing on the larger quantity.

(3) There appears to be no empirical support for a relationship, positive or negative, between collective size and price convergence speed. All groups, whether $I = 4$ or 8, tend to resist price agreement until somewhere near the trial bound, T.

(4) Experiment A3.2 is the only session failing to reach agreement under the stopping rule in a manner that can be interpreted as consistent with incentive incompatibility. The reasons for the failure to reach agreement are clear from chart A3.2. Subjects 2 and 4 held to bids substantially below their LE prices. Each had an LE price of 13, and their final trial bids were $b_2(29) = 6$ and $b_4(29) = 7$, implying a demand for net earnings $v_2(29) = \$69$ and $v_4(29) = \$62$. Since the maximum total surplus was $\$138$ these were unrealistic demands although, of course, the subjects had no way of knowing this. It happened in this experiment that the random assignment of member valuations to subjects gave the two largest marginal valuation schedules to the two most intransigent subjects. Together, at the LE, subjects 2 and 4 accounted for a $\$26$ share of the $\$38$ unit price of the public good, and there was just not enough slack among the remaining members to permit an accommodation to these choices. However, such an accommodation might have been obtained (although not likely) if the group had converged to the quantity 6 instead of 7, for then the final trial bids would have produced the net values, $v_2(29) = \$62$, $v_4(29) = \$56$ leaving a residual surplus of $\$20$ for the remaining six subjects.

(5) Comparing the results of the A1 sessions with those of A2 and A3, there is no evidence to suggest that the Auction process is unable to handle

public good decisions which are "bads" for one or more members of the collective.

(6) Experiment A2.1 was the only session using carefully selected experienced subjects. All four subjects had participated previously in one of the A1 (I = 5) collectives, and by their responses had shown quick ability to master the procedures. From Chart A2.1 it is seen that each member's bids converged asymptotically (but $1 short) to member cost share. Experience seemed to yield a smoother, quicker, play of the game, but did not guarantee equilibrium for the reasons discussed previously.

Experimental Results, Tests of Hypotheses

From Table 5 both the R1 and the A1 sessions produced Lindahl equilibrium quantities (5 or 6). The sample variance of deviations in final prices from the Lindahl optimal prices is $S_A^2 = 6.07$ for the A1 experiments and $S_R^2 = 7.14$ for the R1 experiments. These variances are not significantly different from each other and we are unable to reject the hypothesis that the variability of price outcomes is the same in the Auction and G–L mechanisms.

Hypothesis 5 was tested by estimating the parameters β_0, β in the equation

$$y_{ij} = \beta_0 + \beta x_{ij} + \varepsilon_{ij} \tag{9.1}$$

where y_{ij} is the observed final equilibrium bid of subject j in experiment i, and x_{ij} is the Lindahl optimal price for subject j in experiment i. According to hypothesis 5, $\beta_0 = 0$ and $\beta = 1$, i.e. the mean final equilibrium bids are not significantly different from the theoretical Lindahl prices. Least squares estimates $(\hat{\beta}_0, \hat{\beta})$ were obtained using the method proposed by McGuire, Farley, Lucas and Ring (1968), pp. 1207–1208) when dependent variables

Table 5. Final Trial Price-Quantity Outcomes, G-L and Auction Process Experiments

Subject	$V_i(X^0)$	R1 Sessions, Prices			A1 Sessions, Prices		
		R1.1	R1.2	R1.3	A1.1	A1.2	A1.3
1	3	3	3	3	4	6	4
2	3	8	3	8	6	2	4
3	8	8	8	8	10	9	3
4	13	13	13	8	9	13	15
5	18	13	18	18	16	15+	19
Equilibrium Quantity		6	6	6	5	5	5
Final Trial, t*		16	29	16	30	30	29

+Simulated bid increase by subject chosen at random among those demonstrating willingness to increase.

Table 6

Statistic	$\hat{\beta}_0$	$t(\hat{\beta}_0 - 0)$	$\hat{\beta}$	$t(\hat{\beta} - 1)$	R^2	Var. Error
A1 Sessions	1.761	1.635	0.812	−1.80	0.82	4.458
A2 Sessions	−0.005	−0.17	1.001	0.03	0.97	1.200
A3 Sessions	0.246	0.46	0.948	0.78	0.99	4.131

are subject to add-up constraints (in this case, the stopping rule defining equilibrium requires the final bids to add up to the experimentally defined price of the public good). Using observations from the A1, A2 and A3 sessions shown in Tables 4 and 5, the regression results are summarized in Table 6. The low t-values (especially for the A2 and A3 sessions) under the "null hypotheses," $\beta_0 = 0$, $\beta = 1$, are consistent with hypothesis 5. From the R^2 calculations, approximately 90 percent of the variation in equilibrium bids is explained by the controlled Lindahl price variable in each experiment. The F-values for the three regressions are all highly significant ($P < 0.001$).

From Table 6 the variance of error about the regression line is greater for $I = 8$ (A3) than for $I = 4$ (A2). An F-test of this variance ratio is significant at $P < .05$. This supports hypothesis 6 that replication of a public good economy holding the structure of tastes and costs constant, but increasing (doubling) the number of agents will increase the variability of equilibrium bids.

10. ON SUBJECT ADAPTIVE RESPONSE BEHAVIOR

The research in this paper did not propose any a priori hypotheses regarding the dynamic response behavior of subjects over successive experimental trials. With the large number of subject-trial observations contained in the experiments reported, it is tempting to do some a posteriori analysis in an attempt to obtain some characterizations of subject dynamic behavior in the G-L and Auction Mechanism experiments. Such "fishing" in the data are justified only as a means of suggesting plausible hypotheses about subject dynamic behavior that might be tested by further experiments. In what follows some simple models of subject adaptive response behavior are explored using data from R1 and R2 for the G-L mechanism and data from A1, A2 and A3 for the Auction mechanism.

Adaptive Response in the G-L Experiments

The simplest and most obvious model of subject responses in the G-L experiment is that of Cournot adjustment behavior, i.e., each subject is assumed to choose $x_i(t)$ to maximize $v_i[x_i(t)]$ on the assumption that $S_i(t) = S_i(t-1)$. Thus, the subject's response on trial t is his best reply to trial $t-1$. Since there is little reason a priori to expect such a decision rule to yield group equilibrium for any given experimental design, it is instructive to examine the designs in R1 and R2 for Cournot stability. These two designs yield very different Cournot stability properties.

The payoff matrices in the R1 experiments imply very rapid convergence to the Nash equilibrium (Lindahl optimum) under the Cournot adjustment dynamic from any of a large number of "reasonable" initial choices. An examination of the "Net Membership Value" tables 3.1–3.4 in Appendix I suggests that for subjects 1 and 2 a reasonable initial choice is any element of $\langle -1, 0, 1 \rangle$, while for subjects 3, 4 and 5 any element of $\langle -1, 0, 1, 2 \rangle$ is appealing. Furthermore, if all five subjects choose 0 or 1 initially the Cournot dynamic converges to the Lindahl optimum in one iteration; if the five subjects start at the point $(0, 1, 1, 2, 2)$ or $(0, 1, 1, 1, 3)$ in the choice space they converge in two iterations.

In contrast, I have not found any similar initial points, using the R2 payoff matrices in Tables 3.1–3.7 (Appendix III), that map into the Nash equilibrium. If one plays out the Cournot dynamic assuming initial choices equal to the actual final choices in R2.1, $(-3, 0, -2, 2, 1, 1, 2, 2)$, and in R2.2, $(-4, 3, -1, 1, -1, 3, 0, 2)$, in each case the Cournot process diverges to the boundaries of the subject payoff matrices in two iterations.

Consequently, the R1 design appears to be strongly Cournot convergent, while the R2 design appears strongly Cournot divergent. Yet the subject collectives in R2 reached stopping rule equilibrium about as easily as the R1 collectives. Although the R2 collectives missed the Lindahl optimal quantity by one unit, this did not represent a large sacrifice in economic rent. The decision makers in these experiments seem to perform poorly compared with Cournot simple maximizers in experiments strongly Cournot convergent, but superior to Cournot simple maximizers in experiments strongly Cournot divergent! This suggests a form of gestalt, global, or nonmyopic response behavior that permits collectives to reach agreement where none is possible or likely under a Cournot dynamic. In this respect it is interesting to examine the data from the two sets of expriments for Cournot responses. Of the 230 total subject responses in the R1 experiments 123 were Cournot "best reply" choices. Of the 288 subject responses in the R2 experiments only 67 were Cournot choices. This difference is significant at $P < 0.0001$. Our experimental decision makers appear to use the Cournot rule rather frequently when it will work, and to abandon it when it will not work! However, in both the R1 and R2 experiments there was a smaller number of Cournot responses in the first half of the trials ($56\frac{1}{2}$ in R1, 26 in R2), than in the second half ($66\frac{1}{2}$ in R1, 41 in R2).

"Strategy" Evaluation in the G-L Experiments

One can classify subjects according to whether (i) half or more of their incremental proposal choices, $x_i(t)$, for $t < t^*$, were equal to or greater than their final (equilibrium) choice, $x_i(t^*)$, or (ii) half or more of their $x_i(t)$ were equal to or less than their $x_i(t^*)$ choice. If subjects in the first group are called "cooperative," and subjects in the second group are called "competitive," do "competitive" subjects earn a larger fraction of their Lindahl optimal rent than "cooperative" subjects? (No judgmatic significance should be attached to these labels as one might send "cooperative" responses with the intention of underbidding near the end.) Are these fractional earnings more variable for "competitive" subjects than "cooperative" subjects? The answer to both questions is in the negative based on a t-test comparison of the mean earnings fractions (t = 0.854), and an F-test comparison of the variance (F = 0.694), in the two classifications.

Adaptive Response in the Auction Mechanism

With the exception of A3.2 all the Auction mechanism experiments exhibit strong tendencies to converge to the Lindahl optimal quantity and to bids (cost shares) distributed tightly around means equal to the Lindahl optimal prices. In this section we report the results of an attempt to "explain" or characterize the dynamic adjustment of subject bids in the twelve Auction experiments by means of the linear bid equation,

$$\Delta b_i(t) = \alpha_i[q - B_i(t-1)] + \beta_i \Delta B_i(t-1) + \gamma_i t + \delta_i, \text{ where} \quad (10.1)$$
$$\Delta b_i(t) = b_i(t) - b_i(t-1), \text{ and } \Delta B_i(t-1) = B_i(t-1) - B_i(t-2).$$

Hence, $\Delta b_i(t)$ is the change in subject i's bid from trial $t-1$ to trial t, $q - B_i(t-1)$ is subject i's cost share on trial $t-1$, and $\Delta B_i(t-1)$ is the change in the sum of all bids by subjects $j \neq i$ from trial $t-2$ to $t-1$. The coefficients α_i and γ_i measue the adaptive response, respectively, of bid changes to cost share, and to the passage of "time", i.e., the using up of maximum allowable trials. If $\alpha_i > 0$ then the greater is cost share the larger the adaptive bid increase, while $\gamma_i < 0$ implies a smaller increase in bids as the trial limit approaches. β_i measures the "strategic" response of bid changes to the aggregate of all other bids. If $\beta_i > 0$ then i will (tit for tat) increase his bid if, on balance, there is an increase in the bids of all others.

Least squares estimates of $\hat{\alpha}_i$, $\hat{\beta}_i$, $\hat{\gamma}_i$ and $\hat{\delta}_i$ were computed for 66 of the 67 subjects participating in the three series of Auction experiments. (For subject 5 in A3.4 all coefficients were zero since for $t > 1$ all his bids were identical.)

The results of these regressions provide minimal encouragement for the

Table 7

Experiment Series	Number of Regressions (Subjects)	Number (Percentage) of Significant (P < 0.05) Coefficients		
		$\hat{\alpha}_i$	$\hat{\beta}_i$	$\hat{\gamma}_i$
A1	15	1 (7%)	3 (20%)	0 (0%)
A2	20	1 (5%)	0 (0%)	1 (5%)
A3	31	3 (10%)	3 (10%)	1 (3%)
Total	66	5 (8%)	6 (11%)	2 (3%)

prospect of explaining very much of the dynamics of subject behavior. Of the 66 regressions only 12 of the F statistics were significant at P < 0.05. (This means that about 18 percent of the regressions were significant at a 5 percent level of confidence.) Table 7 lists the number (percentage) of coefficients, excluding the constants, that were significant (P < 0.05) for each of the three series of Auction experiments. Across all experiments 8 percent of $\hat{\alpha}_i$ coefficients were significant, 11 percent of the $\hat{\beta}_i$ and 3 percent of the $\hat{\gamma}_i$. This suggests a weak tendency for the typical subject to relate his bid changes to his cost share, and to make bid changes in response to the bid changes of other subjects. Number of trials has no significant effect on bid response.

In view of these weak quantitative results, Table 8 provides an enumeration of the number of coefficient estimates that were positive or negative. This enables us to test qualitatively whether the positivity of the coefficients is significant. Using the binomial test we reject the hypothesis that α_i is as likely to be positive as negative (P < 0.0001) in the population of subjects. Similarly do we reject the equally likely hypothesis for the signs of β_i (P < 0.02). But for γ_i we cannot reject this null hypothesis (P < 0.16). We

Table 8

Experiment	Number of Regressions (Subjects)	Number of Coefficients with Indicated Signs					
		$\hat{\alpha}_i$		$\hat{\beta}_i$		$\hat{\gamma}_i$	
		+	−	+	−	+	−
A1	15	13	2	10	5	9	6
A2	20	13	7	13	7	11	9
A3	31	26	5	18	13	16	15
Total	66	52	14	41	25	36	30

conclude that $\alpha_i > 0$, $\beta_i > 0$ for the typical subject, but that the magnitude of our estimate of these coefficients is quite small relative to their sampling variability.

11. OTHER EXPERIMENTS IN PUBLIC GOOD DECISIONS

Three previous papers (Bohm, 1972; Scherr and Babb, 1975; Ferejohn and Noll, 1976) report the results of experiments in public good decisions.

Bohm Experiment

In the Bohm (1972) experiment consumers (who had volunteered to come to a TV studio for a payment of Kr. 50) were randomly assigned to six different groups and asked to state how much they were willing to pay under six different cost-sharing rules, to watch a particular TV program that had not yet been shown to the public. The sixth group made hypothetical choices while for the remaining five the program would be shown if and only if the aggregate of the amounts offered were sufficient to cover the cost. However, this outcome rule was not "real" in the sense that each group was led to believe that there were parallel groups in other rooms whose responses were to be merged with theirs. In this way a group, for example of size 23 (treatment I) would find it credible that with offers of only several Kr. each the program cost (Kr. 500) was covered. Unknown to the subjects, the program was to be shown whatever the amount of the offer.

Among the various experimental groups the amounts each consumer paid were as follows (the mean offer in Kr. appears in parenthesis):

I. The amount stated (Kr. 7.61).
II. A percentage of the amount stated, normalized so that cost is just covered (Kr. 8.84).
III. Either the amount stated, a percentage of this amount, Kr. 5, or nothing to be determined by a lottery (Kr. 7.29).
IV. Kr. 5 (Kr. 7.73).
V. Nothing. The costs would be paid by the broadcasting company i.e. out of general taxes (Kr. 8.78).
VI. Nothing. The response was hypothetical (Kr. 10.19).

According to Bohm's analysis only treatment VI led to offers which differed to any (classically) significant degree from the others. Several interpretations and observations seem relevant to this experiment:

1. Treatment I corresponds to the Auction Mechanism applied to an indivisible public good. The theory discussed in section 9 suggests that there are strong incentives for revealing demand under this mechanism and from our experiments we have evidence that in the context of an iterative process

this mechanism produces incentive compatible outcomes. Consequently, Bohm's treatment I should not be expected to yield strong free-rider tendencies unless this is a peculiarity of single trial responses. The theory that has maintained that free-riding will occur in this context has not taken account of the opportunity losses incurred by failure to cover cost.

2. Irrespective of these considerations, if treatment I is regarded as the "free-rider" control experiment against which comparisons are made then the effect of each of the treatments II, IV, V and VI is to raise the average offer, in what might be considered the expected direction. That is, subjects might be expected to offer more in II than in I in the expectation that their share of cost in II is unlikely to exceed that in I. Similarly, IV provides a modest fixed imputation of the cost regardless of one's offer, and similarly for V and VI. If the pre-experimental hypothesis had been that these were the directions in which the treatment outcomes would diverge, then irrespective of the significance tests by classical standards, one would have to conclude that the experimental results increased to some degree the credibility of the hypothesis.

3. The lower offers elicited under treatment III are not in accordance with expectations based upon the above arguments. However, treatment III is by far the most complex or ambiguous, psychologically. The lower average offer in III is consistent with the "ambiguity hypothesis" which would assert that where outcomes are defined by psychologically "rich" (complicated, mysterious, uncertain) processes, subjects are more conservative, or cautious, in their responses. This phenomenon is suggested in a somewhat different context (Ellsberg, 1961; Sherman, 1974) but may have application in the Bohm experiment.

4. The seemingly "high" offers by customer groups across all treatments is consistent with the following "mixed motive" hypothesis: It appears reasonable from the instructions to assume that, since the investigation by the "Research Department" was aimed "...at finding out what viewers think about various TV programs" (Bohn, 1972, p. 127), the subjects may have felt some responsibility for seeing to it that the program was shown, particularly since it was made by the two best-known humorists in Sweden. Consequently, the showing may have been perceived as having private and perhaps broader public values than the immediate utility from the viewing at the TV studio.

5. Each subject was asked for a single response. Although the subjects "accepted the question as...posed and [most]...gave their responses in a matter of a minute or less" (p. 126), the result is not likely to be the same as would obtain if the subjects arrived at a final decision through a process involving many response-outcome iterations. There are many examples of treatment variables, such as price contracting rules in a market (Smith, 1964; Plott and Smith, 1975) in which the effects of the treatment variable

are not felt in the first (or first sequence of) observations, but only in the character of the entire path, or in the final observations.

All the above interpretations, or alternative hypotheses, are conjectures suggested in part by the data of the Bohm experiment or by experience in entirely different experiments. They are not in any scientific sense confirmed by that data. But a source of power in this methodology is the fact that new experiments can always be run to test hypotheses suggested, in part, by previous experiments (Smith, 1975). It is in this spirit that the above comments may be relevant.

Scherr-Babb Experiment

The Scherr-Babb (1975) laboratory experiment was designed to have subjects in collectives of size two (each subject was led to believe that he was paired with one other) reveal demands under the Clarke, Loehman-Whinston (total cost shared equally among agents) and a voluntary contribution plan. Each subject received $10.00 for his participation, and could contribute up to $.50 to each of 14 pricing situations involving an allegedly real Library Fund and a Concert Fund. None of the three pricing methods elicited responses significantly different from the others.

1. As in the Bohm experiment, the single response character of the decisions does not permit reconsideration on the basis of iterative experience although the fact that there were 14 decision situations would have permitted learning to affect decisions later in the sequence. However, the randomization of sequences meant that such effects were averaged across observations so as to not produce systematic bias.

2. The "mixed motive" problem may be particularly severe in this experiment. The highest demands were revealed under the voluntary system. To the extent that subjects perceived fund contribution as having private (altruistic) value, the voluntary system might appear to be the simplest, least mysterious, method of making "donations." Indeed, the use of the word "donations" in the instructions may have suggested a certain congruence between the purpose of the exercise and the voluntary system.

3. The pairing of subjects into two-element collectives may have elicited behavior special to that case. It is well-known in noncooperative oligopoly experiments (Fouraker and Siegel, 1963; Shubik, 1975) that the step from two to three or more is considerable. All the cited experiments, and those reported in this paper, involved larger collectives.

The PBS Station Program Cooperative

In 1974 the Public Broadcasting Service began a three-year experiment to develop a decentralized process for the selection of programs to be broadcast over the noncommercial television network. Some results of the first two seasons of experience with this Station Program Cooperative (SPC) have been reported by Ferejohn and Noll (1976). Approximately 150 participating stations made actual selections from 93 programs in the first experiment, and 136 in the second. The process consisted of 12 iterations (with each station manager communicating through his teletypewriter) and converged rapidly (in seven iterations) to 25 produced programs the first year and (in ten iterations) to 38 produced programs the second year. The cost of program j for station i on trial t was

$$C_j \left[\frac{0.8 b_{ij}(t)}{B_j(t)} + \frac{0.2 n_{ij}(t)}{N_j(t)} \right]$$

where C_j was the producer's cost of program j, b_{ij} is the budget and n_{ij} the population served for any station i selecting program j, and B_j is the aggregate budget and N_j the aggregate population served for all stations selecting program j.

This cost-sharing rule has the essential features of the Auction Mechanism, i.e., (1) each manager risks forfeiting his private net benefit if he fails to "vote for" a program, and (2) he has veto power over the cost allocated to him by the choices of all other stations. However, it has the undesirable characteristic that stations can only accept or reject a program at a bid determined mechanically by the above formula. A station willing to pay some amount for a particular program but less than the formula allocation must perforce decline to select the program, while a station willing to pay more than its formula allocation has no way of signaling this intensity by increasing its bid. It is conjectured that one way to correct these "flaws" is to let each station manager bid whatever he desires on any program irrespective of budget and viewing population, but with the understanding that if equilibrium is not reached by round T his (along with every other) station will not receive the program. This Auction system is incentive compatible is simple and easy to understand, and there is empirical evidence in laboratory settings that it yields bids distributed with means equal to the Lindahl optimum. It would seem that a PBS Auction Mechanism experiment might "work" for essentially the same reasons that the present SPC system is working but with increased flexibility. But the fact that the Ferejohn-Noll-PBS experiment is working to produce decisions in a large collective is an exciting and path-breaking development. Alleged or conjectured improvements in a system, which the station managers themselves find attractive, must be thoroughly tested under suitable controls, bearing in mind that it is a long way from an idea to an operating institution.

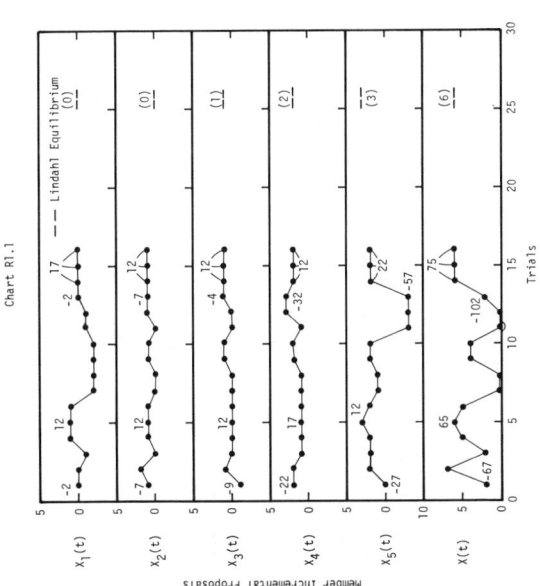

Chart R1.1

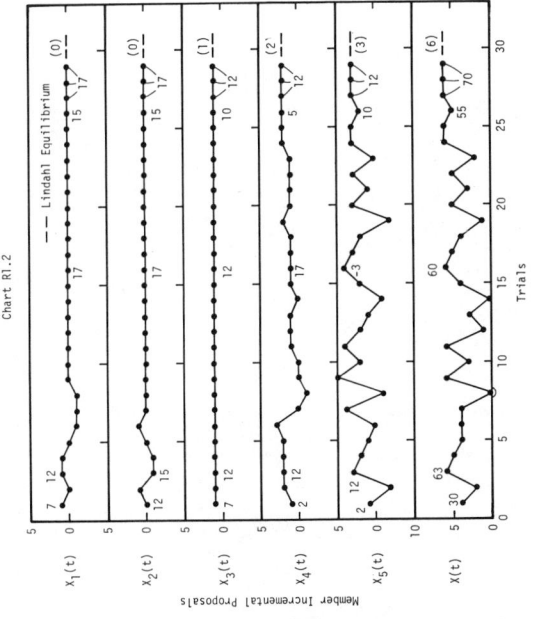

Chart R1.2

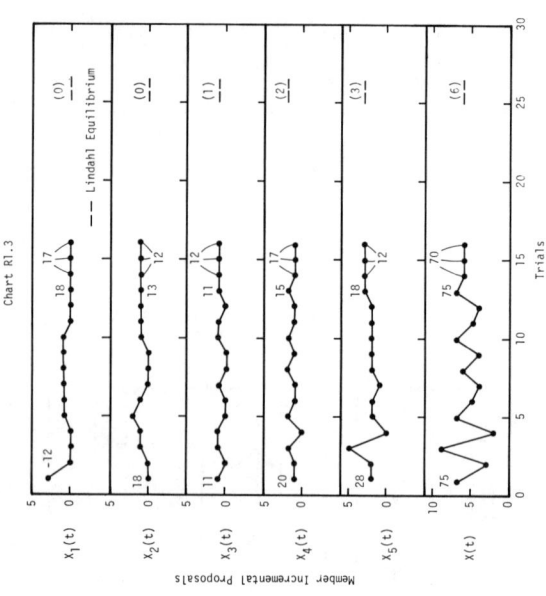

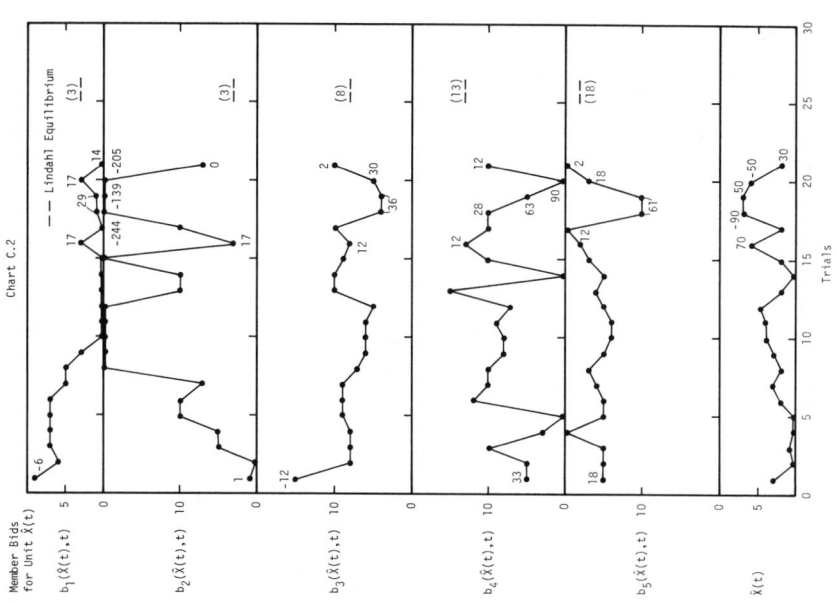

Chart C.2

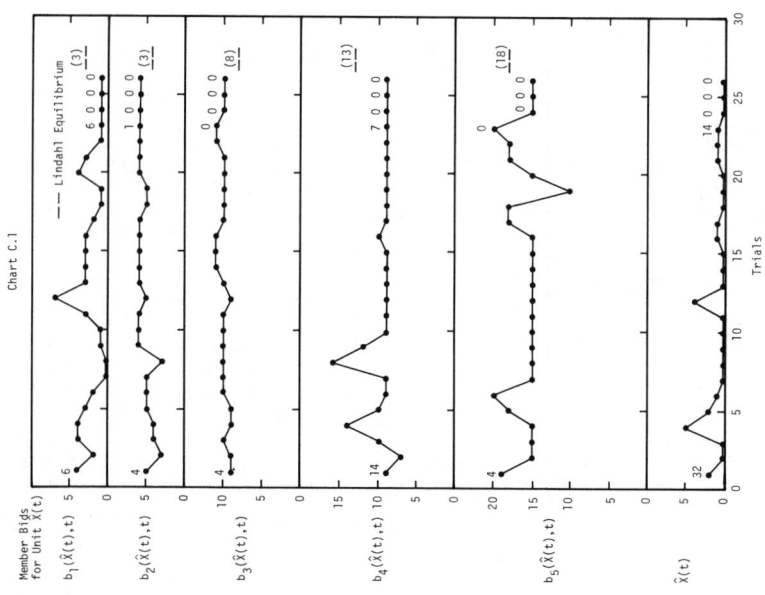

Chart C.1

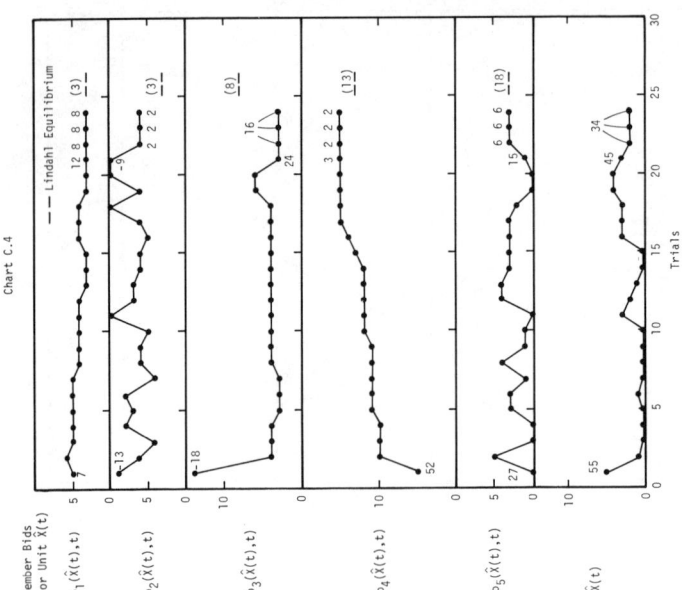

Chart C.4

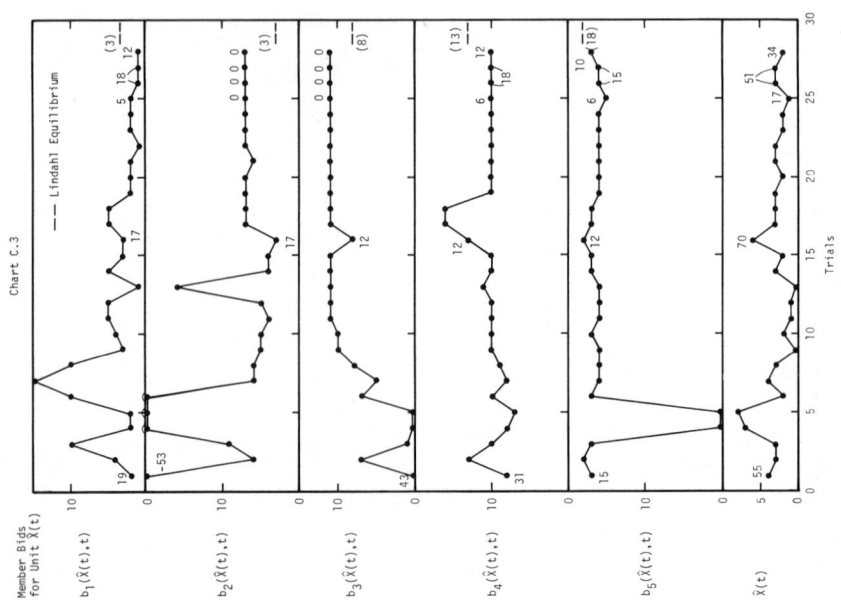

Chart C.3

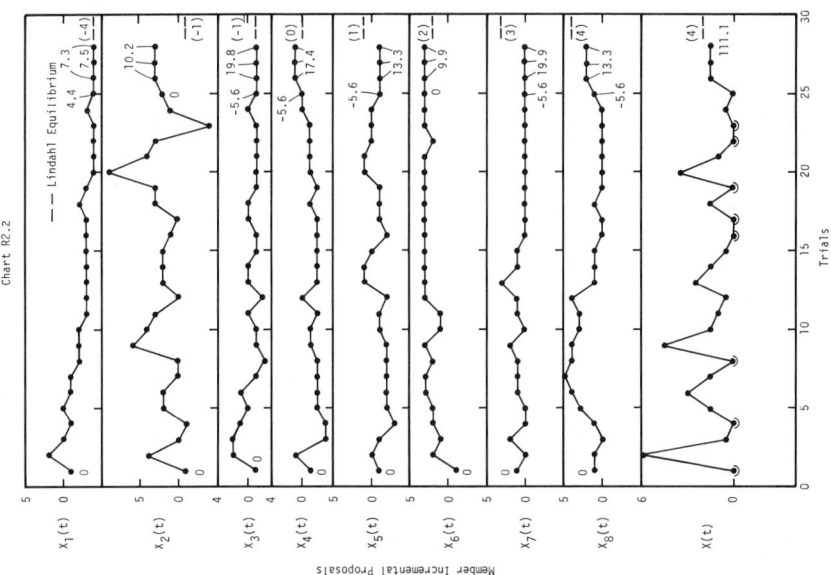

Chart R2.1

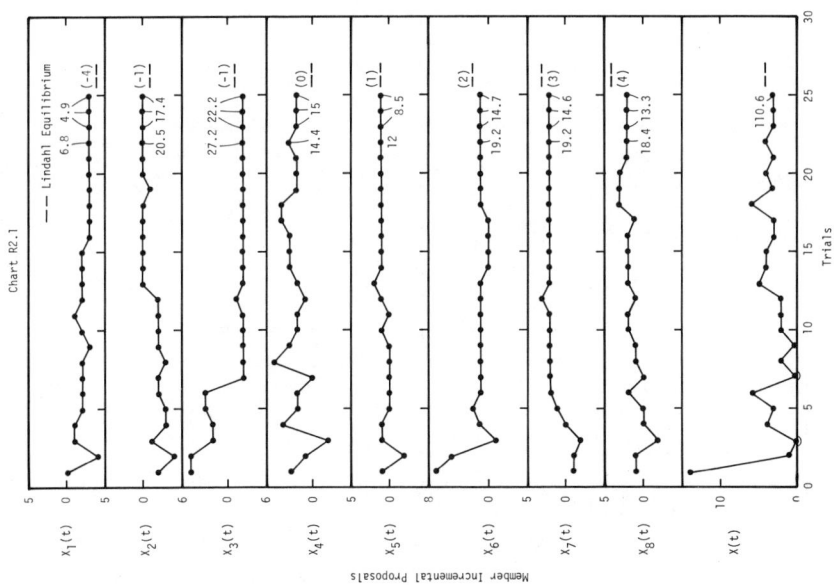

Chart R2.2

101

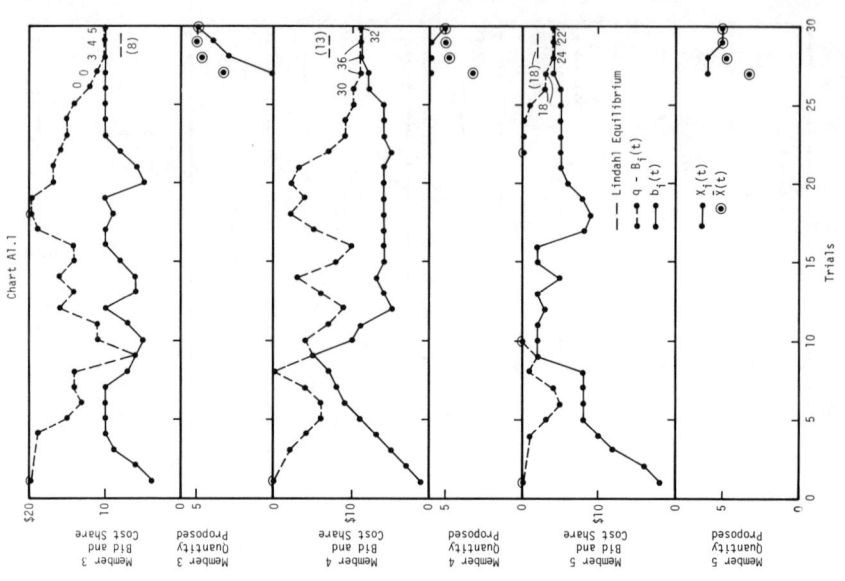

Chart A1.1

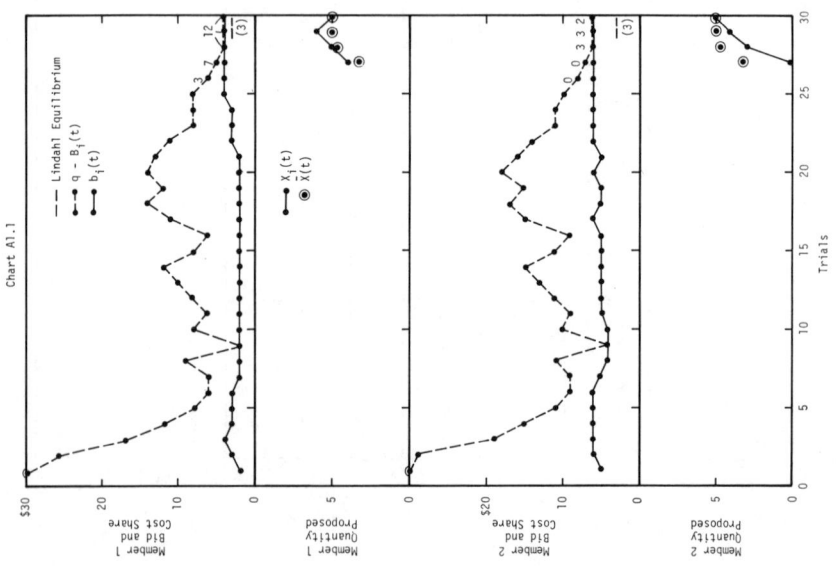

Chart A1.1

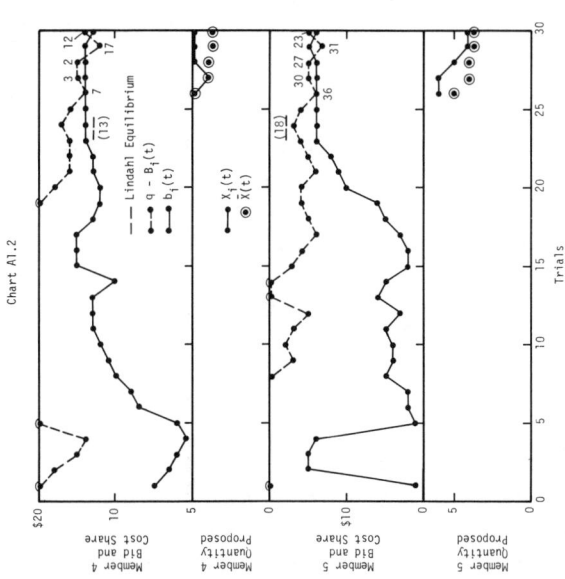

Chart A1.2

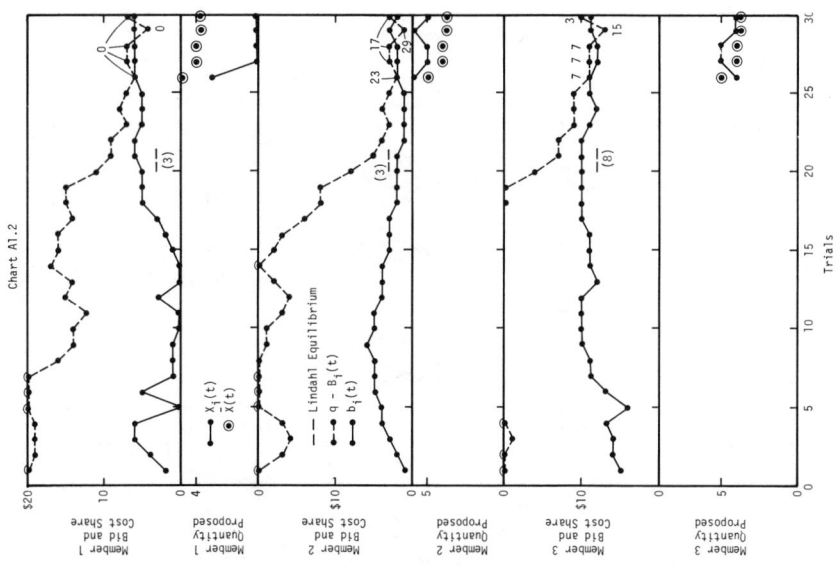

Chart A1.2

103

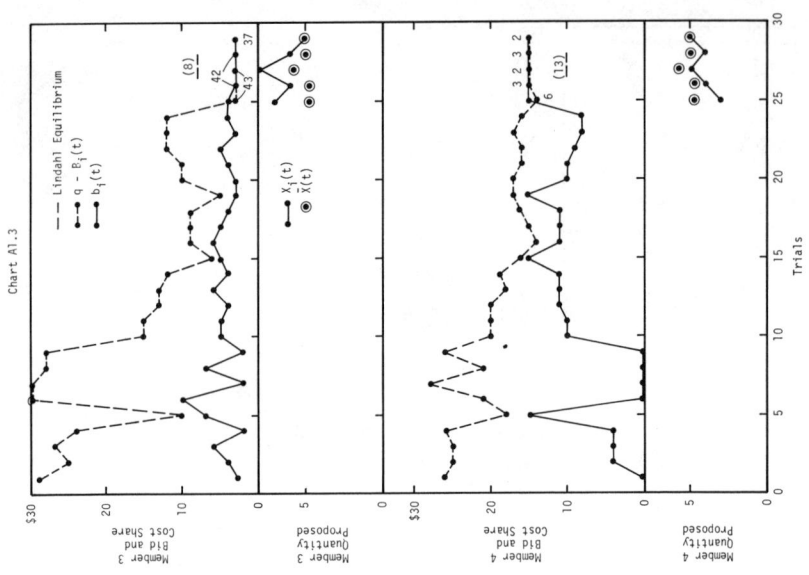
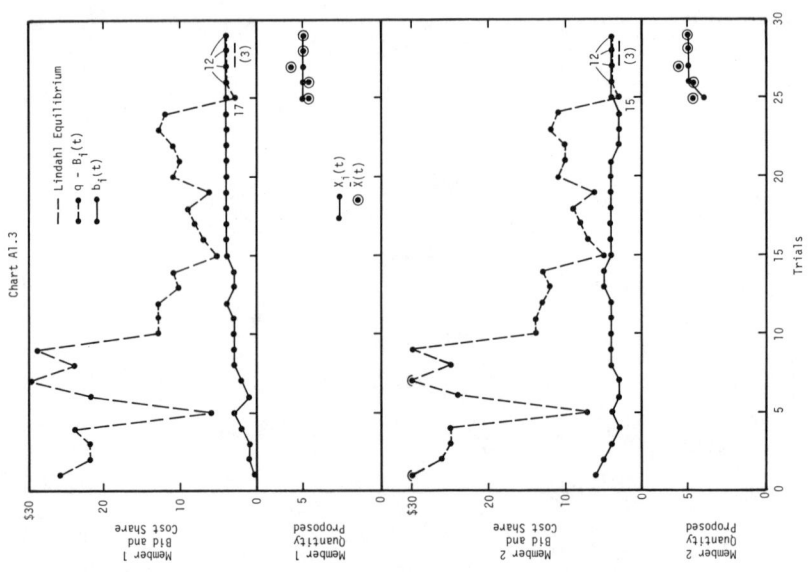

104

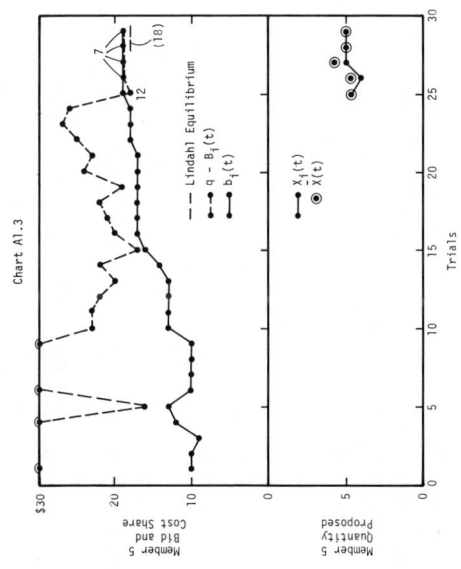

Chart A1.3

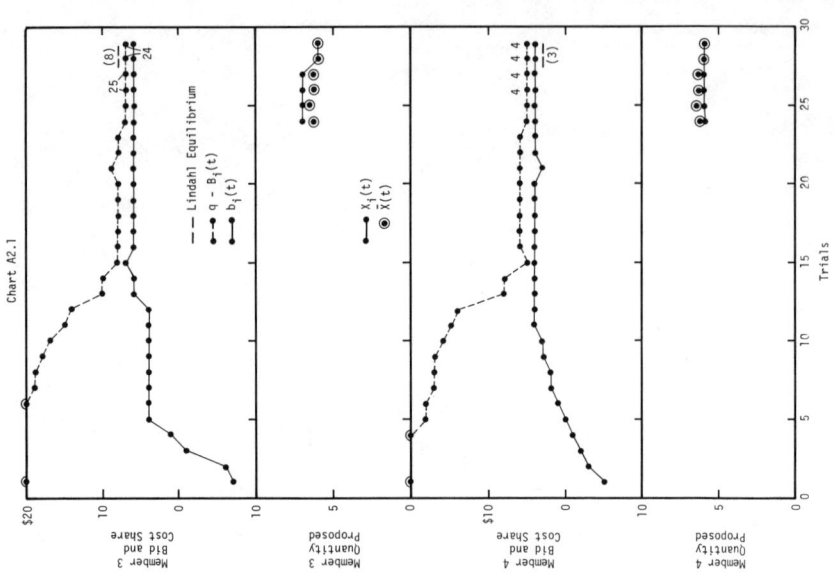

Chart A2.1

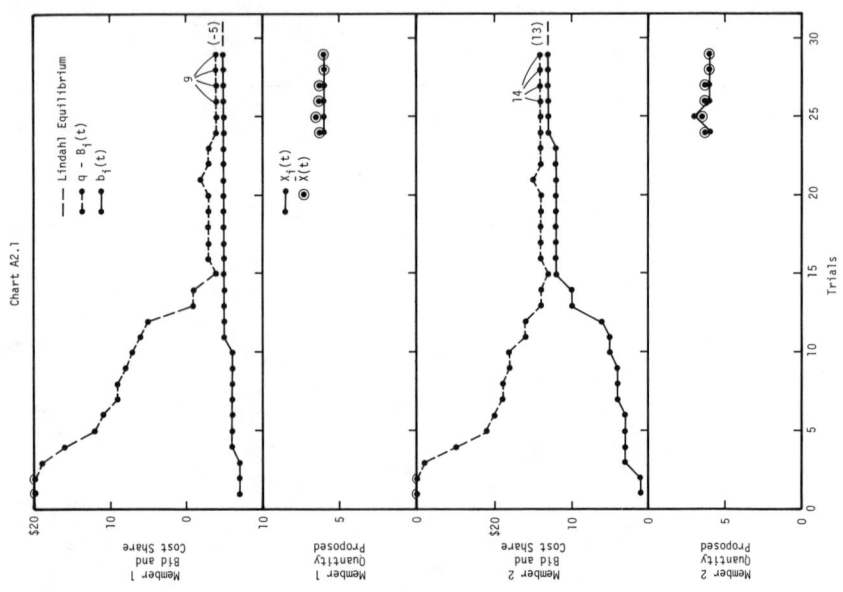

Chart A2.1

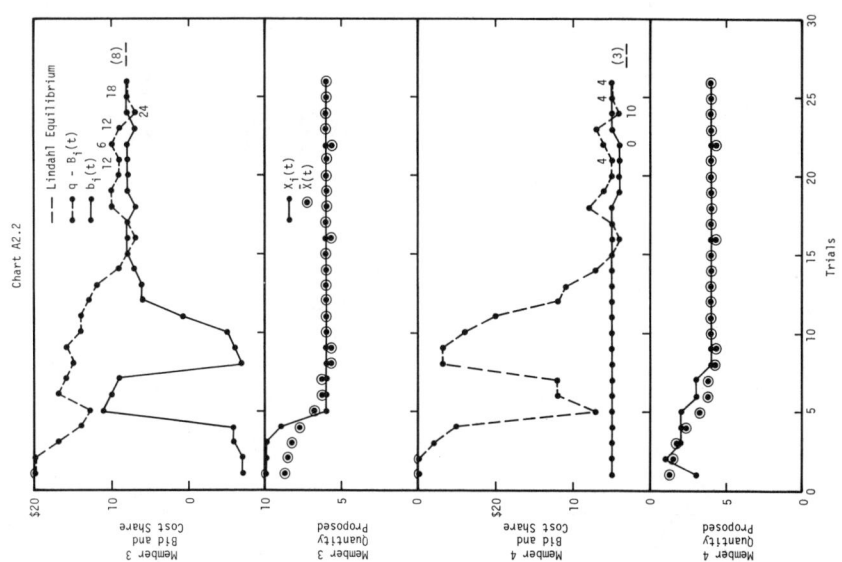
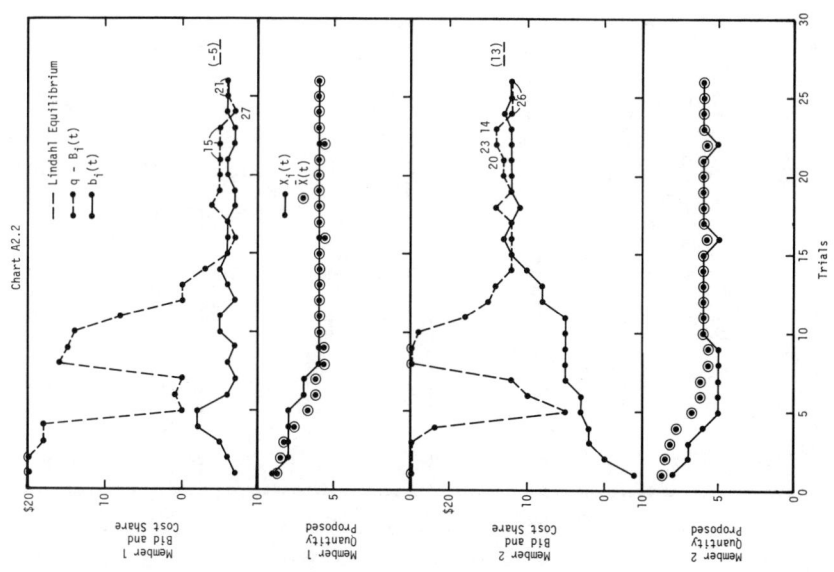

Chart A2.2

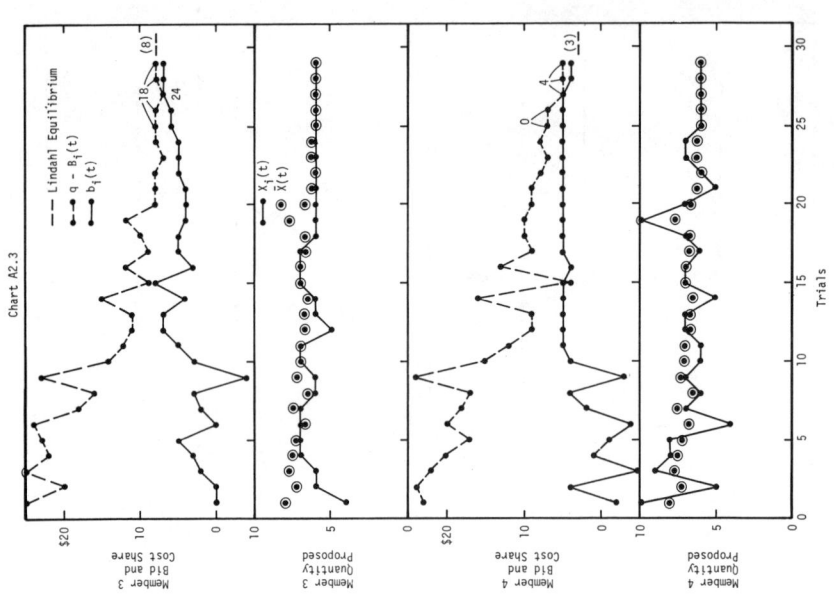
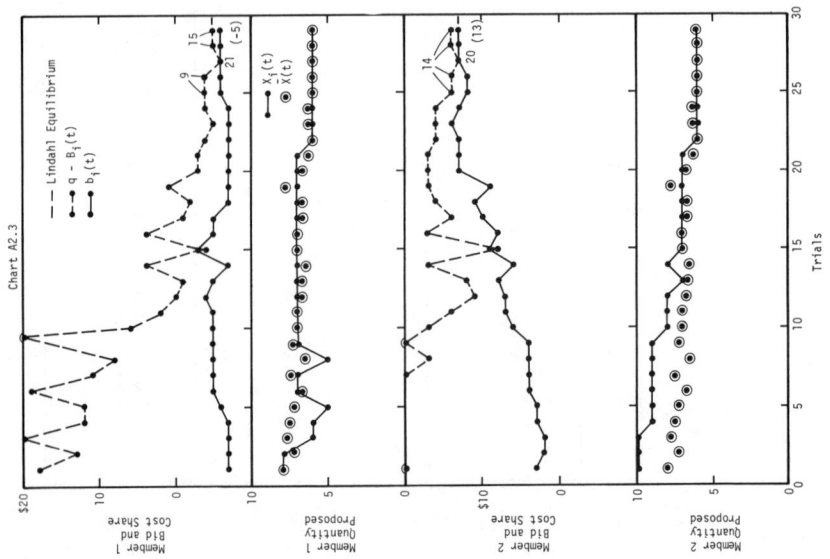

108

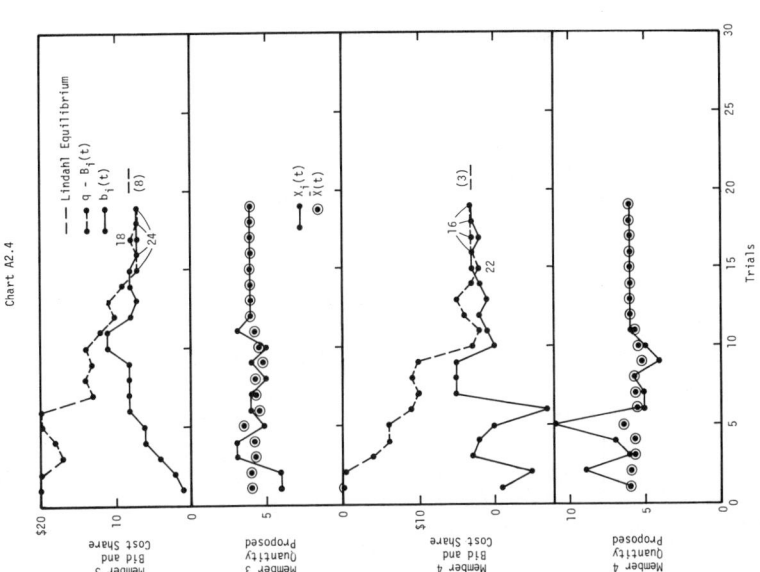

Chart A2.4

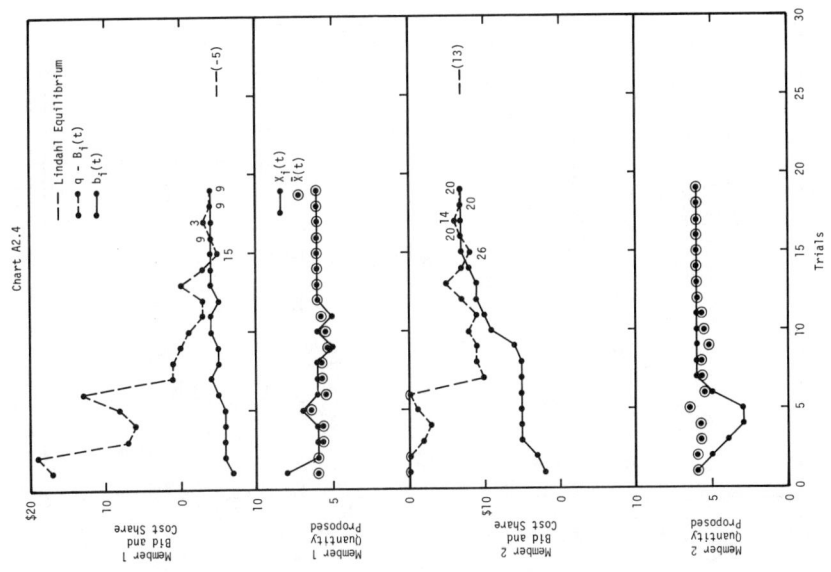

Chart A2.4

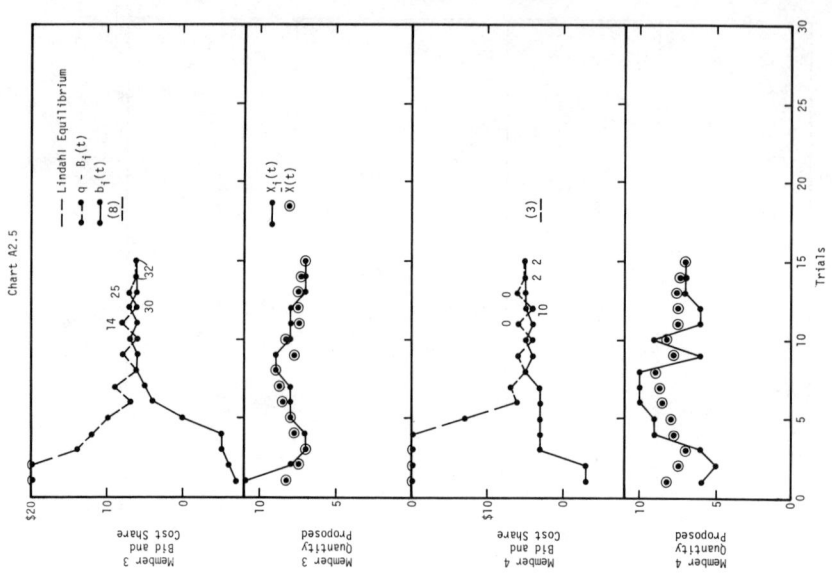
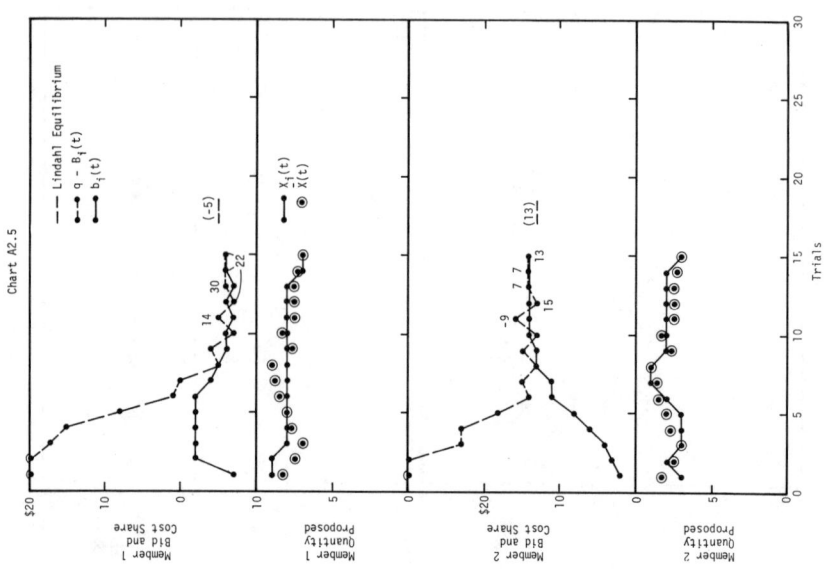

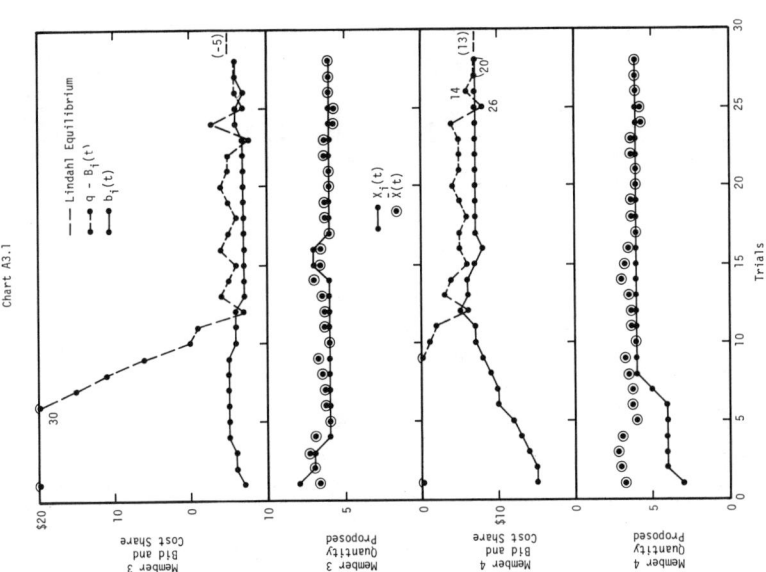

Chart A3.1

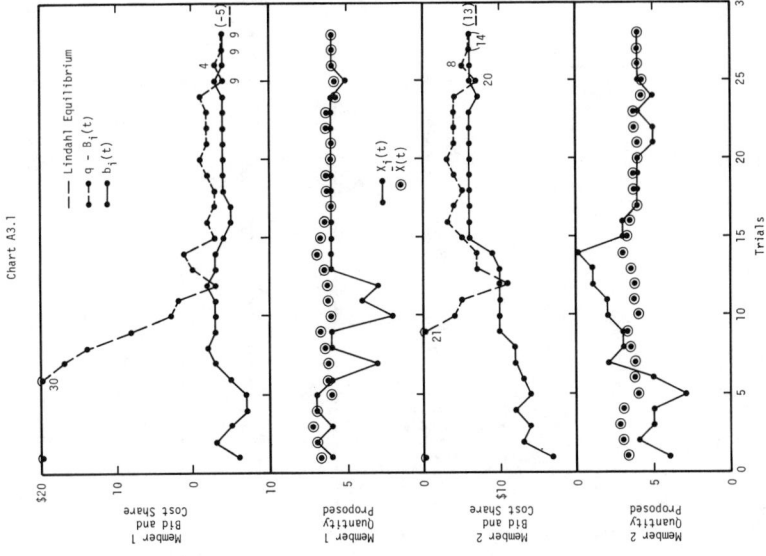

Chart A3.1

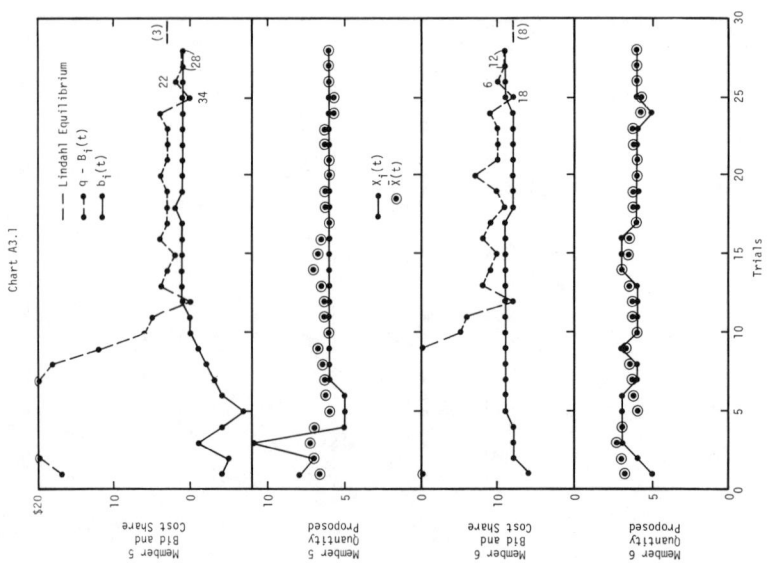

Chart A3.1

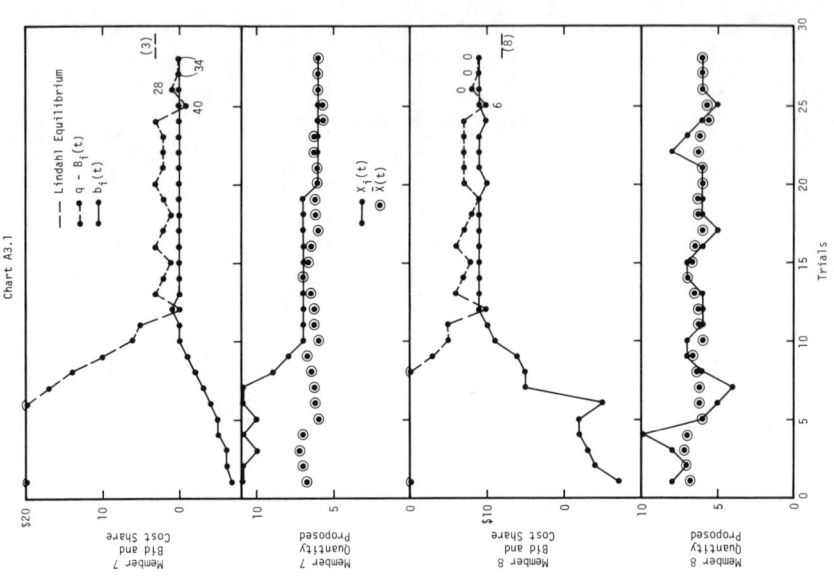

Chart A3.1

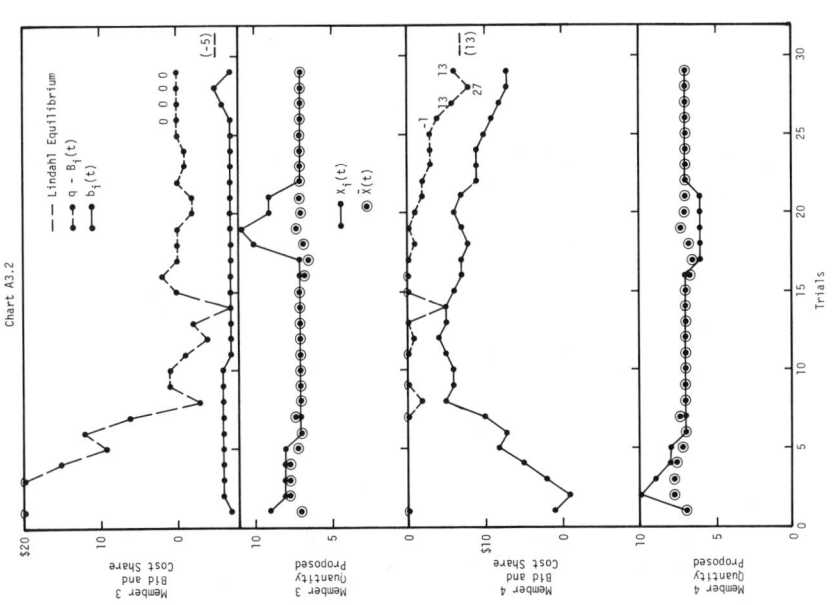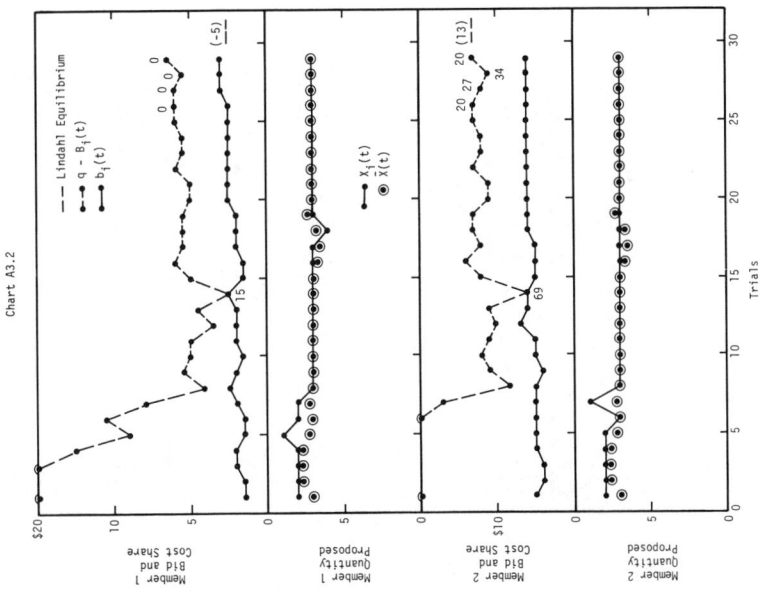

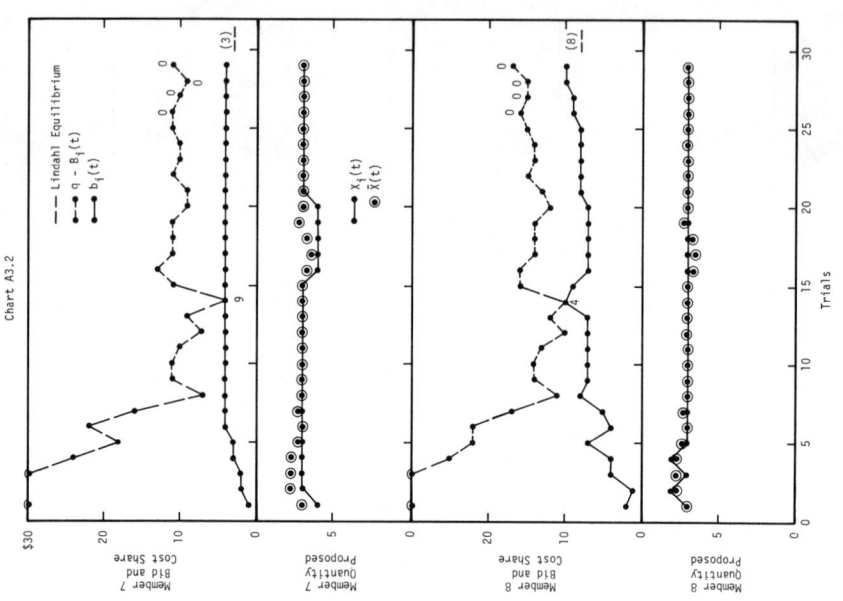

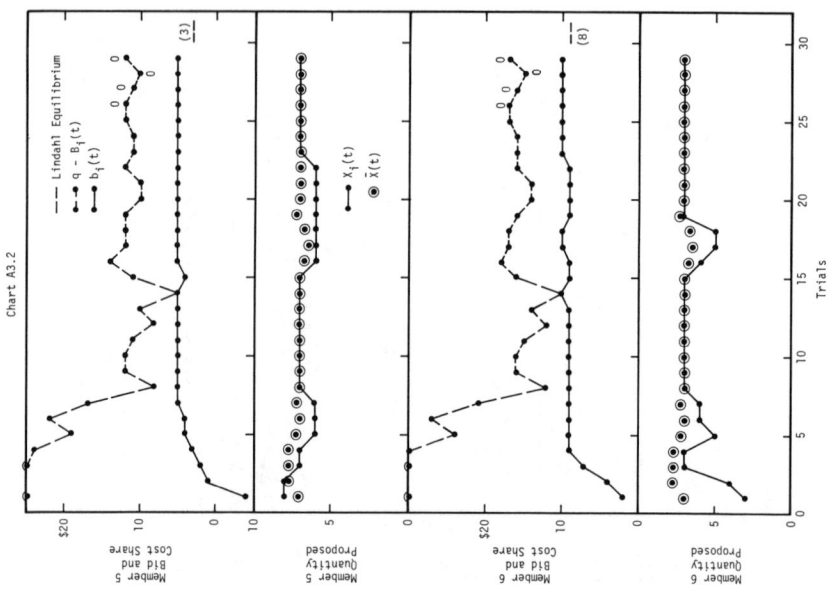

Chart A3.2

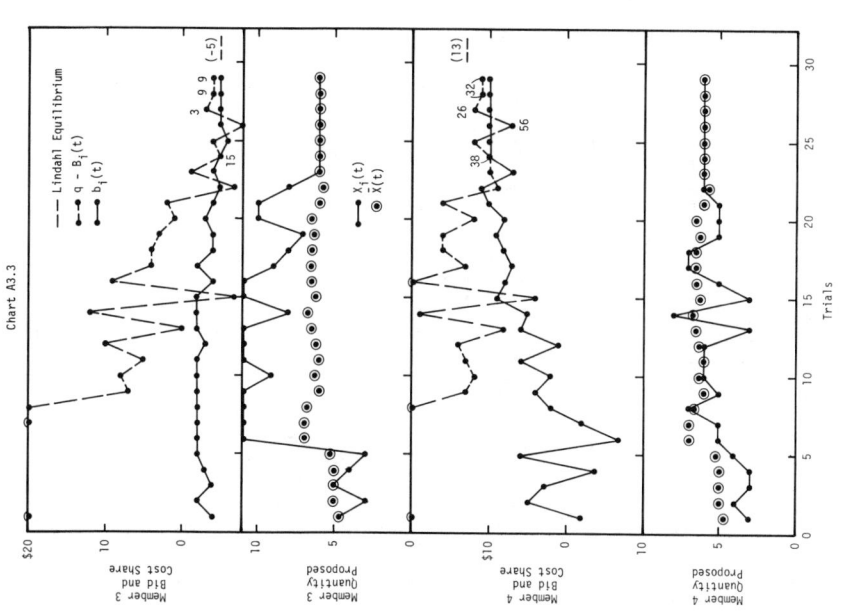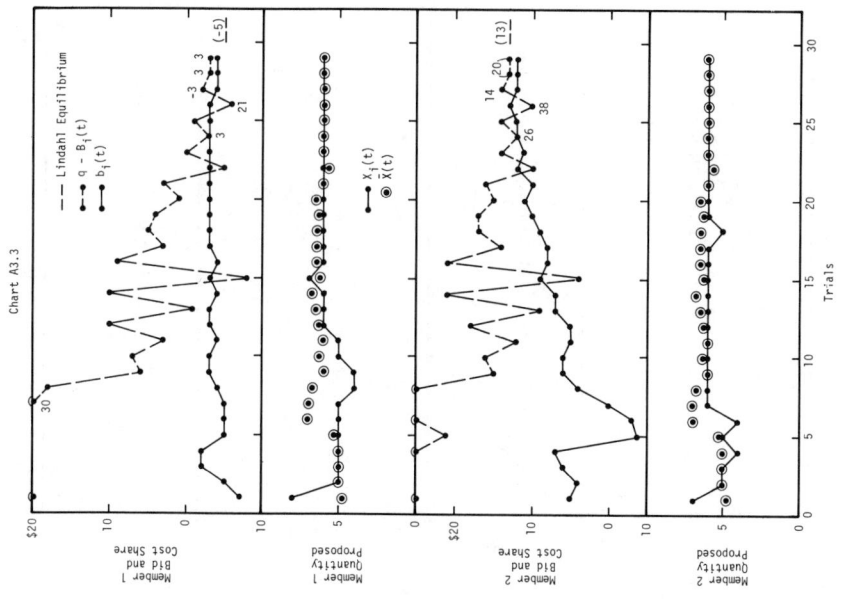

115

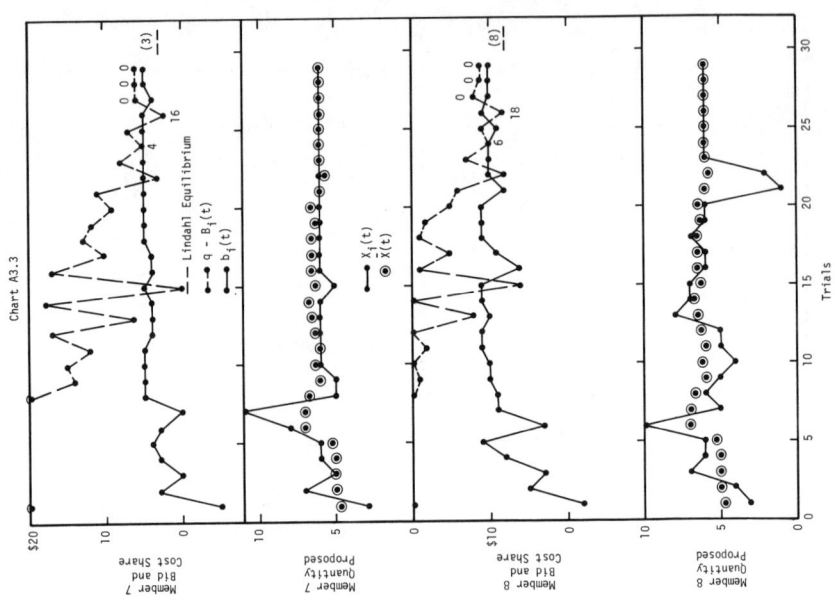
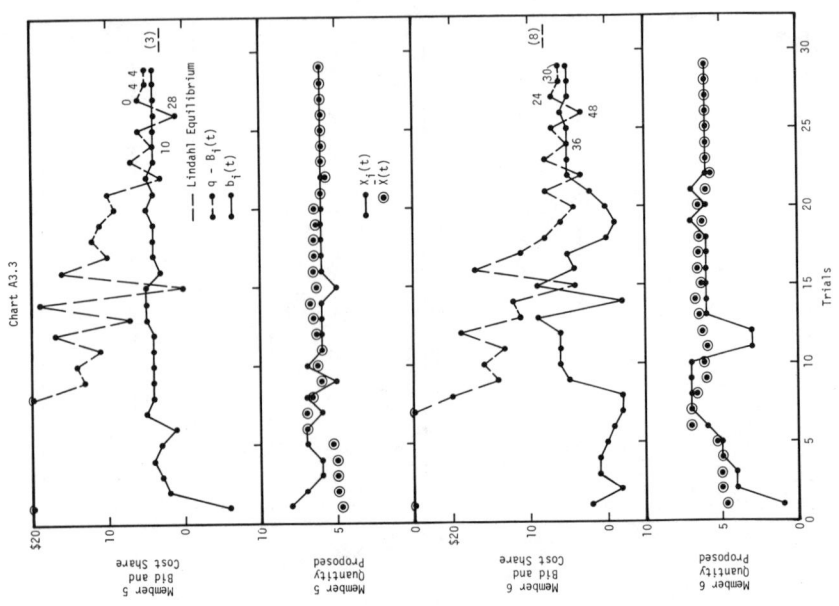

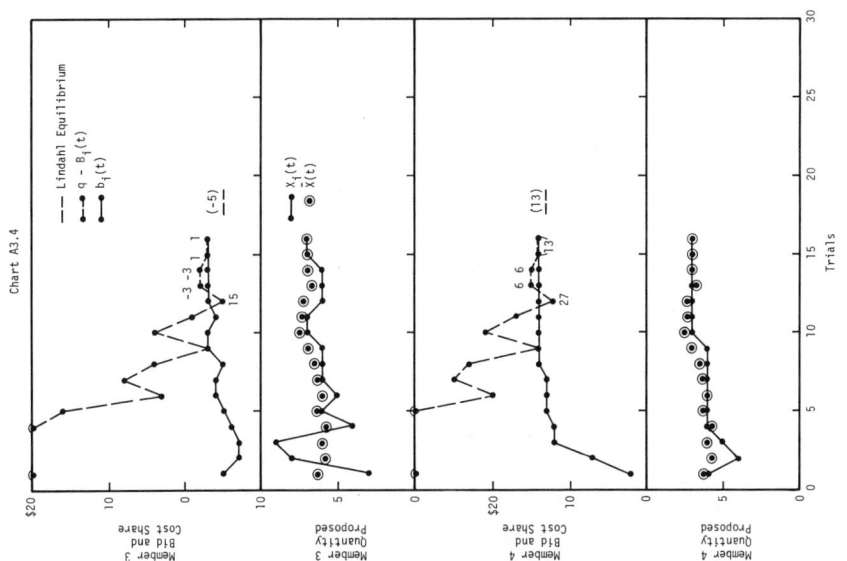
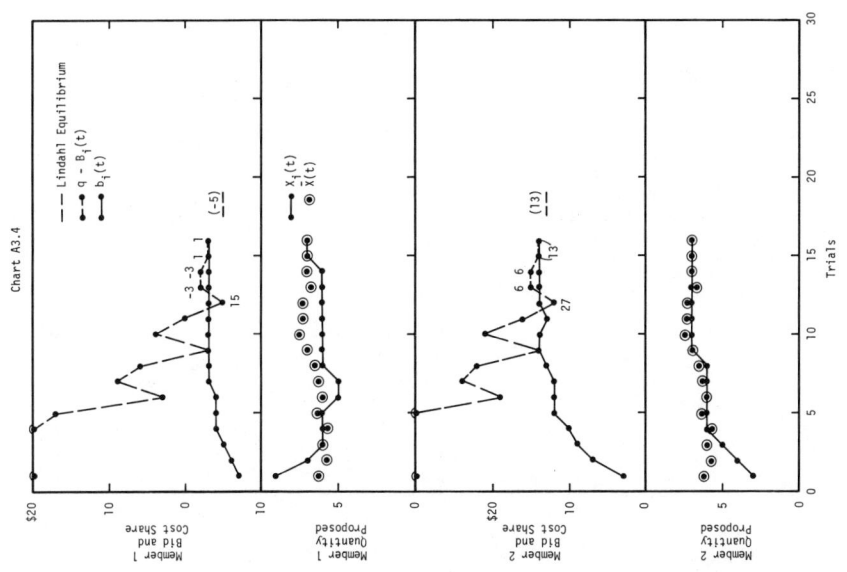

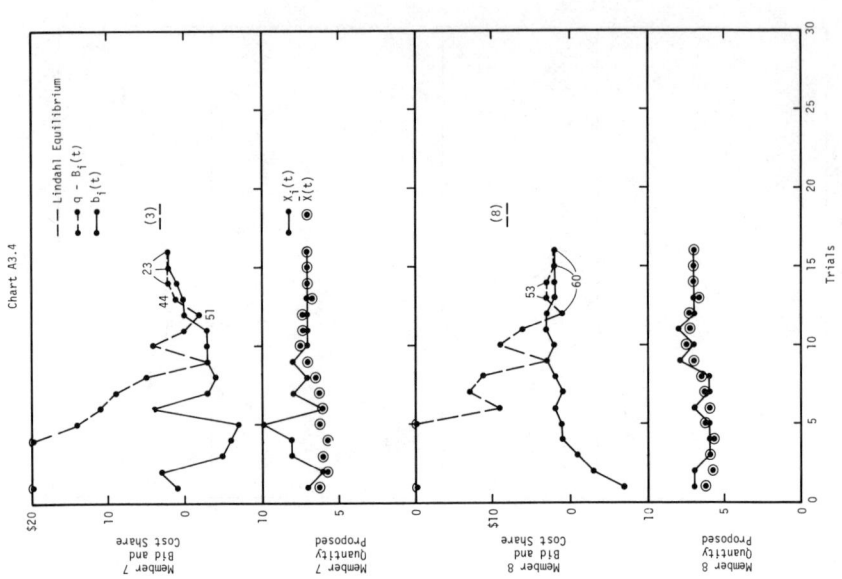
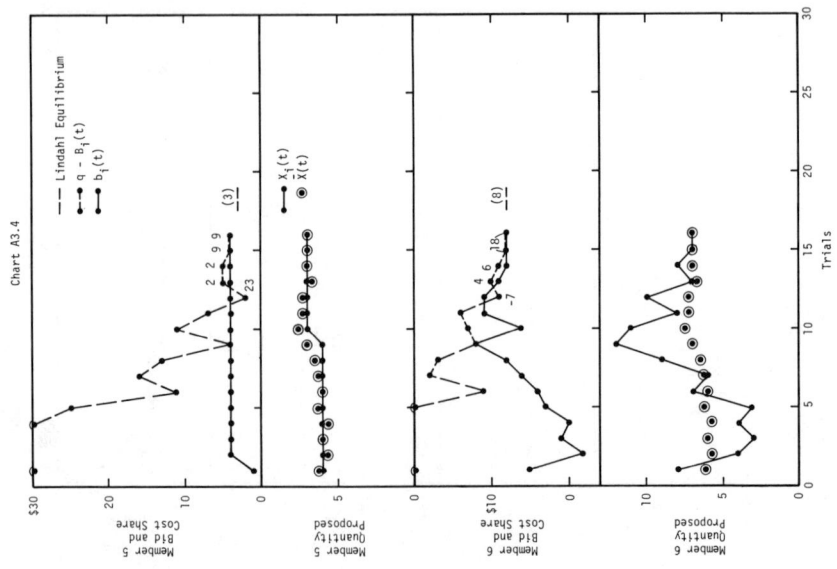

FOOTNOTES

I am happy to acknowledge my indebtedness to S. Reiter for first directing my attention to the path-breaking work of Groves and Ledyard (1974) before the first draft of their work was available for distribution; to T. Groves for inviting me to speak at Northwestern on another topic, but allowing me to use the visit to learn more about the "solution to the free-rider problem"; to T. Groves and J. Ledyard for stimulating my interest in public good experiments; to C. Plott for helping to re-ignite 1973–1974, my long-standing interest in experimental economics; to the dozen or more faculty members at USC, Berkeley, Stanford, Northwestern, and the University of Arizona who allowed me to recruit experimental subjects from their classes; to the 150 or more students who volunteered to participate in some 29 pilot and final experiments; to K. Boles, M. Rached, and S. Wade for computing and charting assistance; to the National Science Foundation for support of a research methodology that does not inspire enthusiasm in every referee, but in enough to be cheering. A preliminary version of this paper, reporting the first two series of experiments discussed below, was presented at the ORSA-TIMS conference in Las Vegas, November 17–19, 1975.

1. In the "second price" auction sealed-bids are tendered (for a single item offered for sale) with the understanding that the highest bidder will be awarded the item, but at a price determined by the second highest bid. Since the price paid is independent of one's bid, each bidder is motivated to bid his full willingness to pay thereby minimizing the chance of "excluding" himself from the award. Actually, the essence of the second price rule in providing an incentive for demand revelation was suggested earlier by Jacob Marschak. I had forgotten the incident until I read Vickrey (1961) recently for the first time. In 1953 Jacob Marschak visited briefly at Harvard. He held informal office hours for the graduate students during that visit. In the course of one of these discussions he noted that there was a very simple device for getting a buyer to reveal what he was willing to pay for anything. The seller privately writes a price on a card and puts it face down on the table. The buyer then makes his bid with the understanding that he is awarded the item at the seller's price if, and only if, his bid exceeds the seller's price. This, of course, is just Vickrey's "second price" auction in which the seller is allowed to bid, and to retain the item if his bid is the highest. This version of the Marschak-Vickrey mechanism does not even depend upon there being two or more buyers. See Marschak (1968) for an "honest asking price" version of the rule.

2. Four pilot experiments with the G-L and Lindahl processes were required before the instructions, tables, recording forms, language, and computing task of the subjects were simple enough to be comprehended by the subjects in a reasonable period of time, and to permit orderly conduct of the experiments. Similarly, four pilot experiments with the Auction Mechanism were run. Numerous revised drafts of the instructions were used in the course of these pilot experiments.

3. Empirically, the condition of privacy may not be sufficient in all cases to control on consumption externalities. A possible example occurred with subject # 3 in experiment A2.1 (see footnote 9).

4. This guarded statement accurately reflects my pre-experimental belief state, but turns out to have been overly cautious. The reason why the enumerated possible difficulties were not of commanding importance is now clearer. There are differences between experiments without monetary rewards, those with rewards on each trial following a series of no-reward practice trials, and those with a final-outcome reward. The absence of monetary rewards may invite inattentive decisions, and/ extraneous gaming utilities. Practice trials, to be followed by reward trials, may produce exaggerated forms of strategic bluffing, i.e., the sending of diversionary messages from which one may hope to gain. Final-outcome reward invokes quite serious choices, especially as the end

approaches and subjects become aware of the need for group coordination to trigger the stopping rule. The opportunity costs of bluffing are high in these final-reward experiments, while bluffing is "free" in pre-reward practice trial experiments. None of these considerations are peculiar to laboratory experiments—they would be directly relevant to any field applications because the behavioral issues are the same.

5. This property explains why the television field experiment reported by Bohm (1972) does not fail because of free-riding. In this application the public good in question is indivisible, bids are therefore constant, and the Lindahl process is not distinguishable from the Auction process in section 8. The same considerations apply to the PBS field experiment reported by Ferejohn and Noll (1976) except that the members of the PBS collective are not free to vary their own bids, only to accept or reject the formula cost imputed to them. This argument suggests that the conventional wisdom which asserts that free-riding will occur in these cases, was wrong from the beginning, and based upon failure to specify a decision mechanism.

6. Obviously, there are many variations on the rule $X_i = \bar{X}$ for obtaining agreement on a common quantity of the public good. Statically equivalent alternatives include $X_i = \max \{X_1, \ldots, X_I\}$, $X_i = \min \{X_1, \ldots, X_I\}$, $X_i = \text{median} \{X_1, \ldots, X_I\}$ and $X_i = \text{mode} \{X_1, \ldots, X_I\}$, but these alternatives may have different dynamic implications.

7. Apparently it has occurred to several scholars that the free-rider "problem" is moderated, or perhaps rendered nonexistent, if economic agents are put in the position either of "filling the cost gap" or losing all utility derivable from the public good. E.g., Kihlstrom (1973, pp. 30, 31) states "From one point of view, the incentives which operate in the (Kihlstrom's) legislative economy ... are the same as ... in the competitive process.... The consumer has an incentive to reveal the truth to avoid ... (accepting) a non-optimal consumption bundle" [Brubaker, 1975, pp. 150–155]. expresses the idea in his concept of "pre-contract group excludability" although his "golden rule of revelation" seems to rely more than is needed on altruistic considerations. Also, when I visited Berkeley to conduct a Lindahl experiment, D. McFadden questioned what might be the effect of making each subject's share of cost depend upon the bids of all other subjects.

8. Except that the $V_i(X)$ were not the same in C and R1 for those values of $X \leq 4$.

9. However, this subject's motives were somewhat mixed for he also indicated after the experiment that he suspected someone in the group must be "cleaning up." When I corrected this impression and reminded him that the instructions state that not all the Tables are the same, he asked if he could participate again in one of the experiments. This interrogation suggests that although privacy keeps each subject from knowing the decisions and payoffs of others during the experiment, it may not keep subjects from having conjectures and suspicions about other's payoffs, with possible external effects.

10. This incentive could be provided by paying a small commission for each unit agreed upon. This commission would then induce a nonzero demand for the marginal unit.

REFERENCES

Bohm, P. (1972), "Estimating Demand for Public Goods: An Experiment,", *European Economic Review* 3: 111–130.

Brubaker, E. R. (April 1975), "Free Ride, Free Revelation, or Golden Rule?", *Journal of Law and Economics* 18, No. 1: 147–161.

Buchanan, J. and Tullock, G. (1962), *The Calculus of Consent*, Ann Arbor: University of Michigan Press.

Clarke, E. H. (Fall 1971), "Multipart Pricing of Public Goods," *Public Choice* 11: 17–33.

Drèze, J. and de la Vallée Poussin, D. (1971), "A Tâtonnement Process for Public Goods," *Review of Economic Studies* 38, No. 2: 133–150.

Ellsberg, D. (November 1961), "Risk, Ambiguity and the Savage Axioms," *Quarterly Journal of Economics* 75: 643–669.

Ferejohn, J. A. and Noll, R. (1976), "An Experimental Market for Public Goods: The PBS Station Program Cooperative," *American Economic Review Papers and Proceedings*: 267–273.

Fouraker, L. and Siegel, S. (1963), *Bargaining Behavior*, New York: McGraw-Hill.

Groves, T. (August 1969), "The Allocation of Resources Under Uncertainty: The Informational and Intensive Roles of Prices and Demands in a Team," Technical Report # 1, Centre for Research in Management Science, University of California, Berkeley, Chapter IV, pp. 71–73.

———. (July 1973), "Incentives in Teams," *Econometrica* 41: 617–33.

Groves, T. and Ledyard, J. (1974), "An Incentive Mechanism for Efficient Resource Allocation in General Equilibrium with Public Goods," Discussion Paper No. 119, The Center for Mathematical Studies in Economics and Management Science, Northwestern University.

——— and ———. (May 1977), "Optimal Allocation of Public Goods: A Solution to the 'Free Rider Problem'," *Econometrica*, 45: 783–809.

Hurwicz, L. (May 1973), "The Design of Mechanisms for Resource Allocation," *American Economic Review, Paper and Proceedings*: 1–30.

Kihlstrom, R. (1974), "A Legislative Mechanism for Achieving Lindahl Equilibrium in a Public Goods Economy," NSF-SSRC Conference on Individual Rationality, Preference Revelation and Computation Cost in Models of General Economic Equilibrium, University of Massachusetts, July 1973. Revised, State University of New York, April 1974.

Loehman, E. and Whinston, A. (Autumn 1971), "A New Theory of Pricing and Decision-Making for Public Investment," *The Bell Journal of Economics and Management Science* 2, No. 2: 606–625.

Malinvaud, E. (March 1971), "A Planning Approach to the Public Good Problem," *Swedish Journal of Economics* 73, No. 1: 96–112.

Marschak, J. (1968), "Decision Making: Economic Aspects," *International Encyclopedia of the Social Sciences*, Vol. 4, New York: Macmillan and Free Press, pp. 42–53.

McGuire, T., Farley, J. Lucas, R. and Ring, L. (December 1968), "Estimation and Inference for Linear Models in which Subsets of the Dependent Variable are Constrained," *Journal of the American Statistical Association*: 1201–1213.

Plott, C. and Smith, V. (April 1975), "An Experimental Examination of Two Exchange Institutions," Social Science Working Paper No. 83, Cal Tech. To appear in *Review of Economic Studies*.

Samuelson, P. (November 1955), "Diagrammatic Exposition of a Theory of Public Expenditure," *The Review of Economic Statistics* 37, No. 4: 350–356.

———. (November 1958), "Aspects of Public Expenditure Theories," *The Review of Economics and Statistics* 40, No. 4: 332–338.

Scherr, B. and Babb E. (Fall 1975), "Pricing Public Goods: An Experiment with Two Proposed Pricing Systems," *Public Choice*: 35–48.

Sherman, R. (February 1974), "The Psychological Difference Between Ambiguity and Risk," *Quarterly Journal of Economics* 88: 166–169.

Shubik, M. (1974), "A Trading Model to Avoid Tatonnement Metaphysics," *Conference on Bidding and Auctioning*, Y. Amihud (ed.), New York: New York University Press, 1976.

———. (May 1975), "Oligopoly Theory, Communication, and Information," *American Economic Review* 65: 280–283.

Smith V. L. (May 1964), "Effect of Market Organization on Competitive Equilibrium," *Quarterly Journal of Economics*: 181–201.
——. (January 1967), "Experimental Studies of Discrimination versus Competition in Sealed-Bid Auction Markets," *Journal of Business* 40: 56–84.
——. (May 1975), "Experimental Economics: Induced Value Theory," *American Economic Review, Papers and Proceedings*: 274–279.
——. (1977), "Mechanisms for the Optimal Provision of Public Goods." *American Re-Evolution/Papers and Proceedings*, R. Auster and B. Sears (eds.), (Tucson: University of Arizona).
Thompson, E. (1965), "A Pareto Optimal Group Decision Process," *Papers in Non-Market Decision-Making* I: 133–140.
Vickrey, W. (March 1961), "Counterspeculation, Auctions and Competitive Sealed Tenders," *Journal of Finance*: 8–37.
Wicksell, Knut (1896), "A New Principle of Just Taxation," translated by J. M. Buchanan, in R. A. Musgrave and A. T. Peacock, *Classics in the Theory of Public Finance*, New York: St. Martin's Press, 1967.
Williams, F. (January 1973), "Effect of Market Organization on Competitive Equilibrium: The Multi-unit Case," *Review of Economic Studies* 40: 97–113.

APPENDIXES I–IV, INCENTIVE COMPATIBLE EXPERIMENTAL PROCESSES FOR THE PROVISION OF PUBLIC GOODS

APPENDIX I

G–L Process, R1.
Instructions

This is an experiment in the economics of group decision making. The instructions are simple, and if you follow them carefully and make good decisions you may earn a considerable amount of money which will be paid to you in cash at the end of the experiment. Various research foundations have provided funds for this research.

You are a member of a group (such as a club, association, or neighborhood) that jointly must decide upon, and bear the cost of, a common facility (examples might be a playground, road, swimming pool, fence, etc.). The group must decide on the size of the commonly shared facility as measured by the number of units, N (which might represent area in square feet, or height in feet, etc.). The total value of the facility to you can be thought of as the amount you could obtain if you were to sell your paid-up membership in the group. This total membership value, corresponding to different facility sizes, N, is listed in the third column of Table 1.1. The membership value for you of each successive unit increase in facility size is listed in the second column of Table 1.1. Net value, which will be paid to you in cash on the final decision, is computed by subtracting from total value your paid-up share of total facility cost.

Your share of total facility cost is determined by the formula tabulated in Table 2.1. The formula applies to the decisions that result on a series of trials using the following process: On each trial a proposed facility size is determined by taking the algebraic sum of the numbers submitted by all members. That is, each member, i, independently selects a number, n_i, representing your proposal as to the number of units to be algebraically added to the sum of the other proposals to determine facility size. Suppose that the sum, S_i, of the proposals of all other members is 4, and the proposal of member i is $n_i = -1$. Then facility size is $N = 3$. Member i's share of total facility cost in dollars is then determined by locating the column for $S_i = 4$, and the row for $n_i = -1$, in Table 2.1; suppose it is $57. If, for member i, the total value of a facility of size 3, is $157, then his net membership value would $100 for that trial. This process will be repeated for at most —— trials. If, at any time in this process each member repeats his choice for three successive trials, the process will be stopped and the net membership value resulting on the last trial will be paid to you in cash.

Otherwise you will be paid a modest wage for the time you have spent. In order to simplify your clerical task, a complete listing of net membership values has been computed for you in Table 3.1.

Your folder includes a record sheet for recording the results of each trial. You are free to select any proposed addition, n_i, between -3 and $+11$, appearing on the left of the rows in Table 3.1. Suppose, for example, that five members independently choose $n_1 = 3$, $n_2 = 3$, $n_3 = 3$, $n_4 = 2$, $n_5 = -3$. Each member writes his choice in the second row of his record sheet for that trial. In the example, member 1 writes $n_1 = 3$. I will go to each member and record his choice on my data sheet, then compute facility size $N = 3 + 3 + 3 + 2 - 3 = 8$ and write it on the blackboard. Each member will record $N = 8$ in the first row of his record sheet for that trial. You then compute S_i, the sum of all other proposals, by subtracting row 2 from row 1 and writing it in row 3. In the example, member 1 records $S_1 = N - n_1 = 8 - 3 = 5$. Each member then locates his net membership value in Table 3.1 by finding the row for n_i and the column for S_i, and recording this number in the fourth row of the record sheet. In the example, member 1 finds the row for $n_1 = 3$, $S_1 = 5$. This process will be repeated on each trial until it is stopped.

Tables 1.1, 2.1, and 3.1 are not the same for all members. They represent your own private information. You are not to reveal them to any other member. Feel free to earn as much cash as you can. Are there any questions?

Table 1.1. Membership Valuation, in Dollars

Member # 1(2)

(1) Facility size (No. of units, N)	(2) Membership Value of Nth unit, in dollars	(3) Total Membership Value of N units, in dollars
0	0	0
1	1	1
2	5	6
3	12	18
4	9	27
5	5	32
6	3	35
7	1	36
8	0	36
9	0	36
10	0	36
11	0	36

Table 1.2. Membership Valuation, in Dollars

Member # 3

(1) Facility size (No. of units, N)	(2) Membership Value of Nth unit, in dollars	(3) Total Membership Value of N units, in dollars
0	0	0
1	6	6
2	8	14
3	15	29
4	13	42
5	10	52
6	8	60
7	4	64
8	3	67
9	2	69
10	1	70
11	0	70

Table 1.3. Membership Valuation, in Dollars

Member # 4

(1) Facility size (No. of units, N)	(2) Membership Value of Nth unit, in dollars	(3) Total Membership Value of N units, in dollars
0	0	0
1	10	10
2	16	26
3	19	45
4	17	62
5	15	77
6	13	90
7	8	98
8	5	103
9	3	106
10	2	108
11	0	108

Table 1.4. Membership Valuation, in Dollars

Member # 5

(1) Facility size (No. of units, N)	(2) Membership Value of Nth unit, in dollars	(3) Total Membership Value of N units, in dollars
0	0	0
1	11	11
2	25	36
3	24	60
4	22	82
5	20	102
6	18	120
7	11	131
8	7	138
9	4	142
10	2	144
11	0	144

Incentive Compatible Experimental Processes

Table 2.1. My Share of Facility Cost, in Dollars

Member # 1(2)

My proposed addition, n \ Sum of proposals of all other members, S	−3	−2	−1	0	1	2	3	4	5	6	7	8	9	10	11
−3								18	23	27	30	32	33	33	32
−2							8	13	17	20	22	23	23	22	20
−1						3	8	12	15	17	18	18	17	15	12
0					3	8	12	15	17	18	18	17	15	12	8
1				8	13	17	20	22	23	23	22	20	17	13	
2			18	23	27	30	32	33	33	32	30	27	23		
3		33	38	42	45	47	48	48	47	45	42	38			
4	53	58	62	65	67	68	68	67	65	62	58				
5	83	87	90	92	93	93	92	90	87	83					
6	117	120	122	123	123	122	120	117	113						
7	155	157	158	158	157	155	152	148							
8	197	198	198	197	195	192	188								
9	243	243	242	240	237	233									
10	293	292	290	287	283										
11	347	345	342	338											

Table 2.2. My Share of Facility Cost, in Dollars

Member # 3

Sum of proposals of all other members, S_3 / My proposed addition, n_3	-3	-2	-1	0	1	2	3	4	5	6	7	8	9	10	11
-3								38	48	57	65	72	78	83	87
-2							23	33	42	50	57	63	68	72	75
-1						13	23	32	40	47	53	58	62	65	67
0					8	18	27	35	42	48	53	57	60	62	63
1				8	18	27	35	42	48	53	57	60	62	63	
2			13	23	32	40	47	53	58	62	65	67	68		
3		23	33	42	50	57	63	68	72	75	77	78			
4	38	48	57	65	72	78	83	87	90	92	93				
5	68	77	85	92	98	103	107	110	112	113					
6	102	110	117	123	128	132	135	137	138						
7	140	147	153	158	162	165	167	168							
8	182	188	193	197	200	202	203								
9	228	233	237	240	242	243									
10	278	282	285	287	288										
11	332	335	337	338											

Incentive Compatible Experimental Processes

Table 2.3. My Share of Facility Cost, in Dollars

Member #4

My proposed addition, n_4 \\ Sum of proposals of all other members, S_4	-3	-2	-1	0	1	2	3	4	5	6	7	8	9	10	11
-3								63	73	82	90	97	103	108	112
-2							48	58	67	75	82	88	93	97	100
-1						38	48	57	65	72	78	83	87	90	92
0					33	43	52	60	67	73	78	82	85	87	88
1				33	43	52	60	67	73	78	82	85	87	88	
2			38	48	57	65	72	78	83	87	90	92	93		
3		48	58	67	75	82	88	93	97	100	102	103			
4	63	73	82	90	97	103	108	112	115	117	118				
5	93	102	110	117	123	128	132	135	137	138					
6	127	135	142	148	153	157	160	162	163						
7	165	172	178	183	187	190	192	193							
8	207	213	218	222	225	227	228								
9	253	258	262	265	267	268									
10	303	307	310	312	313										
11	357	360	362	363											

Table 2.4. My Share of Facility Cost, in Dollars
Member # 5

My proposed addition, n_5 \ Sum of proposals of all other members, S_5	−3	−2	−1	0	1	2	3	4	5	6	7	8	9	10	11
−3								83	93	102	110	117	123	128	132
−2							68	78	87	95	102	108	113	117	120
−1						58	68	77	85	92	98	103	107	110	112
0					53	63	72	80	87	93	98	102	105	107	108
1				53	63	72	80	87	93	98	102	105	107	108	
2			58	68	77	85	92	98	103	107	110	112	113		
3		68	78	87	95	102	108	113	117	120	122	123			
4	83	93	102	110	117	123	128	132	135	137	138				
5	113	122	130	137	143	148	152	155	157	158					
6	147	155	162	168	173	177	180	182	183						
7	185	192	198	203	207	210	212	213							
8	227	233	238	242	245	247	248								
9	273	278	282	285	287	288									
10	323	327	330	332	333										
11	377	380	382	383											

Table 3.1. My Net Membership Value, in Dollars

Member # 1(2)

My proposed addition, n_1 \ Sum of proposals of all other members, S_1	-3	-2	-1	0	1	2	3	4	5	6	7	8	9	10	11
-3								-17	-17	-9	-3	0	2	3	4
-2							-7	-7	1	7	10	12	13	14	16
-1						-2	-2	6	12	15	17	18	19	21	24
0					-2	-2	6	12	15	17	18	19	21	24	28
1				-7	-7	1	7	10	12	13	14	16	19	23	
2			-17	-17	-9	-3	0	2	3	4	6	9	13		
3		-32	-32	-24	-18	-15	-13	-12	-12	-9	-6	-2			
4	-52	-52	-44	-38	-35	-33	-32	-31	-29	-26	-22				
5	-77	-69	-63	-60	-58	-57	-56	-54	-51	-47					
6	-99	-93	-90	-88	-87	-86	-84	-81	-77						
7	-128	-125	-123	-122	-121	-119	-116	-112							
8	-165	-163	-162	-161	-159	-156	-152								
9	-208	-207	-206	-204	-201	-197									
10	-257	-256	-254	-251	-247										
11	-311	-309	-306	-302											

Table 3.2. My Net Membership Value, in Dollars

Member # 3

My proposed addition, n_3 \ Sum of proposals of all other members, S_3	−3	−2	−1	0	1	2	3	4	5	6	7	8	9	10	11
−3								−32	−34	−28	−13	−20	−18	−19	−20
−2							−17	−19	−13	−8	−5	−3	−4	−5	−6
−1						−7	−9	−3	2	5	7	6	5	4	3
0					−2	−4	2	7	10	12	11	10	9	8	7
1				−2	−4	2	7	10	12	11	10	9	8	7	
2			−7	−9	−3	2	5	7	6	5	4	3	2		
3		−17	−19	−13	−8	−5	−3	−4	−5	−6	−7	−8			
4	−32	−34	−28	−23	−20	−18	−19	−20	−21	−22	−23				
5	−54	−48	−43	−40	−38	−39	−40	−41	−42	−43					
6	−73	−68	−65	−63	−64	−65	−66	−67	−68						
7	−98	−95	−93	−94	−95	−96	−97	−98							
8	−130	−128	−129	−130	−131	−132	−133								
9	−168	−169	−170	−171	−172	−173									
10	−214	−215	−216	−217	−218										
11	−265	−266	−267	−268											

Incentive Compatible Experimental Processes   133

Table 3.3. My Net Membership Value, in Dollars

Member #4

Sum of proposals of all other members, S_4 / My proposed addition, n_4	-3	-2	-1	0	1	2	3	4	5	6	7	8	9	10	11
-3								-53	-47	-37	-28	-20	-13	-10	-9
-2							-38	-32	-22	-13	-5	-2	5	6	6
-1					-28	-17	-22	-12	-3	5	12	15	16	16	16
0			-23	-23	-17	-7	-7	2	10	17	20	21	21	21	20
1			-28	-22	-12	-3	2	10	17	20	21	21	21	20	
2		-38	-32	-22	-13	-5	5	12	15	16	16	16	15		
3		-47	-37	-28	-20	-13	2	5	6	6	6	5			
4	-53	-57	-48	-40	-33	-30	-10	-9	-9	-9	-10				
5	-67	-73	-65	-58	-55	-54	-29	-29	-29	-30					
6	-82	-95	-88	-85	-84	-84	-54	-54	-55						
7	-103	-123	-120	-119	-119	-119	-84	-85							
8	-130	-160	-159	-159	-159	-160	-120								
9	-163	-204	-204	-204	-205										
10	-205	-254	-254	-255											
11	-254														

Table 3.4. My Net Membership Value, in Dollars

Member # 5

Sum of proposals of all other members, S_5 / My proposed addition, n_5	−3	−2	−1	0	1	2	3	4	5	6	7	8	9	10	11
−3								−72	−57	−42	−28	−15	−3	3	6
−2							−57	−42	−27	−13	0	12	18	21	22
−1						−47	−32	−17	−3	10	22	28	31	32	32
0					−42	−27	−12	2	15	27	33	36	37	37	36
1				−42	−27	−12	2	15	27	33	36	37	37	36	
2			−47	−32	−17	−3	10	22	28	31	32	32	31		
3		−57	−42	−27	−13	0	12	18	21	22	22	21			
4	−72	−57	−42	−28	−15	−3	3	6	7	7	6				
5	−77	−62	−48	−35	−23	−17	−14	−13	−13	−14					
6	−87	−73	−60	−48	−42	−39	−38	−38	−39						
7	−103	−90	−78	−72	−69	−68	−68	−69							
8	−125	−113	−107	−104	−103	−103	−104								
9	−153	−147	−144	−143	−143	−144									
10	−192	−189	−188	−188	−189										
11	−239	−238	−238	−239											

Incentive Compatible Experimental Processes

Record Sheet, Net Membership Value (Cash earnings on final trial)
Member No. 1 (2–5)

Trial	1	2	3	4	5	6	7	8	9	10	11	12	13	14	15
Item															
1. Facility Size, N															
2. My proposed addition, n_1															
3. Sum of proposals of other members, $S_1 = N - n_1$ (item 1 – item 2)															
4. Net Membership Value (Table 3.1 using column for item 3, row for item 2)															

Trial	16	17	18	19	20	21	22	2†	24	25	26	27	28	29	30
Item															
1. Facility Size, N															
2. My proposed addition, n_1															
3. Sum of proposals of other members, $S_1 = N - n_1$ (item 1 – item 2)															
4. Net Membership Value (Table 3.1 using column for item 3, row for item 2)															

Name_____

APPENDIX II

Lindahl Process, C.
Instructions

This is an experiment in the economics of group decision making. The instructions are simple, and if you follow them carefully and make good decisions you may earn a considerable amount of money which will be paid to you in cash at the end of the experiment. Various research foundations have provided funds for this research.

You are a member of a group (such as a club, association, or neighborhood) that jointly must decide upon, and bear the cost of, a common facility (examples might be a playground, road, swimming pool, fence, etc.). The group must decide on the size of the commonly shared facility as measured by the number of units, N (which might represent area in square feet, or height in feet, etc.). The total value of the facility to you can be thought of as the amount you could obtain if you were to sell your paid-up membership in the group. This total membership value, corresponding to different facility sizes, N, is listed in the third column of Table 1.1. The membership value for you of each successive unit increase in facility size is listed in the second column of Table 1.1. Net value, which will be paid to you in cash on the final decision, is computed by subtracting from total value your paid-up share of total facility cost.

The cost per unit of the facility is $45. Hence, total cost for a facility of size N is 45 times N. Your share of total facility cost is determined from the decisions that result from a series of trial bids using the following process: On each trial each member submits up to eleven bids, arranged in descending order from highest to lowest. [It was explained that "descending" included the option of entering two or more identical bids, so that bids were required to be nonincreasing]. The bids must be expressed in whole dollar amounts and written in the spaces provided on the bid slips in your folder. I will collect these bid slips and compute the sum of all member's # 1 (highest) bids, the sum of all the # 2 bids, then the # 3 bids, and so on. Facility size is determined by finding the largest value of N such that the sum of the # N bids is not smaller than the unit cost, $45. Suppose, for example, that the sum of the # 3 bids is $50 and the sum of the # 4 bids is $40. Then the proposed facility size is 3. Your share of facility cost is then 3 times your lowest accepted bid, # 3. If member 1's # 3 bid is $20, his share of cost is $60. If from column 3 of Table 1.1 member 1's total valuation for a facility of size 3 is $160, then his net membership value is $100 for that trial. This process will be repeated for at most —— trials. If at any time in this process each member's lowest accepted bid is repeated for three successive trials, the process will be stopped and the net membership value resulting on the last trial will be paid to you in cash. Otherwise you will be paid a modest wage for the time you have spent.

Your folder includes a record sheet for recording the results of each trial. After I collect your bid slips and determine the facility size, N, this number will be written on the blackboard. Each member records this number in the first row of his record sheet. I will then go to each member and record his lowest accepted bid ($\# N$) in the second row of his record sheet. Each member will then determine his membership evaluation for facility size N from Table 1.1, column 3, and record it in row 3 of his record sheet. Then in row 4 each member will compute his share of facility cost by taking N times his lowest accepted bid; (row 1) times (row 2). Finally, in row 5, net membership value is computed by subtracting row 4 from row 3.

Table 1.1 is not the same for all members. It is your own private information and is not to be revealed to any other member. Feel free to earn as much cash as you can. Are there any questions?

Table 1.1. Membership Valuation, in Dollars

Member $\# 1(2)$

(1) Facility size (No. of units, N)	(2) Membership Value of Nth unit, in dollars	(3) Total Membership Value of N units, in dollars
0	0	0
1	7	7
2	7	14
3	7	21
4	6	27
5	5	32
6	3	35
7	1	36
8	0	36
9	0	36
10	0	36
11	0	36

Table 1.2. Membership Valuation, in Dollars

Member # 3

(1) Facility size (No. of units, N)	(2) Membership Value of Nth unit, in dollars	(3) Total Membership Value of N units, in dollars
0	0	0
1	11	11
2	11	22
3	11	33
4	10	43
5	9	52
6	8	60
7	4	64
8	3	67
9	2	69
10	1	70
11	0	70

Table 1.3. Membership Valuation, in Dollars

Member # 4

(1) Facility size (No. of units, N)	(2) Membership Value of Nth unit, in dollars	(3) Total Membership Value of N units, in dollars
0	0	0
1	16	16
2	16	32
3	16	48
4	15	63
5	14	77
6	13	90
7	8	98
8	5	103
9	3	106
10	2	108
11	0	108

Incentive Compatible Experimental Processes

Table 1.4. Membership Valuation, in Dollars

Member # 5

(1) Facility size (No. of units, N)	(2) Membership Value of Nth unit, in dollars	(3) Total Membership Value of N units, in dollars
0	0	0
1	21	21
2	21	42
3	21	63
4	20	83
5	19	102
6	18	120
7	11	131
8	7	138
9	4	142
10	2	144
11	0	144

Sample Bid Slip

Member # 1, Trial 30

Bids:

1. ———
2. ———
3. ———
4. ———
5. ———
6. ———
7. ———
8. ———
9. ———
10. ———
11. ———

Record Sheet, Net Membership Value, Member No. _____   Name _____

Row \ Trial	1	2	3	4	5	6	7	8	9	10	11	12	13	14	15
1. Facility Size, N															
2. My lowest accepted bid (Bid N)															
3. My Valuation of Facility, N (Table 1.1, column 3)															
4. My Share of Facility Cost N × low accepted bid (row 1 times row 2)															
5. My Net Membership Value = row 3−row 4															

Row \ Trial	16	17	18	19	20	21	22	23	24	25	26	27	28	29	30
1. Facility Size, N															
2. My lowest accepted bid (Bid N)															
3. My Valuation of Facility, N (Table 1.1, column 3)															
4. My Share of Facility Cost N × low accepted bid (row 1 times row 2)															
5. My Net Membership Value = row 3−row 4															

APPENDIX III

G–L Process, R2.
Instructions

This is an experiment in the economics of group decision making. The instructions are simple, and if you follow them carefully and make good decisions you may earn a considerable amount of money which will be paid to you in cash at the end of the experiment. Various research foundations have provided funds for the research.

You are a member of a group (such as a club, association, or neighborhood) that jointly must decide upon, and bear the cost of, a common facility (examples might be a playground, road, swimming pool, fence, etc.). The group must decide on the size of the commonly shared facility as measured by the number of units, N (which might represent area in square feet, or height in feet, etc.). The total value of the facility to you can be thought of as the amount you could obtain if you were to sell your paid-up membership in the group. This total membership value, corresponding to different facility sizes, N, is listed in the third column of Table 1.1. The membership value for you of each successive unit increase in facility size is listed in the second column of Table 1.1. Net value, which will be paid to you in cash on the final decision, is computed by subtracting from total value your paid-up share of total facility cost.

Your share of total facility cost is determined by the formula tabulated in Table 2.1. The formula applies to the decisions that result on a series of trials using the following process: On each trial a proposed facility size is determined by taking the algebraic sum of the numbers submitted by all members. That is, each member, i, independently selects a number, n_i, representing your proposal as to the number of units to be algebraically added to the sum of the other proposals to determine facility size. Suppose that the sum, S_i, of the proposals of all other members is 4, and the proposal of member i is $n_i = -1$. Then facility size is $N = 3$. Member i's share of total facility cost in dollars is then determined by locating the column for $S_i = 4$, and the row for $n_i = -1$, in Table 2.1; suppose it is $57. If, for member i, the total value of a facility of size 3 is $157, then his net membership value would be $100 for that trial. This process will be repeated for at most —— trials. If, at any time in this process each member repeats his choice for three successive trials, the process will be stopped and the net membership value resulting on the last trial will be paid to you in cash. Otherwise you will be paid a modest wage for the time you have spent. In order to simplify your clerical task, a complete listing of net membership values has been computed for you in Table 3.1.

Your folder includes a record sheet for recording the results of each trial.

You are free to select any proposed addition, n_i, between -4 and $+10$, appearing on the left of the rows in Table 3.1. Suppose, for example, that eight members independently choose $n_1 = 3, n_2 = 3, n_3 = 3, n_4 = 2, n_5 = -3, n_6 = 0, n_7 = 0, n_8 = 0$. Each member writes his choice in the second row of his record sheet for that trial. In the example, member 1 writes $n_1 = 3$. I will go to each member and record his choice on my data sheet, then compute facility size $N = 3 + 3 + 3 + 2 - 3 + 0 + 0 + 0 = 8$ and write it on the blackboard. Each member will record $N = 8$ in the first row of his record sheet for that trial. You then compute S_i, the sum of all other proposals, by subtracting row 2 from row 1 and writing it in row 3. In the example, member 1 records $S_1 = N - n_1 = 8 - 3 = 5$. Each member then locates his net membership value in Table 3.1 by finding the row for n_i and the column for S_i, and recording this number in the fourth row of the record sheet. In the example, member 1 finds the row for $n_1 = 3$, and column for $S_1 = 5$. This process will be repeated on each trial until it is stopped.

Tables 2.1 and 3.1 are not the same for all members. They represent your own private information. You are not to reveal them to any other member. Feel free to earn as much cash as you can. Are there any questions?

Table 1.1. Membership Valuation, in Dollars

Member # 1

(1) Facility size (No. of units, N)	(2) Membership Value of Nth unit, in dollars	(3) Total Membership Value of N units, in dollars
0		10.0
1	−2.6	7.4
2	−2.6	4.8
3	−2.6	2.2
4	−2.6	−0.4
5	−2.6	−3.0
6	−2.6	−5.6
7	−2.6	−8.2
8	−2.6	−10.8
9	−2.6	−13.4
10	−2.6	−16.0

Table 1.2. Membership Valuation, in Dollars

Member # 2(3)

(1) Facility size (No. of units, N)	(2) Membership Value of Nth unit, in dollars	(3) Total Membership Value of N units, in dollars
0		0
1	10.3	10.3
2	7.3	17.6
3	4.3	21.9
4	1.3	23.2
5	− 1.7	21.5
6	− 4.7	16.8
7	− 7.7	9.1
8	− 10.7	− 1.6
9	− 13.7	− 15.3
10	− 16.7	− 32.0

Table 1.3. Membership Valuation, in Dollars

Member # 4

(1) Facility size (No. of units, N)	(2) Membership Value of Nth unit, in dollars	(3) Total Membership Value of N units, in dollars
0		0
1	11.1	11.1
2	8.1	19.2
3	5.1	24.3
4	2.1	26.4
5	− 0.9	25.5
6	− 3.9	21.6
7	− 6.9	14.7
8	− 9.9	4.8
9	− 12.9	− 8.1
10	−15.9	− 24.0

Table 1.4. Membership Valuation, in Dollars

Member # 5

(1) Facility size (No. of units, N)	(2) Membership Value of Nth unit, in dollars	(3) Total Membership Value of N units, in dollars
0		0
1	6.7	6.7
2	5.1	11.8
3	3.7	15.5
4	2.1	17.6
5	0.7	18.3
6	− 0.9	17.4
7	− 2.3	15.1
8	− 3.9	11.2
9	− 5.3	5.9
10	− 6.9	− 1.0

Table 1.5. Membership Valuation, in Dollars

Member # 6

(1) Facility size (No. of units, N)	(2) Membership Value of Nth unit, in dollars	(3) Total Membership Value of N units, in dollars
0		0
1	9.2	9.2
2	7.2	16.4
3	5.2	21.6
4	3.2	24.8
5	1.2	26.0
6	− 0.8	25.2
7	− 2.8	22.4
8	− 4.8	17.6
9	− 6.8	10.8
10	− 8.8	2.0

Table 1.6. Membership Valuation, in Dollars

Member # 7

(1) Facility size (No. of units, N)	(2) Membership Value of Nth unit, in dollars	(3) Total Membership Value of N units, in dollars
0		0
1	10.0	10.0
2	8.0	18.0
3	6.0	24.0
4	4.0	28.0
5	2.0	30.0
6	0.0	30.0
7	−2.0	28.0
8	−4.0	24.0
9	−6.0	18.0
10	−8.0	10.0

Table 1.7. Membership Valuation, in Dollars

Member # 8

(1) Facility size (No. of units, N)	(2) Membership Value of Nth unit, in dollars	(3) Total Membership Value of N units, in dollars
0		0
1	9.1	9.1
2	7.5	16.6
3	6.1	22.7
4	4.5	27.2
5	3.1	30.3
6	1.5	31.8
7	0.1	31.9
8	−1.5	30.4
9	−2.9	27.5
10	−4.5	23.0

Table 2.1. My Share of Facility Cost, in Dollars

Member # 1

My proposed addition, n_1 \ Sum of proposals of all other members, S_1	−4	−3	−2	−1	0	1	2	3	4	5	6	7	8	9	10
−4									5.6	2.9	−0.6	−5.1	−10.4	−16.7	−23.8
−3								5.6	3.7	1.0	−2.7	−7.2	−12.7	−19.0	−26.3
−2							5.6	4.6	2.6	−0.3	−4.0	−8.6	−14.2	−20.7	−28.0
−1						5.6	5.4	4.2	2.1	−0.8	−4.7	−9.4	−15.0	−21.6	−29.1
0					5.6	6.1	5.8	4.5	2.4	−0.7	−4.6	−9.5	−15.2	−21.8	−29.4
1				5.6	6.9	7.4	6.9	5.6	3.3	0.2	−3.9	−8.8	−14.7	−21.4	
2			5.6	7.8	9.0	9.4	8.8	7.3	5.0	1.7	−2.4	−7.4	−13.4		
3		5.6	8.5	10.6	11.8	12.0	11.4	9.8	7.3	4.0	−0.3	−5.4			
4	5.6	9.4	12.2	14.1	15.2	15.4	14.6	12.9	10.4	6.9	2.6				
5	10.1	13.8	16.5	18.4	19.4	19.4	18.5	16.8	14.1	10.6					
6	15.4	19.0	21.6	23.4	24.2	24.1	23.2	21.3	18.6						
7	21.4	24.8	27.3	29.0	29.8	29.6	28.5	26.6							
8	28.0	31.3	33.8	35.3	36.0	35.8	34.6								
9	35.3	38.6	40.9	42.4	42.9	42.6									
10	43.4	46.5	48.8	50.2	50.6										

Incentive Compatible Experimental Processes

Table 2.2. My Share of Facility Cost, in Dollars

Member # 2(3)

My proposed addition, n_2 \ Sum of proposals of all other members, S_2	-4	-3	-2	-1	0	1	2	3	4	5	6	7	8	9	10
-4															
-3															
-2															
-1															
0					5.6	5.6	5.6	5.6	5.6	2.9	-0.6	-5.1	-10.4	-16.7	-23.8
1				5.6	6.9	6.1	5.4	4.6	3.7	1.0	-2.7	-7.2	-12.7	-19.0	-26.3
2			5.6	7.8	9.0	7.4	5.8	4.2	2.6	-0.3	-4.0	-8.6	-14.2	-20.7	-28.0
3		5.6	8.5	10.6	11.8	9.4	6.9	4.5	2.1	-0.8	-4.7	-9.4	-15.0	-21.6	-29.1
4	5.6	9.4	12.2	14.1	15.2	12.0	8.8	5.6	2.4	-0.7	-4.6	-9.5	-15.2	-21.8	-29.4
5	10.1	13.8	16.5	18.4	19.4	15.4	11.4	7.3	3.3	0.2	-3.9	-8.8	-14.7	-21.4	
6	15.4	19.0	21.6	23.4	24.2	19.4	14.6	9.8	5.0	1.7	-2.4	-7.4	-13.4		
7	21.4	24.8	27.3	29.0	29.8	24.1	18.5	12.9	7.3	4.0	-0.3	-5.4			
8	28.0	31.3	33.8	35.3	36.0	29.6	23.2	16.8	10.4	6.9	2.6				
9	35.3	38.6	40.9	42.4	42.9	35.8	28.5	21.3	14.1	10.6					
10	43.4	46.5	48.8	50.2	50.6	42.6	34.6	26.6	18.6						

Table 2.3. My Share of Facility Cost, in Dollars

Member # 4

My proposed addition, n_4 \ Sum of proposals of all other members, S_4	-4	-3	-2	-1	0	1	2	3	4	5	6	7	8	9	10
-4															
-3															
-2															
-1															
0				5.6	5.6										
1				7.8	6.9	5.6									
2			5.6	10.6	9.0	6.1	5.6								
3			8.5	14.1	11.8	7.4	5.4	5.6							
4	5.6	5.6	12.2	15.2	15.2	9.4	5.8	4.6	5.6	2.9	−0.6	−5.1	−10.4	−16.7	−23.8
5	10.1	9.4	16.5	18.4	19.4	12.0	6.9	4.2	3.7	1.0	−2.7	−7.2	−12.7	−19.0	−26.3
6	15.4	13.8	21.6	23.4	24.2	15.4	8.8	4.5	2.6	−0.3	−4.0	−8.6	−14.2	−20.7	−28.0
7	21.4	19.0	27.3	29.0	29.8	19.4	11.4	5.6	2.1	−0.8	−4.7	−9.4	−15.0	−21.6	−29.1
8	28.0	24.8	33.8	35.3	36.0	24.1	14.6	7.3	2.4	−0.7	−4.6	−9.5	−15.2	−21.8	−29.4
9	35.3	31.3	40.9	42.4	42.9	29.6	18.5	9.8	3.3	0.2	−3.9	−8.8	−14.7	−21.4	
10	43.4	38.6	48.8	50.2	50.6	35.8	23.2	12.9	5.0	1.7	−2.4	−7.4	−13.4		
		46.5				42.6	28.5	16.8	7.3	4.0	−0.3	−5.4			
							34.6	21.3	10.4	6.9	2.6				
								26.6	14.1	10.6					
									18.6						

Table 2.4. My Share of Facility Cost, in Dollars

Member # 5

My proposed addition, n_5 \ Sum of proposals of all other members, S_5	-4	-3	-2	-1	0	1	2	3	4	5	6	7	8	9	10
-4															
-3															
-2															
-1															
0					5.6	5.6	5.6	5.6	5.6	2.9	-0.6	-5.1	-10.4	-16.7	-23.8
1				5.6	6.9	6.1	5.4	4.6	3.7	1.0	-2.7	-7.2	-12.7	-19.0	-26.3
2			5.6	7.8	9.0	7.4	5.8	4.2	2.6	-0.3	-4.0	-8.6	-14.2	-20.7	-28.0
3		5.6	8.5	10.6	11.8	9.4	6.9	4.5	2.1	-0.8	-4.7	-9.4	-15.0	-21.6	-29.1
4	5.6	9.4	12.2	14.1	15.2	12.0	8.8	5.6	2.4	-0.7	-4.6	-9.5	-15.2	-21.8	-29.4
5	10.1	13.8	16.5	18.4	19.4	15.4	11.4	7.3	3.3	0.2	-3.9	-8.8	-14.7	-21.4	
6	15.4	19.0	21.6	23.4	24.2	19.4	14.6	9.8	5.0	1.7	-2.4	-7.4	-13.4		
7	21.4	24.8	27.3	29.0	29.8	24.1	18.5	12.9	7.3	4.0	-0.3	-5.4			
8	28.0	31.3	33.8	35.3	36.0	29.6	23.2	16.8	10.4	6.9	2.6				
9	35.3	38.6	40.9	42.4	42.9	35.8	28.5	21.3	14.1	10.6					
10	43.4	46.5	48.8	50.2	50.6	42.6	34.6	26.6	18.6						

Table 2.5. My Share of Facility Cost, in Dollars

Member # 6

My proposed addition, n_6 \ Sum of proposals of all other members, S_6	−4	−3	−2	−1	0	1	2	3	4	5	6	7	8	9	10
−4															
−3															
−2															
−1															
0				5.6	5.6	5.6	5.6	5.6	5.6	2.9	−0.6	−5.1	−10.4	−16.7	−23.8
1				7.8	6.9	6.1	5.4	4.6	3.7	1.0	−2.7	−7.2	−12.7	−19.0	−26.3
2			5.6	10.6	9.0	7.4	5.8	4.2	2.6	−0.3	−4.0	−8.6	−14.2	−20.7	−28.0
3		5.6	8.5	14.1	11.8	9.4	6.9	4.5	2.1	−0.8	−4.7	−9.4	−15.0	−21.6	−29.1
4	5.6	9.4	12.2	18.4	15.2	12.0	8.8	5.6	2.4	−0.7	−4.6	−9.5	−15.2	−21.8	−29.4
5	10.1	13.8	16.5	23.4	19.4	15.4	11.4	7.3	3.3	0.2	−3.9	−8.8	−14.7	−21.4	
6	15.4	19.0	21.6	29.0	24.2	19.4	14.6	9.8	5.0	1.7	−2.4	−7.4	−13.4		
7	21.4	24.8	27.3	35.3	29.8	24.1	18.5	12.9	7.3	4.0	−0.3	−5.4			
8	28.0	31.3	33.8	40.9	36.0	29.6	23.2	16.8	10.4	6.9	2.6				
9	35.3	38.6	40.9	48.8	42.9	35.8	28.5	21.3	14.1	10.6					
10	43.4	46.5	48.8	50.2	50.6	42.6	34.6	26.6	18.6						

Incentive Compatible Experimental Processes

Table 2.6. My Share of Facility Cost, in Dollars

Member #7

Sum of proposals of all other members, S_7 \ My proposed addition, n_7	−4	−3	−2	−1	0	1	2	3	4	5	6	7	8	9	10
−4									5.6	2.9	−0.6	−5.1	−10.4	−16.7	−23.8
−3								5.6	3.7	1.0	−2.7	−7.2	−12.7	−19.0	−26.3
−2							5.6	4.6	2.6	−0.3	−4.0	−8.6	−14.2	−20.7	−28.0
−1						5.6	5.4	4.2	2.1	−0.8	−4.7	−9.4	−15.0	−21.6	−29.1
0					5.6	6.1	5.8	4.5	2.4	−0.7	−4.6	−9.5	−15.2	−21.8	−29.4
1				5.6	6.9	7.4	6.9	5.6	3.3	0.2	−3.9	−8.8	−14.7	−21.4	
2			5.6	7.8	9.0	9.4	8.8	7.3	5.0	1.7	−2.4	−7.4	−13.4		
3		5.6	8.5	10.6	11.8	12.0	11.4	9.8	7.3	4.0	−0.3	−5.4			
4	5.6	9.4	12.2	14.1	15.2	15.4	14.6	12.9	10.4	6.9	2.6				
5	10.1	13.8	16.5	18.4	19.4	19.4	18.5	16.8	14.1	10.6					
6	15.4	19.0	21.6	23.4	24.2	24.1	23.2	21.3	18.6						
7	21.4	24.8	27.3	29.0	29.8	29.6	28.5	26.6							
8	28.0	31.3	33.8	35.3	36.0	35.8	34.6								
9	35.3	38.6	40.9	42.4	42.9	42.6									
10	43.4	46.5	48.8	50.2	50.6										

Table 2.7. My Share of Facility Cost, in Dollars

Member # 8

My proposed addition, n_8 \ Sum of proposals of all other members, S_8	−4	−3	−2	−1	0	1	2	3	4	5	6	7	8	9	10
−4															
−3															
−2															
−1						5.6									
0					5.6	6.1	5.6								
1				5.6	6.9	7.4	5.4	5.6							
2			5.6	7.8	9.0	9.4	5.8	4.6	5.6	2.9					
3		5.6	8.5	10.6	11.8	12.0	6.9	4.2	3.7	1.0	−0.6				
4	5.6	9.4	12.2	14.1	15.2	15.4	8.8	4.5	2.6	−0.3	−2.7	−5.1	−10.4	−16.7	−23.8
5	10.1	13.8	16.5	18.4	19.4	19.4	11.4	5.6	2.1	−0.8	−4.0	−7.2	−12.7	−19.0	−26.3
6	15.4	19.0	21.6	23.4	24.2	24.1	14.6	7.3	2.4	−0.7	−4.7	−8.6	−14.2	−20.7	−28.0
7	21.4	24.8	27.3	29.0	29.8	29.6	18.5	9.8	3.3	0.2	−4.6	−9.4	−15.0	−21.6	−29.1
8	28.0	31.3	33.8	35.3	36.0	35.8	23.2	12.9	5.0	1.7	−3.9	−9.5	−15.2	−21.8	−29.4
9	35.3	38.6	40.9	42.4	42.9	42.6	28.5	16.8	7.3	4.0	−2.4	−8.8	−14.7	−21.4	
10	43.4	46.5	48.8	50.2	50.6		34.6	21.3	10.4	6.9	−0.3	−7.4	−13.4		
								26.6	14.1	10.6	2.6	−5.4			
									18.6						

Table 3.1. My Net Membership Value, in Dollars

Member # 1

My proposed addition, n_1 \ Sum of proposals of all other members, S_1	-4	-3	-2	-1	0	1	2	3	4	5	6	7	8	9	10
-4									4.4	4.5	5.4	7.3	10.0	13.7	18.2
-3								4.4	3.7	3.8	4.9	6.8	9.7	13.4	18.1
-2							4.4	2.9	2.2	2.5	3.6	5.6	8.6	12.5	17.2
-1						4.4	2.1	0.6	0.1	0.4	1.7	3.8	6.8	10.8	15.7
0					4.4	1.3	−1.0	−2.3	−2.8	−2.3	−1.0	1.3	4.4	8.5	13.4
1				4.4	0.5	−2.6	−4.8	−6.0	−6.3	−5.8	−4.3	−2.0	1.3	5.4	
2			4.4	−0.3	−4.2	−7.2	−9.2	−10.3	−10.6	−9.9	−8.4	−6.0	−2.6		
3		4.4	−1.1	−5.8	−9.6	−12.4	−14.4	−15.4	−15.5	−14.8	−13.1	−10.7			
4	4.4	−1.9	−7.4	−12.0	−15.6	−18.4	−20.2	−21.1	−21.2	−20.3	−18.6				
5	−2.7	−9.0	−14.4	−18.8	−22.4	−25.0	−26.8	−27.6	−27.5	−26.6					
6	−10.6	−16.8	−22.0	−26.4	−29.8	−32.3	−34.0	−34.8	−34.6						
7	−19.2	−25.2	−30.3	−34.6	−38.0	−40.4	−41.9	−42.6							
8	−28.4	−34.3	−39.4	−43.6	−46.8	−49.2	−50.6								
9	−38.3	−44.2	−49.2	−53.2	−56.3	−58.6									
10	−49.0	−54.8	−59.6	−63.6	−66.6										

Table 3.2. My Net Membership Value, in Dollars

Member # 2(3)

My proposed addition, n_2 \ Sum of proposals of all other members, S_2	−4	−3	−2	−1	0	1	2	3	4	5	6	7	8	9	10
−4															
−3															
−2								−5.6							
−1					−5.6	−5.6	−5.6	5.8	−5.6						
0			−5.6	−5.6	3.4	4.2	5.0	13.4	6.6	7.4					
1		−5.6	1.8	2.6	8.6	10.2	11.8	17.4	15.0	16.6	18.2				
2		1.0	5.4	7.0	10.2	12.6	15.0	17.6	19.8	22.2	24.6	27.0			
3		3.8	5.4	7.8	8.0	11.2	14.4	14.2	20.8	24.0	27.2	30.4	33.6		
4	−5.6	3.0	1.6	4.8	2.2	6.2	10.2	7.0	18.2	22.2	26.2	30.2	34.2	38.2	
5	0.2	−1.6	−5.8	−1.8	−7.4	−2.6	2.2	−3.8	11.8	16.6	21.4	26.2	31.0	35.8	40.6
6	2.2	−9.8	−17.0	−12.2	−20.6	−15.0	−9.4	−18.4	1.8	7.4	13.0	18.6	24.2	29.8	35.4
7	0.6	−21.8	−31.8	−26.2	−37.6	−31.2	−24.8	−36.6	−12.0	−5.6	0.8	7.2	13.6	20.0	26.4
8	−4.8	−37.4	−50.4	−44.0	−58.2	−51.0	−43.8	−58.6	−29.4	−22.2	−15.0	−7.8	−0.6	6.6	13.8
9	−13.8		−65.4	−65.4	−82.6	−74.6	−66.6		−50.6	−42.6	−34.6	−26.6	−18.6	−10.6	−2.6
10	−26.6														

Table 3.3. My Net Membership Value, in Dollars

Member #4

My proposed addition, n_4 \ Sum of proposals of all other members, S_4	-4	-3	-2	-1	0	1	2	3	4	5	6	7	8	9	10
-4	-5.6	-5.6	-5.6	-5.6	-5.6	-5.6	-5.6	-5.6	-5.6						
-3	1.0	1.8	2.6	3.4	4.2	5.0	5.8	6.6	7.4	8.2					
-2	3.8	5.4	7.0	8.6	10.2	11.8	13.4	15.0	16.6	18.2	19.8				
-1	3.0	5.4	7.8	10.2	12.6	15.0	17.4	19.8	22.2	24.6	27.0	29.4			
0	-1.6	1.6	4.8	8.0	11.2	14.4	17.6	20.8	24.0	27.2	30.4	33.6	36.8		
1	-9.8	-5.8	-1.8	2.2	6.2	10.2	14.2	18.2	22.2	26.2	30.2	34.2	38.2	42.2	
2	-21.8	-17.0	-12.2	-7.4	-2.6	2.2	7.0	11.8	16.6	21.4	26.2	31.0	35.8	40.6	45.4
3		-31.8	-26.2	-20.6	-15.0	-9.4	-3.8	1.8	7.4	13.0	18.6	24.2	29.8	35.4	41.0
4			-44.0	-37.6	-31.2	-24.8	-18.4	-12.0	-5.6	0.8	7.2	13.6	20.0	26.4	32.8
5				-58.3	-51.0	-43.8	-36.6	-29.4	-22.2	-15.0	-7.8	-0.6	6.6	13.8	21.0
6					-74.6	-66.6	-58.6	-50.6	-42.6	-34.6	-26.6	-18.6	-10.6	-2.6	5.4
7															
8															
9															
10															

Table 3.4. My Net Membership Value, in Dollars

Member # 5

My proposed addition, n_5 \ Sum of proposals of all other members, S_5	-4	-3	-2	-1	0	1	2	3	4	5	6	7	8	9	10
-4									-5.6	3.7	12.4	20.5	28.0	34.9	41.2
-3								-5.6	2.9	10.8	18.1	24.8	30.9	36.4	41.3
-2							-5.6	2.1	9.2	15.7	21.6	26.9	31.6	35.7	39.2
-1						-5.6	1.3	7.6	13.3	18.4	22.9	26.8	30.1	32.8	34.9
0					-5.6	0.5	6.0	10.9	15.2	18.9	22.0	24.5	26.4	27.7	28.4
1				-5.6	-0.3	4.4	8.5	12.0	14.9	17.2	18.9	20.0	20.5	20.4	
2			-5.6	-1.1	2.8	6.1	8.8	10.9	12.4	13.3	13.6	13.3	12.4		
3		-5.6	-1.9	1.2	3.7	5.6	6.9	7.6	7.7	7.2	6.1	4.4			
4	-5.6	-2.7	-0.4	1.3	2.4	2.9	2.8	2.1	0.8	-1.1	-3.6				
5	-3.5	-2.0	-1.1	-0.8	-1.1	-2.0	-3.5	-5.6	-8.3	-11.6					
6	-3.6	-3.5	-4.0	-5.1	-6.8	-9.1	-12.0	-15.5	-19.6						
7	-5.9	-7.2	-9.1	-11.6	-14.7	-18.4	-22.7	-27.6							
8	-10.4	-13.1	-16.4	-20.3	-24.8	-29.9	-35.6								
9	-17.1	-21.2	-25.9	-31.2	-37.1	-43.6									
10	-26.0	-31.5	-37.6	-44.3	-51.6										

Incentive Compatible Experimental Processes

Table 3.5. My Net Membership Value, in Dollars
Member # 6

My proposed addition, n_6 \ Sum of proposals of all other members, S_6	-4	-3	-2	-1	0	1	2	3	4	5	6	7	8	9	10
-4									-5.6	6.3	17.0	26.7	35.2	42.7	49.0
-3								-5.6	5.5	15.4	24.3	32.0	38.7	44.2	48.7
-2							-5.6	4.7	13.8	21.9	28.8	34.7	39.4	43.1	45.6
-1						-5.6	3.9	12.2	19.5	25.6	30.7	34.6	37.5	39.2	39.9
0					-5.6	3.1	10.6	17.1	22.4	26.7	29.8	31.9	32.8	32.7	31.4
1				-5.6	2.3	9.0	14.7	19.2	22.7	25.0	26.3	26.4	25.5	23.4	
2			-5.6	1.5	7.4	12.3	16.0	18.7	20.2	20.7	20.0	18.3	15.4		
3		-5.6	0.7	5.8	9.9	12.8	14.7	15.4	15.1	13.6	11.1	7.4			
4	-5.6	-0.1	4.2	7.5	9.6	10.7	10.6	9.5	7.2	3.9	-0.6				
5	-0.9	2.6	5.1	6.4	6.7	5.8	3.9	0.8	-3.3	-8.6					
6	1.0	2.7	3.2	2.7	1.0	-1.7	-5.6	-10.5	-16.6						
7	0.3	0	-1.3	-3.8	-7.3	-12.0	-17.7	-24.6							
8	-3.2	-5.3	-8.6	-12.9	-18.4	-24.9	-32.6								
9	-9.3	-13.4	-18.5	-24.8	-32.1	-40.6									
10	-18.2	-24.1	-31.2	-39.3	-48.6										

157

Table 3.6. My Net Membership Value, in Dollars

Member # 7

My proposed addition, n_7 \ Sum of proposals of all other members, S_7	*−4*	*−3*	*−2*	*−1*	*0*	*1*	*2*	*3*	*4*	*5*	*6*	*7*	*8*	*9*	*10*
−4									−5.6	7.1	18.6	29.1	38.4	46.7	53.8
−3								−5.6	6.3	17.0	26.7	35.2	42.7	49.0	54.3
−2							−5.6	5.4	15.4	24.3	32.0	38.7	44.2	48.7	52.0
−1						−5.6	4.6	13.8	21.9	28.8	34.7	39.4	43.1	45.6	47.1
0					−5.6	3.9	12.2	19.5	25.6	30.7	34.6	37.5	39.2	39.8	39.4
1				−5.6	3.1	10.6	17.0	22.4	26.7	29.8	31.9	32.8	32.7	31.4	
2			−5.6	2.3	9.0	14.6	19.2	22.7	25.0	26.3	26.4	25.4	23.4		
3		−5.6	1.5	7.4	12.3	16.0	18.7	20.2	20.7	20.0	18.3	15.4			
4	−5.6	0.6	5.8	9.9	12.8	14.6	15.4	15.1	13.6	11.1	7.4				
5	−0.1	4.2	7.5	9.6	10.6	10.6	9.5	7.2	3.9	−0.6					
6	2.6	5.0	6.4	6.6	5.8	3.9	0.8	−3.3	−8.6						
7	2.6	3.2	2.7	1.0	−1.8	−5.6	−10.5	−16.6							
8	0	−1.3	−3.8	−7.3	−12.0	−17.8	−24.6								
9	−5.3	−8.6	−12.9	−18.4	−24.9	−32.6									
10	−13.4	−18.5	−24.8	−32.2	−40.6										

Incentive Compatible Experimental Processes

Table 3.7. My Net Membership Value, in Dollars

Member # 8

My proposed addition, n_8 \ Sum of proposals of all other members, S_8	−4	−3	−2	−1	0	1	2	3	4	5	6	7	8	9	10
−4	−5.6	−5.6	−5.6	−5.6	−5.6	−5.6	−5.6	−5.6	−5.6	6.1	17.2	27.7	37.6	46.9	55.6
−3	−1.1	−0.3	0.5	1.3	2.1	2.9	3.7	4.5	5.3	15.6	25.3	34.4	42.9	50.8	58.1
−2	−1.1	2.8	4.4	6.0	7.6	9.2	10.8	12.4	14.0	22.9	31.2	38.9	46.0	52.5	58.4
−1	1.2	3.7	6.1	8.5	10.9	13.3	15.7	18.1	20.5	28.0	34.9	41.2	46.9	52.0	56.5
0	1.3	2.4	5.6	8.8	12.0	15.2	18.4	21.6	24.8	30.9	36.4	41.3	45.6	49.3	52.4
1	−0.8	−1.1	2.9	6.9	10.9	14.9	18.9	22.9	26.9	31.6	35.7	39.2	42.1	44.4	
2	−5.1	−6.8	−2.0	2.8	7.6	12.4	17.2	22.0	26.8	30.1	32.8	34.9	36.4		
3	−11.6	−14.7	−9.1	−3.5	2.1	7.7	13.3	18.9	24.5	26.4	27.7	28.4			
4			−18.4	−12.0	−5.6	0.8	7.2	13.6	20.0	20.5	20.4				
5				−22.7	−15.5	−8.3	−1.1	6.1	13.3	12.4					
6					−27.6	−19.6	−11.6	−3.6	4.4						
7															
8															
9															
10															

APPENDIX IV

Auction Process, A1, A2 and A3
Instructions

1. This is an experiment in the economics of group decision making. The instructions are simple, and if you follow them carefully and make good decisions you may earn a considerable amount of money which will be paid to you in cash at the end of the experiment. Various research foundations have provided funds for this research.

2. You are a member of a group that jointly must decide upon, and bear the cost of, a common facility. The group must decide on the size of the commonly shared facility as measured by the number of units, N. The total value of the facility to you can be thought of as the amount you could obtain if you were to sell your paid-up membership in the group. This total membership value, corresponding to different facility sizes, N, is listed in the third column of Table 1.1. The membership value for you of each successive unit increase in facility size is listed in the second column of Table 1.1. Net value, which will be paid to you in cash on the decision, is computed by subtracting from total value your paid-up share of total facility cost. This is computed in Table 2.1.

3. The cost per unit of the facility is $19. Hence, total cost for a facility of size N is 19 times N. Your share of total facility cost is determined from the decisions that result from a series of trial bids using the following process. (Refer to record sheet in your folder for recording the results of each trial.)

4. On each trial each member independently selects a bid, b_i, expressed in dollars, and a facility size, N_i. You are free to select any $ bid amount appearing at the top of the columns in Table 2.1 and propose any facility size appearing on the left of the rows in Table 2.1. Each member writes his bid choice in the second row of the record sheet, and his proposed facility size in the third row, for that trial. Suppose member 1 bids $b_1 = -3$, and proposes $N_1 = 4$, then he writes the bid -3 in the second row, and the proposal 4 in the third row. I will go to each member and record his bid choice, and his facility proposal. I will compute the sum of the bids, for example $B = 20$ and post it on the blackboard. Each member will record this sum in the first row of his record sheet. You then compute B_i, the sum of all other bids (except yours) by subtracting item 2 from item 1 and writing it in row 5. Member 1 computes $B_1 = 20 - (-3) = 23$ and writes 23 in row 5. Each member's share of unit cost is then computed by subtracting B_1 (item 5) from 19 (item 4) and writing it in row 6. Member 1 computes $19 - 23 = -4$ and writes -4 in row 6. Notice that your individual unit cost is determined by the *bids of all other members not your bid*. Net membership value is then obtained from Table 2.1 by looking up the column for item 6, and the row

for your proposed facility size (item 3). The entries in Table 2.1 are your net membership values. These have been obtained by subtracting your share of total cost $(19-B_i)$ times N from total membership value in Table 1.1 for each N. In the example, member 1 looks up the column for $19-B_1 = -4$, and the row for $N_1 = 4$, yielding, say, a net value of $25. He writes $25 in row 7, which is his net membership value for that trial. Also on each trial I will compute the average proposed facility size and post it on the blackboard for you to record in row 8 of the record sheet. This process will be repeated for at most —— trials. In order that the process stop two events must occur:
    (a) Each member's bid, b_i, in row 2, must match (equal) his share of unit cost, $19-B_i$, in row 6, on two successive trials.
    (b) Each member must propose the same facility size on the last trial, by matching the average proposal.

5. Hence, group agreement requires each member to indicate his acceptance of his share of unit cost by bidding this amount, and to make the same proposal.

6. If the process stops by these rules then the net membership value resulting on the final trial will be paid to you in cash. Otherwise you will be paid a modest wage for the time you have spent.

7. Tables 1.1 and 2.1 are not the same for all members. They represent your own private information and are not to be revealed to any other member. Feel free to earn as much cash as you can. Do not speak to any other participant. Are there any question?

These instructions, as printed, were used in experiments A2.2–A2.5.

In the A1 experiments unit facility cost was $45, and in the illustration of paragraph 4, $b_1 = 1$, $B = 40$, with B_1 and $45-B_1$ changed accordingly. In the A3 experiments unit cost was $38, $b_1 = -3$, $B = $39 with B_1 and $38-B_1$ changed accordingly.

In experiments A1.1–A1.3 and A2.1, the instructions in paragraph 4 did not require choice of N_i on each trial, and paragraph 5 had the following sentence added: "If, and when, each member's bid equals his share of unit cost, I will give the group information on your average proposed facility size so that the individual proposals can be adjusted to equal each other."

Table 1.1. Membership Valuation, in Dollars

Member # 1

(1) Facility size (No. of units, N)	(2) Membership Value of Nth unit, in dollars	(3) Total Membership Value of N units, in dollars
0	0	0
1	−1	−1
2	−2	−3
3	−2	−5
4	−3	−8
5	−3	−11
6	−4	−15
7	−5	−20
8	−6	−26
9	−7	−33
10	−9	−42
11	−11	−53

Table 1.2. Membership Valuation, in Dollars

Member # 2

(1) Facility size (No. of units, N)	(2) Membership Value of Nth unit, in dollars	(3) Total Membership Value of N units, in dollars
0	0	0
1	11	11
2	16	27
3	20	47
4	19	66
5	17	83
6	15	98
7	13	111
8	8	119
9	5	124
10	3	127
11	2	129

Table 1.3. Membership Valuation, in Dollars

Member # 3

(1) Facility size (No. of units, N)	(2) Membership Value of Nth unit, in dollars	(3) Total Membership Value of N units, in dollars
0	0	0
1	2	2
2	8	10
3	18	28
4	15	43
5	13	56
6	10	66
7	8	74
8	4	78
9	3	81
10	2	83
11	1	84

Table 1.4. Membership Valuation, in Dollars

Member # 4

(1) Facility size (No. of units, N)	(2) Membership Value of Nth unit, in dollars	(3) Total Membership Value of N units, in dollars
0	0	0
1	1	1
2	2	3
3	6	9
4	11	20
5	9	29
6	5	34
7	3	37
8	1	38
9	0	38
10	0	38
11	0	38

Table 2.1. My Net Membership Value, in Dollars
Member # 1

My proposed facility size, N_1 \ My share of unit facility cost, $19-B_1$ $	-7	-6	-5	-4	-3	-2
0	0	0	0	0	0	0
1	6	5	4	3	2	1
2	11	9	7	5	3	1
3	16	13	10	7	4	1
4	20	16	12	8	4	0
5	24	19	14	9	4	-1
6	27	21	15	9	3	-3
7	29	22	15	8	1	-6
8	30	22	14	6	-2	-10
9	30	21	12	3	-6	-15
10	28	18	8	-2	-12	-22
11	24	13	2	-9	-20	-31

Table 2.2. My Net Membership Value, in Dollars

Member # 2

My proposed facility size, N_2 \ My share of unit facility cost, $19-B_2$ \$	-7	-6	-5	-4	-3	-2	-1	0	1	2	3	4	5	6	7	8	9	10	11	12	13	14	15	16
0	0	0	0	0	0	0	0	0	0	0	0	0	0	0	0	0	0	0	0	0	0	0	0	0
1	18	17	16	15	14	13	12	11	10	9	8	7	6	5	4	3	2	1	0	-1	-2	-3	-4	-5
2	41	39	37	35	33	31	29	27	25	23	21	19	17	15	13	11	9	7	5	3	2	0	-2	-4
3	68	65	62	59	56	53	50	47	44	41	38	35	32	29	26	23	20	17	14	11	8	5	2	-1
4	94	90	86	82	78	74	70	66	62	58	54	50	46	42	38	34	30	26	22	18	14	10	6	2
5	118	113	108	103	98	93	88	83	78	73	68	63	58	53	48	43	38	33	28	23	18	13	8	3
6	140	134	128	122	116	110	104	98	92	86	80	74	68	62	56	50	44	38	32	26	20	14	8	2
7	160	153	146	139	132	125	118	111	104	97	90	83	76	69	62	55	48	41	34	27	20	13	6	-1
8	175	167	159	151	143	135	127	119	111	103	95	87	79	71	63	55	47	39	31	23	15	7	-1	-9
9	187	178	169	160	151	142	133	124	115	106	97	88	79	70	61	52	43	34	25	16	7	-2	-11	-20
10	197	187	177	167	157	147	137	127	117	107	97	87	77	67	57	47	37	27	17	7	-3	-13	...	
11	206	195	184	173	162	151	140	129	118	107	96	85	74	63	52	41	30	19	8	-3	-14	...	...	

Table 2.3. My Net Membership Value, in Dollars
Member # 3

My proposed facility size, N_3 \ My share of unit facility cost, $19-B_3$ $	−7	−6	−5	−4	−3	−2	−1	0	1	2	3	4	5	6	7	8	9	10	11
0	0	0	0	0	0	0	0	0	0	0	0	0	0	0	0	0	0	0	0
1	9	8	7	6	5	4	3	2	1	0	−1	−2	−3	−4	−5	−6	−7	−8	−9
2	24	22	20	18	16	14	12	10	8	6	4	2	0	−2	−4	−6	−8	−10	−12
3	49	46	43	40	37	34	31	28	25	22	19	16	13	10	7	4	1	−2	−5
4	71	67	63	59	55	51	47	43	39	35	31	27	23	19	15	11	7	3	−1
5	91	86	81	76	71	66	61	56	51	46	41	36	31	26	21	16	11	6	1
6	108	102	96	90	84	78	72	66	60	54	48	42	36	30	24	18	12	6	0
7	123	116	109	102	95	88	81	74	67	60	53	46	39	32	25	18	11	4	−3
8	134	126	118	110	102	94	86	78	70	62	54	46	38	30	22	14	6	−2	−10
9	144	135	126	117	108	99	90	81	72	63	54	45	36	27	18	9	0	−9	−18
10	153	143	133	123	113	103	93	83	73	63	53	43	33	23	13	3	−7	−17	...
11	161	150	139	128	117	106	95	84	73	62	51	40	29	18	7	−4	−15	...	...

Incentive Compatible Experimental Processes

Table 2.4. My Net Membership Value, in Dollars
Member #4

My proposed facility size, N_4 \ My share of unit facility cost, $19-B_4$ $	-7	-6	-5	-4	-3	-2	-1	0	1	2	3	4	5
0	0	0	0	0	0	0	0	0	0	0	0	0	0
1	8	7	6	5	4	3	2	1	0	-1	-2	-3	-4
2	17	15	13	11	9	7	5	3	1	-1	-3	-5	-7
3	30	27	24	21	18	15	12	9	6	3	0	-3	-6
4	48	44	40	36	32	28	24	20	16	12	8	4	0
5	64	59	54	49	44	39	34	29	24	19	14	9	4
6	76	70	64	58	52	46	40	34	28	22	16	10	4
7	86	79	72	65	58	51	44	37	30	23	16	9	2
8	94	86	78	70	62	54	46	38	30	22	14	6	-2
9	101	92	83	74	65	56	47	38	29	20	11	2	-7
10	108	98	88	78	68	58	48	38	28	18	8	-2	-12
11	115	104	93	82	71	60	49	38	27	16	5	-6	-17

Record Sheet, Net Membership Value (Cash Earnings)

Member # 1

Item	Trial	1	2	3	4	5	6	7	8	9	10
1.	Sum of all bids, B.										
2.	My bid, b_1 (any $ amount at top of Columns, Table 2.1).										
3.	My proposed facility size, N_1 (Table 2.1, choose a row for N_1)										
4.	Unit cost of facility.										
5.	Sum of bids of other members, $B_1 = B - b_1$ (Item 1 – Item 2)										
6.	My share of unit facility cost, $19 - B_1$ (Item 4 – Item 5)										
7.	My net Membership Value (Table 2.1, using column for item 6, and row for item 3)										
8.	Average proposed Facility Size										

VOLUNTEER ARTIFACTS IN EXPERIMENTS IN ECONOMICS: SPECIFICATION OF THE PROBLEM AND SOME INITIAL DATA FROM A SMALL-SCALE FIELD EXPERIMENT

John H. Kagel and Raymond C. Battalio,
TEXAS A & M UNIVERSITY

James M. Walker, UNIVERSITY OF ARIZONA

INTRODUCTION

Controlled experiments in economics have been criticized on a number of grounds. Central to many of these criticisms is a nagging suspicion that the particular *subjects* studied are somehow inappropriate models for studying economic behavior. For example, voting experiments (Fiorina and Plott, 1978) have been criticized on the grounds that volunteers (mostly college students) may be fundamentally different from "real" politicians and, as a consequence, the results obtained might differ systematically and significantly from results obtained using legislators as subjects. Similarly, in some work on the economic effects of marihuana smoking (Kagel et al.,

1976) the results have, at times, been dismissed on the grounds that, given the "small" samples involved (n < 20), one can't possibly hope to extrapolate the results to the population of marihuana smokers in general, who number in the millions in the United States alone. Although these questions can be studied in a scientific manner, quite often these assertions about the inadequacies of experimental subjects involve belief statements on the part of the critic and, as such, do not admit to scientific inquiry; viz., a critic may simply not be able to "feel" that the behavior of the experimental subjects provides reliable indications of the behavior of more "normal" individuals under more "normal" circumstances.

The social psychology research classified under the heading of volunteer artifacts, or volunteer bias, echoes the same concern with the suitability of volunteer subjects. Here, however, we find active experimentalists concerned with the discovery and specification of those characteristics and situational determinants associated with volunteering for psychology experiments, and determining how these factors affect experimental outcomes, either by themselves or in combination with the treatment variables of interest. The purpose of the present paper is to begin to relate the research on volunteer artifacts in psychology to economic experiments. This will be done in two parts. First, we specify the issues involved in the question of volunteer artifacts. These remarks are of necessity brief and interested readers will find a more complete and, in many ways, more precise explication of the concepts developed in the references cited. In the second half of the paper we pursue the issues raised as they apply to a small scale study of electricity demand (Battalio et al., 1976; Winett et al., 1975). To our knowledge this analysis is the first investigation to date of volunteer artifacts in an experiment which, in effect, took place in subjects' homes over a period of several months.

I. SPECIFICATION OF THE PROBLEM

The logic of scientific inference shows that experiments cannot prove theories, but can only falsify them. For every theory-corroborating experimental result there are an infinity of alternative explanations available, a few of which must be investigated either because they receive support from independent research results or because they have a "plausibility" comparable to that of the theory in question. A major class of these rival hypotheses are methodological artifacts, where an artifact is defined as an uncontrolled factor producing a spurious, but consistent, relationship between the variables of interest (Campbell, 1969); e.g., experimenter-subject interactions were an apparent artifact in the studies of the relationship between working conditions and output conducted at the Hawthorne plant of the Western Electric Company (Roethlisberger and Dickson, 1939). As a rule such artifacts are theory specific and are discovered, as in the Hawthorne studies, in the course of identifying experimentally the precise factors responsible for generating a given set of results. But general-purpose controls are discovered for recurrent classes of artifacts which then become the empirically developed methodological requirements of a field (Campbell, 1969).

In this chapter we are concerned with potential artifacts arising in human experiments from the fact that these experiments typically involve subjects who have voluntarily presented themselves. Questions concerning the status of subjects in a study are but a subset of the infinity of questions that can be raised about the results of any piece of empirical research, be it experimental or nonexperimental.[1] Such questions are of special concern in experimental research to the extent that: (1) a number of subject characteristics and situational determinants are reliably associated with volunteering for such studies, and (2) hypotheses concerning the relationship between such factors and the behavior under study consistently provide insight into the results reported.

While there are few characteristics which unequivocally differentiate volunteers from nonvolunteers, social psychologists have identified a number of subject characteristics and situational determinants which are reliably associated with volunteering for social psychology experiments; e.g., volunteers tend to be higher in socioeconomic status and more interested in the subject under investigation than nonvolunteers (see Rosenthal and Rosnow, 1969, for an excellent summary of this research). Since economic experiments involve a different subject matter from social psychology experiments and, unlike most social psychology experiments, commonly involve nontrivial monetary payments to subjects (Manning et al., 1976; Smith, 1976), these situational determinants and subject characteristics may not generalize across disciplines. However, to the extent that they do, or that volunteers for economic experiments reliably display different subject characteristics, one can develop a number of "plausible" hypotheses relating these factors to economic variables of interest. For example, to the extent that volunteers for economic experiments tend to be higher educated and of higher social status than nonvolunteers, as they frequently are in social psychology experiments, they will have higher incomes; a variable of significant importance in a number of economic studies.

In discussing the question of volunteer artifacts it is useful to distinguish between two separate questions of interest raised in the social psychology literature. First is the extent to which the situational determinants and characteristics affecting volunteer status affect subjects' responses to experimental treatments so that the laws of behavior established under experimental conditions fail to be maintained for these same or similar subjects under comparable non-experimental conditions; i.e., will the results generalize to nonexperimental conditions for the same, or similar subjects?

Second, is the question of representativeness. That is, to the extent that reliable situational determinants and subject characteristics are associated with volunteering, will the behavioral laws developed generalize to other groups of subjects not displaying these characteristics or responding to the situational determinants in question, under either experimental or non-experimental conditions?

Generalizability from Experimental to Nonexperimental Conditions

This single most widely documented effect related to volunteer status is the tendency for volunteers to behave as alert and cooperative individuals or as "good subjects." While not all subjects will behave this way, and being a "good subject" undoubtedly means different things to different people, it involves a tendency on the part of volunteers to do what is expected of them and to help make the experiment work by behaving in ways which are consistent with the hypothesis under investigation, independent of the experimental variables under study (Orne, 1969; Rosenthal and Rosnow, 1973). Social psychologists refer to the cues which govern expectations as the *demand characteristics* of an experiment, and the tendency on the part of volunteers to conform to these demand characteristics as *demand induced effects*.

In social psychology experiments demand-induced effects are routinely controlled for by calculated efforts to deceive subjects with respect to the hypothesis under investigation, by withholding information, by introducing control groups explicitly designed to elicit the demand characteristics but not embodying the variable of interest, etc.[2] The pervasiveness of this problem in social psychology experiments suggests that definite steps be taken to control for it in economic experiments. Failure to do so complicates the interpretation and evaluation of results. For example, in the study by McCrimmon and Toda (1969) the potential effects of the demand characteristics introduced by an extensive training session, in which subjects were instructed on indifference curves and the implications of intersecting curves, makes it difficult to evaluate the impact of the experimental payment procedures used in generating the indifference curves reported. In this case, it would be interesting to know the separate effects of the training session and the payment procedure. Similar questions arise when the subjects in an economic experiment are familiar with the economic theory being tested where this familiarity could affect the responses reported.

This cooperative behavior on the part of volunteers is not all bad. It can be exploited to increase the motivation of subjects in performing the experimental task (Orne, 1969). For example, in auction market experiments cues to subjects to maximize profits may be used as a supplement to monetary rewards for inducing known (to the experimenter) supply and demand values on individual subjects (Smith, 1976), and undoubtedly provided the source of induced valuation in the early auction market studies when subjects did not receive monetary rewards for participation (Smith, 1962). We hasten to add that since subjects in auction market experiments are typically ignorant of demand and supply valuations other than their own, these cues can only motivate them to behave in accordance with the induced valuations and do not, by themselves, generate the results reported; i.e., the cues do not guarantee that market prices and quantities will converge to their equilibrium values, nor that they will be stable around these values once they have been attained.

Experiments involving very high participation rates—some have approached 80–90 percent of the population pool the subjects were recruited from (see below)—do not necessarily eliminate the potential for such demand-induced effects. Within the context of our Western culture the role of research subject in an experiment is well understood by most normal adults. For example, when experimentally naive high school students were asked, "How do you think the typical human subject is expected to behave in a psychology experiment?" over 70 percent circled characteristics labeled cooperative and alert (Rosenthal and Rosnow, 1973, pp. 136–137). Consequently, one would expect these stereotypic role expectations to be operative in volunteers irrespective of method of recruitment or percentage of the targeted sample recruited.

Comparable questions of generalizability to non-experimental conditions also arise when nonvolunteers are marshaled into an experiment. Only, in this case, demand-induced characteristics of a different sort may come into play. For example, in the Federal Energy Administration-sponsored experiment on peak-load pricing in Arkansas, subjects (who were all conscripted) were assigned to either a control group or experimental condition, with the experimental group facing price increases of as much as 600 percent for extended periods when air-conditioning demands were at their maximum.[3] While off-peak rates in this experiment were designed so that on average subjects would be no worse off, some of them were. This has resulted in a number of very angry consumers and unusually high failure rates in the equipment used to monitor use. While "naturally" occurring increases in utility rates have led, in recent years, to outspoken protests from numbers of consumers and scattered reports of increased tampering with utility meters, the artifact question has to do with whether the frequency of these events is unusually high in Arkansas as a result of subjects' knowing that they are an experiment, or whether the frequencies reported are what one would expect to see under universal implementation of these same tariff rates.

Sample Representativeness

Given that experiments quite frequently draw subjects from a distinct subset of the population, it is useful to distinguish between applications of theories designed to estimate parameter values of some finite, well defined, population vs. research aimed at the development and testing of theoretically derived behavioral hypotheses (Kruglanski, 1973). In the first case, where accuracy in estimating parameter values is usually of primary importance, even small deviations of the sample characteristics from the relevant underlying population may result in an unacceptable bias in the estimated parameter values. It is important to recognize that in deciding what constitutes a representative sample one must be dealing with a well developed empirically interpreted theory, since the characteristics one wants represented are theory dependent; i.e., the term "unrepresentative" is only meaningful for a given referent. In the second case, that of testing and developing economic theories, the investigation is concerned with falsification of premises of universal import (statements of the type, for all x, if p then q where p and q designate more or less complex relations or properties) and consequently, "representativeness" is something to be frequently avoided in initial tests since it is likely to introduce confounds of unknown importance. For example, laboratory experiments using rats typically suffer from unrepresentativeness since genetic strains developed for such studies may not be very good models for typical rodents or even wild rats (Rosenthal and Rosnow, 1973, p. 2). However, the use of such strains are explicitly chosen to control for genetic variability and thereby eliminate this factor as a potential confound in the results reported. The pragmatic basis underlying this approach is the recognition that the research process boes not end with any single study, but slowly develops by introducing additional variables suggested by both the theory and empirical observations. This process includes using enlarged subsamples of the population exhibiting different characteristics and, in comparative research programs, using different species. Of course, one can never be sure, a priori, that behavioral laws will generalize to such expanded populations. But, if they don't, the search for the factors responsible has been substantially reduced.

The economic efficiency of using "non-representative" groups to experimentally narrow down and screen hypotheses is not limited to very "basic" or "abstract" research questions, but is a practical research strategy commonly employed in "applied" problems. For example, the National Institute of Drug Abuse (NIDA) has sponsored a number of small scale studies (n < 50) of the health effects of marihuana smoking, even though the director of the NIDA cautions, "They were studies where people who had many of the health problems which might have been related to mairhuana use were excluded through the sample selection process" ("Marihuana...," 1976). However, such studies are conducted "Because they narrow down the parameters for the discussion. It's no longer credible to say that *all* marihuana smokers have an x or y negative health outcome. That's a limited but valuable finding" (ibid., italics in orginal). Such experiments, while of considerable value in their own right, also provide a sound basis for designing and evaluating the potential cost effectiveness of longer term, and considerably more expensive, epidemilogical studies that are more fully representative of the population of interest.

Dealing with Potential Artifacts

The phenomena of demand induced effects is but one of several pervasive sources of artifacts found across broad domains of experimental research in psychology (see Rosenthal and Rosnow, 1973, for a review of this research). Once a source of artifact has been identified, safeguards against it can be developed and become a routine part of the research method in the subject area of investigation. In this respect, artifacts in experimental research are akin to specification errors in time series analysis—once they have been identified they can usually be avoided.[4]

In conducting experiments the presence or absence of artifacts are frequently identified via the process of replicating research results reported and then designing experiments to resolve any observed differences. Alternative, but equally important, research strategies include conducting covert experiments, using covert control groups and generating data explicitly designed to identify the presence or absence of factors confounding experimental treatments. Plott and Levine's (1975) application of voting agenda manipulation theories to a real flying club's decisions represents an outstanding example of a covert experiment in economics. Additional examples are provided in the second part of the present paper where we investigate the question of volunteer bias in the context of an energy experiment.

There is virtually no limit to the potential for artifacts in experimental research. The potential would cease to exist only if there were no logical possibility for multiple explanations of the outcomes of an experiment, in which case our theories and methods would be tautologies, explaining everything and nothing (Brunner, 1967). As a matter of practical research strategy individuals doing experiments have an important stake in identifying the presence or absence of artifacts, for we can only devise practical research methods to overcome them once they have been identified. On an equally practical level the research process dictates that the burden of proof be on the critical reader to demonstrate confounds in a research design in terms of well established empirical evidence or well established *empirically interpreted* theories. The burden of proof does not lie with the experimenter in demonstrating the absence of biases *if* the methodological conventions for handling known sources of artifacts have been employed, for one can imagine potential biases a lot faster and easier than one can investigate them. The failure to publish internally consistent and methodologically sound results would only thwart the research process (Campbell, 1957).

The remainder of the paper is devoted to investigating volunteer bias in a small scale field experiment of electricity demand. The data reported are part of a larger project which has not yet been completed. The analysis conducted represents one of the first systematic investigations of volunteer bias in a small scale field experiment, as most of the social psychology literature is devoted to experiments of limited duration (session lengths of an hour or so) in laboratory settings.

II. VOLUNTEER ARTIFACTS IN AN ELECTRICITY DEMAND EXPERIMENT

In the summer of 1975, we recruited volunteer families from the community for a study of electricity demand. The experiment was aimed at assessing the impact of changes in prices, weekly feedback and energy conservation information on electricity use. The experiment lasted 12 weeks, covering most of the hot-weather months of June through August when air conditioning was the major source of electricity demand. A description of the experimental procedures employed and the outcome(s) of the experiment, as well as a discussion of the rationale for using experimental procedures in favor of more familiar regression analysis of nonexperimental data sets, is reported elsewhere (Battalio et al., 1976; Winett et al., 1978) and goes beyond the scope of the present paper. What we do here is describe the recruitment procedures employed and analyze questions of volunteer bias within the framework developed in the previous section.

For the reader short on time, we summarize our findings on the question of volunteer artifacts as follows: (1) The volunteers were no different, at the 5 percent confidence level, with respect to the key (observable) population characteristic of interest, kilowatt-hours of electricity used, than a random sample of nonparticipants drawn from the population pool used to recruit the volunteers, although the volunteers did use approximately 10 percent more electricity than the comparison group. (2) The data examined indicate that electricity use during the baseline period, after the subjects had volunteered but prior to their assignment to an experimental condition, provides an externally valid referent against which to evaluate experimental treatment effects. These data also show that those volunteers assigned to the control group condition behaved no differently during the experimental period than a comparison group of nonvolunteers. Thus, although it was difficult to disguise the goals of the experiment, and volunteering was to some extent motivated by general concerns about the "energy crisis," the level of experimenter-subject interaction maintained throughout the experiment did not, by itself, result in any demand induced effects on electricity use. (3) Comparing *changes* in the past levels of electricity use for the volunteers (prior to their volunteering) and the random sample of nonparticipants, we found a statistically significant decrease in electricity use of about 7 percent for the volunteers between the summer of 1973 and 1974. This relative reduction in electricity use, which occurred prior to our contact with the volunteers, appears to be a result of differential responses to the OPEC oil embargo and mass media concern with the "energy crisis" and not to changes in the relative cost of electricity. These results are analyzed in terms of their implications for evaluating the outcomes of the experiment under study, for designing additional experiments, and for understanding economic behavior in general.

Recruitment Procedures

Letters of invitation to participate in the study were sent to 496 families selected at random from the utility district's records. The families selected were limited to those households that had electric service at the same residence for a minimum of one year. Since our goal was to register about 100 families in the study, and we had no basis for forecasting the response rate to the invitations, the letters were sent out in three staggered mailings, each of which contained about one third of the sample.

The letters asserted (see Appendix A) that the purpose of the study was "to find out whether household energy use is affected by lowering prices as energy use is reduced and providing consumers with energy conservation information." The letter asked those who were interested to phone in to arrange a metting where further information would be given to them and we could obtain certain essential information, including permission to read electric meters (Appendix A). All households were promised a price reduction plan and/or a package of energy conservation material and were told that participation would simply require attending the one meeting, having the electric meter read weekly for 13 weeks, and returning a postcard each week indicating what days the house had been empty and any changes in the number of people living in the house. The letters were followed by two phone call attempts to reach nonrespondents (Appendix C), which proved to be the primary means of getting families to enroll in the study. A second mailing to those who did not respond to the first staggered mailing and who did not have telephone listings provided virtually no response and was discontinued.

Actual enrollment in the study took place at a series of meetings at the continuing education center at Texas A&M University during which time household information was collected and permission was obtained to read electric meters and to obtain past electricity use records. Baby-sitting services were offered at the meetings and households unable to attend meetings were enrolled in a home visit by a member of the research team. After all three mailings were made, a total of 129 households had enrolled in the study. Of the 129 families, eight were enrolled through home visits. About 50 percent of all eligible households contacted by phone agreed to be in the study.[5] Front-page coverage of the study in the local newspaper and news spots on a local radio station between the first and second mailings seemed to help substantially with recruitment.

The recruitment efforts employed stand in marked contrast to procedures employed in other small scale field studies of electricity demand. For example, Winett and Nietzel (1975) recruited on the basis of a call for volunteers in a newspaper article, Hayes and Cone (1977) went door to door for the few subjects studied, while Heberlein (1975) and Seaver and Patterson (1976) simply read meters and administrated treatments with no formal recruitment procedures. These differences in procedures reflect, in part, differences in the technically feasible options open in terms of the goals of each study, the financial resources available, and the observational requirements of the dependent variable, energy use. For example, Heberlein studied the effect of energy conservation information in an apartment complex with meters located outside the apartments in the basement, so that reading them involved no intrusion on subjects property and the experimental contingencies required minimum contact with the subjects.[6] In contrast, in our study, and the Winett and Nietzel experiment, meters were located on private property and administering rebates for reduced electricity use required a higher contact level with subjects. The similarity of research outcomes between the several studies (Battalio et al., 1976; Winett et al., 1978) under markedly different recruitment procedures involving substantial differences in the degree with which subjects voluntarily presented themselves suggests an absence of any major biases in results arising from factors motivating volunteering. In other words, since voluntary status varied across studies but there were no major differences in research outcomes, the factors motivating volunteering are unlikely to have strongly effected the results reported (Campbell, 1969).

A Comparison Group

To assist in investigating the question of volunteer artifacts in the College Station experiment, a second random sample was drawn from the same population used to recruit the volunteers for the experiment itself. The second random sample, referred to as the *comparison group*, was designed to exclude those households originally sent letters of invitation to participate in the experiment; i.e., the comparison group is representative of the parent population that the volunteers were solicited from and is *not* made up of those households sent letters of invitation but refusing to volunteer.[7] Monthly electricity use records for these households were recorded, where possible, back to May 1972, before the period of national concern with energy shortages. Also, as of that time, the nominal cost of electricity had remained unchanged for about six years.

Representativeness of Volunteers vs. Comparison Group

There are a number of characteristics against which representativeness can be evaluated.[8] One important characteristic in the present study would be actual electricity use during the hot-weather summer months. Using average electricity consumption for the summer preceding the experiment— June, July, and August 1974—empirical cumulative distribution functions for the volunteers and the comparison group were computed. These distribution functions, shown in Figure 1, describe the percentage of subjects in each group having average summer electricity use at or below a given kilowatt-hour usage.

Using a Smirnov test to compare the two distributions (Conover, 1971), we find no difference between them under a two-tailed test at the 5 percent confidence level (max. difference = .10, $p > .20$).[9] The Smirnov test is explicitly designed to compare two independent random samples, is

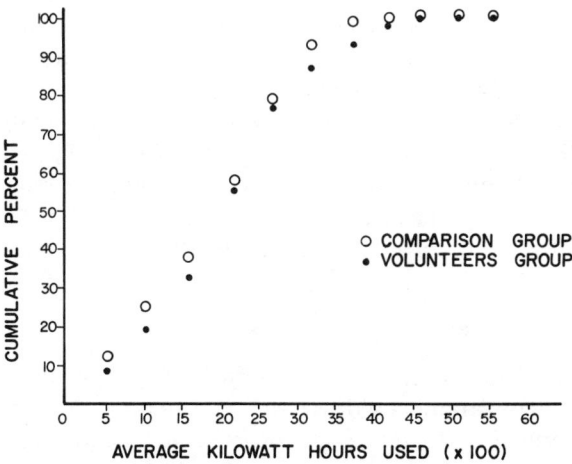

Figure 1. Cumulative distribution functions of electricity use for the volunteers and comparison group. Electricity use is averaged over the summer of 1974 and is measured in hundreds of KWH's. The maximum difference between the groups occurs at 2850 KWH's.

Table 1. Mean Electricity Use of Volunteers vs. Comparison Group

	Volunteers	Comparison Group
Mean kwh[a]	1903.7	1731.1
Standard Deviation of Sample	994.1	905.8
Sample Size	124	177

[a]Average monthly kilowatt-hour of electricity used June, July, and August 1974.

distribution free, and is sensitive to differences in both means and variances between the two samples. As shown in Figure 1, the volunteer group appears to underrepresent families using less than 750 kwh in the summer (primarily households without air conditioning) and to overrepresent large users with 2,800 kwh or more per month. A good deal of prior research indicates that volunteers tend to have higher educational and occupational status than nonvolunteers (Rosenthal and Rosnow, 1973). Since these factors tend to correlate positively with income, which in turn correlates with house size and electricity use, the differences in kilowatt-hours used between the two samples are to be expected. However, they are not sufficiently accentuated to yield statistically significant results under the Smirnov test.

Table 1 shows mean electricity use for the two samples. Consistent with Figure 1 and the remarks above, volunteers had a higher mean kilowatt-hour use than nonvolunteers. However, using a Mann-Whitney nonparametric test for differences between means (Conover, 1971), we cannot reject the null hypothesis of equal means at the 5 percent confidence level (T = 10, 158, n = 177, m = 124, p = .30, two-tailed test).[10]

We have yet to explore relevant dimensions of representativeness with respect to other characteristics commonly thought to affect electricity use such as income, frequency of central air conditioning, household size, etc. However, to the extent that electricity use correlates with income (and the presence or absence of air conditioning) the data above are indicative of what we are likely to find.

Demand Induced Effects During Baseline

In determining the effects of the experimental treatments on electricity use, the dependent variable used was the percentage change in use relative to a pre-experimental (baseline) period. During the baseline volunteers had already agreed to be in the experiment and had given permission for their meters to be read, but had yet to be assigned to treatment groups. The use of a baseline period against which to evaluate treatment effects is a common research strategy designed to reduce between subject variability.

It was employed, rather than directly modeling electricity use, because earlier research had indicated that the residual variation, even for quite detailed models, would be quite large (Mayer and Robinson, 1975).

The use of a baseline period against which to evaluate treatment effects poses no threat to the internal validity (direct replicability) of the results reported since subjects were randomly assigned to the several treatment conditions only at the end of the baseline period. However, to the extent that volunteering for an experiment affects behavior prior to the application of any explicit treatment conditions, the use of such a baseline jeopardizes external validity or generalizability to nonexperimental settings. The volunteer bias literature suggests several reasons why the act of volunteering might affect baseline behavior. For one, demand-induced effects might lead to altered baseline use patterns if the subjects perceived the experimenter's goals and attempted to conform to them independent of experimental contingencies. Alternatively, signing up to be in the experiment could have involved a self-commitment to reduced electricity use which, again, could affect behavior during the baseline period independent of any treatment effects. To guard against these possibilities, subjects were instructed not to do anything differently after the meetings, being told that the experiment proper would not start for a while (no dates given) but that we would be around to read meters in order to give our meter readers "practice." Further, during the meetings themselves conscious efforts were made to dissuade subjects from assuming any well-defined set of priors the experimenters held—"If we knew the outcome of the study we wouldn't be conducting it in the first place." In addition, subjects were not given any details of treatment conditions and a number of questions were turned back with the explanation that the information requested could not be provided at that time. People seemed to accept this evasiveness readily (they also had the option to withdraw from the study at anytime); only one couple left a meeting without giving permission to be in the experiment. Nevertheless, baseline use could have been affected, and, if so, one might guess in favor of reduced use.

Two sets of data are relevant with respect to this question. First, in another small-scale study of electricity use (Hayes and Cone, 1977) covert meter readings were obtained prior to approaching and signing subjects up for study.[11] Baseline meter readings were then collected in much the same way that we did. *No* differences between covert and overt readings were found, indicating in this study at least, volunteering did not effect baseline use. The second set of data is a byproduct of our comparison of the week-by-week behavior of the experimental control group, relative to a covert control. These data, presented below, provide indirect evidence that the baseline use readings were relatively uncontaminated.

Demand Induced Effects During the Experiment

Conducting an electricity experiment in Texas during the summer months required having a control group of some kind to provide a basis for sorting out the effects of weather (and other potential threats to internal validity) from the behavior of interest (Campbell and Stanley, 1966). However, anytime such a group is made up of subjects who have volunteered for an experiment they have received a treatment condition of some kind, call it X', consisting of some proper subset of the complex set of conditions, X, which comprise the treatment condition of interest. For example, in the College Station experiment members of the control group all signed up for the experiment, had their electric meters read weekly, and mailed in weekly postcards, all part of the treatment conditions the other groups received. Such a control group does provide a standard against which to evaluate the variables of interest, thus insuring the internal validity (replicability) of the results reported. However, since the control group has been exposed to an experimental treatment called control, which may effect behavior for the reasons discussed in the previous section on baselines (and other reasons readers can undoubtedly imagine on their own), it is useful to have some basis against which to evaluate the effects of the control treatment (Campbell, 1957).

To provide this we sought a covert control. This was achieved in the form of a main feeder line made up of over 70 percent residential customers which serviced a large section of the community the volunteers were drawn from. The meter readers read the meter on this line weekly at the same time

Table 2. Mean Percentage Change in Electricity Use Relative to Baseline: Feeder Line vs. Control Group

Week	Feeder Line	Control Group[b]
1	−.099	−.054
2	.188	.228
3	−.037	−.042
4	.086	.091

[a]Percentage change calculated as

$$\frac{Bsl - Use_i}{\frac{Bsl + Use_i}{2}}$$

where Bsl is baseline use and Use_i is use in week i of the experiment.

[b]Control group includes all subjects assigned to this treatment condition.

they read residences. Table 2 shows electricity use for the control group and main feeder line over the first four weeks of the study, before the control group was switched over to an information condition [see (Battalio et al., 1976) for the motivation underlying the switch-over and the resulting analysis of the data]. Both sets of numbers move parallel week by week as electricity use swings by as much as 25 percent owing to changes in weather conditions and their resulting effects on air-conditioning use. Further, they are at virtually the same level, well within the tolerance limits set by the between subject variance for the control group ($\sigma^2 = .06$, n = 28). These data indicate that the experimenter-subject interactions maintained throughout the experiment did not, by themselves, result in any demand induced effects on weekly changes in energy use, and that the control group provides an externally valid referent against which to evaluate the treatment effects.[12] The parallel movements between the two sets of figures over time is also consistent with the results of the previous section, since, if baseline electricity use changed in response to volunteering, it seems likely that these responses would have faded out for the control group over the six-week period following the initial meeting, during which minimum contact was maintained with these subjects. Electricity use at the feeder line continued to move parallel to that of the average for the experimental subjects as a whole up to the last week of the experiment when there was an abrupt change; which turned out to be the power load shift of the feeder line the utility company had earlier informed us was scheduled near the end of the study.

Energy Conservation Behavior Prior to the Experiment

One of the most reliable findings in the social psychology research on volunteers is that they are typically more interested in the topic under investigation than nonvolunteers (Rosenthal and Rosnow, 1975). While national concern with the "energy crisis" undoubtedly made it a topic of considerable interest for large numbers of people, thus easing problems of recruitment, this concern may have biased the volunteers towards including those whose concern had already resulted in energy saving behavior, or toward including those who were particularly interested in reducing, and able to reduce, electricity use. Subjects' self-reports indicated that well over 50 percent of all volunteer households had taken major steps to reduce electricity consumption, including raising air conditioning thermostat settings, prior to the time the study began.[13]

Whether these self reports were exaggerated and/or represent a frequency of energy conservation behavior reflective of the community at large is a question of some interest with implications for generalizing the experimental results to the community at large. To investigate this we compared changes in electricity use between the volunteers and the comparison group for the

Table 3. Mean Percentage Change in Electricity Use 1972–1973 and 1973–1974: Volunteers vs. Comparison Group

	1972–1973		1973–1974	
	Volunteers	Comparison Group	Volunteers	Comparison Group
Mean Change[a]	−.073	−.079	−.062	.009
Standard Error of Mean	.028	.025	.022	.019
Sample Size	78	97	101	147

[a]Change calculated as: $\dfrac{KWH_t - KWH_{t-1}}{\dfrac{KWH_t + KWH_{t-1}}{2}}$

where kilowatt-hours are average use for June, July, and August, with the subscript t indicating the year in question. Negative numbers indicate a reduction in use from year t − 1 to t. Data not corrected for heating degree day differences between years.

two summers prior to the experiment. These data are reported in Table 3. Between the summers of 1972 and 1973, we find no differences between the two groups (t = .16, df = 173). However, between the summers of 1973 and 1974 the volunteers *reduced* use about 7 percent more than the comparison group (t = 2.48, df = 246, p < .02, two-tailed test). The 1973–1974 difference continues to be statistically significant using a Mann-Whitney nonparametric test (T = 8455, n = 142, m = 101, p < .02, two-tailed test).

The differential changes in electricity use between volunteers and the comparison group between 1973–1974 appear to be, in large measure, a differential response to the OPEC oil embargo which occurred in the fall of 1973, and associated government and mass media concern with the "energy crisis." One is hard pressed to explain this behavior strictly in terms of differential responses to increases in the relative price of electricity since the real price of electricity increased only 3 percent during this period, while substantially larger increases in real prices of 30 percent between the summer of 1974 and 1975 resulted in no differential response in electricity use between the two groups (t = .69, df = 277, p = .49, two-tailed test).[14] By the same line of reasoning, it is difficult to explain this differential response strictly in terms of nominal price increases. In addition, one must explain why a nominal price increase of 6 percent between the summer of 1972–1973 resulted in no differential response, while a nominal price increase of 17 percent between 1973–1974 resulted in the differential response reported.

A good deal of independent evidence supports the conclusion that the OPEC embargo and associated mass media appeals, or some interaction between these factors and the changes in the nominal price of electricity, were primarily responsible for the differential changes in electricity use observed. First, when volunteers are given written information (feedback) on electricity use, such plans appear to result in statistically significant reductions in use only when the feedback is on a daily basis (Battalio et al., 1976). Daily feedback schemes involve high levels of prompting, or normative appeals from the experimenters (rather than the government or the media) for reduced energy use, while the most effective scheme to date has involved explicit prompting in the form of color-coded feedback slips with an ascending series of frowning faces for increases in use, and smiles for decreases electricity consumption (Winett et al., 1977). Second, Seaver and Patterson (1976) report that while infrequent feedback did not affect fuel oil consumption, when feedback was combined with social commendation in the form of a small energy saver decal, small but statistically significant reductions in use were observed. Third, the theoretical explanation for demand-induced effects in experiments, as well as the effects of advertising (which is what mass media appeals for reduce energy use are), is that human beings are sensitive to the coercive demands of whatever propriety norms may be operating in a given situation (Rosnow and Aiken, 1973). Finally, the hypothesis that our volunteers may simply be an "unusual" sample is ruled out since comparable reductions in household energy use (in this case gas for home heating) have been reported for a large complex of townhouses in New Jersey (Mayer, 1977) coincident with the OPEC oil embargo but prior to any sizable increases in the nominal or real price of gas.

Having found this differential response to energy use prior to entry into the experiment, it remains to determine the implications relative to the external validity of the results reported. On the one hand, it can be argued the reduction in use resulted in less responsiveness to the experimental incentives for reduced use (the rebates) than would otherwise have been the case, as subjects had already taken a number of steps to reduce electricity use. However, one may also argue that the volunteer households, having already made a greater effort to reduce electricity use, were more prepared in both outlook and experience to take further actions in response to the rebates. Since we cannot determine, without considerably more research, what "the correct" alternative is, we would propose, in the interim, to adjust the response bounds reported in the experiment upward and downward to reflect either extreme of potential bias. Such adjustments would do nothing to our lower-bound price elasticity estimates since they were zero to begin with. For upper-bound price elasticity estimates this would involve adding the 7 percent differential reported here to the experimentally induced treatment group differentials.[15] In contrast, the results reported on the effects of feedback and information on energy use would remain unaltered as they have been replicated in comparable small scale studies not employing volunteer subjects (Battalio et al., 1976).

This differential change in electricity use between the volunteers and the comparison group has implications for energy research, and economic behavior in general, beyond any issues of volunteer bias. In this respect we note that the rate of volunteering in our experiment consisted of about 25 percent of all households sent letters of recruitment and approximately 50 percent of households contacted by phone who claimed to be eligible for the study. In either case, the volunteers represent a sizable fraction of the parent population who responded to appeals in the mass media for reduced energy use. Statistical tests of such responses for the population as a whole, however, may well not reach standard significance levels, as preliminary analysis of our comparison group data indicate a sizable fraction of the population apparently did not respond to these media appeals. This is illustrated in Peck and Doering's (1976) investigation of voluntary reductions in gas use in rural Indiana following the OPEC oil embargo, where a 4.78 percent mean reduction in gas use is not statistically significant at the 5 percent confidence level, but is at the 10 percent level (one-tailed t-test). These data represent important field documentation, in the area of economic behavior, of social psychology experiments which indicate that people do respond to alterations in social norms (Rosnow and Aiken, 1973). It is a phenomenon that certainly deserves further study.

Summary and Conclusions of Analysis

We have reached several conclusions regarding volunteer artifacts in the College Station experiment that are of general interest. First, the data indicate that the strategy of recording baseline observations after subjects have volunteered is effective in the sense that the act of volunteering, by itself, did not appear to have measurable effects on electricity use during this period. Second, the close match between electricity use patterns over time for the control group and the residential feeder line indicate that the control group provided an effective measure of nonexperimental behavior patterns. Both results suggest an absence of demand induced effects simply as a result of experimenter-subject interactions where it was difficult, if not impossible, to disguise the main hypotheses of interest (although we did not, of course, reveal our priors as to experimental outcomes and severly limited information regarding the design of the experiment). Part of the explanation for the absence of such effects is, we suspect, that the experiment took place within the context of the volunteers' carrying out their usual activity patterns in their homes. At such a level of experimental intrusion any desires on the part of subjects to meet some assumed set of experimenter's expectations would receive relatively low priority since the experimental contingencies were but a small part of the total environmental contingencies subjects faced. This is consistent with models (Rosnow and Aiken, 1973) of mediating factors involved in eliciting demand induced effects in laboratory experiments.

These data do not, of course, demonstrate an absence of demand induced effects in the responses reported for the other experimental groups; e.g., the members of the rebate groups may have responded to the rebates, in part, to be "good subjects" and to reduce energy use "like they knew they should." Further, one might anticipate greater price responsiveness in an experiment as a result of subjects hightened awareness of price contingencies as compared to utility mandated price changes. Consequently, there is a need to estimate what, if any, degree of bias might be present in experimental estimates of price elasticity values. Such estimates are difficult to come by, as covert experiments involving price increases face obvious ethical and legal problems (Rivlin and Timpine, 1975), while covert price reductions financed with government funds may face opposition from producers of competing products or those consumers not enjoying the reductions. In one of the few studies of its kind, Nevin (1974) reports an effort to evaluate the external validity of laboratory-generated estimates of price induced changes on brand demand. His results suggest that for the type of laboratory studies investigated, simulated shopping trips and paired-preference experiments, there is a tendency to overstate price responsiveness when price awareness is relatively low outside the laboratory setting. While this result is certainly suggestive, particularly in the area of household demand for electricity where price awareness has, until recently, been virtually non-existent (Hoffman, Brown and Baxter, 1975), it is obviously of limited generality, indicating the need for more research along these lines.

The finding that volunteers reduced electricity use significantly more than the comparison group prior to enrollment in the study is consistent with the fact that volunteers tend to be more interested in the topic under study than nonvolunteers. If these results are replicated; i.e., if volunteers in field studies are generally found to already have done something with respect to the variable of interest prior to investigation, important implications for conducting such experiments may be drawn. First, as a routine matter investigators would be obliged to obtain measures of the changes in question to determine if they are present, and if so, to use the measures to provide upper and lower bounds for the response variables in question. Second, to the extent that such activities are consistent with modern ethical and legal standards for experimentation, increased emphasis would be placed on investigating elements of the problem of interest using nonvolunteers such as in the energy information studies cited. Third, efforts should be made to evaluate the costs and benefits, in terms of reducing the bias in question, of more intensive recruitment procedures, such as door-to-door canvassing. The rule of thumb here is the more effort devoted to recruitment and the greater the monetary returns for volunteering, the larger the percentage of potential subjects who volunteer. For example, in the Rand study of peak-load electricity pricing in Los Angeles (Manning, Mitchell and Acton, 1976) the large monetary inducements for volunteering, in combination with several repeat phone calls to nonrespondents and door-to-door soliciting where necessary, have resulted in a sign-up rate of about 90 percent of all eligible households (Manning, personal communication). Using door-to-door solicitation, Winett, et al., (1977) achieved volunteer rates of between 70–75 percent of all households targeted for contact although subjects received no gifts or monetary remuneration for participation in the study.

Achieving these high rates of volunteering virtually eliminates potential biases resulting from sample representativeness or behavior prior to enrolling in the study. They do not, of course, eliminate potential biases resulting from being in an experimental environment. Further, since high rates of volunteering are usually associated with increased costs, these benefits must be weighed against alternative uses of the resources. Consequently, the optimal strategy will depend upon the nature of the questions being investigated (Campbell and Stanley, 1966, especially p. 23–24), and the resources available for obtaining answers.

APPENDIX A

The energy crisis is affecting us all in different ways and has led to a massive program throughout the country to find ways to save energy. The Economics Department at Texas A&M University is part of this program. We are about to begin a project here in College Station which aims to find out whether household energy use is affected by *lowering prices* as energy use is reduced and by providing consumers with *energy conservation information*.

At present, the price of the energy we use is actually reduced if we use a lot. We want to see what happens if the reverse occurs. Part of our study will therefore involve *paying participants as they reduce the amount of energy they use*. The second part of the study will be aimed at finding out what happens to household energy use when participants are given the various *packages of information currently prepared by the government and by utility companies*.

Participants in the project will receive different combinations of the price reduction and information schemes at different times.

The names of participants receiving the different combinations would be pulled out of a hat randomly. All participants in the study will, however, receive at various times price reductions and/or a package of energy conservation information.

The study will be conducted over the summer, from approximately mid-June to mid-August, and is supported by College Station Utilities and the National Science Foundation.

If you wish to be included in the study, please call the Energy Project Secretary, Department of Economics, Texas A&M University at 845–7351. We will then arrange a time when we can meet with you to discuss further details.

Your participation in the study will involve coming to an initial meeting, allowing us to read your electricity meter, and leaving a brief questionnaire in your mailbox each week for our meter readers to pick up. This questionnaire will be concerned with aspects of energy use only. The information would be mailed to you and the payments would also be mailed to you.

We cannot include as participants people who plan to be on vacation for more than 2 weeks during the period the project is running. Also, we cannot include households which have converted to central air conditioning since last summer or have added an addition to the house during this period. Apart from this, however, we would like to have as broad a cross section of people as possible in our study. We ask you to please consider seriously being part of our project to find ways to conserve energy. This is one way you can help solve the national energy crisis while helping yourself directly at the same time.

This letter has been sent to a large number of households in College Station who were drawn at random through the cooperation of College Station Utilities. Your privacy will be carefully safeguarded throughout the study.

We thank you for your interest and look forward to hearing from you.

Sincerely,

R. C. Battalio
Assistant Professor of Economics

R. C. Winkler
Visiting Associate Professor of Economics

APPENDIX B

Telephone Instructions

Thank the person for calling.
After person gives commitment, take:
  1. Name
  2. Address
  3. Telephone Number
  4. Note day, time of call
  5. Note on record sheet

When arranging meeting, use the following as a guide:

"We are arranging a meeting where we can meet with you. At the meeting, we can answer more questions than we can over the phone, and will ask you to sign a permission slip allowing us to read your meter. We would also like to get some information from you about vacation plans, the various things in the house that use energy and so on. Once we have gotten together at this meeting, we can start the project. All we need is a responsible adult from your household who can sign a permission form to attend but it doesn't matter who it is. We will have facilities to look after children, if necessary. The meeting will last about an hour."

  **Note in "comments section" of record sheet if they are bringing children.
  Tell them to check the location of their electricity meter before attending meeting, as we will ask them to draw a sketch to help us find it.

Meeting Times: (offer the following meeting times)

Tuesday, May 20, 8 p.m.	Room 401 Rudder Center
Thursday, May 22, 8 p.m.	*Offer these times first*
Friday, May 23, 10 a.m.—or—2:30 p.m.	
Monday, May 26, 8 p.m.	Room 501 Rudder Center
Wednesday, May 28, 10 a.m.—or—2:30 p.m.	Offer these times as an alternative only if they cannot make any of the first three.
Thursday, May 29, p.m.	
Monday, June 2, 10 a.m.	Room 140 MSC
Tuesday, June 3, 3:30 p.m.—or—8 p.m.	

If a person says or implies they want more information before saying yes, answer questions. If questions are asked only out of curiosity, suggest they can be answered at a meeting: phone is busy. When answering questions, use the following as a guide:

Purpose: "We want to find out what happens when/what the effects of price reductions for energy reduction and information packages are."

Work on their part: Stress *minimal work required:* One meeting, permission to read meter, brief form in mailbox once a week, rest done by us.

Have a copy of letter of invitation handy for reference, re: (1) length of time of study, (2) when starts, (3) vacation, recent air conditioning added, new room added. As far as possible repeat information in letter.

If someone asks about *how much the payment will be*, say:

"That will depend on how much electricity you use—you could get a reduction in your electricity bill of $5 to $10 per week if you are in the price-reduction group."

Source of funds: National Science Foundation and Department of Economics.

Comments: Include under *comments section* any special problems involved in the caller as a participant in the study, and any other special points you feel should be noted about the call.

If a person calls and then decides not to be involved, record name and note under meeting arranged—NO. If the person says why he/she decided no, record under comments.

APPENDIX C

Telephone Call for Nonresponders

Use the following as a guide:

Introduce yourself: "Good afternoon/evening, my name is —————, from the Department of Economics, Texas A&M."

"Recently we sent a letter inviting you to participate in a project we are running on household energy use. We wondered if you had received the letter and had a chance to look at it." (If not received or remembered, very briefly summarize the letter—see attached.)

If received, person may volunteer yes or no to participation. If no volunteered response: "Have you made a decision yet whether you would like to be part of the project?"

If *not* decided, ask if need any further information. If can't answer from letter, buzz Battalio or Kagel. If no questions or questions answered, ask if we should call them back in a few days or would they prefer to call us back. Note response on sheets next to person's name.

If have decided *yes*, follow instruction sheet for telephone acceptance, attached.

If have decided *no*, that's fine. "Thank you for your time. I hope I haven't disturbed you."

1. Record day and time of call, opposite person's name.
2. Record yes or no response. If yes, make sure name is recorded for meeting arranged.
3. Note any relevant comments, e.g., did the person seem to mind the letter or call? Was he/she interested but couldn't be involved for some discernable reason; was he/she disinterested for some discernable reason?

Try to speak to an adult in the house. If no one answers, make two attempts at different times, then if no response, record time of day of attempts, plus not reachable.

Summary of Letter

The project is designed to find out how household energy use is affected by *lowering prices* as energy use is reduced and by providing consumers with *energy conservation information*.

At present, the price of the energy we use is actually reduced if we use a lot. We want to see what happens if the reverse occurs. Part of our study will therefore involve paying participants as they reduce the amount of energy they use. The second part of the study will be aimed at finding out what happens to household energy use when participants are given the various packages of information currently by the government and by utility companies.

Participants in the project will receive different combinations of the price reduction and information schemes at different times.

Your participation in the study will involve coming to an initial meeting, allowing us to read your electricity meter, and leaving a brief questionnaire in your mail box each week for our meter readers to pick up. This questionnaire will be concerned with aspects of energy use only. The information would be mailed to you and the payments would also be mailed to you.

FOOTNOTES

We thank the City Manager and Staff of the City of College Station for their essential support in this research. Ken Avio provided particularly useful comments on an earlier draft of this paper which was presented at the University of Arizona Conference on Experimental Economics, March 1977. Research was partially supported by NSF Grant GS 32057 and a Texas A&M University mini-grant.

1. A particularly clear example, using nonexperimental data, of the importance of the characteristics of the population from which samples are drawn is illustrated in Garfinkel (1973).

2. The widespread use of deceit in psychology experiments has generated discussion concerning the ethicality of the procedures employed and how to adequately protect subjects' rights while maintaining a nontrivial social science (see Campbell, 1969, especially pp. 370–372).

3. Based on Mr. John Pickett's remarks at the University of Missouri-Missouri Energy Council Conference on Energy, October 12–14, 1976. Mr. Pickett is a commissioner for the Arkansas Public Service Commission.

4. See Campbell and Stanley (1966) for an interesting specification of potential artifacts in time series analysis not present in experimental studies. "Pure" or uninterpreted theories avoid these problems for the very reason that they are empty of any factual content until a specific system of rules has been established for connecting the theoretical concepts to measurement procedures (Basmann, 1975; Brunner, 1967).

5. The 50 percent figure is quite rough (± 10 percent error) since the telephone logs (see Appendix C) are incomplete or have double counting. The figures are based on the first and second mailing for which more complete records were maintained. In calculating these percentages, households are excluded if no telephone contact was made, accounting for about 30 percent of all households that were mailed letters of invitation.

6. Anytime one uses such nonobstrusive measures of behavior, questions arise concerning the ethicality of the procedures involved. See Campbell (1969) for a discussion of these questions.

7. The random sample of households that were sent letters to participate in the experiment was obtained by taking approximately one in every eight residences (exclusive of trailers) as they appeared in the meter reader books, beginning with the same (randomly determined) start point in each book. In cases where the eighth household did not have continuous electric service at the residence for a year, we went forward and backward for a maximum of two households (the initial direction of movement determined by whether the eighth household's address was even- or odd-numbered) until the first household was met that satisfied this criteria. The comparison group was obtained in a similar manner but taking approximately one in every 16th name in the meter reader books and using a different start point in order to avoid overlapping. (In drawing

the original sample some of the meter readers books were inadvertently sampled at a rate exceeding 1 in 8. In these cases the comparison group was obtained by drawing names from these books at a correspondingly higher rate.) The use of a random sample from the population of interest to compare the volunteers to, rather than a sample of those original residences not volunteering, is somewhat unusual in the volunteer bias literature. This was done because a large number of those households contacted but not in the study had indicated that their reason for declining to be in the study was that they did not meet the eligibility criteria, which consisted of being on vacation no more than two weeks during the experiment and of having made no major alterations to their homes within the past year (Appendix A). Consequently, to have used these subjects would have biased the comparison group, relative to a second random sample, toward observing large changes in electricity use between 1974 and 1975 independent of price changes or other common environmental factors. Further, the very nature of the question being asked—how do volunteers differ from the community at large with respect to factors affecting electricity use—would appear to require a random sample from the community at large.

8. The question being asked here is the representativeness of the volunteers relative to residential electricity users in the College Station utility district. The question of representativeness with respect to the population of residential electricity users in the U.S. or even Texas lies well beyond the scope of the present paper.

9. Results of the Smirnov test excluding the eight households recruited through home visit leaves the results reported in the text unchanged, although mean kilowatt-hours of electricity used increases to 1,959.3 compared to 1,903.7 as reported in Table 1.

10. A Mann-Whitney test was used in preference to the usual t-test because the normality assumption (with respect to kilowatt-hours of electricity used) underlying the parametric test appears questionable and the nonparametric test is almost as efficient given the sample sizes involved.

11. In surreptitiously reading meters, Hayes and Cone did not face a privacy problem since the meters were exposed in the basement of the apartment complex the study was done in.

12. This special case of demand-induced effects is what a number of writers seem to mean when referring to Hawthorne effects in experiments; i.e., the attention subjects receive as a result of being in an experiment alters behavior independent of any particular changes in experimental contingencies. The routine use of control groups allows the investigator to control for the possibility of these responses thereby insuring the internal validity of the results reported (Campbell, 1969).

13. Incredibly, 95 percent of all subjects returned the completed questionnaire following two telephone prompts. This leaves very little room for bias in these data.

14. All prices are marginal prices for the lowest block rate (which most households pay in the summer) indexed to 1972 with the average difference between summers reported in the text. This comparison includes the summer of the experiment during which members of the experimental group were receiving treatments which significantly increased the price of electricity. This biases the data in favor of rejecting the null hypothesis of no differences between the groups.

15. This yields revised *upper-bound* price elasticity estimates of $-.50$ and $-.21$ for the low- and high-price rebate groups, respectively, compared to the old upper-bound estimates of $-.32$ and $-.16$. See Battalio et al. (1976), for how to compute these price elasticities and details of the rebate plans.

REFERENCES

Basmann, R. L. (1975), "Modern Logic and the Suppositious Weakness of the Empirical Foundations of Economic Science," *Schweiz Zeitschrift für Volkswirtschaft und Statistik* 2: 153–175.

Battalio, R. C., Kagel, J. H., Winkler, R. C., and Winett, R. A. (December 1976), "Residential Electricity Demand: An Experimental Study," Texas A&M University, to appear in *Review of Economics and Statistics*.

Brunner, K. (1967), "A Case Study of the Importance of the Appropriate Rules for the Competitive Market in Ideas and Beliefs," *Schweiz Zeitschraft fur Volkswirtschaft und Statistik* 2: 173–189.

Campbell, D. T. (1957), "Factors Relevant to the Validity of Experiments in Social Settings," *Psychological Bulletin* 54: 297–312.

———. (1969), "Prospective: Artifact and Control," in *Artifacts in Behavioral Research*, ed. by R. Rosenthal and R. L. Rosnow, New York: Academic Press.

———, and Stanley, J. C. (1966), *Experimental and Quasi-Experimental Designs for Research*, Chicago: Rand McNally.

Conover, W. J. (1971), *Practical Nonparametric Statistics*, New York: John Wiley and Sons.

Fiorina, M. P., and Plott, C. P. (1978), "Committee Decisions Under Majority Rule: An Experimental Study," *American Political Science Review*.

Garfinkel, J. (1973), "On Estimating the Labor-Supply Effects of a Negative Income Tax," in *Income Maintenance and Labor Supply*, ed. by G. C. Cain and H. W. Watts, Institute for Research on Poverty Monograph Series.

Hayes, S. C. and Cone, J. D. (1977), "Reducing Residential Electricity Energy Use: Payments, Information and Feedback," *Journal of Applied Behavioral Analysis*.

Heberlein, T. A. (1975), "Conservation Information, the Energy Crisis and Electricity Consumption in an Apartment Complex," *Energy Systems and Policy* 1: 105–117.

Hoffman, L., Brown, F. L., and Baxter, J. D. (1975), "Towards More Accurate Measurements of Customers Response to Electrical Price Changes," *Electrical World* 184: 52–54.

Kagel, J. H., Battalio, R. C., and Miles, C. G. (1976), "Marihuana and Work Performance: Results from An Experiment," Texas A&M University, Department of Economics Working Paper.

Kruglanski, A. W. (1973), "Much Ado About the 'Volunteer Artifacts'," *Journal of Personality and Social Psychology* 28: 348–354.

MacCrimmon, K. R., and Toda, M. (1969), "The Experimental Determination of Indifference Curves," *Review of Economic Studies* 36: 433–451.

Manning, W. G., Jr., Mitchell, B. M., and Acton, J. F. (November 1976), "Design of the Los Angeles Peak Load Pricing Experiment for Electricity," The Rand Corporation, R-1955-DWP.

"Marihuana: A Conversation with NIDA's Robert L. DuPont" (May 1976), *Science* 192: 647–649.

Mayer, L. S. (June 1977), "Estimating the Effect of Price on Energy Demand: Econometrics versus Exploratory Data Analysis," Technical Report No. 123, Series 2, Department of Statistics, Princeton University.

———, and Robinson, J. A. (April 1975), "A Statistical Analysis of the Monthly Consumption of Gas and Electricity in the Home," Center for Environmental Studies Report No. 18, Princeton University.

Nevin, J. R. (1974), "Laboratory Experiments For Estimating Consumer Demand: a Validation Study," *Journal of Marketing Research* 11: 261–268.

Orne, M. T. (1969), "Demand Characteristics and the Concept of Quasi-Control," in *Artifact in Behavioral Research*, ed. by R. Rosenthal and R. L. Rosnow, New York: Academic Press.

Peck, A. E. and Doering, O. C. III (1976), "Voluntarism and Price Response: Consumer Reaction to the Energy Shortage," *The Bell Journal of Economics* 7: 287–292.

Plott, C. R. and Levine, M. E. (April 1975), "On Using the Agenda to Influence Group Decisions: Theory, Experiments and Applications," Cal. Tech. Social Science Working Paper 66.

Rivlin, A. M., and Timpine, P. A., eds. (1975), *Ethical and Legal Issues of Social Experimentation*, Washington, D.C.: Brookings Institution.

Roethlisberger, F. J. and Dickson, W. J. (1939), *Management and the Worker*. Cambridge, Mass: Harvard University Press.

Rosenthal, R. and Rosnow, R. L. (1969), *Artifact in Behavioral Research*, New York: Academic Press, 1969.

——— and ———. (1973), *The Volunteer Subject*, New York: John Wiley and Sons.

Rosnow, R. L. and Aiken, L. S. (1973), "Mediation of Artifacts in Behavioral Research," *Journal of Experimental Social Psychology* 9: 181–201.

Seaver, W. B. and Paterson, A. H. (1976), "Decreasing Fuel-Oil Consumption Through Feedback and Social Commendation," *Journal of Applied Behavior Analysis* 9: 147–152.

Smith, V. L. (1962), "An Experimental Study of Competitive Market Behavior," *Journal of Political Economy* 70: 111–137.

———. (1976), "Experimental Economics: Induced Value Theory," *American Economic Review* 66: 274–279.

Winett, R. A., and Nietzel, M. T. (1975), "Behavioral Ecology: Contingency Management of Consumer Energy Use," *American Journal of Community Psychology* 3: 123–133.

———. (1978), Kagel, J. H., Battalio, R. C., and Winkler, R. C., "The Effects of Monetary Rebates, Feedback, and Information on Residential Electricity Conservation," *Journal of Applied Psychology*.

———. (1977), Neale, M., Williams, K., Yokley, J., and Kauder, H., "Preliminary Report on the Use of Feedback Conservation," Institute for Behavioral Research, Silver Spring Md.

ON THE THEORY AND PRACTICE OF OBTAINING UNBIASED AND EFFICIENT SAMPLES IN SOCIAL SURVEYS AND EXPERIMENTS

Carl Morris, Joseph P. Newhouse, and Rae Archibald, RAND CORPORATION

I. INTRODUCTION

Classical experimental design has been developed for studies that use cross-sectional techniques; that is, those that seek to make inferences about a population at one point in time. Such designs frequently attempt to satisfy the criteria of efficiency (minimum variance) and unbiasedness, and in doing so they often assume that certain attributes of the population can be measured costlessly, instantly, and without error.

Field experiments (or social experiments) that involve economic phenomena frequently will violate these assumptions. Time must pass to gather data (e.g., data on labor supply in the income maintenance experiments, data on medical care and electricity consumption in the health insurance and peak-load pricing experiments); thus, measurements are not made on a population at one point in time. Furthermore, it is impossible in field experiments to measure individual or family attributes costlessly or instantly, and the presence of error in such measurements can substantially reduce the gains in efficiency that an optimal design purports to achieve.

As a result of these constraints and of the practical difficulties of administering large-scale social experiments in real time, experimental design issues arise that have not been well addressed in the literature. Our purpose in raising them here is twofold: to give those who will design field experiments the benefits of our experience in designing and implementing the experimental portion of the Health Insurance Study (HIS); and to encourage the scientific community to rethink the criteria and methods needed for design in these complicated situations. Before turning to the main issues of the paper, a brief description of the HIS may be helpful for the reader.[1]

The HIS has several objectives, including: (1) to measure the insurance elasticity of demand for medical care services (i.e., the response to varying the portion of the expenditure that the participant must pay out-of-pocket); (2) to determine if the insurance elasticity of demand interacts with permanent income; (3) to determine what effects on health, if any, are observed from variation in the consumption of medical care services due to differences in amount paid out-of-pocket. To achieve these ends, nearly 2,800 families have been enrolled in the experiment; these families are located in six geographic locations (Dayton, Ohio; Seattle, Washington; Fitchburg-Leominster, Massachusetts; Franklin County, Massachusetts; Charleston, South Carolina; Georgetown County, South Carolina). The families are enrolled in one of eleven health insurance plans that vary the fraction of the total expenditure that the participant must pay; that fraction is either 0, 25, 50, or 95 percent. In addition, the family's financial exposure is limited to a certain amount in any one year; this amount is called the Maximum Dollar Expenditure (MDE). Generally the MDE is set as a fraction of income, but in one plan it is $150 per person. Some families also are assigned to a Health Maintenance Organization (HMO) (prepaid group practice), and their care is free to them so long as it is received at the HMO. Families participate for either three years (70 percent) or five years (30 percent) in order to measure transitory behavior at the beginning and end of the experiment. Several years were needed to allow for transitory demand to disappear (i.e., rates of consumption that do not reflect steady-state behavior, for example, restorative dentistry that would be done on a one-time basis) and for health status effects to appear.

During the period of participation in the experiment, families do not use their own health insurance; rather, they assign the benefits of that insurance to the experiment. They are paid lump sums (not based on utilization) to ensure that they will not be worse off financially by participating in the experiment. They do not have a choice of insurance plan within the experiment, but instead are faced with an all-or-nothing offer to participate using the plan to which they have been assigned.

Families were enrolled using the following procedure: (1) A screening interview was administered to determine eligibility (the aged and certain other populations are not eligible). (2) A baseline interview was administered to the eligible families to elicit certain information; in particular, information about health insurance policies. This information was verified with the employer or insurance company and used as the basis for the guarantee to the families that they will not be worse off by participating. (3) Following verification of the insurance information, families were selected, assigned to insurance plans (experimental treatments), and made an offer to enroll.

The experiment is well underway. All families are enrolled, and approximately 60 percent of the ultimate number of person-years have been completed (as of December 1978).

II. LONGITUDINAL SURVEYS OF NONSTATIONARY POPULATIONS

Difficulties arise in the practice of repeated interviews of nonstationary populations. These difficulties are not effectively dealt with by the existing theory and practice of survey sampling, which usually assumes a stationary target population. A description of some of these difficulties encountered in the HIS appears in part A, which follows. While our purpose here is to call attention to these problems, and not to solve them, we do discuss in part B some practical methods which can reduce the difficulties. Real progress, however, will be achieved only when new theory, methods, and standards are developed to deal directly with the complications of surveying nonstationary populations.

A. Sampling Problems Peculiar to Longitudinal Surveys

Contact with families in the HIS begins with a longitudinal (panel) survey before the experimental phase and is followed by the longitudinal experiment, lasting from three to five years. The preexperimental portion is longitudinal, i.e., involves reinterview of subjects, because families are administered screening (preliminary, ten-minute) interviews, then baseline (longer, in-depth) interviews, and finally enrollment (when the insurance offer is made) interviews. Our concern here is focused primarily on problems arising from these preexperimental surveys, which in the HIS take a total of six to nine months to complete, and which might be expected to result in an unbiased sample for the experiment.[2]

The theory and practice of cross-sectional (only one interview) survey sampling is now highly developed and widely used to obtain nearly unbiased samples from specified target populations. When the target population (e.g., a specified subset of individuals in a city) can be enumerated and located, only the refusing respondents prevent obtaining an unbiased sample. If the refusal rate is low, the sample can be used with confidence. When a human population cannot be enumerated and located readily, standard practice requires listing dwelling units and then sampling from that list as a basis for locating individuals. The occupants of a dwelling at the time of the "first knock" are considered to be in the sample; they are followed if they move to another dwelling before the interview is actually conducted. Hence, the sample switches from a dwelling sample to a sample of individuals at the first knock. This method works well provided almost all individuals are associated with exactly one dwelling unit at any one time, provided individuals who move can be found, and provided the survey period is short relative to changes in the population (due to vital events, leaving the sampling area, etc.).

The successes of cross-sectional sampling lead to expectations that longitudinal sampling should produce equally good results. This is unrealistic, except in cases of relatively stationary populations. Longitudinal surveys cannot do as well. Even the concept of the "target population" becomes ambiguous. The target population consists of those individuals about whom the survey is to make inferences (in the HIS these would be the populations in the six HIS experimental sites at the end of the experiment who satisfy certain age and other eligibility constraints). The "survey population" is the set of individuals who make up the sampling frame during the (preexperimental) survey period. These two populations often coincide for cross-sectional (one interview) surveys, since the period of analytical interest is the sampling period, or nearly so. They cannot coincide for longitudinal surveys of nonstationary populations.

Suppose the site has a transitory population and the experimental period is lengthy. Only by constantly replenishing the sample during the experimental period is it possible to maintain an unbiased sample corresponding to the target population. This is infeasible in the HIS because the survey population is the cross-section of eligible people in each site at the time of the preexperimental surveys and must remain fixed during the experiment. New entrants (save for newborns and adopted children) are not allowed into the sample during the experiment for two principal reasons. First, a minimum number of years of participation is required to allow long-term changes in health status to occur. Individuals who have been used to replenish the sample will not show these effects. Second, transitory behavior may occur at the outset and at the end of the HIS if the participant's own insurance differs from that provided by the experiment. For example, the experimental insurance usually is more generous in that it covers both dental and psychiatric expenses. To the extent that these are durable goods, experimental families may purchase dental and psychiatric care at the beginning and end of the experiment in greater quantity than they would if their coverage were unchanging. Thus, their behavior differs from steady-state behavior. That individuals must be enrolled for a substantial period of time also has implications for cross-over designs; these are taken up in Section IV.

A second difference with cross-section surveys arises because the three surveys for the HIS during the preexperimental period (screening, baseline, enrollment) make the survey population hard to define. The screening survey can, and does in the HIS, provide a "first knock" cross-sectional sample that is acceptably representative of the community by cross-sectional survey standards. The survey population at that time is the "eligible" community during the screening period; thereafter it must be modified. (In the HIS, the eligible community excludes certain families, on the basis of income exceeding $25,000 [1973 dollars], the aged, the institutionalized, and certain students. Those whose current insurance cannot be verified [e.g., held by an employer who will not cooperate with the HIS] also are excluded. In a broader context, eligibility also requires meeting certain space and time restrictions, namely, that the individual reside within the sampling area during the preexperimental surveys.)

The first new difficulties arise when the interviewer returns to administer a second survey, the baseline survey, to an eligible family that already has been screened. It may happen that

(a) the family has moved out of the sampling area;
(b) the entire family, or perhaps some of its members, has changed eligibility status since the screening period;
(c) the family has reconfigured; births, adoptions, deaths, marriages, divorces, or a member coming of age and becoming a separate family, all act to produce family reconfigurations (which may include the formation of new families within the household).

The screening and baseline interviews are followed by the enrollment interview occurring several months after the baseline. The sampling problems occur again in this third interview. Sampling problems (a) through (c) occurred frequently in the HIS. As shown in Table 2 (p. 222), nonrefusal losses from the sample (moved, unable to locate, ineligible, unable to verify insurance) were about 22 percent and the final enrollment sample in the HIS was slightly more than 105 percent of the original sample due to the discovery of new families.

In the presence of these events, the survey cannot be dated to the screening period. If no effort is made to recoup moving and eligibility losses, the sample will be biased toward the more stable population that is eligible and within the site for both interviews. It is expensive and of negligible value to follow out-of-area movers in pursuit of an unbiased sample at the screening period. The HIS opted instead to administer both screening and baseline interviews to new families occupying those dwellings that housed out-of-area movers, and to follow only in-area movers. This partly atones for loss of the moving population, although not perfectly, because out-of-area movers are replaced by new families from both out-of-area and within the area. It also moves the survey target population closer to the eligible population at the baseline period. Of course, the survey population cannot be updated entirely to the baseline period without returning to all households that during the screening period refused, were never at home, were vacant, or were not even contacted, and attempting again to complete screening and baseline interviews. Further, it would be required to return to households occupied by ineligible persons to determine if their eligibility status had since changed. All these moving, eligibility and reconfiguration difficulties cause the baseline to oversample the population that is stable during both the screening and baseline periods. The nonconstancy and nonpredictability of eligibility characteristics causes this. By contrast, ineligibility due to age does not cause this problem (ignoring deaths), because future ages are totally predictable.

The "unbiased" method for treating the problem created by family reconfigurations is to ignore new persons joining the family between the screening and the baseline interviews. The HIS, however, is especially interested in families, because the family is the economic decision-making unit, and because national health insurance may well apply to the family unit. To take an example, suppose a widower and his child are insured by the HIS, but the stepmother is not because she married into the family after the screening interview. This family's behavior will match neither that of three-person, man-woman-and-child families with all members insured (since the woman's expenditures in such families affect whether the family meets the deductible), nor the two-person, father-and-child families (since the stepmother shares income and also is likely to influence the child's demand for health care). Furthermore, national health insurance is unlikely to exclude some family members, especially the mother. A sampling procedure that attempts to produce an unbiased sample by excluding new family members therefore could lead to bias in the analysis of HIS experimental data. On the other hand, if some sampling bias is accepted in order to enroll families as a unit, the utilization of health services as a function of family characteristics actually may be estimated with reduced bias. In the preceding example, inclusion of the new spouse clearly would aid the analysis. In fact, an estimate of the conditional distribution of utilization from a biased sample may be unbiased. The point is this: *A sampling design must consider the combined effects of two sources of bias, through sampling biases and through limitations (here, the incomplete family) imposed on the analysis.* An unbiased sample may not minimize bias of inferences concerning population parameters.[3]

B. Some Practical Methods for Reducing Longitudinal Sampling Problems

Our primary purpose here is to call attention to the increased difficulties of sampling populations longitudinally, not to resolve them. A solution will be achieved only when the research community explicitly recognizes the longitudinal problem and provides generally acceptable standards and methods for dealing with it. We think the standards should be concerned with minimizing some function of both bias and variance in relation to cost. Acceptable sampling frames must include broader concepts than a specified population at a particular point in time.

While we will not attempt to make general recommendations, certain methods for reducing the magnitude of the problem have come to our attention in the course of designing the HIS. Related ideas in the context of assigning treatments are presented in Section V. Some of the following suggestions were used in the HIS and others were not. We are not claiming that we always made the proper choices for the HIS or that we would make the same choices now. When reasons for choice are given below, they are those that applied at the time of decision.

1. *Sample Replenishment.* As attrition takes place, new members with characteristics matching those lost can be brought into the study. This can reduce or eliminate sampling bias, but it also can be difficult, costly, and lead to incomplete data for subjects. A minor example of sample replenishment in the HIS was replacing out-of-area movers during the preexperimental survey period by the families who moved into the vacated dwelling units.

2. *Sample Compensation.* If certain groups eventually will be underrepresented, then it may be profitable to overrepresent them initially. In the HIS, those recently discharged from the military or leaving college could have been oversampled, since their cohorts will not be picked up later.[4] While data were gathered at the baseline stage on those soon to be discharged or graduated, this oversampling strategy was not followed because these categories include only a minor segment of the population, and because a proper oversampling rate was not known.

3. *Techniques for Shortening the Preenrollment Survey Period.* In the first HIS site, the screening survey preceded the baseline by several months. In all other sites, a "doorstep screener" was used. The interviewer attempted at first knock to complete the screening interview. After establishing family eligibility, a randomization table (the randomization was based on income and family size for the purpose of oversampling low-income families) was

used to determine whether to administer a baseline interview. If so, the family was asked to continue at that time or for an appointment to complete the baseline interview. By shortening the survey period, and sometimes reducing the number of interview contacts, this strategy significantly reduced costs, fielding time, and potential biases. It requires more training of interviewers to make correct eligibility and randomization decisions, since they cannot be made centrally.

Another similar tactic was used in the Los Angeles peak-load electricity pricing experiment (Manning et al., 1976) for the purpose of shortening the time to enrollment. A random two-thirds of the households were asked to participate in the experiment on predesignated treatments at the end of the first interview. The remaining households were assigned optimally to treatments later, after baseline data were available for the entire sample. This method appears to be very cost-effective, although it does restrict the ability to make optimal assignments of subjects to treatments.

The method used by the peak-load pricing experiment was not applicable to the HIS because the HIS families had to have their insurance formally verified (which took at least six weeks) before an offer could be made. However, the HIS moved the enrollment period closer to the baseline period by selecting a portion of the enrollment sample before the baseline period was complete. Care must be taken when doing this; problems encountered are discussed in Section V.

4. *Crossover Designs with Pre-Enrollment in Control Group Status.* In experimental situations, even though the treatments cannot be assigned immediately after completion of the baseline interview, it may be advantageous to preenroll interviewees in control group status at that time. If this can be done, then transitory effects attributable solely to participating in an experiment may diminish before assignment of the treatments. While this does not alleviate many of the difficulties attributable to longitudinal sampling, it can lead to better comparisons among the treatments because some early attrition would be forced due to forms burden, and some refusals would occur before assignment of treatments. Other advantages are that participants will serve as their own control group while on the experimental measurement system, that the size of the entire control group is increased, and that analysis of those who refuse the offer of the experimental treatment is facilitated. The HIS did not use this method (except for a two-year pre-enrollment group for part of the sample in South Carolina) primarily because of the additional risk of bias attributable to possible nonrandom attrition from the control group, unless quite large payments were made to the families. (By contrast, the magnitude of benefits received leads to low attrition during the experimental period.) Secondarily, it was costly to make preexperimental data available quickly for assignment of treatments.

5. *Rules for following Movers and Reconfigured Families.* Standard survey practice is to follow individuals within the sampling area if this is possible. What if it is impossible? Under what circumstances should the person who moves into the vacated dwelling be interviewed instead? Which procedure is cost-effective? These issues become more complex if family units are to be sampled when divorce, separation, remarriage, and coming-of-age leads to reconfiguration and to creation of new family units.

Randomization, in conjunction with a change of viewpoint away from preserving a population of individuals and toward preserving the characteristics of the initial sample, offers one possibility. For example, if a husband and wife divorce and both remarry during the sampling period, then if the survey unit is the individual, both would be followed and their new spouses ignored. When the survey unit is the family, it may be preferable to follow the husband with probability one-half, and the wife with probability one-half, incorporating the new spouse, and ignoring the unselected family. Even though the new spouse has a second chance of being enrolled, certain characteristics are maintained: the wholeness of one husband-wife family is retained instead of changing the sample to include two partially enrolled families. This example is straightforward, but the matter becomes complex when one must consider the myriad combinations involving children and other members in the old and new family units, the inability to follow some members, and multiple family dwellings. We believe that much useful research could be carried out here.

6. *Connecting Cross-sectional Surveys with the Panel Survey.* A cross-sectional survey of the site made after a panel has been selected will include two groups: those who might have been (or are) panel members because they were present and eligible during the preenrollment period; and those who could not have been because they were ineligible at the time (lived out-of-area, etc.). Questions can be included on the cross-sectional survey that would provide information about which group included the interviewee. Analysis of such data would provide information about biases that might obtain because the panel was constrained to the more stable population. In particular, those biases due to selection of a nonrepresentative population along measurable dimensions (e.g., the stable population is older) can be relatively well estimated. However, any interaction between the experimental treatment and the transitory population cannot be measured using a later cross-sectional sample.

In concluding this section, we wish to reiterate the main point: that longitudinal surveys are more difficult to carry out than cross-sectional surveys and these difficulties and differences need to be more widely recognized by the scientific community so that appropriate standards can be agreed upon and appropriate sampling methods developed. Longitudinal surveys are not always more informative than cross-sectional ones, and for many purposes can be less informative. They gain because they permit estimation when experimental effects are time-dependent. Even when these models are not of interest, longitudinal experiments may be required if the number of experimental subjects is limited, if costs per year are constrained (but several years' support is available), if recall error requires frequent interview (e.g., asking a panel about consumption every month rather than asking once for annual consumption), if transitory behavior is expected, or if long-term effects are to be measured. But if these objectives or difficulties are not encountered, then a cross-sectional analysis will produce results earlier and also may be more accurate (in steady-state, a mean estimated from two positively correlated measurement periods on one subject has greater variability than a mean estimated from one measurement period on two subjects).

Sampling goals should be to minimize a function of both variances and bias of the estimates finally generated by the analysis, subject to prescribed cost constraints. Hence, sampling errors are just one component of the total error, and some sampling bias may be acceptable if this leads to decreased errors in the fitted analytical model, or reduced costs. We hope that research on methods and standards for reinterview sampling will be forthcoming.

III. CONSTRAINTS ON OPTIMIZATION OF SURVEYED POPULATIONS

Because the HIS sponsors had greater interest in the effects of insurance on the low (permanent) income population than on other income groups, it was agreed that the HIS would oversample low-income families. This oversampling amounts to optimizing by not sampling proportionately because of the increased interest in the low-income group. Since oversampling is required, survey costs also could be reduced by overselection of low-income neighborhoods. Under certain circumstances, both kinds of oversampling can be effective, but *our purpose here is to show that without strong modeling assumptions, the gains from each can be negligible or even negative.*

(A) Optimization with Classification Errors

There is a fundamental difference between oversampling with respect to a variable that varies randomly with time, as income does over the several-year experimental period of the HIS, and one that is constant or completely predictable, such as race, sex, or age. Oversampling a group is desired for values of a variable that will occur during the experiment, but only the preexperimental values are available for this purpose. If the preexperimental variable is not perfectly correlated with the experimental value, then two difficulties arise. First, there will be some regression to the mean so that the experimental value will not be oversampled as strongly as the preexperimental value, causing the result to be less efficient than desired. Second, unless researchers are in a position to asert that no latent variables (omitted variables which are partially correlated with the oversampling variable) exist, then an analysis of experimental data must account simultaneously for the separate oversampling rates due to the preexperimental and to the experimental variables. This degrades precision, possibly to the extent that proportional sampling would be more efficient than oversampling. Of course, weighted analyses also are more cumbersome to conduct because the weights must be carried throughout.

We shall illustrate these ideas with a simple example which will permit numerical evaluation of the efficiency gains and losses. Suppose each family falls into a "low-income" or "high-income" category on the basis of their income for the year immediately preceding the experiment, and that each of these two categories represents one-half of all families. Similarly, the average income of each family during the life of the experiment (permanent income would be another candidate for the variable of interest) falls into "low" and "high" categories, and again each is assumed to include one-half of all families. The assumption that each category corresponds to one-half the population is made for convenience only. While more general situations may be treated, we keep matters simple here because our purpose is only to illustrate the problem caused by classification errors.[5]

The only data available for oversampling are preexperimental incomes, so the fraction f is designated as the proportion of the sample that is to have low preexperimental income, while 1-f will have high income. Let c be the probability of correct classification. Because of the symmetry in this example, c is the probability that a preexperimental low (or high) income family is low (or high) during the experiment and 1-c is the probability of changing income categories during the two periods. The case $c = 1$ corresponds to variables like race, age, and sex (assuming no errors in measurement of these variables). Ordinarily, c is greater than one-half, with $c =$ one-half meaning that the preexperimental and experimental classifications are independent. Figure 1 contains the assumptions used for this presentation. Note in particular that the proportion of low-income families actually experienced, f_c, is closer to one-half than f, since $f_c = cf + \bar{c}\bar{f}$. For convenience, we also denote $\bar{f}_c = 1 - f_c = \bar{c}f + c\bar{f}$ to be the fraction of families with high incomes during the experiment.

The population means μ_{ij} are estimated unbiasedly by $\bar{x}_{ij}$, the mean response in cell i, j. Assume that $\text{var}(\bar{x}_{ij}) = \sigma^2/n_{ij}$ and that a total of N families are used so that $n_{00} = cfN$, $n_{10} = \bar{c}fN$, $n_{01} = \bar{c}\bar{f}N$, and $n_{11} = c\bar{f}N$. With these definitions, the mean responses during the experiment and the two quantities to be estimated, are $\mu_0 \equiv c\mu_{00} + \bar{c}\mu_{10}$ for the low-income group and $\mu_1 \equiv \bar{c}\mu_{01} + c\mu_{11}$ for the high-income group.

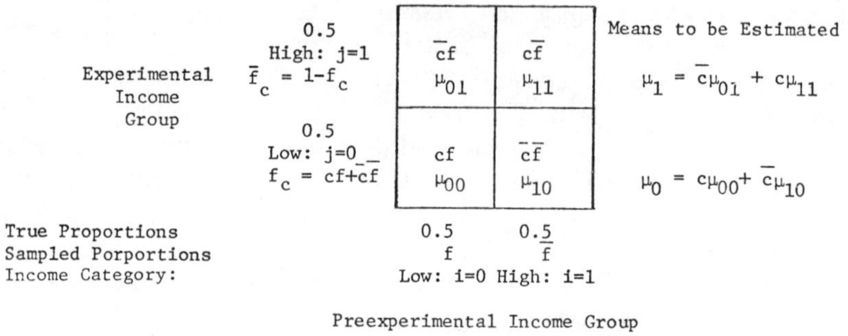

		Means to be Estimated
Experimental Income Group	0.5 High: j=1 $\bar{f}_c = 1-f_c$	$\bar{cf}$ μ_{01}	$\bar{cf}$ μ_{11}	$\mu_1 = \bar{c}\mu_{01} + c\mu_{11}$
	0.5 Low: j=0 $f_c = cf+\bar{c}\bar{f}$	cf μ_{00}	$\bar{c}f$ μ_{10}	$\mu_0 = c\mu_{00} + \bar{c}\mu_{10}$
True Proportions Sampled Proportions Income Category:		0.5 f Low: i=0	0.5 $\bar{f}$ High: i=1

Preexperimental Income Group

Figure 1. Sampling proportions and responses μ_j and μ_{ij} for crossed income categories. $\bar{c} \equiv 1 - c$, $\bar{f} \equiv 1 - f$, μ_{ij} = mean of response of interest when preexperimental income group is i, experimental group is j. μ_j = mean response when experimental group is j. Naturally occurring fraction is 0.5. Sampled fractions are f, $1-f$ preexperimentally and f_c, $1-f_c$ during experiment.

If $\mu_{00} = \mu_{10}$ and $\mu_{01} = \mu_{11}$, so that the response for each income group during the experiment is independent of the preexperimental income categorization, then $\mu_0 = \mu_{00} = \mu_{10}$, $\mu_1 = \mu_{01} = \mu_{11}$, and *unweighted*[6] estimates may be used.

$$\hat{\mu}_0 = \frac{n_{00}\bar{x}_{00} + n_{10}\bar{x}_{10}}{n_{00} + n_{10}} \tag{3.1}$$

$$\hat{\mu}_1 = \frac{n_{01}\bar{x}_{01} + n_{11}\bar{x}_{11}}{n_{01} + n_{11}} \tag{3.2}$$

These estimates are unbiased if $\mu_{00} = \mu_{10}$ and $\mu_{01} = \mu_{11}$. If not, let $\delta_0 \equiv \mu_{00} - \mu_{10}$, $\delta_1 \equiv \mu_{01} - \mu_{11}$. Then (3.1) and (3.2) are biased by the amounts

$$E\hat{\mu}_0 - \mu_0 = \frac{c\bar{c}(2f-1)}{f_c}\delta_0, \quad E\hat{\mu}_1 - \mu_1 = \frac{c\bar{c}(2f-1)}{\bar{f}_c}\delta_1 \tag{3.3}$$

which are not zero unless c = 1 (or c = 0) or proportional sampling ($f = \frac{1}{2}$) has been used. Whether the estimates are biased or not, their variances are

$$\text{Var}(\hat{\mu}_0) = \frac{\sigma^2/N}{f_c}, \quad \text{Var}(\hat{\mu}_1) = \frac{\sigma^2/N}{\bar{f}_c}. \tag{3.4}$$

If δ_0 and δ_1 cannot be assumed to be zero, because the preexperimental income category is partially correlated (given experimental income) with the response, then although (3.1) and (3.2) are biased, the following *weighted* estimates are unbiased for μ_0 and μ_1:

$$\hat{\hat{\mu}}_0 = c\bar{x}_{00} + (1-c)\bar{x}_{10}, \quad \hat{\hat{\mu}}_1 = (1-c)\bar{x}_{01} + c\bar{x}_{11}. \tag{3.5}$$

Their variances are

$$\text{Var}(\hat{\hat{\mu}}_0) = \frac{\sigma^2 \bar{f}_c}{N \bar{ff}}, \quad \text{Var}(\hat{\hat{\mu}}_1) = \frac{\sigma^2 f_c}{N \bar{ff}}. \qquad (3.6)$$

The values (3.6) are always larger than the corresponding ones in (3.4) unless $c = 1$ or $f = \frac{1}{2}$. If $f = \frac{1}{2}$ weighted and unweighted estimates are the same, so

$$\text{Var}(\hat{\mu}_0) = \text{Var}(\hat{\hat{\mu}}_0) = 2\sigma^2/N, \quad \text{Var}(\hat{\mu}_1) = \text{Var}(\hat{\hat{\mu}}_1) = 2\sigma^2/N. \qquad (3.7)$$

When $f = \frac{1}{2}$, the variances (3.7) therefore are independent of the correct classification probability c, and furthermore, unweighted estimates are unbiased, c.f. (3.3). These are two strong advantages of choosing $f = \frac{1}{2}$ in this case, and in more general situations of sampling proportionally.

We now are in a position to compute the variance of the weighted estimates with $f \geq \frac{1}{2}$ from (3.6), relative to the variance in (3.7) for $f = \frac{1}{2}$. These values

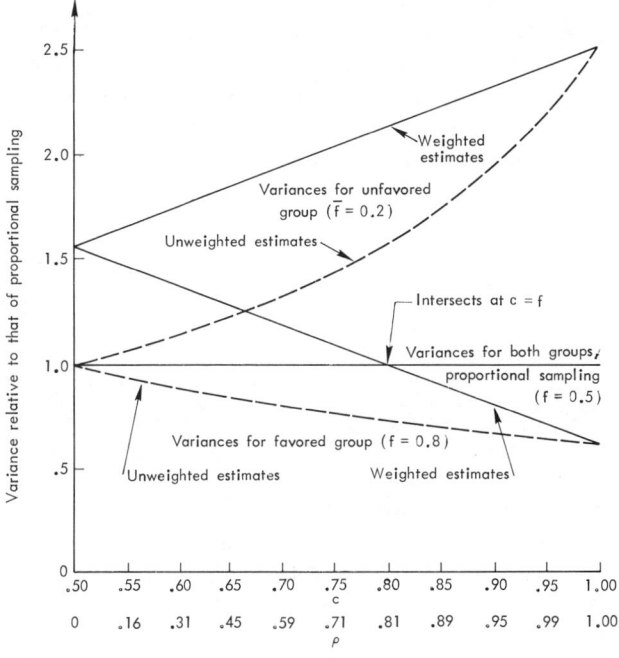

Figure 2. Variances of weighted and unweighted estimates for the case $f = 0.8$, relative to variances resulting from proportional sampling. Horizontal axis is the classification probability c, or the corresponding correlation coefficient $\rho = \cos(\pi(1 - c))$ between the preexperimental and experimental values of the classification variable.

Table 1. Ratio of Variances of Weighted Estimates for values of $f \geq \frac{1}{2}$, Formula (3.6), Relative to the Variances When $f = \frac{1}{2}$, Formula (3.7)

	Low Income (favored) Group ($f \geq \frac{1}{2}$)			High Income (Unfavored) Group ($\bar{f} \leq \frac{1}{2}$)	
	Variance Ratio			Variance Ratio	
f	$c = 0.5$	$c = 1$	$\bar{f}$	$c = 0.5$	$c = 1$
0.5	1.00	1.00	0.5	1.00	1.00
0.6	1.04	0.83	0.4	1.04	1.25
0.7	1.19	0.71	0.3	1.19	1.67
0.8	1.56	0.63	0.2	1.56	2.50
0.9	2.78	0.56	0.1	2.78	5.00
1.0	∞	0.50	0	∞	∞

appear in Table 1 for both income groups for the two cases $c = .5$ and $c = 1.0$. Since this ratio is linear in c, variance ratios for other values of c can be obtained by linear interpolation, as illustrated in Figure 2.

Table 1 illustrates the major result of this section, that the variance for the unfavored group is always increased by oversampling, and for c near to 0.5 oversampling even harms estimation of the favored group. In fact, since the simple average of the two variance ratios for any value of c is $1/(4f\bar{f})$, independent of c, we may define this amount to be the overall increase in variance accepted in order to produce lower variances for the favored group. It is easy to see that even the favored group has larger variance than for proportional sampling if $c < f$. Hence: *oversampling leads to uniformly higher variances if the oversampling rate exceeds the correct classification probability*.

These ideas are illustrated for the case $f = 0.8$ in Figure 2. The horizontal line going through 1.0 is the variance available if proportional sampling is used. The two solid sloped lines, which meet at 1.56 for $c = 0.5$ (see Table 1), are the variances from using the weighted estimates (3.5) when 80 percent of the sample is low income (preexperimentally) and 20 percent is high income (preexperimentally). If $c \leq 0.8$, even the favored group does not improve on the variance for proportional sampling; hence the lines cross there. The variances of the unweighted estimates (3.1), (3.2) are the dashed curving lines, whose two values always average in excess of 1.0. The gains for the favored group are small for c near to 0.5 because substantial misclassification produces experimental samples that nearly match the population proportions. At $c = 1$ the unweighted and weighted estimates are the same, and so their variances also agree. At $c = 0.5$ the unweighted estimates have variance independent of the oversampling rate f (since $f_{.5} = 0.5$ for all f), and therefore have relative variance equal to 1.

The horizontal axis is indexed not only by c but also by ρ, the value of the correlation coefficient that is consistent with c. It is computed from the formula $\rho = \cos(\pi(1-c))$, and is the correlation required between two normally distributed observations in order that the conditional probability of the second exceeding its median is c, given that the first exceeds its own median. (This formula is exact only for the case of two categories, each having probability one-half as in the example.) Thus, in the case $f = 0.8$ of Figure 2, correlations between preexperimental and experimental income less than 0.81 will lead to higher variances than for $f = 0.5$, *even for the favored group*.

The value ∞ for $f = 1$ and $c = 0.5$ in Table 1 raises an interesting point. If low incomes are the only ones of interest to the study, and if $c < 1$, then either it is necessary to postulate that $\mu_{00} = \mu_{10}$ (that there are no latent variables partially correlated with preexperimental income) or to sample both preexperimental categories. That is, if $\delta_0 \neq 0$ in (3.3), any attempt to study low income preexperimental families by restricting the sample to low preexperimental incomes would be biased because families with high preexperimental income, whose incomes drop later, would be excluded.

In summary, strong assumptions can eliminate the need to use weights based on the preexperimental variables. In that case oversampling can be efficient if the probability of correct classification is high. If a weighted analysis is needed, then oversampling may degrade precision relative to proportional sampling, even for fairly high probabilities of correct classification. An additional reason to avoid oversampling is that a weighted analysis is more cumbersome to conduct than an unweighted one. This is quite important if many different analyses and dependent variables are being considered, because the weights must be used each time, even for those dependent variables whose prediction is not improved by the oversampling.

B. Problems Derived from Oversampling Neighborhoods

If it is decided to oversample certain categories, possibly because classification errors are small, then it may appear to be efficient to obtain the sample by oversampling neighborhoods that are abundant with the desired characteristics. This strategy reduces cost by decreasing the number of screening interviews needed to produce the desired sample proportions. If the analytical models legitimately can ignore the neighborhood effects, the savings are real. Even when this simplifying assumption cannot be made with confidence, such a sampling procedure may be required and some bias accepted to keep costs within reasonable bounds for studies that focus on individuals with uncommon characteristics.

But oversampling in order to reduce screening costs may not be cost effective. If the study must oversample low income families, then the income distributions in census tracts can be estimated from census data. This information could be used to reduce the number of screening interviews substantially if the between census tract variation in income is large relative to the within tract variation. However, a biased sample will result if low-income families in low-income tracts differ systematically in their responses from low income families in high-income tracts. For example, low-income families in high-income neighborhoods often are young, single people living with their high-income parents. These people probably differ in their responses from low-income families in low-income neighborhoods having different age, family size, and employment characteristics. Therefore, a weighted analysis would be required to avoid bias, and as stated earlier, this increases variances of estimates. We have constructed many models, similar to those presented in Part A, where the fractional increases in variance resulting from this kind of strategy substantially exceeds the fractional decrease in costs, and hence such strategies are not cost effective for a given budget. Furthermore, oversampling of neighborhoods has other disadvantages: derivation of a proper sampling scheme is costly, quite difficult, and if done improperly can produce biases; and weighted analyses are more difficult to conduct.

To summarize this section, two examples were considered where oversampling of a population in which the analyst has greater interest may be undesirable. Oversampling is common in these situations. More discussion of the problems of oversampling, involving treatment assignment, appears in Section V. Our view is that oversampling should be used only after reviewing the additional modeling assumptions required to make the exercise advantageous and the likelihood of classification error.

IV. DIFFICULTIES WITH OPTIMAL ALLOCATION OF SUBJECTS TO TREATMENTS IN SOCIAL EXPERIMENTS

In the preceding two sections we discussed the difficulties of getting unbiased samples of transitory populations and of oversampling subpopulations in the presence of classification errors. In experimental situations there also are opportunities to control the manner in which subjects are allocated to treatments, the purpose being to produce a more cost-effective experiment. In this section we briefly consider three of these options: A. Choosing the sample to be nonrepresentative of the survey population; B. Making unbalanced assignments of subjects to treatments; and C. Using a crossover design. In each of these cases extra modeling assumptions are required to avoid bias, assumptions we were unwilling to make in the context of the Health Insurance Study.

A. Nonrepresentative Samples

Certain experimental subjects may be more valuable for the estimation of parameters or less costly than others, and therefore be preferred for allocation to treatments. A simple example of this occurs if a linear response to one independent variable is to be estimated, in which case subjects with extremely low or high values on this variable (e.g., income) are much more informative than those with intermediate values. When more subjects are available for selection than are needed for assignment to treatments, the preferred subjects may be assigned to treatments and the others excluded from the sample. A proper analysis may be derived from such assignments either if the assumed functional form is correct, or in the absence of such assumptions, if every member of the target population has positive probability of being assigned to the treatments and in the analysis subjects are weighted inversely to their selection probability. Of course, the weighted analysis may be inefficient.

More hazardous yet are samples with some subjects having no possibility of selection. This occurs in the simple linear response example. The exclusion of the intermediate subjects makes the estimation of a nonlinear model very difficult, and no weighted analysis can rectify the situation. The HIS did not follow this procedure by excluding middle-income families, for example. While such a procedure would reduce variances for estimating a linear income effect, we have no assurances that responses are linear in income, and there is a strong likelihood that middle-income families differ importantly along other critical dimensions that are correlated with income.

Note that the problem here is one of determining a priori the appropriate functional form. Unfortunately, economic theory rarely gives much help with respect to functional form. Conlisk (1973) has proposed a decision-theoretic approach to this problem in which the analyst assigns probabilities to functional forms and then minimizes expected loss. While attractive conceptually, it is not clear how one proceeds in practice to assign zero probability to functional forms one will not consider, nor how one should think about appropriate probabilities (in some cases information from other studies can be helpful). In the absence of information concerning functional form, a self-weighting (representative) sample appears to us to have desirable properties.

B. Unbalanced Assignments of Subjects to Treatments

If the cost of including a subject in the experiment depends jointly on his characteristics and on the treatment to which he is assigned, then it may be possible to increase the sample size and precision of the experiment by exploiting this relationship. The allocation model of Conlisk and Watts (1969) provides a means for computing the optimal imbalance based on such a cost function, assuming a functional form is specified.

For example, the cost of the Health Insurance Study could have been reduced by assigning those who had good insurance before the experiment to the generous experimental insurance plans, and those with little or no insurance to the less generous plans. This would have eliminated the "worst-case" participation incentives paid to compensate those families whose experimental insurance was inferior in any way to their preexperimental insurance. It also would have been unwise. Families in poor health tend to purchase better insurance than they would were they in good health (Phelps, 1976). Generous insurance plans therefore would be overrepresented by unhealthy families and as a result, comparisons between treatments would be biased.

The New Jersey Negative Income Tax Experiment provides a second example. The designers of this experiment found it less costly to put higher income families on generous plans and lower income families on less generous plans, and so generosity of the treatment and family income are correlated. Of course the modeling assumption that income does not interact with treatment generosity and that responses are linear with income provides one way to unravel these effects. Presumably, such assumptions were made during the design of the New Jersey experiment when it was decided that unbalanced assignment of incomes would be cost effective. The alternative to making these modeling assumptions is to use a weighted analysis. But this will yield less efficient estimates than would have resulted from balanced assignments of subjects to treatments.

C. Crossover Designs

Thus far, we have considered designs in which subjects are exposed to one treatment only. In a long experiment it may be possible to expose subjects to several treatments, one at a time—a crossover design. If valid responses can be elicited in this fashion, then increased precision for estimating treatment effects can be expected because each subject acts as his own control. That is, comparisons between treatments can be made directly by observing the changed responses of each subject as he changes treatments. This eliminates accounting for the differences between subjects. Variances are reduced by a factor $1 - R^2$ if every subject is exposed to every treatment for an equal length of time, where R^2 is the portion of the total variance of the response of subjects attributable to differences between subjects. Hall (1975) has argued that a crossover design could have reduced the necessary sample size by a factor of six in the New Jersey Negative Income Tax Experiment. We doubt this. The responses from crossover experimentation will be invalid if there is transitory behavior at the beginning or end of each treatment period that is not accounted for. Transitory behavior may exist for a variety of reasons. Learning effects produce transitory behavior if it takes time for the subject to become familiar with all the benefits of the treatment and to develop ways to take advantage of them (e.g., to find dentists or psychiatrists in the HIS). Put another way, the actual response may be lagged. Or if the treatment benefits permit subjects to purchase durable goods, they may engage in transitory behavior in crossover situations by waiting to purchase these goods until they are on a generous treatment (e.g., elective surgery, dental work, and psychiatric care are likely to be purchased in greater quantity per unit time by a subject who is on a generous health insurance plan for only a short period than by one who has generous insurance for a long time). Changes in behavior resulting from the subject's heightened awareness of the experiment are more likely if the treatment is changed frequently.

In the face of time-varying experimental responses, the design must either: (a) allow sufficient time within each treatment for transitory effects to disappear; this amount of time is likely not to be known a priori and additional calendar time may be necessary to estimate it; or (b) estimate the rate of change in behavior and extrapolate to a steady-state value. The first solution in practice will defer the results in time, and therefore a larger sample with no crossover (but earlier results) may well be preferred; the second solution requires strong assumptions.

Unfortunately, time-varying experimental responses appear to be common. In the peak-load pricing experiment for electricity, it takes time to adjust the household's stock of appliances; in the income maintenance experiments, it takes time to search for a new job; in the housing demand experiments, it takes time to locate new housing. Further, all involve aspects of durable goods. Thus, while crossover designs can be very useful, we doubt that they will prove to be desirable as a general design for the types of social experiments considered here.

V. OPTIMAL BALANCE OF ASSIGNMENTS TO TREATMENTS AND THE DIFFICULTIES OF ACHIEVING IT WITH FIELD CONSTRAINTS

For reasons just mentioned, imbalances between the treatment assignments and the target population, or imbalances between treatments, can lead to poor estimates of the treatment effects. Suppose then that it is desired to balance subjects across treatments as carefully as possible. The time-honored and simplest method for doing this is by simple random sampling (S.R.S.): The available subjects are assigned at random to treatments in accord with the required sample size for each treatment, *without* regard to any pre-experimental measurements made on the subjects. Of course some imbalance of the preexperimental measurements still occurs, but it is random; and if

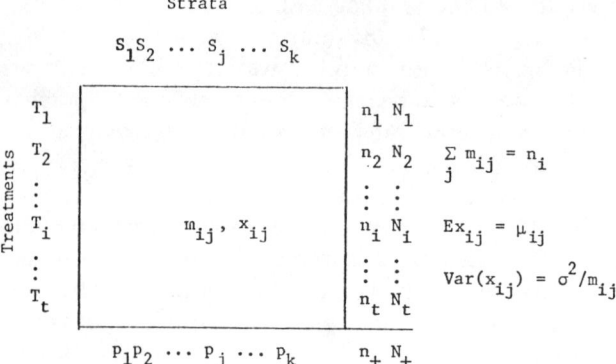

Figure 3. Notation for assignment of subjects from k strata to t treatments.

large samples are assigned to each treatment, only minor increases in variance are experienced relative to a perfectly balanced assignment. If sample sizes are not large, however, then the imbalances from S.R.S. can be substantial, and more control over the sample is desired.

Classical ways to use preexperimental measurements to improve balance over S.R.S. include proportional stratification and blocking. In the Health Insurance Study, the "Finite Selection Model" (FSM) was used as an alternative because it can handle more independent variables than the classical methods and does not require converting continuous variables, like income, to categorical variables (Morris, 1975). The method of proportional stratification involves dividing the sample into k strata on the basis of the preexperimental variables and then assigning subjects to treatments separately from each stratum, in proportion to the treatment size, using simple random sampling. Blocking, a special case of proportional stratification, can be used only if all the treatments are the same size, or if all treatment sizes are small integer multiples of the smallest treatment. The entire sample then would be broken into homogeneous groups of the proper size, and each group assigned to the treatments in proportion to their size by simple random sampling.

Because the calculations can be carried out conveniently for proportional stratification, that case is treated in our examples here. Proportional stratification includes blocking as a special case, while it in turn is a special case of the FSM.

The notation needed is given in Figure 3.

Subjects are classified into k strata $S_1,\ldots,S_k$ on the basis of their preexperimental measurements and are to be assigned to treatments $T_1,\ldots,T_t$, with N_i subjects assigned to treatment T_i. Hence $\Sigma N_i = N_+$ is the total number of subjects in the pool. The proportion of subjects available for selection in stratum j is p_j, so $\Sigma p_j = 1$. Because there may be refusals of the offer or other failures to enroll assigned subjects on treatments, n_i (with $n_i \leq N_i$) is the number actually enrolled in T_i. The number actually enrolled in T_i from stratum j is m_{ij}, $\Sigma_j m_{ij} = n_i$. The true mean response to T_i in S_j is μ_{ij}, which is to be estimated by the sample mean x_{ij} of the m_{ij} observations in that cell. We assume

$$Ex_{ij} = \mu_{ij}, \quad Var(x_{ij}) = \sigma^2/m_{ij}. \quad (5.1)$$

The average response to T_i among these subjects is

$$\mu_i = \sum_j p_j \mu_{ij} \quad (5.2)$$

which is estimated unbiasedly by

$$\hat{\mu}_i = \Sigma p_j x_{ij} \quad (5.3)$$

with variance

$$Var(\hat{\mu}_i) = \sigma^2 \sum_j p_j^2/m_{ij} \quad (5.4)$$

The variances for making comparisons between treatments are determined by formula (5.4). For example, the difference in effects of T_1 and T_2 is estimated by $\hat{\mu}_1 - \hat{\mu}_2$ with variance $Var(\hat{\mu}_1) + Var(\hat{\mu}_2)$.

Suppose first that all assigned subjects actually enroll, so that $n_i = N_i$. Assuming that $(n_1, \ldots, n_k)$ is given, the uniformly best assignment scheme for all treatments, subject to $\Sigma_j m_{ij} = n_i$, is proportional stratification:

$$m_{ij} = n_i p_j \quad (5.5)$$

for all i, j, in which case

$$Var_{PROP}(\hat{\mu}_i) = \sigma^2/n_i \quad (5.6)$$

is the optimal variance. This is proved by minimizing (5.4) subject to $\Sigma_j m_{ij} = n_i$. Of course an exact identify for (5.5) may be impossible for any treatment because $n_i p_j$ may not be an integer. We ignore this complication.

Now suppose that some selected subjects fail to participate. If these subjects can be replaced by others from the same stratum, perfectly proportional samples still will be achieved. This sequential procedure was infeasible in the context of the HIS for reasons described later. Instead it was necessary to select N_i subjects, in excess of the n_i desired for each treatment $(N_i > n_i)$, permitting the imperfect acceptance rate $\pi < 1$ to yield approximately the desired number n_i. Our purpose is to demonstrate how much the variance (5.6) increases when this happens. As a first step, the expected precision from simple random sampling will be determined.

We are supposing that the $\{p_j\}$ are defined by the sample, based only on the N_+ observations, and not on the entire universe. The variances realized from simple random sampling therefore will be reduced because of finite sampling, as we shall see. Comparisons between S.R.S. and the results of proportional stratification also will be made conditionally on the value of $\{n_i\}$, since the random mechanism that operates to produce these values is the same for either design method.

The sample is assumed to have been constructed as follows. The universe is assumed to be large (e.g., a city) and a simple random sample of N_+ subjects, eligible for treatment assignment, is obtained. The numbers $\{N_i\}$ are fixed in advance, $\Sigma N_i = N_+$ subjects are assigned to T_i either at random, or by the method of proportional stratification. Let m_{ij}^* be the number of subjects assigned to T_i from S_j at this step, with $\Sigma_j m_{ij}^* = N_i$. If S.R.S. is used, m_{ij}^* is random, while $m_{ij}^* = N_i p_j$ if proportional stratification is used. These subjects are enrolled with probability π, so given m_{ij}^*, the number that actually accept on T_i from S_j are $m_{ij} \sim$ Binomial(m_{ij}^*, π). (This notation means that the random variable m_{ij} has the Binomial distribution with mean $m_{ij}^* \pi$ and variance $m_{ij}^* \pi(1 - \pi)$.) Of course, it is m_{ij}, not m_{ij}^*, that acts to reduce variances in (5.4). We wish to compute the expected value of (5.4), i.e., $\sigma^2 E \Sigma p_j^2 / m_{ij}$, conditionally on this sampling scheme, on $\{n_i\}$, and on the sample of N_+ subjects, for both simple random sampling and proportional sampling. Formally, these expectations do not exist unless m_{ij} cannot be zero, but we shall interpret the expectations as conditional on the event that $m_{ij} \geq 1$. The approximate method used to obtain these expectations takes care of this problem. The results that follow are proved in the appendix.

Theorem 5.1. The expected value of (5.4) under random sampling is approximately

$$E_{SRS} \operatorname{Var}(\hat{\mu}_i) \doteq \frac{\sigma^2}{n_i}\left(1 + \frac{k-1}{n_i}\left(\frac{N_+ - n_i}{N_+ - 1}\right)\right). \tag{5.7}$$

Since σ^2/n_i is given by (5.6) as the variance for proportional stratification, the factor

$$1 + \frac{k-1}{n_i}\left(1 - \frac{n_i - 1}{N_+ - 1}\right) \tag{5.8}$$

is the expected fractional increase in variance from S.R.S. relative to proportional stratification. When N_+ is large in relation to n_i, (5.8) simplifies approximately to

$$1 + (k-1)/n_i. \tag{5.9}$$

Note that (5.9) is the S.R.S. variance for sampling from the universe, while (5.8) is smaller, because sampling without replacement from a universe of size N_+ is more efficient than from one of infinite size. Formulas (5.8) and (5.9) illustrate the well-known fact that S.R.S. becomes less efficient as the number of subjects per treatment per stratum, n_i/k, decreases. S. R. S. is asymptotically optimal as n_i/k becomes very large. But we believe that as n_+ increases in experiments as costly as the HIS that more treatments and more strata will be created, so that n_i/k ordinarily would not be large.

Turning to proportional stratification with $m_{ij}^* = N_i p_j$, formula (5.6) no longer will obtain because of random nonacceptances. Instead, conditional on n_i (the number of acceptances of T_i) the expected variance would be given by the following theorem.

Theorem 5.2. The expected value of (5.4) assuming random acceptance of proportionally stratified offers ($m_{ij}^* = N_i p_j$ made to T_i from S_j) is

$$E_{\text{PROP}} \text{Var}(\hat{\mu}_i) \doteq \frac{\sigma^2}{n_i}\left(1 + \frac{k-1}{n_i}\left(\frac{N_i - n_i}{N_i - 1}\right)\right). \quad (5.10)$$

To interpret Theorem 5.2, define

$$\psi_i \equiv \frac{n_i - 1}{N_i - 1} \cdot \frac{N_+ - N_i}{N_+ - n_i}, \quad (5.11)$$

which depends on the acceptance rate n_i/N_i, and on N_i and N_+, but not on k or σ^2. If $n_i = N_i$ then $\psi_i = 1$, if $n_i = 1, \psi_i = 0$, and in most instances ψ_i is slightly less than, but fairly close to, the acceptance rate π. We may rewrite (5.10) in terms of ψ_i and (5.7) as

$$E_{\text{PROP}} \text{Var}(\hat{\mu}_i) \doteq (1 - \psi_i) E_{\text{SRS}} \text{Var}(\hat{\mu}_i) + \psi_i \text{Var}_{\text{PROP}}(\mu_i), \quad (5.12)$$

where $\text{Var}_{\text{PROP}}(\hat{\mu}_i) \equiv \sigma^2/n_i$ is the variance achieved by proportional sampling (5.6). The quantity ψ_i therefore shows how much a random acceptance rate would be expected to cut into the gains due to proportional stratification. Roughly, the improvement over S.R.S. would be reduced by a factor equal to the nonacceptance rate, $1 - \pi$.

To illustrate this improvement, the acceptance rate was about 0.58 in the HIS with losses caused by refusal of the offer, refusal of the final interview, and because families had moved, become ineligible, couldn't be found, etc. A detailed breakdown of the HIS enrollment experience is shown in Table 2. Note that one-half of the 42 percent sample loss is due to nonrefusal attrition, and the other half is due to refusal of the enrollment interview or the actual offer of enrollment.

If $N_+ = 800$ families, a typical value, then for values of N_i at 10, 40 (where ψ_i is maximum), 75, 120, 180, the corresponding values of ψ_i are 0.531, 0.557, 0.550, 0.537, and 0.515. Taking 0.54 as a typical value here, slightly less than the 58 percent acceptance rate, we would expect to have gained only about 54 percent of the improvement over S.R.S. nominally available had proportional stratification been used in the HIS. In fact, proportional stratification was not used because it was infeasible with the large number of covariates considered in the HIS design, and the Finite Selection Model was used instead. We believe that 54 percent of the nominal gain also provides

Table 2. Disposition of the Health Insurance Study Enrollment Sample

	Dayton		Seattle[a]		Massachusetts[b]		South Carolina[c]		Total	
	No.	%	No.	%	No.	%	No.	%	No.	%
Families who completed baselines and were assigned to treatments	528		2054		1068		1232		4882	—
Families added to sample at enrollment interview[d]	[e]		101	5.2	46	4.5	89	7.8	236[f]	5.1[f]
Attrition due to nonrefusals (moved, unable to locate, ineligible, unable to verify insurance)	106	20.1	414	20.2	264	24.7	245	19.9	1029	21.1
Enrollment refusals	32	6.1	404	19.7	238	22.3	356	28.9	1030	21.1
Enrolled	390	73.9	1236	60.2	566	53.0	631	51.2	2823	57.8
Families interviewed for enrollment	422	79.9	1640	79.8	804	75.3	987	80.1	3853	78.9
Refused interview	4	0.9	147	9.0	108	13.4	125	12.7	384	10.0
Refused offer to enroll	28	6.6	257	15.7	130	16.2	231	23.4	646	16.8
Enrolled	390	92.4	1236	75.4	566	70.4	631	63.9	2823	73.3

[a] Includes a fee-for-service sample, a health maintenance organization sample, and a control group.
[b] Fitchburg-Leominster and Franklin County.
[c] Charleston and Georgetown County (includes a preexperimental control group sample).
[d] Line z is a subset of line 1.
[e] Not available.
[f] Excluding Dayton. The percentage figure is calculated as 236/(4882−236).

a rough percentage for the actual improvement over S.R.S. provided by the FSM after sample reduction in the field.

Two points need to be made in relation to (5.12). First, while the expected variance of $\hat{\mu}_i$ is given by (5.7), the actual amount varies randomly. When many treatments are involved, it is likely that some treatment effects will be estimated with much larger variance than (5.7) suggests. This is an additional argument against S.R.S. However, proportional stratification, even in the context of random nonacceptances, not only reduces the expected variance of the treatment effects, but it also reduces the variability of the actual precision from that expected. This is highly desirable, especially so in view of criticism that would be likely to occur if after the sample was selected it was observed that the actual assignments to treatments from strata were unbalanced (i.e., if m_{ij}/n_i is substantially different from p_j for some treatment stratum combinations). A second point is that the variances in (5.12) obtain with respect to the strata defined on the basis of the pre-experimental observations. The gains from proportional stratification with respect to the experimental observations would be diminished if the correlation between the two sets of observations is imperfect. Of course, S.R.S. does not suffer from this phenomenon.

If the variance of x_{ij} is not given by (5.1), but instead by v_{ij}/m_{ij} (i.e., depends upon stratum and treatment), or if the objective function (5.4) is replaced by a more general one, such as

$$\text{Var}(\hat{\mu}_i) = \sum_j W_{ij} \text{Var}(x_{ij}) \qquad (5.13)$$

with $W_{ij} \geq 0$ and fixed, then proportional stratification is not optimal. However, proportional stratification still is uniformly better than S.R.S., and formula (5.12) holds for the objective function (5.13). That is, even in this more general situation, the variance afforded by proportional sampling is a $(\psi_i, 1 - \psi_i)$ mixture of the proportional sampling variance resulting from no refusals, and of the expected S.R.S. variance.

The discussion thus far has treated the n_i as given. Let n_i^* be the desired value for n_i, i.e., the desired number of subjects to be assigned to treatment T_i. If π is the acceptance rate then $N_i = n_i^*/\pi$ selections would be made. Suppose the actual number of acceptances are random, so that n_i has a binomial distribution with parameters N_i and π. Then the mean of n_i is n_i^*, but since it would vary around this value, some loss of overall precision would be expected. Suppose the n_i^* were derived by minimizing a weighted sum of the variances of $\hat{\mu}_i$, each given by (5.6), subject to a cost constraint that assumes c_i is the cost of observing each subject on T_i. It is proved in the appendix under the assumptions just made, that the weighted variance achieved for the optimal n_i^* is increased approximately by the factor

$$1 + \frac{1-\pi}{E_c n^*}, \quad E_c n^* \equiv \frac{\sum n_i^* c_i}{\sum c_i}. \qquad (5.14)$$

This ordinarily is fairly small. For example, with $\pi = 0.58$ and $E_c n^* = 35$ being the approximate average number of families enrolled on each HIS insurance plan, a 1.2 percent increase in variance results.

We conclude this section by describing field constraints that acted in the Health Insurance Study to diminish the gains provided by the FSM. We have just showed that an imperfect acceptance rate reduces precision gains, unless the nonaccepting subjects are replaced by others from the same stratum. The sequential procedure needed to replace losses by subjects from the same stratum requires close contact with the field. Although it is worth some effort to implement, this is more difficult than it may seem for the following five reasons.

First, the enrollment process is more efficient if enrollers have many cases to work at any one time rather than a few, with replacements arriving only as cases are closed. Thus, the majority of the cases to be assigned (N_+ in Figure 3) should be assigned at the beginning of the enrollment period.

Second, at any particular time, families selected in the field are in one of four categories: they have dropped out of the sample because of ineligibility, etc.; they have accepted; they have refused; or they are in an indeterminant state because the field has not attempted to contact them; they have been hard to contact, their eligibility is being verified; there has been a change in family composition since the baseline interview; they are pondering the offer; and so on. The indeterminant category tends to be large through most of the enrollment period, and until it diminishes significantly, backup selections are not useful.

Third, a long time, sometimes six weeks, transpired after the field declared that a family could not be enrolled before a replacement selection could be fielded. While quicker communications could have been designed, some of the clerical and data processing procedures necessary to maintain control in administering such a large survey would have had to be circumvented. Processing data about the refusal, making the new selection, preparing legal documents for the newly selected family, and integrating the new selections into the field schedule involved coordination among Rand and two subcontractors that required careful control procedures, and inevitably, time.

Fourth, in the HIS the end of the field enrollment period came not long after most families had achieved a final enrollment/nonenrollment status, and by that time it was too late for the field to enroll those new families with enrollment complications. Replacing families near the end of the enrollment period could create a bias, because unless enrollers are given sufficient time to work on those families with enrollment complications (e.g., replacing those families who moved out, those changing composition, and those contemplating the offer), the experiment would be overloaded with problem-free families, and the acceptance rate would be lowered. Obviously, the responses of problem-free families to the treatments may well differ from the target population.

Fifth, the number of available backup families tends to be small in any stratum, unless large amounts are spent generating baseline interviews to purchase protection. Even if the true nonacceptance probability is the same for every stratum, random differences in the actual acceptance rate would deplete some strata of the necessary reserves, forcing some nonproportional stratification at the backup stage.

We will not consider the case in which the acceptance rate varies by stratum, or worse yet, varies on the basis of some unmeasured variable. The former problem can be corrected by using the true acceptance probabilities (although defining and estimating them may be difficult); the unmeasured variable problem is much harder.

The full benefits of proportional stratification in the HIS were reduced further by the need to make selections in "bursts." Burst is a term used in the HIS to refer to the fact that selections were made not one at one time, but in stages. The baseline period ended close to the beginning of the enrollment period in order to reduce the number of transitory changes in the sample, to reduce cost, and to get the experimental data as early as possible. Because of the time lag between administration of the baseline and availability of machine-readable data for selection (often several months), it was necessary to make selections before all baseline data were available. Thus, selections were made in stages; each stage was called a "burst." The number of bursts ranged from one to nine in the sites. Families that were harder to reach or whose insurance took longer to verify tended to appear in the later bursts. Since they are likely to differ systematically from other families (e.g., families living in multiple family units tended to be associated with later bursts), the burst itself was considered as a stratum. That is, each family was identified with a burst, and assignment of families to treatments was made proportionally from each burst. More bursts degrade efficiency gains of proportional sampling relative to random sampling because they reduce the number of options available for balancing the sample.

The final constraint that we will mention here is that the overall acceptance rate π is not known until after enrollment is complete, and one must work with an estimate $\hat{\pi}$. In the H.I.S. π differed from site to site, so that we were operating under uncertainty in every case. Furthermore, in the early bursts, one can not know for sure how many eligible families, which we shall call N_E, eventually will become available.

These two uncertainties make it uncertain what portion of families should be assigned to treatments in early bursts, and what portion should be withheld. Substantial penalties are paid for significant errors in either direction. Too few assignments cause field schedules to slip and lead to low field morale because enrollers are ready to work but don't have enough to do. Eventually they will be overworked near the end of the enrollment period, and therefore a full effort will not be made on the families selected with the final bursts. In this case some bias will result from undersampling those families. Of course, when it is realized later that more families should have been assigned from the early bursts, these selections would be made, but it is the release of these families that overburdens the field. On the other hand, too many selections from an early burst leads to overenrollment of that group, and if the enrollment targets (and budget) are not to be exceeded, the situation cannot be corrected later. If π and N_E are known, and if n_+ is the number of acceptances desired in the site, then the fraction of the burst that should be assigned is

$$\frac{(n_+/\pi)}{N_E} \tag{5.15}$$

since n_+/π is the number of selections that eventually would have to be made to get n_+ acceptances, and N_E is the number of families eventually eligible for selection. Therefore the product must be estimated. The conservative approach would choose a high value for this product, making undersampling of the burst much more likely than oversampling, and compensating later. This means the field period must be extended enough to provide time to pursue the replacement families from the early bursts as the actual number needed becomes known later.

Our recommendation is to protect against this situation by earmarking a balanced fraction of the enrollments (we used 20 percent in the last sites) and instructing the field office to set them aside until the other enrollment selections have been fielded and followed up. This keeps options open until near the end of the fielding period and eliminates the lag time in the likely event that some of the remaining selections must be used.

To summarize this section, blocking, proportional stratification, and the Finite Selection Model all can be used to improve the balance and precision of the estimates from an experiment. But the gains that they provide relative to simple random sampling are reduced by random nonacceptances, approximately in proportion to the nonacceptance rate. We discussed the principal reasons why, in the context of the HIS, a sequential procedure designed to replace nonaccepting families with others from the same stratum was infeasible, even though, if successful, such a procedure would reclaim the precision losses due to nonacceptances.

APPENDIX

By Carl Morris

Definition: Given k, n_+, and $(N_1,\ldots,N_k)$, the random vector $(n_1,\ldots,n_k)$ of nonnegative integers with $\Sigma n_i = n_+$ is distributed as the *Multivariate Hypergeometric Distribution*, $MGH_k(n_+; N_1,\ldots,N_k)$, if

$$P(n_1 = n_1^*,\ldots,n_k = n_k^*) = \frac{\binom{N_1}{n_1^*}\cdots\binom{N_k}{n_k^*}}{\binom{\Sigma N_i}{n_+}}. \tag{A.1}$$

The first two moments of $MHG_k(n_+; N_1,\ldots,N_k)$ are

$$En_i = n_+ p_i, \quad Var(n_i) = n_+ p_i(1-p_i)\frac{N_+ - n_+}{N_+ - 1} \tag{A.2}$$

where $N_+ \equiv \Sigma N_i$, $p_i \equiv N_i/N_+$. The expected value of the reciprocal of the i-th coordinate of MHG_k does not exist if $P(n_i = 0) > 0$, but

$$E\left(\frac{1}{n_i}\Big| n_i \geq 1\right) \doteq (1 + \gamma_i^2)\frac{1}{En_i} \tag{A.3}$$

with γ_i^2 being the squared coefficient of variation of n_i given by

$$\gamma_i^2 = \frac{Var(n_i)}{E^2 n_i} = \frac{1-p_i}{n_+ p_i}\frac{N_+ - n_+}{N_+ - 1}. \tag{A.4}$$

Formula (A.3) is determined by noting that for any random variable X with mean μ that since

$$\frac{\mu}{X} = 1 - \left(\frac{X-\mu}{\mu}\right) + \left(\frac{X-\mu}{\mu}\right)^2 - \left(\frac{X-\mu}{\mu}\right)^3\frac{\mu}{X}$$

that

$$E\frac{\mu}{X} = 1 + \frac{Var(X)}{\mu^2} - E\left(\frac{X-\mu}{X}\right)\left(\frac{X-\mu}{\mu}\right)^2.$$

The remainder term $E\left(\frac{X-\mu}{X}\right)\left(\frac{X-\mu}{\mu}\right)^2$ is ignored, which is legitimate for the expectation in (A.3) involving the hypergeometric distribution, provided $P(n_i = 0)$ is small and γ_i is small. In the examples we have looked at, satisfying $n_+ p_i \geq 4$ and $\pi \geq 0.5$ (note that $1 - \pi \doteq (N_+ - n_+)/(N_+ - 1)$ in (A.4)), the right-hand side of (A.3) is lower than the left-hand side, but by less than 4 percent, with diminishing error as $n_+ p_i$ increases. In Theorems (5.1) and (5.2) these errors are averaged over all strata, with smaller weights for small strata, thereby improving further the approximations in those theorems.

We turn to the proof of Theorems (5.1) and (5.2). Under the assumption of Theorem (5.1), N_i subjects are chosen at random from the N_+ available for treatment T_i. Then n_i accept at random from the N_i. Hence the accepting subjects also are a random sample of size n_i from the N_+ available. Since the stratum sizes available are $(p_1 N_+, \ldots, p_k N_+)$, the conditional distribution of the numbers selected for T_i, i.e., of $(m_{i1}, \ldots, m_{ik})$, subject to $\Sigma_j m_{ij} = n_i$ with n_i given, is

$$(m_{i1}, m_{i2}, \ldots, m_{ik}) \sim MHG_k(n_i; p_1 N_+, \ldots, p_k N_+). \tag{A.5}$$

It follows from (A.2), (A.3) and (A.4) that

$$\sigma^2 E_{SRS} \Sigma p_j^2 / m_{ij} \doteq \sigma^2 \Sigma p_j^2 \frac{1}{n_i p_j} \left(1 + \frac{1-p_j}{n_i p_j} \cdot \frac{N_+ - n_i}{N_+ - 1}\right), \tag{A.6}$$

and this reduces to (5.7).

Under the assumption of n_i random acceptances from N_i offers, where proportional stratification requires $m_{ij}^* = N_i p_j$ assignments to be made from S_j to T_i, then

$$(m_{i1}, \ldots, m_{ik}) \sim MHG_k(n_i; p_1 N_i, \ldots, p_k N_i). \tag{A.7}$$

This is formally equivalent to (A.5) with N_i replacing N_+. Theorem (5.2) therefore follows from Theorem (5.1) with N_+ replaced by N_i.

Finally, (5.14) needs proof. If n_i^* minimizes $\sigma^2 \Sigma w_i / n_i$ subject to the budget constraint $\Sigma c_i n_i = C$, then

$$n_i^* \propto (w_i / c_i)^{\frac{1}{2}}. \tag{A.8}$$

With $n_i \sim$ binomial $(n_i^* / \pi, \pi)$, then $E n_i = n_i^*$, $Var(n_i) = n_i^*(1-\pi)$. The approximation (A.3) also holds for the binomial distribution, and therefore $E \, 1/n_i \doteq (1 + (1-\pi)/n_i^*)/n_i^*$. It follows that

$$\sigma^2 E \Sigma w_i / n_i \doteq \sigma^2 \Sigma w_i / n_i^* (1 + (1-\pi)/n_i^*)$$
$$= \sigma^2 \Sigma w_i / n_i^* \left(1 + (1-\pi) \frac{\Sigma w_i / n_i^{*2}}{\Sigma w_i n_i^* / n_i^{*2}}\right)$$
$$= \sigma^2 \Sigma w_i / n_i^* (1 + (1-\pi)/E_c n^*) \tag{A.9}$$

since $w_i / n_i^{*2} \propto c_i$. Formula (5.14) follows.

FOOTNOTES

The research reported herein was performed pursuant to the Health Insurance Study grant from the U.S. Department of Health, Education, and Welfare, Washington, D.C. The opinions and conclusions expressed herein are solely those of the authors and should not be construed as representing the opinions or policy of any agency of the United States Government.

1. A detailed description can be found in Newhouse (1974).
2. We use the term unbiased sample loosely to mean that the probability of selection is not affected in unknown ways.
3. The problem is analogous to the theory of the second best. Imposing the requirement of an unbiased sample when there are resulting limitations on analysis is analogous to insisting that one marginal condition be satisfied when another cannot be.
4. A HIS participant who enters the military is suspended; therefore, those with military experience will be underrepresented. College dormitories were not sampled because of the mobility of students and the likelihood that students would continue to use a student health service even if national health insurance were enacted; as a result, college students will also be underrepresented.
5. The problem discussed in this section arises whether the classification variable is continuous (e.g., income) or discrete (e.g., employment status), so long as the preexperimental values are not perfectly correlated with the experimental values.
6. We say "unweighted" because (3.1) and (3.2) are the simple averages ignoring the preexperimental income category; i.e., total response divided by total number of subjects in each experimental income vategory.

REFERENCES

Conlisk, John (July 1973), "Choice of Response Functional Form in Designing Subsidy Experiments," *Econometrica* 41(4): 643–656.

——, and Harold Watts (1969), "A Model for Optimizing Experimental Designs for Estimating Response Surfaces," *Proceedings of the Social Statistics Section*, American Statistical Association, pp. 150–156.

Hall, Robert E. (1975), "Effects of the Experimental Negative Income Tax on Labor Supply," in *Work Incentives and Income Guarantees*, ed. Pechman, Joseph, and Timpane, P. Michael (1975) Washington, D.C.: Brookings Institution. pp. 115–147.

Manning, Willard G., Bridger M. Mitchell, and Jan P. Acton (November 1976), "Design of the Los Angeles Peak-Load Pricing Experiment for Electricity," The Rand Corporation, R-1955-DWP.

Morris, Carl (1975), "A Finite Selection Model for Experimental Design of the Health Insurance Study," Proceedings of the Social Statistics Section, American Statistical Association, pp. 78–85.

Newhouse, Joseph P. (March 1974), "A Design for a Health Insurance Experiment," *Inquiry* 11(1): 5–27.

Phelps, Charles E. (1976), "Demand for Reimbursement Insurance," in *The Role of Health Insurance in the Health Services Sector*, ed. Richard Rosett New York: National Bureau of Economic Research.

LABOR SUPPLY BEHAVIOR OF ANIMAL WORKERS: TOWARDS AN EXPERIMENTAL ANALYSIS

Raymond C. Battalio, TEXAS A&M UNIVERSITY

John H. Kagel, TEXAS A&M UNIVERSITY

Leonard Green, WASHINGTON UNIVERSITY

Recently we have begun to carry out a series of experimental studies of labor supply behavior using laboratory animals as subjects. While experimental studies using nonhumans as subjects are relatively new to economics, a considerable history of this type of research exists in other disciplines; particularly in psychology and behavioral biology. Since our experimental paradigm is, in part, based on the accumulated research results and laboratory technologies from these other disciplines, which we do not anticipate that many economists are familiar with, our primary goal in this paper so to summarize this research as it is relevant to studying labor supply behavior. In addition, we will present the design and some results from our initial series of experimental studies in this area, and indicate how the procedures can be extended to investigate a wide range of issues that are of general interest to economists.

We begin with a discussion of the experimental procedures under which we are able to study the labor supply behavior of animal workers; i.e., we present the interpretation used for the basic concepts of wage rate, quantity of labor supplied, income, and the effort price of income under which we propose to study the labor supply behavior of animal workers. This is followed by a presentation of empirical results from experimental studies in psychology and biology which indicate that the interpretation system used captures the essential properties of the labor supply process as presented in economics. In the concluding section we outline the design of the labor supply experiments we are currently doing and suggest extensions of the procedures used to other areas, such as studies of income distribution and multiple job holding.

I. EXPERIMENTAL PARADIGM

As early as 1953, B. F. Skinner suggested that the fixed-ratio schedules being used to study the behavior of laboratory animals and humans could be viewed as piecework wage rates. Under a fixed-ratio (FR) schedule the organism receives payment only after making a fixed number of responses.[1] For example, with a FR 10 every 10th response results in a payment being made. The responses required can be of any form (subject to biological constraints) such as lever presses, pecks, revolutions of a running wheel, or deposting marbles. In this respect a FR schedule can be compared to wage payment schemes based on the number of units of output produced, such as the number of shirts sewn, boxes packed, or operations of a machine or engines assembled. In both cases, the total payment depends directly on the worker's output rather than the hours worked or the speed of work per se.

In using laboratory animals as workers it is technically possible in most cases to use some form of money or other conditioned reinforcer in making wage payments, e.g., chimpanzees work to earn money in the form of poker chips after they have learned that the poker chips can be spent to purchase primary reinforcers, such as grapes, from a vending machine. However, in most cases, pragmatic considerations result in making wage payments to these subjects directly in the form of consumption goods or services. Such is the case in our studies using rats, where training these animals to handle money or another conditioned reinforcer would result in a considerable increase in the cost of the experiments conducted. In view of the fact that using direct wage payments in the form of goods does not result in any essential differences in the interpretation or measurement of real wages and income within economic theory, the increased costs of introducing a form of money in these experiments does not seem to be warranted at this time.

In the experimental paradigm presented below, the piecework output is a lever press, and wage payments are made directly in the form of fixed units of a single commodity. The subject is placed in an experimental chamber for a fixed period each day. The experimental chamber contains a lever and a dispenser for liquid or food mounted on the front panel of the chamber. Operation of the lever a predetermined number of times results in the delivery of a fixed amount of the fluid or food. No restrictions are placed on either the amount of labor supplied or the total income earned during an experimental session. The predetermined length of the experimental session is the only constraint. Under this interpretation the real wage is the quantity of the commodity received per lever press and the total labor supplied during an experimental session is the total lever presses per session. (We assume that the time for a response is constant, although inter-response times may vary.) Total income earned during a session is calculated by multiplying the total labor supplied (the total number of lever presses) by the real wage rate (the quantity of some commodity obtained per lever press).

Consider the case where a subject is required to lever press ten times (FR 10) to receive payment of 0.10 ml. of some fluid such as sucrose solution or root beer. Under the interpretation system proposed, the rat faces a real wage of 0.10 ml. of fluid per 10 lever presses. If we double the work requirement (FR 20) while keeping payment constant (0.10 ml.) the real wage will be halved. Similarly, if we halve the work requirement (FR 5) while keeping payment constant, the real wage will double. Since the absolute value of the real wage rate depends on the units of measurement chosen for the unit of payment and the unit of work, we will adopt the convention of presenting real wages as an index with a value of 100 based at about the midpoint of the real wage changes studied. For the above example the real wage index would be equal to 100 for FR 10, 50 for FR 20 and 200 for FR 5.

The labor-leisure constraints for the example used above are shown in Figure 1. The constraint $Z°$ corresponds to a real wage index of 100 (10 presses per 0.10 ml.). If the subject chooses the income-leisure bundle A with a total quantity of labor supplied equal to 1,000 lever presses, the total income earned will be 10 ml. of fluid. Constraint Z'' corresponds to a real wage index of 50 (FR 20) with the choice of point B involving a total quantity of labor supplied of 600 lever presses and an earned income of 3.0 ml. of fluid. Similarly, if we double the initial wage (FR 10 to FR 5) we obtain constraint Z' with real wage equal to 200. A total labor supplied of 750 lever presses now results in an income of 15 ml. of fluid. In terms of the changes in the labor-leisure constraint, *increases* in the fixed ratio correspond

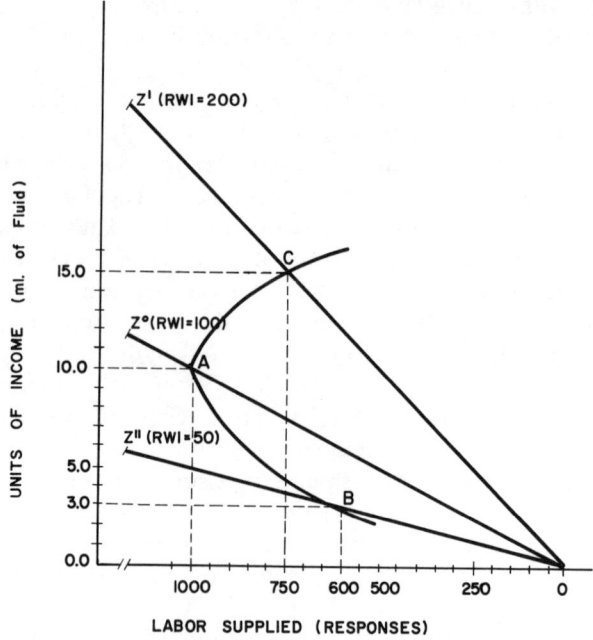

Figure 1. Labor-Leisure Choice Space.

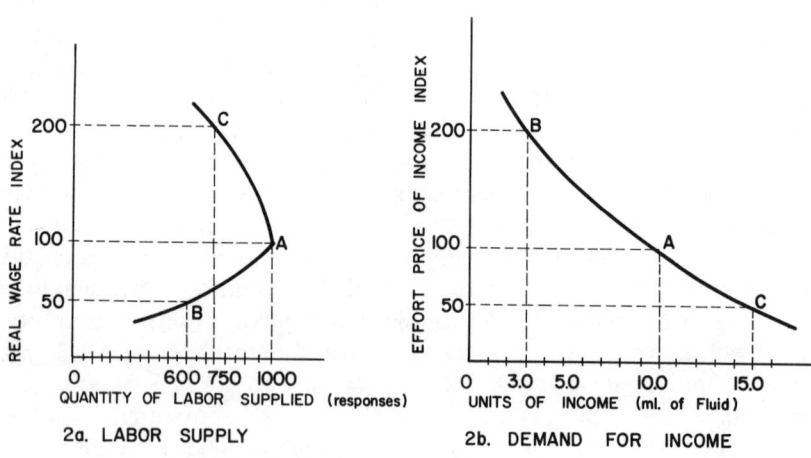

2a. LABOR SUPPLY

2b. DEMAND FOR INCOME

Figure 2.

to *decreases* in the real wage rate, and *decreases* in the fixed ratio correspond to *increases* in the real wage rate and will be referred to as such.

Although the diagram in Figure 1 is useful to illustrate changes in the budget constraint associated with experimental changes in the real wage rate, labor supply schedules are usually presented in the form shown in Figure 2a, where we have plotted the three data points from the numerical example used in Figure 1 and sketched a labor supply curve through these points.

In addition to the qualitative shape of the labor supply schedule we will also examine the relationship between the real wage rate and the level of earned income. The conceptual approach taken here follows that introduced by L. Robbins (1930) in that we examine the relationship between the effort price of income and the demand for income. Under our interpretation, the effort price of income is the number of lever presses (amount of labor) required to earn a given unit of income. This is, of course, the reciprocal of the real wage rate defined above. Indexing the effort price at 100 for 10 lever presses per 0.10 ml. of fluid, Figure 2b shows the relationship between effort price and demand for income for the example used in Figure 1. These illustrative data indicate an important empirical regularity in the data to be presented below; an inverse relationship exists between the effort price of income and the demand for income throughout most of the range of wage rates studied. The relationship between this "law of demand" for income and the shape of the labor supply schedule is: (1) when the elasticity of the labor supply curve is positive, such as between points B and A in Figure 2a, the demand for income is always inversely related to the effort price of income and (2) when the elasticity of labor supply is negative, such as between points A and C, in Figure 2a, it must be between 0 and -1 to obtain a downward-sloping demand curve for income.

Since the behavioral response being interpreted as work, lever pressing, was also present in our earlier studies of consumer demand behavior with the work component being largely ignored, it is worthwhile to discuss how we made such a transformation. Several comments are relevant. First, in a technical sense, spending one's income always involves some component of energy expenditure or effort. The decision of whether or not to ignore this in organizing consumption behavior is always a pragmatic decision based on some idea of the relative importance of this component for the particular problem under investigation. In the consumer demand studies the work component has been kept at minimum levels. In addition, subjects always faced an effective binding constraint on their lever presses; i.e., they would have lever pressed a greater number of times if the constraint were removed. In contrast, in the labor supply experiments reported total lever-pressing requirements per session are considerably greater than those required in the consumer demand studies and, more importantly, no constraint is placed on the number of effective lever presses. Subjects in the labor supply studies can, and do, change their income levels in response to changes in the work (lever pressing) requirements. Therefore, the subject's behavior can be characterized by a labor-leisure model where increased income earnings are traded off against reduced leisure, with leisure interpreted as the time spent on nonwork activities such as self-cleaning, sleeping, etc. Furthermore, an explicit accounting of the work components in the consumer demand studies would only result in changing the absolute value of the prices and not in changing their relative values. However, irrespective of both our considerations in adopting this interpretation and the empirical results reported, the efficiency of retaining this interpretation in future consumer demand studies remains open to further empirical investigation.[2]

A second point to consider in interpreting the lever pressing response as work is that no activity is work (or leisure) per se. Activities such as fishing, golfing, woodworking, or research are, at times, classified as work and, at other times, classified as leisure. While economics does include studies of the total allocation of time to alternative activities, the concept of work in the labor supply literature is usually interpreted as those activities performed in exchange for income. In this context any activity is interpreted as work if wage payments are associated with the activity. This point is dramatically illustrated in token economy research where labor supply behavior in response to changing wage rates are remarkably similar across such diverse jobs as self-care activities, floor mopping and factory assembly-type jobs (Kagel et al., 1977).

Although the range of activities grouped under the heading of work may be diverse, there are certain basic characteristics common to the economic concept of work which animal workers also display. For example, when given a choice between two similar jobs (say, two levers to press) providing qualitatively similar sources of income earnings (say, the same kind of food pellets), changes in the relative wage rates (ratio requirements) of the jobs always results in the animal's increasing the quantity of labor supplied to the job whose relative wage rate has increased. Further, work is exclusively confined to the job with the higher real wage rate when the differential approaches 3 or 4 to 1 (Herrnstein, 1958; Herrnstein and Loveland, 1975). This response to changing relative wage rates is predicted on the basis of the matching law in psychology (Herrnstein, 1958; Rachlin, 1976), and has also been observed for human workers in token economies (Kagel et al., 1977). Since complete specialization typically does not occur until the wage rate differntial approaches 3 or 4 to 1, economic theory would posit the existence of a difference in the nonpecuniary or psychic income associated with the jobs (Becker, 1971, p. 170). Evidence supporting the presence of such returns is provided by the fact that in the absence of any wage rate differentials animals typically work one of the jobs a disproprotionate amount of the time.

One can find a number of basis for such nonpecuniary returns reported in the literature, e.g., mice exhibit definite signs of left or right-handedness which, other things being equal, would not make them indifferent between two jobs (levers) situated at different locations in the experimental chamber (Collins, 1975).

We have also found in our laboratory that if a dish of food pellets is left on the cage floor, or if a water tube is hung on the door of the experimental chamber, the amount of lever pressing that pays off in that currency is greatly diminished, although the response rate does not drop to zero provided that lever pressing still results in income being earned. The existence of positive work levels in the presence of "free" income of the same kind would also be explained, within economic theory, in terms of non-pecuniary returns associated with the job tasks in question. However, in this case the evidence would suggest that such non-pecuniary returns are learned and are a result of some sort of classical conditioning or secondary reinforcer effects in terms of lights and sounds associated with the delivery of payments in the past (Koop et al., 1976; Wallace et al., 1973).

It is, of course, quite clear that there are no *exact* physical analogs in advanced industrialized economies to the experimental procedures described above for studying income-leisure choices for animals. However, what we argue is that these procedures define a choice process which contains all of the characteristics required to define a logically consistent interpretation system for a simple Slutsky-Hicks labor supply model. Having operationalized this labor-leisure choice process in the laboratory, one can use it to examine certain essential properties of the model such as the negativity of own substitution effects. The frequently made assumption that leisure (not working) is a superior good can be examined throughout the choice set. Further, having thoroughly explored behavior under these simplified conditions, we can add more complex characteristics to the process under investigation.

For example, alternative kinds of job tasks can be studied, including ones that exhibit nonpecuniary returns (nonzero response rates in the absence of explicit payoffs), and highly preferred (or multiple) commodities can be introduced into the animal's choice set, including nonfood items, to overcome any potential "satiation" problems. (We use the term "satiation" advisedly here since, for a given work requirement, animals are known to work and consume significantly greater amounts of more preferred commodities.) Suggestions as to the nature of these extensions of the experimental procedures are reserved for the concluding section.

The data presented below is taken from several experimental studies reported in the psychology and physiology literature. Each of these studies was designed to examine particular questions other than labor supply behavior per se and, as a result, the experimental designs (including the commodities used) reflect the particular questions under study. Although the questions examined in these studies and the overall results obtained are interesting, given the goals of this paper they will not be reported here. (Interested readers are directed to the sources cited.) We will only report those aspects of the experimental design and results that are relevant to evaluating labor supply behavior. That is, our goal in surveying this literature is to provide the experimental results that have guided us in designing our experimental studies of labor supply behavior using laboratory animals.

II. RESULTS FROM OTHER STUDIES

a. Labor Supply with Ethanol Payments: Meisch and Thompson (1973)

This study was conducted to examine various aspects of behavior under self-administered ethanol (ethyl alcohol) (Meisch and Thompson, 1973). The subjects were male rats that were individually housed in home cages with water always available. During the experimental sessions the animals were housed in experimental chambers with two levers, a food magazine, and a dipper for presenting liquid. Each operation of the dipper mechanism made available 0.25 ml. of liquid for four seconds. Operations of the lever controlling the food magazine produced no effect, i.e., this lever was inoperative during the experimental sessions. The experimental procedures consisted of placing a rat in the experimental chamber for six hours each day. During the experimental sessions in which the animals were food deprived, they were maintained at 80 percent of their free feeding weight. For the nondeprived experimental series food was always available in the home cages.

The experimental design consisted of making 8 percent (W/V) ethanol available during the six-hour experimental session every third day, with water available during the remaining sessions. Each animal was exposed to ethanol for two or more sessions at each wage rate (fixed-ratio value) and was not switched to the next wage rate until the quantity of labor supplied (responding) stabilized. Wage rates were changed in a decreasing order and the sequence of wage rate changes were run first when the animal was food deprived and then under nondeprived conditions.

The quantity of labor supplied per session under food deprived and nondeprived conditions is shown in Table 1. Several general characteristics are apparent in these data. In most cases, the maximal quantity of labor supplied is observed at an intermediate level of real wages, producing the general shape of a "backward bending" labor supply schedule. In addition, the maximal quantity of labor supplied by each subject is substantially greater than the quantity observed for the same subject at very high and/or very low wage rates. Comparing the two labor supply schedules for each

Table 1[a]. Real Wages and Labor Supplied

Real Wage Index[b]	Labor Supplied per Session (Responses)							
	Subject 856		Subject 861		Subject 864		Subject 865	
	Food Dep.	Non Dep.	Food Dep.	Non Dep.	Food Dep.	Non Dep.	Food Dep.	Non Dep.
1,600	61	28	67	55	122	48	88	40
800	140	55	130	101	175	75	142	65
400	260	75	326	136	410	180	438	104
200	456	216	536	432	552	317	624	197
100	584	187	1,000	795	1,184	208	1,704	187
50	416	139	1,616	597	1,248	160	2,512	213
25	—[c]	—	2,496	811	640	—	3,808	—
13	—	—	1,344	683	—	—	896	—
6	—	—	256	—	—	—	640	—

[a]The data is for responses that were reinforced and is the average of the final sessions reported in Meisch and Thompson (1971), Tables 1–6. The initial and final sessions at wage equal 1,600 were averaged together.
[b]The real wage index was based on a lever pressing requirement of FR 16. The actual FR values used were 1, 2, 4, 8, 16, 32, 64, 128 and 256.
[c]The "—" indicates insufficient total responses to receive any fluid.

subject reveals that under food deprivation the quantity of labor supplied is greater at all wages with the "backward bending" portion beginning at a lower real wage rate. Although ethanol's caloric value may be a factor in the greater labor supply observed during food deprivation, rats' intake of morphine solution—which has no caloric value—also approximately doubles under food deprivation. In addition, since considerable ethanol is consumed under nondeprived conditions, this suggests that there are other factors, in addition to caloric value, which act to determine ethanol consumption (Meisch and Thompson, 1971; Meisch and Thompson, 1973).

Figure 3a presents the labor supply data from Table 1 for subject # 856. In Figure 3b the demand for income in terms of the effort price of income index is shown for the same subject. The inverse relationship between the effort price of income and the demand for income shown in Figure 3b is a common characteristic of all four subjects as indicated by the data in Table 2. In both figures above the curves were sketched freehand to indicate their characteristic shapes. This general tendency for income to increase as real wages increase (i.e., the effort price of income falls) is replicated in all of the data sets reported below. [Discussion of the occassional reversals reported at very high wage rats (FR $\leq$ 10) is deferred until the rest of the data has been presented.]

Two additional results from this study are relevant to our interpretation of the data reported above. First, during the experimental days that water

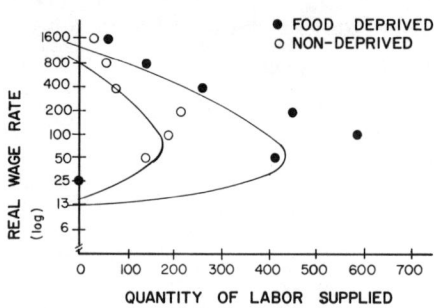
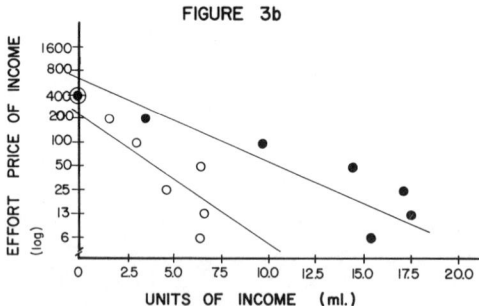

Figure 3. Labor Supply and Income Demand.

Table 2. Demand for Income

Effort Price of Income[b]	Income[a] Earned per Session [ml. of 8% (W/V) Ethanol]							
	Subject 856		Subject 861		Subject 864		Subject 865	
	Food Dep.	Non Dep.	Food Dep.	Non Dep.	Food Dep.	Non Dep.	Food Dep.	Non Dep.
1,600	—	—	0.25	—	—	—	0.63	—
800	—	—	2.63	1.33	—	—	1.75	—
400	—	—	9.75	3.16	2.50	—	14.88	—
200	3.25	1.08	12.63	4.67	9.75	1.25	19.63	1.67
100	9.13	2.92	15.63	12.42	18.50	3.25	26.63	2.92
50	14.25	6.75	16.75	13.50	17.25	9.92	19.50	6.17
25	16.25	4.67	20.38	8.50	25.63	11.25	27.38	6.50
13	17.50	6.92	16.25	12.67	21.88	9.33	17.75	8.17
6	15.30	6.88	16.75	13.71	30.44	11.96	22.06	9.96

[a]Income calculated by using the response data in Table 1 and valuing each dipper cup presentation as 0.25 ml.
[b]The effort price of income index is based at the same FR value as in Table 1.

replaced ethanol as the source of income payment the level of labor supplied was substantially smaller, with no subject earning any income at a wage rate index of 25 or lower even under the food deprived condition. The maximal labor supplied by any subject was about 120 responses for subject # 864 when the wage rate index was 100 and the subject was food deprived. One factor accounting for this difference between the response rates for water and ethanol is that the subjects were deprived of ethanol in their home cages while having unlimited access to water. Independent research by Premack (1965), reported below, indicates that the greater the level of deprivation of a given commodity or activity in the home cage, the greater the quantity of labor supplied during the experimental session at each wage rate to gain access to that commodity or activity, other things equal.[3] However, independent of the factors accounting for this behavior, this data clearly demonstrates that the quantity of labor supplied is not independent of the income payment. Further evidence for this proposition is contained in the experiment by Collier and Jennings (1969) reported on below.

Second, since the experimental chamber had an additional lever with no programmed consequence, this served as a control for nonspecific lever pressing. Three of the subjects had modal values of zero responses on this lever and one subject, # 861, had modal values of 3 and 1 during food deprivation and nondeprivation, respectively. These low levels of responding indicate that the labor supply patterns reported in Tables 2 and 3 were a result of experimentally inducing value on the arbitrary job task and not simply some random response pattern. While these results may not be surprising, they are important in terms of our interpretation of the underlying income-leisure choice process being studied.

The basic characteristics of the labor supply behavior reported above have been systematically replicated over the higher wage rates shown in Table 1 for nondeprived subjects using 32 percent (W/V) ethanol solution as the wage payment (Meisch and Thompson, 1972).[4] In addition, the experimental sessions were of one hour duration in contrast to the six-hour sessions reported above. The similarity in the underlying labor supply behavior observed across experimental sessions of quite different durations is an important regularity that will be discussed further below.

b. Labor Supply with Two Types of Sucrose Payments: Collier and Jennings (1969)

Two series of experiments were run on groups of 9 rats; one group using a 16 percent sucrose solution for the wage payment and another group using a 64 percent sucrose solution (Collier and Jennings, 1969). Each dipper presentation contained 0.12 ml. of sucrose solution. All subjects were given a total caloric intake each day equal to 64 percent of the ad lib

Table 3[a]. Real Wages, Labor Supplied and Income Demand

Real Wage Index[b]	Labor Supplied		Effort Price of Income	Income-ml. of Fluid	
	16% Sucrose	64% Sucrose		16% Sucrose	64% Sucrose
400	650	550	800	0.01	0.19
200	862	975	400	0.11	0.76
100	675	1279	200	0.63	1.87
50	422	1249	100	2.03	3.84
25	150	1010	50	5.17	5.85
13	20	500	25	7.80	6.60

[a] Data from Collier and Jennings (1969) and will contain some errors of interpolation. These errors are not however, large relative to the intended use of the data in this paper.

Data are for the 16% and 64% groups with a 12.5 gm. bar weight. Each column is an average of 9 subjects and includes those subjects that failed to complete ratio runs at the lowest two wage rates, FR 160 and FR 320.

[b] The real wage index and the effort price of income index were calculated with FR 40 as base.

intake, with additional food provided in the home cages as needed. The experiment consisted of 30 min. sessions daily with the wage index varying from 400 to 13 (FR values of 10, 20, 40, 80, 160 and 320) presented in descending order. The number of sessions at each wage rate varied between 10 and 14, depending upon when stability was reached. The data reported are the average values for the last three sessions at each wage rate.

The total quantity of labor supplied, presented in Table 3, for the 64 percent concentration is generally greater at each wage rate than for the 16 percent solution. Under both concentrations the labor supply schedule is "backward bending." The relationship between the two labor supply schedules is similar to that reported by Meisch and Thompson (1971) above in that the labor supply schedule with the greatest quantity of labor supplied over most wage rates (the 64 percent concentration) reaches its maximum at a lower wage rate. Since the subjects did not have access to sucrose solutions in their home cages, these data provide support for the proposition that changes in the choice set available from income earnings can be used to change the position and shape of the labor supply schedule.[5] We note in closing that in both cases the demand for income is inversely related to its effort price.

c. Labor Supply with Food Payments: Collier, Hirsch and Hamlin (1972)

In this experiment two rats were continuously housed in separate experimental chambers for 24 hours a day except for a brief time each day when they were weighed and commodities were replenished (1972). Each subject obtained all of its food by lever pressing with each operation of the food dispenser producing one (standard) 45 mg. rat pellet. Water was available continuously from a drinking tube. The real wage rate index was decreased from 1000 to 4 (FR values of 1, 5, 10, 20 followed by increments of 20 until FR 240 reached). Each schedule remained in effect 10 days. Two additional control animals were fed 45 mg. rat pellets ad lib and two more were fed Purina rat chow ad lib.

Both experimental subjects increased their labor supplied sufficiently to maintain constant income earnings through a wage rate of 50 (Fr 20), with the quantity of labor supplied increasing from about 500 to about 10,000 responses per day. Further reductions in wage rates were always associated with decreases in income even though the labor supplied continued to increase up until the lowest 4 wage rates studied (FR $\leq$ 160). Beyond Fr 160 (wage index $\leq$ 6) some decreases in the quantity of labor supplied were observed. Remarkably enough, normal growth rates were maintained for wage rates of between 50 to 13 (FR 20 to FR 80) even though income was falling. Beyond this point, further wage decreases and the associated income reductions resulted in the subjects no longer maintaining normal growth rates compared to the control animals.[6] Although this study differs from the previous studies, both in the nature of the commodity used for the wage payment and in the length of the session, the labor supply behavior observed has the same general characteristics. These results have been replicated using Guinea Pigs as subjects (Hersch and Collier, 1974).

d. Labor Supply with Ethanol Payments and Human Subjects: Bigelow and Liebson (1972)

The study by Bigelow and Liebson (1972) differs from the above experiments in that human subjects were employed. Two male, skid row, chronic alcoholic volunteers were housed in a hospital behavioral research ward. The subjects earned alcohol for consumption by operating a lever mechanism similar in function to those used in the above experiments. When a subject had completed the fixed-ratio requirement on the lever a sonalert tone sounded and a drink, consisting of 1 oz. of 95-proof ethanol in 2 oz. of orange juice, was dispensed. (An upper limit of 3 drinks per hour and 24 drinks per day was imposed.) The fixed-ratio requirements varied between 100 and 5,000 responses per drink with each value in effect for three or four days.

The data in Table 4 indicates that the labor supply schedules for these human subjects have the same basic characteristics as the labor supply schedules for the laboratory animals in the earlier ethanol experiments. In fact, plotting the data for subject H (Figure 4) and comparing it to the earlier figure for rat # 859 shows very few differences; the major one being the greater number of data points for the laboratory animal which reflects the relatively lower costs of conducting experiments using nonhumans as

Table 4[a]. Real Wages, Labor Supplied and Income Demand

Real Wage Index[b]	Labor Supplied (Responses)		Effort Price of Income	Income-Number of Drinks	
	Subject H	Subject St		Subject H	Subject St
1,000	1,700	2,400	500	2.00	2.00
100	15,250	21,500	300	8.00	9.00
33	24,000	27,000	100	15.25	21.50
20	10,000	10,000	10	17.00	24.00

[a]Data from Figures 1 and 2 in Bigelow and Liebson (1972) and will contain some small errors in interpolation.
[b]The fixed-ratio values were FR 5000, FR 3000, FR 1000 and FR 100. The index is based at FR 1000.

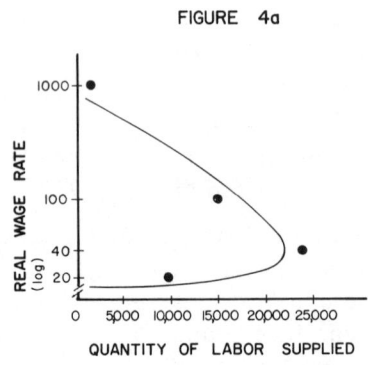

FIGURE 4a

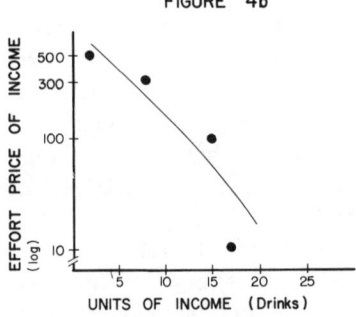

FIGURE 4b

Figure 4. Labor Supply and Income Demand.

compared to human subjects. In this instance it is quite clear that over the range of real wage rates studied the ethanol-leisure preference relationship is not lexical, with substantial reductions in work taking place at the lowest wage rate for both subjects. The income data for both subjects also show an inverse relationship between the effort price of income and income earnings.

e. Summary and Implications

Although the studies reported above were not designed to examine the labor supply behavior of laboratory animals, when taken together they provide considerable data that is of relevance in designing labor supply experiments using animal workers. With respect to the individual's labor supply schedules, we found that the quantity of labor supplied varies with the real wage rate in a systematic manner producing characteristic "backward bending" labor supply schedules. This relationship between wages and quantity of labor supplied was found across several species under a variety of experimental conditions. Furthermore, the resulting demand for income was inversely related to the effort price of income over most of the effort prices studied, as L. Robbins (1930) conjectured a number of years ago. Subject to the possible limitations discussed below, these results suggest that the "Law of Demand" for income be added as an empirical premise in theories of labor supply behavior similar to the way the "Law of Demand" for consumer goods is employed in consumer demand theory. In this context it is of interest to note that laboratory animals also obey the law of demand for commodities (Kagel et al., 1975).

As indicated in Figure 3 and Tables 2 and 3 above, at very high wage rates the demand for income in terms of the effort price of income is very inelastic, with occasional reversals in the inverse relationship for the mean data reported. Although we do not know why the demand for income asymptotes out at the particular real wage rates it does in the above studies, our own research indicates that the day to day variability in income is likely to be relatively large at these wage rates ($FR \leq 10$). In view of the small changes in the mean income earned associated with the changes in effort price over this range of wage rates and the relatively large day-to-day variability in income earnings, determining the precise relationship between the effort price of income and the demand for income at these wage rates is likely to be a relatively expensive research task.[7] Although determining this relationship may be an interesting problem, for present purposes research economy dictates that we study labor-leisure choice processes under conditions where the effect of the changes in real wage rates on earned income is large relative to the day-to-day variability.

A further empirical regularity of note is the similarity in labor supply responses obtained under experimental sessions of differing durations.

Since shorter session lengths allow for more than one subject per day to be run with the same fixed capital, discovering these similarities in experimental results under varying session lengths is of great pragmatic value. That is, although it appears that the position of the labor schedule may shift with the length of the session, e.g., a greater number of eating or drinking bursts may occur during longer sessions, it also appears that the underlying behavioral process is such that a one or two hour session is adequate to examine most questions posed.

Finally, the use of foods and liquids as the form of wage payment might be expected to impose severe limitations on the labor supply process studied. In this respect it is important to note that considerable variation in consumption can be induced by changing the characteristics of the commodities used. For example, Ernits and Corbit (1973) have shown that rats will consume 20–30 ml. of such "good tasting" commodities as sucrose, sodium saccharin or glucose during a one-hour session even though they have ad lib access to water the remaining 23 hours of the day. Further, total fluid consumption increased from about 45 ml. per day when water was available during the one-hour session to about 65 ml. per day when the alternative fluids were available during the one-hour session. We have obtained similar results when root beer was introduced as a fluid with water concurrently available. Indeed, under certain concentrations of a combined mixture of sodium saccharin and glucose, rats will regularly consume over 200 ml. of fluid per day, with occasional 24-hour periods during which they consume greater than their own body weight (Smith et al., 1976). These data show that there is considerable room for studying income-leisure choice using animal workers with foods and/or liquids as the form of income payments. In addition, food and liquid are not unique with respect to their ability to increase the level of responding on some arbitrary task, e.g., wage payments in the form of access to an activity wheel or intercranial self-stimulation have been used to increase the level of work (lever pressing). Premack's (1973) experiments showing that one can readily change in "job" task to a "consumption good" by altering home cage deprivation levels also support this, as well as indicating a method for operationalizing job tasks with high "nonpecuniary" returns.

III. TESTS OF CONSISTENCY AND EXTENSIONS

While the studies reported above are certainly suggestive that the kinds of labor-leisure trade-offs we talk about in economics are present for animal workers there is still substantial room for testing the processes specified within the theory. In designing our initial experiments we have decided to test the strong axiom of revealed preference as it applies in the labor-leisure

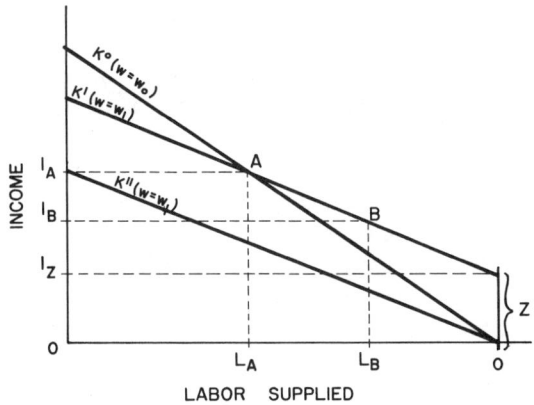

Figure 5. Experimental Design.

context. The basic structure of these experiments is shown in Figure 5, where budget line K° represents a baseline (initial) wage rate, W_0, with zero nonwage income. Suppose that the labor-leisure bundle $A(L_A, I_A)$ is selected under these conditions. Then by selecting a new wage rate lower than the initial wage rate ($W_1 < W_0$) and increasing the nonwage income to I_Z a new budget line K' can be made to pass through the original bundle A. Consistent behavior now requires that the new equilibrium bundle contain less income than I_A and less labor than L_A, i.e., some point on budget line K' to the right of A such as B. Removal of the non-wage income would result in a parallel shift in the budget line from K' to K''.

In experiments underway with pigeons as workers, subjects work (key peck) for limited access to a feeder magazine containing grain. In these experiments variable-ratio schedules are used where the labor supply requirement for any given wage payment varies randomly with a predetermined average value; e.g., in a variable-ratio schedule 50 (VR 50) payment is made on average for every 50 responses rather than on every 50th response as it would be under an FR 50 schedule. Variable-ratio schedules were chosen, rather than fixed-ratio schedules, for two reasons: (1) for the session lengths used the response rate is typically greater than for corresponding value fixed-ratio schedules and (2) less time is required to reach stability when large changes in the ratio values are made.

The point labeled A on budget line K° in each of the four panels of Figure 6 show the income-leisure choices for the four pigeons used in this study under baseline wage rate conditions of VR 50. (Mean values over the last five days of each condition are reported throughout.) The experimental sessions last for 40 minutes in each case with time at the food hopper (time spent consuming) not counting in the session time. Each bird is maintained at 80 percent of normal body weight throughout the experiment to remove the weight variable as a confounding factor in the behavior observed. This is done by either providing the birds with some grain in their home cages following a session or skipping a day's session, as the case requires. Extensive research suggests that the high rate of discount attached to delayed consumption maintains high levels of work output during an experimental session even when subjects are consistently fed following the session to maintain a given body weight. While the rate of time discount varies across pigeons, since sessions are started at approximately the same time each day the discounted value of the free food possibilities at the end of the session remains approximately the same from session to session along with the subject's body weight. (Rachlin and Green, 1972).

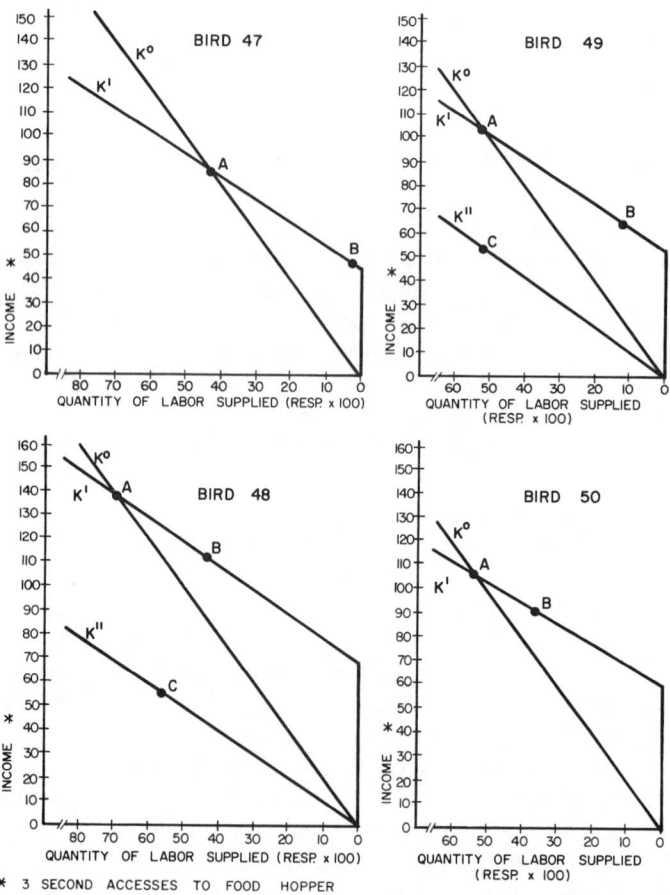

*3 SECOND ACCESSES TO FOOD HOPPER

Figure 6. Experimental Results.

Following the establishment of stable baseline conditions each bird was given half of its average baseline income earnings in the form of nonwage payments programmed for delivery on a randomized time schedule throughout the session. At the same time wage rates were halved so that the new budget line would pass through the original equilibrium point, A, in each case. This given each bird budget line K' in Figure 6 with the new equilibrium income-leisure point shown by the letter B in each case.

We note two things about the behavior reported in Figure 6. First, the birds behave consistently with the theory in each case. That is, food-deprived birds maintained at 80 percent of normal body weight substitute leisure for income under an income-compensated wage rate change, with the magnitude of substitution being quite substantial in two of the four cases. Second, there is a good deal of variability between subjects in the quantity of labor supplied under the same (baseline) experimental conditions with the magnitude of substitutability also varying substantially across birds in response to the income compensated wage rate changes.

One additional data point is reported for subjects number 48 and 49. (Subjects number 47 and 50 are under a different experimental sequence and have not yet been run under this condition.) The nonwage income received under budget line K' was eliminated resulting in budget line K''. In both cases the quantity of labor supplied and income earned under budget line K'', point C, is greater than under K', point B, indicating that over this range of the choice space leisure is a "normal" good, consistent with the relatively large substitution effects reported under budget line K'. It is also of interest to note that a comparison of point A on budget line K° (VR 50) and point C on budget line K'' (VR 100) shows that the demand for income is inversely related to the effort price of income, thus replicating this relationship found in the studies reported on above.

The data reported in Figure 6 is for mean responses over the last 5 days of an experimental condition, each of which lasted a minimum of 28 days with the stipulation that the last nine days of a condition showed no trends in response rates. Examination of session-to-session data leading up to the equilibrium points reported in Figure 5 show considerable movement in the choice space prior to settling down. For example, subject 47, who had the greatest reduction in the quantity of labor supplied under budget line K', started out supplying 2,240 responses (averaged over the first five days of the experimental condition) with the quantity of labor supplied gradually decreasing to about 200 responses as reported in Figure 6.

Additional changes in experimental conditions are underway continuing to explore the labor-leisure choices of these subjects. We are extremely cautious about too hasty generalization of the results reported in Figure 6 in terms of the magnitude of substitutability likely to be observed at other points in the choice space under these same experimental conditions or at a comparable point in the choice space under changed conditions. As noted earlier, the available data suggests that the length of the experimental session affects the location and turning points of the labor supply schedule, although not its general characteristics. It follows from this that the responses reported in Figure 6 under the particular wage rates employed are probably not invariant to the length of the experimental session or, what amounts to the same thing, that the substitution effects with constant session lengths are likely to vary with changing wage rates. Further, as in the consumer demand experiments, the response patterns observed are likely to be a condition of the items in the choice set. The effects of introducing more than one commodity to spend income on and/or commodities with different tastes and other characteristics that induce consumption above and beyond any survival requirements of the animal, as well as augmenting the quantity and quality of "leisure" time activities within the experimental chamber, remain to be explored.

In closing we note that the experimental procedures developed here can be extended to a wide range of questions of general interest to economists. For example, the genetic similarity between subjects and the ability to exert a relatively high degree of experimental control over the environmental conditions suggests that groups of these subjects (say $n \geq 20$) can be used to examine some basic questions in the area of income distribution. That is, once the distribution of income is obtained under some baseline condition, we can examine the effects of changes in real wage rates, changes in the consumption set to include nonessential items, or changes in the jobs available on the observed income distribution. Under these conditions, an examination of the resulting income distributions provides direct information about the importance of the underlying intersubject differences on the observed income earnings since the institutional-environmental conditions are held constant.

The experimental procedures can also be extended in directions that will help to provide a basis for the further integration of research results in other disciplines. Two illustrations will make this type of extension clear: (1) the introduction of the multiple jobs into the above experimental procedure results in an experimental design that is similar to that used in psychology in studies of the matching law and (2) the introduction of multiple consumption goods results in an experimental design that is similar to that used in biology to study predator-prey switching (Herrnstein, 1970; Covich, 1974). In both cases, experiments conducted under these extensions would help to integrate the empirical behavioral relationships in these other disciplines with economic theory.[8] Extending the range of circumstances in which economic concepts are known to be able to organize individual subject behavior would be of obvious value for economic science.

FOOTNOTES

This research was partially supported by NSF Grant GS 32057. An earlier version of this paper was presented at the Conference on Experimental Economics, Tucson, Arizona, April 1977.

1. For a good introduction to schedules of reinforcement and modern behavioral psychology in general see Rachlin (1976).
2. Preliminary results from consumer demand experiments in which responses are reduced to a simple indication of choice by using time to constrain the choice set for pigeons also show substitutability.
3. As the length of the experimental session is increased sufficiently, this behavior may asymptote out. For example, although three-spined sticklebacks (a kind of fish) increased their rate of eating during the first hour of access to food under longer levels of deprivation (16 hours deprivation compared to 40, 64, and 88 hours), they all ate about the same amount during the entire test day (Curio, 1976; Ernits and Corbit, 1973).
4. It is also of interest to note that Henningfield and Meisch have replicated these basic results under conditions where the real wage rate was increased by increasing the size of the income payment while holding the FR value constant (Henningfield and Meisch, 1975). The volume of the dipper cup was increased from 0.034 ml. to 0.274 ml. while maintaining a constant fixed-ratio ($FR = 1$). As the effort price of income decreased (the volume of the dipper cup was increased), more income was earned.
5. This statement must be qualified on the grounds that the data presented are for different groups of nine subjects, each under one concentration, whereas the theory is for individual labor supply behavior. However, related research has shown that individual rats consume significantly different amounts of sucrose (as well as glucose, sodium saccharin and sodium chloride) as the concentrations are varied, indicating that the behavior will replicate under a within subjects design (Ernits and Corbet, 1973). (Data for individual subjects was made available by Dr. Ernits.) It is interesting to note that in these studies the maximal fluid intake occurred in the general vicinity of isotonicity for the sugars and sodium chloride but the maximal intake in terms of the quantity of sucrose, glucose and sodium chloride ingested occurred at a much higher concentration.
6. Due to the weight loss of one subject, its series was terminated at FR 220. We note that fixed-ratio increases over the range FR 1 and FR 20 had little effect on either the total food consumed or water consumed from the water tube. The work levels observed over this range are about four times as large as the maximal work levels required in any of our consumer demand studies.
7. Other factors may be at work as well, such as the sequence of wage rate changes implemented, the stability criteria employed in a given study, etc. Sorting out these issues is far from trivial and would undoubtedly tie up a good deal of capital and labor for considerable periods of time. Consequently, the decision to undertake such studies depends upon the particular research question being asked [See Sidman (1960), Chapter 6, esp. pp. 252–53].
8. For a brief introduction to the growing literature in biology and ecology, using economic concepts, see the recent papers by Hirschliefer (1976), Rapport and Turner (1977), and Covich (1974).

REFERENCES

Becker, G. S. (1971), *Economic Theory*, New York: Knopf.
Bigelow, G., and Liebson, I. (1972), "Cost Factors Controlling Alcoholic Drinking," *The Psychological Record*, 22: 305–314.

Collier, G., Hirsch, E., and Hamlin, P. (1972), "The Ecological Determinants of Reinforcement in the Rat," *Physiology and Behavior* 9: 705–716.

———, and Jennings, W. (1969), "Work as a Determinant of Instrumental Performance," *Journal of Comparative and Physiological Psychology* 68, no. 4: 659–662.

Collins, R. L. (January 11, 1975), "When Left-Handed Mice Live in Right-Handed Worlds," *Science* 187: 181–184.

Covich, A. (1974), "Ecological Economics of Foraging Among Coevolving Animals and Plants," *Annals of the Missouri Botanical Garden* 61, No. 3: 794–805.

Curio, E. (1976), *The Ethology of Predation: Zoophysiology and Ecology*, Vol. 7, Berlin, Heidelberg, New York: Springer-Verlag.

Ernits, T., and Corbit, J. (1973), "Taste as a Dipsogenic Stimulus," *Journal of Comparative and Physiological Psychology* 83, No. 1: 27–31.

Henningfield, J. E., and Meisch, R. A. (1975), "Ethanol-Reinforced Responding and Intake as a Function of Volume Per Reinforcement," *Pharmacology Biochemistry and Behavior* 3: 437–441.

Herrnstein, R. J. (1958), "Some Factors Influencing Behavior in a Two-Response Situation," *Transactions of the New York Academy of Sciences* 21: 35–45.

———. (1970), "On the Law of Effect," *Journal of Experimental Analysis of Behavior* 13: 243–266.

———, and Loveland, D. (1975), "Maximizing and Matching on Concurrent Ratio Schedules," *Journal of Experimental Analysis of Behavior* 24: 107–117.

Hirsch, E., and Collier, G. (1974), "The Ecological Determinants of Reinforcement in the Guinea Pig," *Physiology and Behavior* 12, No. 12: 239–249.

Hirschleifer, J. (September 1976), "Economics and Sociobiology," UCLA Department of Economics Working Paper No. 80.

Kagel, J. H., Battalio, R. C., Rachlin, H., Green, L., Basmann, R. L., and Klemm, W. R. (March 1975), "Experimental Studies of Consumer Demand Behavior Using Laboratory Animals," *Economic Inquiry* 13, No. 1: 22–38.

———, ———, Winkler, R., and Fisher, E. J. (July 1977), "Job Choice and Total Labor Supply: An Experimental Analysis," *Southern Economic Journal* 44, No. 1: 13–24.

Koop, J., Bourland, G., Tarte, R. and Vernon, C. (1976), "Acquisition of Bar Pressing in Nondeprived Rats," *The Psychological Record* 26: 49–54.

Meisch, R. and Thompson, T. (1971), "Ethanol Reinforcement: Effects of Food Deprivation, Fixed-Ratio Size, and Concentration," Reports from the Research Laboratories, Department of Psychiatry, University of Minnesota, No. PR-71–2.

——— and ———. (1972), "Determinants of Ethanol Intake in Rats: Food Intake and Ethanol Concentration," Reports from the Research Laboratories, Department of Psychiatry, University of Minnesota, No. PR-72–3.

——— and ———. (1973), "Ethanol as a Reinforcer: Effects of Fixed-Ratio Size and Food Deprivation," *Psychopharmacologia* (Berlin) 28: 171–183.

Premack, D. (1965), "Reinforcement Theory," *Nebraska Symposium on Motivation*, D. Levine (ed.): 123–188.

Rachlin, H. (1976), *Behavior and Learning*, San Francisco: Freeman.

———, and Green L. (1972), "Commitment, Choice and Self-Control," *Journal of the Experimental Analysis of Behavior* 17: 15–22.

Rapport, D., and Turner, J. (January 28, 1977), "Economic Models in Ecology," *Science* 195: 267–273.

Robbins, L. (June 1930), "On the Elasticity of Demand for Income in Terms of Effort," *Economica* 29: 123–129.

Sidman, M. (1960), *Tactics of Scientific Research*, New York: Basic Books.

Skinner, B. F. (1953), *Science and Human Behavior*, New York: Macmillan.

Smith, J. C., Williams, D. P., Jue, S. S. (January 23, 1976), "Rapid Oral Mixing of Glucose and Saccharin by Rats," *Science* 191: 304–305.

Wallace, R., Osborne, S., Norborg, J. and Fantino, E. (December 7, 1973), "Stimulus Change Contemporaneous with Food Presentation Maintains Responding in the Presence of Free Food," *Science* 182: 1038–1039.

INTERTEMPORAL COMPETITIVE EQUILIBRIUM: ON FURTHER EXPERIMENTAL RESULTS

Arlington W. Williams, UNIVERSITY OF ARIZONA

This paper and much of the analysis that follows is a replication and extension of research initially conducted by Ross M. Miller, Charles R. Plott, and Vernon L. Smith, published under the title "Intertemporal Competitive Equilibrium: An Empirical Study of Speculation." Their paper was "based upon the conjecture that the information conditions that yield a competitive equilibrium in stationary markets will also yield an intertemporal competitive equilibrium in a seasonal market with cyclical but unknown shifts in demand and a stationary supply" (Miller, Plott, and Smith, 1975, p. 2).

Briefly, the theory of intertemporal competitive equilibrium in a two season market is that, in equilibrium, prices in the two markets (P_1^0, P_2^0)

will differ only by any carryover cost, T,

$$P_2^0 = P_1^0 + T \tag{1}$$

and the excess supply at the season 1 equilibrium price (the amount carried over) will equal the excess demand at the season 2 equilibrium price

$$S_1(P_1^0) - D_1(P_1^0) = D_2(P_2^0) - S_2(P_2^0). \tag{2}$$

In experiment I that follows[1] subjects designated as "traders" have the exclusive right to make speculative purchases in season 1 (blue) for resale in season 2 (yellow). They have no knowledge of market, or any individual, supply or demand in either season, and are thus unsure about their season 2 resale prices at the time of their season 1 purchases.

Supply and demand schedules are constructed for each trading period in accordance with the theory of induced valuation. Buyers received cash payments equal to the difference between their marginal valuation (to be thought of as resale or redemption value) and the purchase price for each unit bought plus a five-cent "commission." Sellers received cash payments equal to the difference between the sale price and the marginal cost for each unit sold plus a five-cent "commission." It was stressed that no buyer should pay more for a unit than its marginal valuation and no seller should sell a unit for less than its marginal cost. The additional five-cent payment on each transaction was to overcome subjective transaction costs associated with making and executing decisions and thereby induce the exchange of marginal units. No attempt was made to add realism to the market by giving the abstract experimental commodity a particular name or to simulate the circumstances of any particular market. Such suggestions could give rise to possible changes in induced values and lessen the experimental control on individual valuation. The sole source of valuation was limited to the explicitly stated reward structure as far as possible.[2]

The institution of contract is the oral double auction. Buyers are free at any time to make an oral bid to buy one unit of the commodity and any seller is free to make an oral offer to sell one unit. Any buyer is free to accept the offer of any seller, and any seller is free to accept the bid of any buyer. Upon acceptance of a bid or offer a binding contract is made between the buyer and seller. There are no rules governing the bid-offer sequence.[3]

EXPERIMENT I:
SPECULATIVE MARKET REPLICATION
Subjects and Market Design

The subjects were eleven undergraduate and three graduate students at the University of Arizona. None had previously participated in an auction

Table 1

Season	Marginal Valuation			
	Blue		Yellow	
Unit	1st	2nd	1st	2nd
Buyer 1	3.20	1.00	4.80	2.60
Buyer 2	3.00	1.20	4.60	2.80
Buyer 3	2.80	1.40	4.40	3.00
Buyer 4	2.60	1.60	4.20	3.20
Buyer 5	2.40	1.80	4.00	3.40
Buyer 6	2.20	2.00	3.80	3.60
Seller 1	1.60	3.80	1.60	3.80
Seller 2	1.80	3.80	1.80	3.80
Seller 3	2.00	3.40	2.00	3.40
Seller 4	2.20	3.20	2.20	3.20
Seller 5	2.40	3.00	2.40	3.00
Seller 6	2.60	2.80	2.60	2.80

market experiment. Subjects were seated at intervals throughout a classroom and then randomly distributed "record sheets" (see Appendix I) designating them as buyer # (1–6), seller # (1–6), or trader # (1, 2). Space was provided for the recording of each transaction and the calculation of profits. Buyers and sellers were also given their marginal valuations for each of two units in both the blue and yellow seasons. Detailed instructions[4] were then read aloud to the group describing the functioning of buyers, sellers, and traders after which questions were answered. The market was carried out over seven trading "years"[5] composed of a blue and a yellow season. Each season lasted five minutes, with a bell at four indicating that trading would end in one minute.

Table 1 shows the marginal valuations induced on the six buyers and six sellers resulting in the seasonal market demand and supply curves shown in Chart 1.[6] Traders could carry purchases in the blue season over to the yellow season at zero storage cost. No purchases could be carried over from a yellow season into the next year's blue season (or any later season). Each trader received a $3.00 capital endowment to cover potential losses.

The autarky price-quantity equilibrium is $2.40, with five units exchanged in the blue season and $3.20 with nine units exchanged in the yellow season. The intertemporal equilibrium price is $2.80 with seven units produced in each season and four units carried over by "traders."

Experimental Results

Chart 1 (also see Appendix II) plots the prices at which contracts occurred by transaction number and shows the tendency for contract prices to

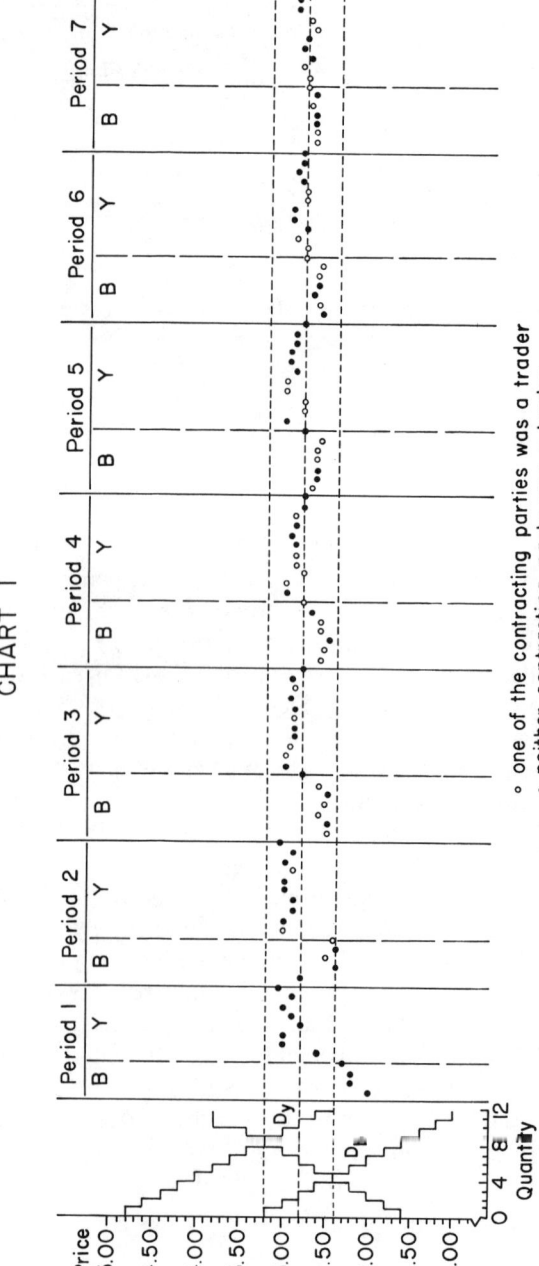

CHART I

Table 2. Experiment I (Speculation)

Period	$\bar{P}_b$	$\bar{P}_y$	$\bar{P}$	S_e	α	$\bar{P}_y - \bar{P}_b$	Q_b	Q_y	Q
1	2.17	2.90	2.67	.39	14.0	.73	4	8	12
2	2.51	2.96	2.81	.24	8.4	.45	5	10	15
3	2.58	2.92	2.79	.18	6.5	.34	7	11	18
4	2.62	2.90	2.79	.16	5.6	.28	7	11	18
5	2.67	2.91	2.82	.14	4.9	.24	7	11	18
6	2.67	2.86	2.78	.12	4.2	.19	7	11	18
7	2.72	2.84	2.79	.09	3.2	.12	7	11	18

gradually converge to the intertemporal equilibrium with the maximum number of exchanges occurring in periods 3–7. In period 4 the marginal buyer and seller were replaced by an extra unit carried over by a trader. The narrowing of contract prices between seasons and their movement toward the intertemporal equilibrium is further revealed in Table 2. There is a successive reduction of both the difference between the mean yellow and mean blue season price ($\bar{P}_y - \bar{P}_b$) as well as α, the "coefficient of convergence." α is the ratio of the standard deviation of exchange prices around the predicted equilibrium price (rather than the mean exchange price), S_e, to the predicted equilibrium price, P_e; the entire ratio being expressed as a percentage: $\alpha = 100(S_e/P_e)$.[7] Thus α is a measure of exchange price variation expressed as a percentage of the predicted theoretical equilibrium price. In period 7 the pooled seasonal mean contract price, $\bar{P}$, is $2.79. Contract price standard deviation around the intertemporal equilibrium, S_e, is $.09, interpreted by α as being 3.2 percent of the equilibrium price.

For ease of comparison Table 3 displays the same statistics as Table 2 but calculated using the results of the experiment conducted by Miller, Plott, and Smith. The convergence of their market to a price slightly above the intertemporal equilibrium price of $2.80 and a quantity exchanged of 17 rather than 18 was not repeated and would seem to be due to sampling variation. Convergence in the Miller, Plott, and Smith experiment, as reflected by S_e and α, was much more rapid than in this replication. This is

Table 3. Miller, Plott, and Smith (Speculation)

Period	$\bar{P}_b$	$\bar{P}_y$	$\bar{P}$	S_e	α	$\bar{P}_y - \bar{P}_b$	Q_b	Q_y	Q
1	2.35	2.79	2.64	.30	10.6	.44	5	10	15
2	2.66	2.75	2.72	.14	4.9	.09	6	10	16
3	2.74	2.89	2.83	.09	3.2	.15	6	10	16
4	2.84	2.89	2.87	.08	2.7	.05	7	10	17
5	2.84	2.88	2.87	.07	2.6	.04	7	11	18
6	2.87	2.88	2.87	.08	2.8	.01	7	10	17

Table 4

	Season	U.D.*	T.D.*	U.S.*	T.S.*	E.M.*
Theoretical Autarky Equilibrium	B	—	2.60;2.40	2.60;2.80	—	92%
	Y	3.00;2.80	—	—	3.00;3.20	
Period 1	B	2.80	2.60;2.40	2.40 2.60;2.80	—	90%
	Y	3.20 3.00;2.80	—	—	3.00	
Period 2	B	—	—	2.60;2.80	—	98%
	Y	2.80	—	—	3.00	
Period 3	B	—	—	—	—	100%
	Y	—	—	—	—	
Period 4	B	2.80	—	—	—	100%
	Y	—	—	2.80	—	
Period 5	B	—	—	—	—	100%
	Y	—	—	—	—	
Period 6	B	—	—	—	—	100%
	Y	—	—	—	—	
Period 7	B	—	—	—	—	100%
	Y	—	—	—	—	

*U.D. = Limit prices of *untraded* marginal and intramarginal *demand* units
T.D. = Limit prices of *traded* extramarginal *demand* units
U.S. = Limit prices of *untraded* marginal and intramarginal *supply* units
T.S. = Limit prices of *traded* extramarginal *supply* units
E.M. = Efficiency Measure.

probably due to sampling variation and the fact that some subjects in their experiment had prior experience in other auction market experiments.

An index of efficiency[8] to judge market performance is shown in Table 4. Inefficiencies occur when extramarginal units are traded and when intramarginal units fail to be traded. One hundred percent efficiency occurs if, and only if, subjects receive maximum available consumer plus producer surplus. The index of efficiency is the ratio of actual payments to maximum available under the intertemporal equilibrium price ($20.00 per period) expressed as a percentage. The speculative market averaged 98.3 percent over periods 1–7 and was 100 percent efficient in periods 3–7; perfect autarky equilibrium would be 92 percent efficient.

As done in the Miller, Plott, and Smith study a test of the null hypothesis that in the final trading period the mean contract prices in each season are equal to the seasonal autarky prices was conducted using the t-statistic.

Intertemporal Competitive Equilibrium

The sample mean, number of transactions (prices), and autarky equilibrium in the ith season ($i = y, b$) are given respectively by $\bar{P}_i, n_i$, and P_i^*:

$$H_0 : (\bar{P}_y - \bar{P}_b) = (P_y^* - P_b^*)$$
$$H_A : (\bar{P}_y - \bar{P}_b) \neq (P_y^* - P_b^*)$$

$$t(n_y + n_b - 2) = \frac{(\bar{P}_y - \bar{P}_b) - (P_y^* - P_b^*)}{S\sqrt{(1/n_y) + (1/n_b)}}$$

S^2 is the pooled estimate of the population variance over both seasons in the final period and is of the form:

$$S^2 = \frac{\sum_{j=1}^{n_y} (P_{yj} - \bar{P}_y)^2 + \sum_{j=1}^{n_b} (P_{bj} - \bar{P}_b)^2}{(n_y + n_b - 2)}$$

Calculation of t using the above yields $t = -19.46$ (compared with -59.8 in the Miller, Plott, and Smith experiment), hence we reject the null hypothesis with better than a .001 confidence level. It would seem that speculation was once again an effective "treatment" variable. Ideally, the experiment should be rerun without seasonal carryover and then the final period mean experimental autarky prices used in the test as well as their standard deviation rather than the theoretical autarkic market equilibria. It is to this potentially much more rigorous test of the research hypothesis that we now turn.

EXPERIMENT II: AUTARKIC MARKET

Subjects and Market Design

The subjects were twelve undergraduate students at the University of Arizona, none of whom, as in Experiment I, had any prior experience as a subject in an auction market experiment. Experiment II was conducted in a manner identical, insofar as possible, to that of Experiment I except that the role of the two traders (or speculators) was eliminated. Subjects were spatially seated, distributed record sheets randomly, then read instructions identical to those in Experiment I (deleting the section specifically directed to traders). Individual marginal valuations and hence market supply and demand remained the same as in Experiment I. Autarky price quantity equilibria were $2.40 with five exchanged in the blue season and $3.20 with nine units exchanged in the yellow season.

Experimental Results

Chart 2 (see also Appendix III) shows the gradual convergence of contract prices toward the seasonal autarky equilibria. Maximum autarkic market

CHART 2

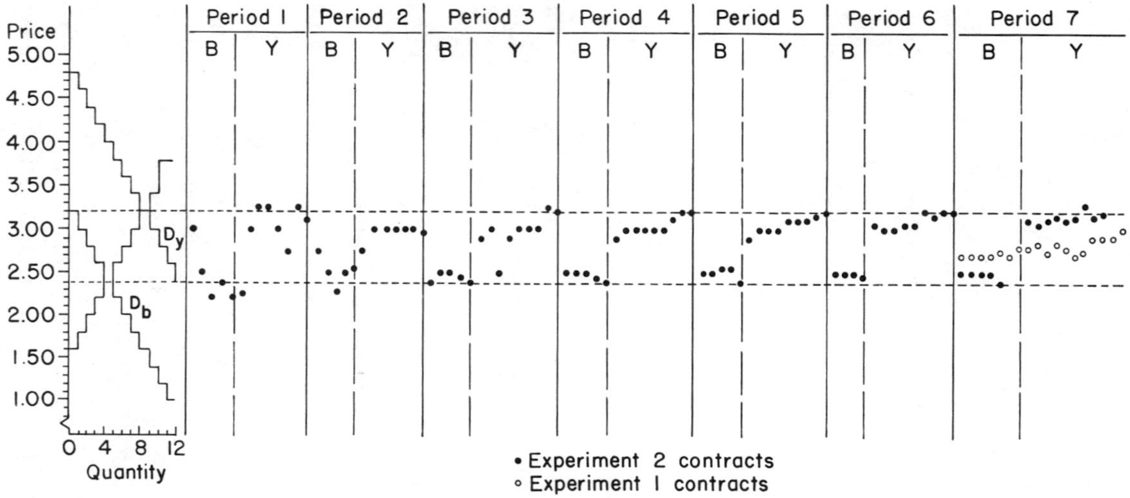

Table 5. Experiment II (Autarky)

Period	$\bar{P}_b$	S_e^b	α_b	$\bar{P}_y$	S_e^y	α_y	$\bar{P}_y - \bar{P}_b$	Q_b	Q_y	Q
1	2.46	.30	12.5	2.98	.39	12.1	.52	5	8	13
2	2.52	.19	7.9	2.96	.25	7,8	.44	5	7	12
3	2.45	.07	2.8	2.97	.30	9.5	.52	5	9	14
4	2.47	.08	3.4	3.04	.18	5.7	.57	5	9	14
5	2.50	.11	4.8	3.06	.16	5.1	.56	5	9	14
6	2.49	.09	3.7	3.10	.13	4.0	.61	4	9	13
7	2.48	.09	3.7	3.14	.09	2.8	.66	5	9	14

efficiency occurs in periods 3–7 (in period 6 the marginal buyer and seller were not able to come to terms, so although the maximum number of exchanges did not occur no surplus was forfeited and hence there was no inefficiency). Table 5 reveals the divergence of seasonal contract prices by increases in the difference between the mean blue season contract price and the mean yellow season price. Table 5 also presents seasonal standard errors calculated around the respective autarky equilibrium price (S_e^i, i = b, y), seasonal coefficients of convergence (α_i, i = b, y), and exchanges made in each season (Q_i, i = b, y).

Note that α_b, S_e^b, and $\bar{P}_b$ are all at a minimum in period 3 and tend to diverge from the autarky equilibrium levels as the yellow season market stabilizes over periods 4 and 5. In periods 6 and 7 both seasonal markets tend to converge to their respective equilibrium contract price, with period 7 standard errors being nearly equal between seasons ($S_e^b = .089$, $S_e^y = .088$) and mean contract prices deviating from predicted equilibrium values by $.08 in the blue season and $.06 in the yellow season ($\bar{P}_y - \bar{P}_b = \$.66$ rather than the autarkic equilibrium value of $.80). Presumably the formation of cross-seasonal expectations (and their gradual expiration) about potential contract prices (and profits) were an important factor in the shaping of the market participants' bargaining behavior. It would seem that the fairly rapid initial convergence of blue season contract prices to a level near the autarkic equilibrium as well as most sellers' willingness to accept contracts of around $3.00 in the yellow season (at a greater profit than in the blue season) tended to make convergence in the yellow season a very gradual process. Expectations of yellow season contract prices and profits were slowly extinguished when the highest marginal valuation sellers (4 and 5) were able to come to terms in the last two contracts of periods 3 and 4. By not accepting sellers' offers at the end of the yellow season of periods 1 and 2, buyer 6 (period 1) and buyer 4 (period 2) forfeited substantial profits. Such decisions are not entirely consistent with the premise upon which the theory of induced valuation is based in that it is doubtful that the obvious concrete opportunity costs of not coming to contract were outweighed by any psychic "punitive" benefits derived by the buyers. The experimenter must conclude that some confusion may have existed as to the role and proper functioning of the subject in the market place. Situations such as this are nearly inevitable in experimental markets. The initial market periods are educationally functional not only with regard to informational yields concerning market structure (necessary to the bargaining process) but also as a clarification through individual participation and observation of the subject's role in the experiment. Perhaps the disutility derived by shy or unsure subjects' participation in verbal bargaining is simply outweighed very rapidly by the thought of substantial profits foregone.

A test of the research hypothesis using the period 7 experimental seasonal mean autarky prices and the associated "noise" yields $t = -10.72$; we can still reject the null hypothesis with better than a .001 level of confidence.[9] Recalculation of the t-statistic using the period 7 autarky experimental data for the Miller, Plott, and Smith experiment yields $t = -18.49$. It might be mentioned at this juncture that any non-parametric test based on "runs" would be an exercise in arithmetic since there were no overlapping period 7 contract prices in either the blue or yellow seasons between experiments as can be noted by inspection of Chart 2.

Conclusion

The combined results of Miller, Plott, and Smith and this experimenter would indicate that the inclusion of speculators in a market with unknown seasonal fluctuations in demand *is* an effective treatment variable resulting in a significant narrowing of interseasonal contract prices. Further, the results would indicate that a replication of the general characteristics of an experimental market can be accomplished by independent experimenters drawing subjects from entirely different populations.

APPENDIX I. SAMPLE RECORD SHEETS

Record Sheet, Buyer # ――

Record of Purchases and Profits

Trading Year Season	1		2		3		4		5		6		7	
	B	Y	B	Y	B	Y	B	Y	B	Y	B	Y	B	Y
1 1st unit redemption value														
2 Purchase price														
3 Profit (row 1–row 2)														
4 Profit + 5¢ commission (row 3 + 5¢)														
5 2nd unit redemption value														
6 Purchase price														
7 Profit (row 5–row 6)														
8 Profit + 5¢ commission (row 7 + 5¢)														
9 Total Profit (row 4 + row 8)														

Total Profit, All Trading Periods――――

Name――――――――

Record Sheet, Seller # ――

Record of Sales and Profits

Trading Year Season	1		2		3		4		5		6		7	
	B	Y	B	Y	B	Y	B	Y	B	Y	B	Y	B	Y
1 Sale Price														
2 Cost of 1st unit														
3 Profit (row 1–row 2)														
4 Profit + 5¢ commission (row 3 + 5¢)														
5 Sale Price														
6 Cost of 2nd unit														
7 Profit (row 5–row 6)														
8 Profit + 5¢ commission (row 3 + 5¢)														
9 Total Profit														
9 (row 4 + row 8)														

Total Profit, all trading periods――――

Name――――――――

Record of Transactions and Profits, Trader # ———

Unit		Trading Year Number	1	2	3	4	5	6	7
1	1	Sale Price (Yellow Period)							
	2	Purchase Price (Blue Period)							
	3	Profit (row 1–row 2)							
	4	Profit + 5¢ Commission							
2	5	Sale Price (Yellow Period)							
	6	Purchase Price (Blue Period)							
	7	Profit (row 5–row 6)							
	8	Profit + 5¢ Commission							
3	9	Sale Price (Yellow Period)							
	10	Purchase Price (Blue Period)							
	11	Profit (row 9–row 10)							
	12	Profit + 5¢ Commission							
4	13	Sale Price (Yellow Period)							
	14	Purchase Price (Blue Period)							
	15	Profit (row 13–row 14)							
	16	Profit + ¢ Commission							
5	17	Sale Price (Yellow Period)							
	18	Purchase Price (Blue Period)							
	19	Profit (row 17–row 18)							
	20	Profit + 5¢ Commission							
6	21	Sale Price (Yellow Period)							
	22	Purchase Price (Blue Period)							
	23	Profit (row 21–row 22)							
	24	Profit + 5¢ Commission							

Total Profits, All Periods ———
Name ————————

Intertemporal Competitive Equilibrium 267

APPENDIX II. Bids, Offers and Contracts for Experiment I (B, S, T indicates Buyer, Seller, Trader)

Number	Bid	Offer	Taker	Number	Bid	Offer	Taker
\multicolumn{4}{	l	}{1 Blue}	S4		2.40	
B2	1.50			B5	(2.20)		
S5		2.80		B1	.80		
S6		2.60		B6	2.00		
B6	1.60			S4		2.30	
S5		2.50		B3	2.20		
B5	1.80			S4		(2.30)	S3
B1	(2.00)			B3	2.20		
B6	1.90			S5		2.50	
S2	(2.20)			B6	2.10		B4
B2	1.95			\multicolumn{4}{	l	}{1 Yellow}
B5	2.00	2.50	S1	B2	(2.60)		
B6				B1	(3.00)		
S3		2.50		B5	(3.00)		S5
B5	2.10			B6	2.50		S4
B6	2.25			B3	(2.80)		S6
S5		2.50		B2	2.50		
B1	1.00		S2	S2		3.00	
S4		2.40		B1	1.60		
B1	.40			B6	2.90		
B3	2.00			B5	(3.00)		S1
B1	.60			B1	2.00		S2
B2	.90			B4	2.80		
B5	1.00			S5		3.20	
S2		4.00		B6	2.60		
S6		3.00		S2		4.00	
S5		2.50		B2	2.70		
B6	2.00			S5		3.10	
B5	2.10						

Number	Bid	Offer	Taker	Number	Bid	Offer	Taker
B3	2.75	4.00		B6	2.00		
S2			S3	B3	2.40		S2
B4	(2.90)			T2	(2.50)		
B6	2.90			B6	2.00		
B1	2.30			B3	2.40		
B2	2.60			S5		2.60	S1
B3	2.75	3.80		B5	2.30		
B6	2.90	3.10		B3	(2.40)		
S4				B5	2.20		
S5				S5		2.60	
B6	3.00	3.80		B4	2.30	3.50	
S2				S3			
B6	3.00	3.10		B6	2.00	2.70	
S5			S5	S6		2.60	
B6	(3.05)			S5		2.60	
B3	2.75	3.80		S6			
S4		3.80		B6	2.20	2.60	
S2				B5	2.30		
B2	2.75	3.50		S5			
S4				B4	2.40	2.60	
B4	2.90			S6			
\multicolumn{4}{	l	}{2 Blue}	B2	2.20		
B6	1.50			B5	1.20		
B1	2.00	2.80		B6	1.50	2.50	
B2	2.30			B5	2.20	3.20	
S6				B6	2.20		
B1	2.50	3.00	S3	S3			
S2	(2.80)			B5	2.30		
B1	2.00	2.85		S5		2.45	
B5		2.50	S4	B5	2.35		
S2				B4	2.40		
S5				B6	2.19	2.45	
B2	(2.40)			S5			

3 Yellow

Number	Bid	Offer	Taker
B5	(3.00)		
B6	2.80		
B1	(3.00)		
B2	2.90	3.00	S3
S5			
B2	(2.95)		T2
B6	(2.90)		T1
B4	(2.90)		S5
B5	(2.90)		S4
B2	2.80		T1
B3	(2.90)		
B6	2.80		
B2	2.90		
B3	2.80		S1
B6	(2.95)		
S2		2.85	
B4	(2.90)		
S5		3.00	S6
S6		3.25	
B6	2.90	3.00	T1
S2		2.95	
B6	(2.92)	3.05	S6
S5		3.00	
S2	2.60	3.00	
B2	2.80	2.90	
S2		2.90	
B2	2.80	2.85	
S2	(2.80)	3.05	S2
B2			
S5			

Number	Bid	Offer	Taker
S4		(2.60)	T1
S6		2.70	
B3	2.40	2.75	
S5	2.20		
B6	2.40	2.70	T1
B3		(2.55)	S3
S6	(2.50)		
S5	2.20		
B2	2.30		
B6	2.45		
B5	2.50	2.65	
B3	2.55		T1
S6	2.40	(2.60)	
B4		4.00	
B3	2.55	3.90	
S6		3.10	
B3	1.20	3.00	
S2		3.45	
B3	2.25		
S1	2.60	2.90	S6
S5	1.00		
B2	2.20	2.85	
S6	2.70		
S3	(2.80)		
B5			
B3			
S6			
B1			
B6			
B3			

2 Yellow

Number	Bid	Offer	Taker
B5	2.35		
B4	2.40		
S5		(2.45)	T1
B4	2.50		
B2	2.60		T2
B5	(3.00)		S5
B1	(3.00)		S4
B3	2.80		
B2	(2.90)	3.25	S1
S2		(3.00)	B6
B3	2.80	(3.00)	B5
B4	(2.90)		
S6			T1
S2	2.00		
B1	2.50		
B6	2.60		
B2	(2.90)	3.40	S6
B3	2.50	3.20	
B6	2.80		
B4	2.85		
B3	(3.00)	3.10	S3
S4	2.70		
S6	2.80		
B6	2.90		
B2	2.70	3.10	
B3	(2.90)		
B4	2.00		
S5			
B2			
B3			
B2			
S5			

3 Blue

Number	Bid	Offer	Taker
B4	3.00	3.05	
S5	2.80	3.40	
B2		3.05	S5
S4	2.50		
S5	(3.05)		
B2	2.60	4.00	
B4		3.50	
B2			
S2	2.80		
S4		3.50	
B2	2.80	3.25	
S3			
S4			
B2			
S3	2.00	3.00	
B6	2.10		
B5	2.20	2.80	T2
S6	2.30		
B2	2.40	(2.50)	
B3	2.20	2.80	
S2	2.40	2.60	S1
B1			
S6			
B6	2.20		
S5	2.40		
B2	(2.50)		
B1	2.20		
B6	2.30	2.70	
B5	2.50		
S6	2.40		
B2			
B4			

Intertemporal Competitive Equilibrium

5 Yellow / 6 Blue

Number	Bid	Offer	Taker	Number	Bid	Offer	Taker
S5		2.75		B5	(3.00)		T1
B1	2.60	2.70		B2	2.70		
S2			S1	S1	2.80		
B3	(2.65)		S2	B3	(2.90)	3.10	S4
B1	(2.65)		S5	B4	2.80		
T2	(2.65)			B6	2.85		
B2	2.50		T1	B3	(2.95)		S6
S4		(2.65)		B6	2.90		S2
S6		2.85		S1	(2.95)	3.00	
B4	2.55		T2	B6	2.80		
S3		(2.60)		B2			
B6	2.20			S1		3.00	
B2	2.60			S6	2.85	2.90	
S6		2.80		B3	2.80		
B2	2.65			B2			
S6		2.80		S1	(2.90)	2.95	S6
B2	2.50			B6	2.80		
B2	2.70			B2	(2.90)		
S5		3.05		S1		3.00	S3
S6		2.80		B3	2.80	2.95	
B2	2.70			S1	2.80	2.95	
B5	2.40			B2			
S6		2.80		S1	2.80	2.85	
B2	2.75	(2.80)	B2	B2	(2.80)		
S6				S5		3.05	S1

5 Yellow // 6 Blue

Number	Bid	Offer	Taker	Number	Bid	Offer	Taker
S5		(3.00)	B5	B2	2.50	2.90	
B2	2.70	3.10	T1	S4		2.80	
S1	(2.80)			S5		2.70	
B2	2.70		T2	S6			
B6	(2.80)		T2				
B4	(3.00)						
B1							
B3	2.80						

4 Blue / 4 Yellow

Number	Bid	Offer	Taker	Number	Bid	Offer	Taker
B4	2.00			B1	(3.00)		S5
S2		2.60		B5	(3.00)		T2
S6		2.10		B2	(2.80)		T1
B5	2.30			B3	(2.90)		T2
B2	2.45			B6	2.80		
B1	2.50			B5	(2.90)		T1
S2		(2.60)	T1	B6	2.80		S4
S5		(2.55)	T2	B4	(2.90)		
B2	(2.50)		S1	B2	2.60		S1
B1	2.50			B6	(2.95)		
S6		2.70	T1	B2	2.60		
S4		(2.60)		B4	2.80		
B1	2.50			B3	(2.90)	3.00	S6
B3	2.55			S2			
B2	1.20			B4	(2.90)	2.90	T1
B6	2.20			B6	2.85	2.95	
B4	2.50			S2			
S6		(2.60)	T2	S3		3.00	S2
B1	2.60			B6	(2.80)	2.90	
S3		2.75	B1	B2	2.75		
B3	2.65			S3			
S3		(2.70)		S6			
B6	2.20			B2	(2.80)	2.90	S3
B3	2.50			S6		2.85	
B5	1.50		T1	S6			
B3	2.65						
B5	2.00						
S6		(2.80)					
S5	2.75	3.05					

5 Blue

Number	Bid	Offer	Taker
S5		2.80	
B2	2.50		
B1	2.50	2.75	
S5			
B2	2.40		
B3	2.55	(2.70)	T1
S6			

Number	Bid	Offer	Taker
B3	2.50		
S3		3.05	
S5	2.75	3.05	

Number	Bid	Offer	Taker
S5		3.05	
S3		2.95	S3
B3	(3.00)		
S5		3.05	
S5		3.00	
S3		3.40	

Number	Bid	Offer	Taker
S4		(2.75)	T1
S3		2.80	
B4	2.60		
B3	2.70		
S6		2.80	
T2	2.75		
S3		(2.70)	B3
S6		2.80	
S5		3.05	
S6		2.80	
T2	2.75		
S6		(2.80)	T1

7 Yellow

Number	Bid	Offer	Taker
S3		3.00	
B2	2.60		
S5		2.90	
B6	2.70		
S2		2.90	
B2	(2.80)		T1
B5	(2.85)		T2
B6	(2.75)		S6
B2	2.80		
B2		(2.85)	B1
S5			S6
B4	(2.80)		T1
B6	(2.70)		B5
B2	(2.75)		
S4	2.85		
S2		(2.90)	
B2		2.95	B3
S1		(2.90)	
S2		2.95	S2
B4	(2.90)		

Number	Bid	Offer	Taker
B2	(2.60)		S1
S2	2.60	(2.65)	T1
S4		(2.70)	B1
B4	2.65		
B3		(2.65)	S6
S5			T1
B2	1.20		
B6	2.20		
B4	2.40		
S6	2.50		
S3		2.85	T2
S6		(2.60)	
B5		2.80	
B4	2.40		
S6	2.60		
T2	2.65	2.80	
T1	2.70		
S6		2.80	
S3		3.40	
S6		2.80	
B5	1.80		
T2	2.70		
S6		(2.80)	T1
S5		3.05	

6 Yellow

Number	Bid	Offer	Taker
B2	2.70	3.00	
S5			T2
B6	2.75		T1
B2	(2.80)		B4
B5	(2.90)		
S5		(2.80)	
B6	2.70		

Number	Bid	Offer	Taker
B3	2.80		
S4		(2.95)	B5
S2		(2.95)	B1
B2	(2.80)		T1
B6	(2.80)		T1
S1		2.95	S6
B3	(2.85)		
S3		3.00	
B4	2.80		
S1		2.95	S1
B3	(2.90)		S6
B6	2.75		
B4	(2.85)		
B6	2.80		
S5		3.05	S3
S3		2.90	
B6	2.80		
S3		2.90	
B6	(2.85)		
S5		3.05	
S5		3.00	

7 Blue

Number	Bid	Offer	Taker
S6		3.00	
B2	2.60		
B3	2.65		T1
S5		2.75	T2
S2		(2.70)	
S5		(2.70)	
S4		2.80	
B2	(2.70)		S1
B1	(2.70)		S6
S3		2.80	
B3	2.70		

Intertemporal Competitive Equilibrium 271

APPENDIX III. Bids, Offers and Contracts for Experiment II (B, S indicates Buyer, Seller)

Number	Bid	Offer	Taker
1 Blue			
B5	1.25		
S5		6.00	
S1		5.00	
B1	(3.00)		
S5		4.00	
S4		3.50	
B2	2.00		
B5	2.25		
S1		3.25	
S2		3.00	
S4		2.90	
S3		2.85	
S1		(2.50)	S6
B4	(2.20)		
S5		2.70	
B3	(2.40)		
S6		2.90	
B5	2.10		
S4		2.60	B2
B5	2.15		S3
S1		8.00	
S4		2.50	S2
B5	(2.20)		
S5		2.60	
S1		6.00	
S2		4.50	S4
B3	1.00		
S3		3.80	

Number	Bid	Offer	Taker
B5	1.20		
B3	1.25		
B4	1.30		
1 Yellow			
S3		4.25	
S6		4.00	
B5	2.00		
B6	(2.25)		
S5		(3.00)	S4
S6		4.00	B4
B5	2.25		
S1		3.50	
S3		(3.25)	B5
S6		(3.25)	B2
S1		(3.00)	B3
S2		(2.75)	B1
S6		(3.25)	B5
B4	3.00		
S5		3.50	
S4		3.35	
B1	2.50		
S1		6.00	
S5		3.25	
B2	2.80		
S3		3.82	
S4		3.30	
S2		3.80	
S3		3.64	

Number	Bid	Offer	Taker
S1		4.25	
B3	2.85		
B6	3.00		
S3		3.52	
S5		3.20	
B3	2.90		
S1		3.80	S5
B4	(3.10)		
B1	2.60		
S3		3.50	
B3	2.95		
S4		3.25	
S2		3.80	
2 Blue			
B5	1.40		
S5		5.00	
S3		4.50	
S1		3.30	
B1	1.50		
S2		3.00	S2
B5	1.75		
B1	2.00		
B5	2.20		
B2	2.25		
S5		2.90	
B1	2.30		
S2		2.75	
S4		2.90	
B1	(2.75)		
S5		2.80	S3
B2	(2.50)		
S6		3.00	
S1		2.75	

Number	Bid	Offer	Taker
B3	2.40	2.70	
S5	2.45	3.80	
B3	(2.30)		
S3		3.80	S1
B5		3.75	
S6		3.40	
S3		3.00	
S4		2.65	
S6			
B5	1.00		
B5	2.00		
B4		3.80	
S1	2.20		
B3		3.50	
S4			
B5	1.50	3.45	
B3	2.45	3.20	
S3			
S6			
B5	1.75		
B4	(2.50)		
B3	(2.55)		
B5	1.80		
S6		2.65	
B6	2.00		
S1		3.80	S4
			S5
2 Yellow			
B5	2.00		
B3	2.50		
B6	(2.75)		
B3	2.75		
S5		3.40	S3
S6		(3.00)	B5

Table 1 (top left, upper)

Number	Bid	Offer	Taker
S1		3.80	
S6		3.00	
S4		2.85	
B5	2.30		B5
S4		(2.40)	
S6		2.70	
S1		3.80	
S6		2.70	

3 Yellow

Number	Bid	Offer	Taker
B5	1.95		
B3	2.90		
B5	2.00		
B3	(2.90)		
S1		(3.00)	S2
B5	(2.50)		B3
B1	2.55		S3
S5		(2.90)	
S1		4.50	B2
B4	(3.00)		
B1	2.75		S4
S6		3.00	
B2	2.80		
S1		4.00	S6
B1	2.90		
B5	(3.00)		S6
S5		3.25	
B1	(3.00)		S5
B4	3.00		
B6	(3.25)		
B6	3.00		
S1		4.00	
S4		3.30	
B4	3.10		

Table 2 (top right)

Number	Bid	Offer	Taker
S2		3.20	
S4		3.25	
S1		4.00	
S2		3.80	B4
B4	3.15		
S4		3.20	
S4		3.80	
S1		(3.20)	
S3		3.80	
B6	3.20		
S1		3.60	
S3		3.80	
S1		3.55	
B6	3.25		
S3		3.80	
S3		3.45	

4 Blue

Number	Bid	Offer	Taker
B5	1.40		
B2	2.00		
S1		3.50	
B5	2.20		
B3	2.40		
S5		3.00	
S6		3.25	
S1		2.95	
B5	2.25		
S2		2.90	S3
B2	(2.50)		
B1	2.25		
B5	2.30		
S6		2.70	
S4		2.60	
B5	2.35		

Table 3 (bottom left)

Number	Bid	Offer	Taker
S5		3.20	
S1		(3.00)	
S6		3.20	
S2		(3.00)	
S6		(3.00)	
S5		(3.00)	
B5	(2.95)		
S2		3.80	
B2	2.80		
S5		3.50	
S1		4.00	
B3	2.95		
S4		3.30	
S2		3.80	
B3		3.25	
B3	3.00		
S2		3.80	
S3		3.50	
S4		3.25	
S5		3.20	
S1		3.80	
B1	2.60		
S5		3.10	
S4		3.25	
B3	3.00		

Number	Bid	Offer	Taker
S2		2.75	
B1	2.25		
B2	(2.40)		
S1		3.00	S3
S5		2.70	
B5	2.25		
B4	2.30		
B3	2.40		
S2		2.65	
B1	(2.50)		
S6		3.20	
S1		3.00	
S2		2.95	S5
B5	2.25		
B4	2.40		
S1		2.75	
S2		2.65	
B3	(2.50)		
S1		3.00	
S2		2.90	
B5	2.30		
B4	2.40		
S1		2.55	S2
S4		2.50	
S1		(2.45)	
S6		3.00	
B5	2.20		
S6		2.75	
B3	1.25		
S1		4.00	
S3		3.95	B4
B5	2.40		
S5		3.25	
S6		3.00	
S4		2.80	

3 Blue

Number	Bid	Offer	Taker
B1	2.00		
S1		3.25	
S2		3.15	
S5		3.00	
B2	2.40		
B5	2.00		
B3	2.35		
S5		2.80	

Intertemporal Competitive Equilibrium

Number	Bid	Offer	Taker		Number	Bid	Offer	Taker
S1	3.00	3.80			B5	2.30		
B3		3.80			B4	2.40		
S2	1.00				S3		2.95	
B1		9.00			S5		2.70	
S2		3.80			B1	2.50		
S1		3.50			S1		3.90	
S3	3.00				B5	2.40		
B3					S4		2.80	
	5 Blue				S5		2.60	
B5	2.00	2.75			B1	(2.55)	3.00	S3
S1	2.40				S6	2.50		
B3	2.50				B4		4.00	
B2	2.25				S1		2.60	
B5	2.40	2.70			S5	1.25	2.75	
S2	(2.50)	2.60			B3	(2.55)		
S1	2.50		S2		B4	2.30	4.00	S5
B1	2.30	3.50			S6		3.80	
B3	2.50	2.55			B5	1.30	3.00	
B2	2.50	2.54			S3	2.40	2.75	
S1	2.40	2.70			S1			
B1		2.55			B3			
S4					B5	2.00	(2.40)	B5
S1	2.40	2.60	S1		S6			
B5	(2.50)				S4			
B2	2.50	4.00				5 Yellow		
S6		3.25			B3	2.90	3.50	
B1					B5	1.95	3.25	
S1					S2			
S6					S1	2.00		
					B1	2.50		
					B5			

Number	Bid	Offer	Taker		Number	Bid	Offer	Taker
S2	2.40	2.60				4 Yellow		
B1	2.45				S1		3.25	
B3					B6	(2.90)		S4
S2	(2.50)				B2	2.80		
B3	2.25	2.60			B5	2.00		
S1	2.30	2.55			S5		3.10	
B5	2.40		S5		S6		(3.00)	B5
B4		2.75			S5		3.10	
B1					S5		3.05	
S2	2.45	2.60			S1		(3.00)	
S1		2.55			S2		(3.00)	B4
B1	2.40	2.50	B1		B5	2.50	(3.00)	B6
S2	2.45	(2.50)			S1			B5
B5		5.00			S5		3.50	
B1		3.50			B2	2.90	3.25	
S2	2.00	3.00			S3		4.00	
S6					S4		4.25	
B5	2.40	2.90			S1			
S5		2.65			B3	2.95	3.80	S6
S5					B4	(3.00)	3.25	S3
S1		2.60	S1		B1	(3.10)	3.20	
B4	2.20	2.55			S2			
S4	2.45	2.50			S5	3.00	3.25	
S1					S1		3.20	
B5					B2			
B4	2.40	2.60			S3	2.10	3.80	B2
S6	(2.45)	2.45	B5		B3		3.60	
S4		3.80			S5			
S1		(2.40)			B3	3.10	3.25	
B5		3.00			S1		4.00	
S4		2.75			S4	3.15	(3.20)	B3
S6					S3		3.60	
S6								

274 ARLINGTON W. WILLIAMS

Number	Bid	Offer	Taker
S1		3.10	
B2	3.00		B4
B5	2.00		S4
S1		(3.05)	
B5	2.90		S6
B2	(3.00)	3.25	S2
S6	(3.00)		
B6	3.00		S6
B3	(3.05)	3.25	
B1	3.00		
S6	(3.05)		
B5	3.00		
B4	(3.05)		S3
B3	3.05	3.30	
S3	(3.20)	3.20	
B5			S5
S5	3.10		
B6	3.00		
B5	(3.15)	3.80	
B3	3.10		
S1	3.15	3.80	S5
B5		3.25	
B6			
S1	(3.20)	3.80	S4
S4	3.10	3.25	
B5			
B6	(3.20)	3.80	
S1		3.70	
S3	3.00		
B3	3.00	3.80	
S2			
B3			

Number	Bid	Offer	Taker
B3	1.90		
B5	1.80		
B1	2.25		
B5	2.00		
B5		3.10	
S6			
B5	1.95		
B3	2.40		
S2		2.60	S3
B4	(2.50)		
B3	2.50		
S2		2.60	B3
B5	2.25		
S5		2.55	
S2		(2.50)	
S6		2.75	
B5	2.10		
B1	2.25		
B5	2.30		
S6		2.70	
S5		2.60	
S4		2.55	
B5	2.30		
B1	2.40		
B5	2.25	3.50	B1
S2		(2.45)	
S4		3.00	
S6		2.50	
S5			
B5	2.40	2.45	
B5	2.40		

6 Yellow

| B3 | 2.90 | | |
| B6 | 2.95 | | |

Number	Bid	Offer	Taker
B5	6 Blue		
B5	1.95		
B6	2.00		
S6		2.60	
B1	2.00		
B4	2.40		B2
S1		(2.50)	
S2		2.65	
B5	2.15		
B3	2.45		
B4	2.40		
B1	2.15		
B5	2.20	3.50	
S6		2.90	
S4			
B5	2.00		
B3	1.90		
B5	1.80	3.55	
B1	2.00	3.00	
S3			
S2			
B5	2.25		
B3	2.40		
B4	2.45		
B5	2.20	2.60	
S4			
S6			
B5	2.10		
B1	2.25		
B5	2.30		
B3	2.40		
B4	2.45	3.50	
S6			
B5	2.00		

Number	Bid	Offer	Taker
B3	(2.90)		S4
B4	(3.00)		S2
B5	(3.00)		S6
B2	(3.00)		S1
B3	3.00		
B6	(3.10)		
S5		3.20	
B5	3.00	4.00	S6
S1			
B3	3.00	3.20	
S4			
B5	(3.10)		
B4	(3.10)	3.80	
S1			
B1	3.10	3.30	S5
S5		3.20	S3
S4			
B6	(3.15)		
B3	3.00		
B1	3.10	3.20	S5
S4		3.80	
S1			
B1	3.15	3.20	
S4			
B1	3.10		
S2		3.80	B1
B3	3.00		
B1	3.15	(3.20)	
S4		3.65	
S3	3.00	3.80	
B3			
S2			
B3	3.00	3.50	
S3			

Table 1

Number	Bid	Offer	Taker
B5	3.00		
B4	3.05		
B5	3.10		
S6		3.50	
S2		(3.15)	B2
B6	(3.10)		S6
S5		3.20	
B4	3.10		
B5	(3.15)		
S1		3.80	
B3	3.00		
B1	3.15		
S4		3.25	S5
B5	(3.30)		
S1		3.80	
B4	3.10		
S4		3.30	
S4		3.25	S3
B4	3.15		
S1		3.80	
B3	3.00		
S4		3.20	
B4	3.15		
S5		3.20	
B3	3.00		
B4	(3.15)		
B3	3.00	(3.20)	S5
S4			
B3	3.00	3.80	B1
S2			

Table 2 — 7 Yellow

Number	Bid	Offer	Taker
B5	2.40	3.00	
S6			
B5		3.80	
B1	2.00	3.75	
S2	2.15	2.75	
S6		2.70	
B5	2.35		
S3		2.60	
S6			
B5	2.40		
B5	2.30		
S3		2.60	
S5		3.10	
S4		3.20	
S6		3.15	
S5		3.10	
B5	2.30		
S6	(2.40)	3.15	S3
B5		3.00	
S6			

7 Yellow

Number	Bid	Offer	Taker
B6	2.95	3.45	
B3	3.00		
S1	3.00	3.15	
B5	3.05	(3.10)	B4
B6		3.10	
S1	3.00		
S4	2.05		
S1	(3.05)		S1
B5	(3.10)		S6
B2			
B3			
B6			

Table 3 — 7 Blue

Number	Bid	Offer	Taker
B5	2.25		
S1		2.75	
B2	2.40		
B5	2.00	2.75	
B3	1.90	3.20	
S1		2.60	
S6	2.00		
S2	2.40		
B5	2.45	(2.50)	B2
B3		3.00	
B4	2.30		
S4		2.55	S2
S6	2.45	(2.50)	B1
B5	(2.50)		
S1	2.35		
B3		2.55	
S5	2.45		
B5	2.40		
B3	2.45	2.85	B3
S3	2.25		
B5		5.00	
S6	2.45	(2.50)	
B3	2.30	3.10	
B5			
S5	2.30	3.05	
S6	2.25		
B5			
B1			
S5			

FOOTNOTES

I am grateful to the National Science Foundation for providing the funds necessary for this research. Special thanks to Vernon L. Smith whose comments, insights, encouragement, and enthusiasm aided me in the preparation of this paper. Final responsibility for the analysis and opinions expressed herein rests solely with the author.

1. This experiment is a replication of "Experiment 2" in Miller, Plott, and Smith.
2. See V. L. Smith (1976b) for a formal discussion of induced valuations using cash payoffs.
3. For a discussion of the double auction and other institutions of contract and their potential effect as a treatment variable in experimental markets, see V. L. Smith (1976a).
4. Identical to those in Miller, Plott, and Smith, Appendix 2.
5. Miller, Plott, and Smith use only six trading "years."
6. The induced marginal valuations for individual buyers differs somewhat from those in Miller, Plott, and Smith (1975). This was done in an effort to equalize the expected payoffs, but does not affect the *market* demand schedule and hence should not constitute an effective treatment variable. Buyer marginal valuations in the Miller, Plott, and Smith experiment are as follows:

	\multicolumn{4}{c}{Marginal Valuation}			
Season	\multicolumn{2}{c}{Blue}		\multicolumn{2}{c}{Yellow}	
Unit	1st	2nd	1st	2nd
Buyer 1	2.20	1.00	4.80	3.60
Buyer 2	2.40	1.20	4.60	3.40
Buyer 3	2.60	1.40	4.40	3.20
Buyer 4	2.80	1.60	4.20	3.00
Buyer 5	3.00	1.80	4.00	2.80
Buyer 6	3.20	2.00	3.80	2.60

The expected payoff (profit) per trading year (excluding commissions) in each experiment using the intertemporal equilibrium as the transaction price ($2.80) is as follows:

	M.P. & S.	Experiment I
Buyer 1	2.80	2.40
Buyer 2	2.40	2.00
Buyer 3	2.00	1.80
Buyer 4	1.60	1.80
Buyer 5	1.40	1.80
Buyer 6	1.40	1.80
Total	11.60	11.60

7. The "convergence coefficient," α, is identical to that used by V. L. Smith (1962). Note that α depends not only on S_e but also on P_e and is thus affected by any variation in market structure which would change P_e; the absolute value of α is not meant for

cross-market comparison but rather as an inter-period intramarket indicator of relative convergence.

8. As done in Miller, Plott, and Smith (1975) pp. 7, 8 and discussed in Plott and Smith (1975) pp. 14–19. However, I do not feel it is proper to include transaction commissions as part of the available rent in such an analysis as is done in these two studies. Thus no inefficiency occurs if a marginal unit is not traded. Miller, Plott and Smith use \$21.40 as the figure for maximum available rent per period. This figure includes commissions to buyers and sellers but ignores those to traders. This seems to be an inconsistency since traders are an essential part of the market process. For comparison, the efficiency measures (in Table 4) calculated taking into account buyer and seller commissions are as follows:

Theoretical Autarky Equilibrium	92.5%	*Miller, Plott & Smith*
Period 1	89.7%	94.9%
Period 2	97.7%	99.5%
Period 3	100.0%	99.5%
Period 4	99.5%	94.4%
Period 5	100.0%	94.9%
Period 6	100.0%	94.4%
Period 7	100.0%	—
Average over all periods	98.1%	96.3%

9. Formally:

$$H_O: (\bar{P}_y - \bar{P}_b) = (\bar{P}^*_y - \bar{P}^*_b)$$
$$H_A: (\bar{P}_y - \bar{P}_b) \neq (\bar{P}^*_y - \bar{P}^*_b)$$

where $\bar{P}_i$ $(i = y, b)$ are mean seasonal contract prices from period 7 of Experiment I (with speculation) and $\bar{P}^*_i$ $(i = y, b)$ are mean seasonal contract prices from period 7 of Experiment II (autarky).

$$t(n_y + n_b + n^*_y + n^*_b - 4) = \frac{(\bar{P}_y - \bar{P}_b) - (\bar{P}^*_y - \bar{P}^*_b)}{S\sqrt{(1/n_y) + (1/n_b) + (1/n^*_y) + (1/n^*_b)}}$$

where n_i and n^*_i $(i = y, b)$ are season exchange quantities in Experiments I and II respectively, and S^2 is the pooled estimate of the population variances. Given by:

$$S^2 = \frac{\sum_{j=1}^{n_y} (P_{yj} - \bar{P}_y)^2 + \sum_{j=1}^{n_b} (P_{bj} - \bar{P}_b)^2 + \sum_{j=1}^{n_y^*} (P^*_{yj} - \bar{P}^*_y)^2 + \sum_{j=1}^{n_b^*} (P^*_{bj} - \bar{P}^*_b)^2}{(n_y + n_b + n^*_y + n^*_b - 4)}$$

The above pooling assumes equal variance. Recalculation of the test statistic and degrees of freedom using separate variance estimates does not affect the conclusion of any tests of hypotheses reported in this paper.

Tests of the following null and alternative hypotheses were also performed for period 7:

(A) $H_O: \bar{P}_b = \bar{P}_b^*$
$H_A: \bar{P}_b > \bar{P}_b^*$
(t = 9.92)

(B) $H_O: \bar{P}_y = \bar{P}_y^*$
$H_A: \bar{P}_y < \bar{P}_y^*$
(t = −8.48)

(C) $H_O: \bar{P}_b^* = \bar{P}_y^*$
$H_A: \bar{P}_b^* \neq \bar{P}_y^*$
(t = −18.41)

(D) $H_O: \bar{P}_b = \bar{P}_y$
$H_A: \bar{P}_b \neq \bar{P}_y$
(t = −3.27)

In cases A, B, and C the null hypothesis is rejected at a .0005 significance level. Case D requires that the null hypothesis *not* be rejected at .0005 and .001 levels, but can be rejected with a confidence level of .01.

REFERENCES

Miller, Ross M., Plott Charles R., and Smith, Vernon L. (1975), "Intertemporal Competitive Equilibrium: An Empirical Study of Speculation," California Institute of Technology Social Science Working Paper No. 87. Forthcoming in *Quarterly Journal of Economics*.

Plott, Charles R. and Smith, Vernon L. (April 1975), "An Experimental Examination of Two Exchange Institutions," California Institute of Technology Social Science Working Paper No. 83. Forthcoming in *Review of Economic Studies*.

Smith, Vernon L. (April 1976), "An Experimental Study of Competitive Market Behavior," *Journal of Political Economy* 70: 111–137.

———. (May 1964), "Effect of Market Organization on Competitive Equilibrium," *Quarterly Journal of Economics* 78: 181–201.

———. (August 1965), "Experimental Auction Markets and the Walrasian Hypothesis," *Journal of Political Economy* 73: 387–393.

———. (1976), "Bidding and Auction Institutions: Experimental Results," in *Bidding and Auctioning for Procurement and Allocation*, Yakov Amihud, ed., New York: New York University Press, pp. 274–279.

———. (May 1976), "Experimental Economics: Induced Value Theory," *American Economic Association Papers and Proceedings* 66: 274–279.

SEALED-BID AUCTIONS: EXPERIMENTAL RESULTS AND APPLICATIONS

Meyer W. Belovicz, WAKE FOREST UNIVERSITY

THE THEORY OF SEALED BID AUCTIONS

A sealed bid auction is an economic mechanism for the sale of a fixed quantity of a homogeneous commodity by a single seller. More of this commodity is offered for sale than any one buyer desires to purchase.[1]

In the case in which only one unit of the commodity is offered for sale, the distinction (to be drawn later) between discriminative and competitive rules is eliminated. This case is not of interest since the study focuses on a comparison of the discriminative and competitive auction.

Figure 1 illustrates the sealed bid auction in terms of supply and demand. nn' is the vertical supply curve corresponding to the offer quantity. bb is the

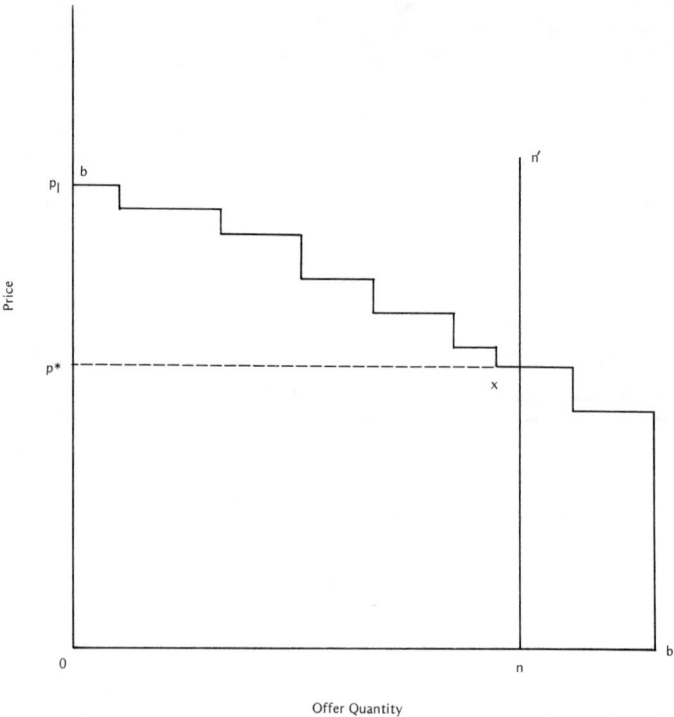

Figure 1. Supply and Demand Curves for Bill Auction.

bidding array, which for the present we can consider as corresponding to a "demand curve." The bids to the left of point x are filled at the bid prices or P*, respectively, for discriminative and competitive auctions. The revenue would be the area under the portion bx of bb for the discriminative rules and the rectangle P*xnO for the competitive rules. For a competitive auction to produce greate revenues, the observed bidding array must be above the observed bidding array for the discriminative section at a quantity of n. This is illustrated in Figure 2; dd is the discriminative bidding array and cc the competitive bidding array. The area B is revenue gained with competitive rules but lost with discriminative rules, and area A the revenue lost with the competitive rules, but gained with discriminative rules. For the competitive auctions to produce greater revenue, A must be greater than B.

A description of the auction mechanism can be in dynamic terms as well as static terms. A static framework may not exist, though, in a particular institutional framework. The market may be one of continual adjustment where this adjustment is related to both prior periods of this same auction and current and prior behavior in related markets. In the next section we shall give some examples of sealed bid auctions.

Sealed-Bid Auctions

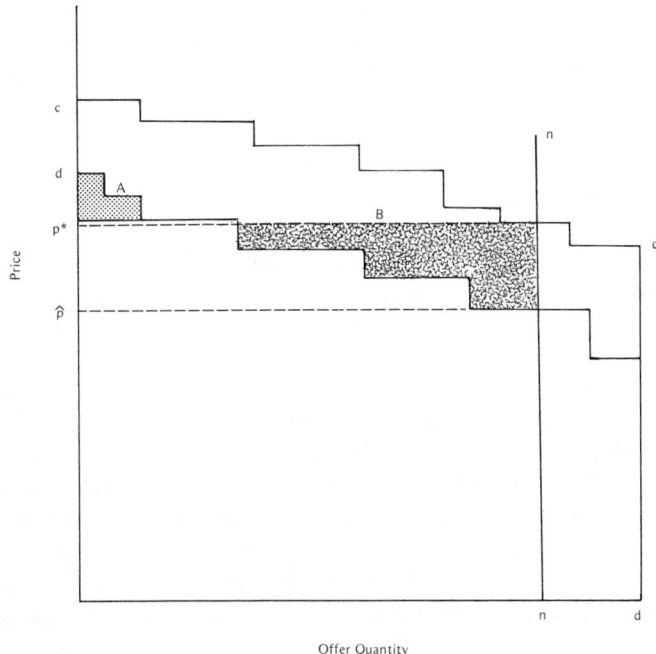

Figure 2. Price Determination in the Bill Auction.

Examples of Sealed Bid Auctions

The sealed bid auction is, for example, a device used to purchase equipment for a municipality, to purchase x number of busses, to let contracts for new road construction (where no contractor can build the required roads in the stated or required time period), to market a bond issue, etc.

Possibly the single most important sealed bid auction run on a continual basis is the Treasury's bill auction. It is described elsewhere (see Belovicz, 1967; Smith, 1967; and Rieber, 1963; 1964). An important controversy regarding the auction method has been discussed extensively (see Brimmer, 1962; Carson, 1959; Friedman, 1960, 1964; Goldstein, 1962; and Rieber, 1963; 1964a; 1964b). The basic question facing the Treasury is whether the competitive or discriminative auction would produce greater revenue.

The Relationship of Theory to Real World and Experimental Equivalents

The theoretical formulation of the problem is a way of condensing the problem into a number of variables and interrelationships of such magnitude that we can meaningfully comprehend the problem and derive implications of the interactions among the pertinent variables. Discussion of real world equivalents of theoretical formulations should, in principle, include a description of the environment in which they are found. The institutions will differ; the extent of the market and the nature of the commodity might have effects. The real world equivalents are influenced by many more factors than can be controlled or accounted for. Elimination of those factors which a priori appear to have the least promise in explaining the phenomena is necessary. This is essentially a theoretical analysis.

An experimental study is also based upon the theory. The theory has experimental equivalents in which a greater number of factors can be held constant. Greater control over the situation can be exercised in the laboratory than in field studies.

The controversy exists as to the relative efficiency in obtaining revenue (or, conversely, reducing the cost to the Treasury) of a discriminative auction vs. a competitive auction in the sale of Treasury bills. There are essentially two ways to determine which one produces greater revenue. The Treasury could at different times run the Treasury bill auction as a competitive and as a discriminative auction. In order to have a valid comparison under those conditions one of two things would be necessary: (1) sufficient trials made under each condition so that the effects of the market at different times could be considered a random distrubance or, (2) the hypothesis maintained that the environment or conditions of the market were comparable when each test was made. In either event we would have a valid comparison of the two methods.

A second approach is to ask a more general question: What would we expect in general by varying the conditions (discriminative vs. competitive) in the theoretical mechanism of a sealed bid auction? How would we expect this to affect the revenue? This can be approached with other analytic techniques and with the experiments designed specifically to correspond to this theoretical mechanism. We would be able to control those variables considered relevant and the environment; therefore, we would be able to test the relative efficiency of the two methods of obtaining revenue. The conclusions we can draw are of course more limited.

These experiments, run in the more limited, controlled environment, must be generalized with care to environments in which similar market mechanisms are operating. They do, however, allow us a close look at what we consider to be the relevant variables and relevant interactions. Revenue is not the only consideration in this instance. The question of collusion has arisen and can be considered in the experimental setting. The significant advantage of the experimental approach for the study of economic theory, in general, is that it affords us an opportunity to gain more insights into the interactions of a small number of relevant variables and their relationships that is not provided by studying a larger system. It is not a substitute for field studies. The insights gained in experimental studies can then help us to alter our analysis of field studies and our theoretical groundworks. These are the purposes of the experimental studies presented here.

EXPERIMENTAL DESIGN

Procedure

The basic experimental design described here was based on that of Smith (1967). A description of the experimental design, based upon the sealed bid auction paradigm, follows.

The experimental design has a single seller (E). At the beginning of each market period E stated the offer quantity of the fictitious commodity. The buyers were (with two exceptions) all students from economics classes and varied in number depending upon the precise experimental conditions. 444 subjects were used in all. Each buyer in the original set of experiments was allowed to bid for two units of the fictitious commodity and the seller (experimenter) offered 18 units of the commodity for sale in each period. The supply (offer quantity) was held constant for all the experiments. It is a variable which can be systematically studied.

The subjects, acting as buyers, were given a set of instructions, which were read simultaneously by the subjects and the experimenter (E). These instructions are presented in Appendix A. A trial period was run after the instructions were read to insure that they had been understood. These instructions described how the sealed bid auction functions, the role of the buyer, the role of the seller, and the meaning of the information regarding the auction results which the buyer would receive. Subjects were told that the seller (E) would announce, prior to the opening of each market period, the quantity being offered that period. Subjects were instructed to enter two bids. E announced to the subjects the highest bid entered and the lowest bid accepted and wrote these on the blackboard. (The resale price was then announced.) This was the feedback the subjects received with respect to the bidding section of the auction, and roughly corresponded to the information published for Treasury bill auctions.

Buyers must be able to buy and then resell a commodity if a profit potential is to exist. The resale market, in the original experiments, consisted of a random drawing from resale prices of $1.15 to $1.95 rectangularly distributed with 10-cent intervals. Uncertainty exists in most real markets and a rectangular resale distribution simulates an uncertain market.

After the resale price was announced, each subject could determine his profits. Subjects participating in a discriminative auction knew that they had purchased one unit at the bid price for each of their bids which exceeded the low accepted bid. When bids equaled the low accepted bid, subjects were told which bids had been accepted and which rejected. A subject's profit then equaled the resale price minus the bid price for each unit if the bid had been accepted, and zero if the bid had not been accepted. During the trial period and after the first period the method of calculating the profits was reiterated by E to assure understanding by the subjects.

Under the competitive condition, profit was equal to the resale price minus the low accepted bid (stop-out price) for each bid accepted and zero if the bid was not accepted.

At the end of each trial, the seller made the statement: "In the next period x eighteen units are offered for sale." The quantity offered was equal to 18 for all of the original experiments and, with a few exceptions, for the other 27 experiments.

Subjects were not informed when the last period would take place. It seems likely, however, that subjects commonly anticipated the end of the experiment since most of the experiments were run during class periods. As the class hour approached completion it probably became obvious to subjects that the experiment could not last much longer.[2]

Independent Variables

The variables and conditions under study in the first set of expriments by Smith were: (1) a comparison of the discriminative and competitive methods of auctioning, and (2) the excess demand (ED). Excess demand is defined as the number of bids entered minus the supply offered. Each bidder in the original experiments was allowed to enter two bids. Three excess demand conditions were used: 13 buyers (ED = 8), 15 buyers (ED = 12), and 17 buyers (ED = 16). Each excess demand condition experiment was run under both competitive and discriminative rules. The experimental conditions are presented in Table 1.

The variables manipulated and considered in these experiments were the bidding rules and the excess demand. Several other variables were held constant for all the experiments. These were: the number of bids per bidder, the number of bidders, the supply (offer quantity), the method of resale,

Table 1. Experimental Conditions in Original Experiments

Experiment Identification	Rules	Number of Bidders	Bids per Bidder	Excess Demand
DR(13,2)	Discriminative	13	2	8
CR(13,2)	Competitive	13	2	8
DR(15,2)	Discriminative	15	2	12
CR(15,2)	Competitive	15	2	12
DR(17,2)	Discriminative	17	2	16
CR(17,2)	Competitive	17	2	16

other supplementary information given the buyers, and communications between the buyers.

It can be seen then that in the original experiments there were three levels of excess demand, defined as the total number of bids minus the supply quantity. Since there were 13, 15 and 17 subjects, respectively, each subject submitting two bids, there were $(2 \times 13) - 18$, or 8 units of excess demand for the lowest condition, and 12 and 16 units for the middle and high excess demand conditions, respectively. One question that can arise in this context is whether the quantity defined as excess demand is in itself a meaningful quantity or whether it is the composition of the quantity which has significance. For example, an excess demand of 8, given a supply of 18, could be obtained in many ways: by 26 subjects entering one bid per subject, by 13 subjects entering two bids per subject, by four subjects entering five bids per subject, and one subject entering six bids, etc. It becomes apparent then that by varying the number of bids per bidder and the number of bidders, we can simulate different market structures. The competitive market, in the standard sense, is approached most closely by the situation with one bid per bidder and the maximum number of bidders for a given excess demand. We can systematically vary the parameters, number the bidders and number of bids per bidder.

A second element that can be varied is the condition under which resale takes place. In the original experiments the resale price had a rectangular distribution with a mean of $1.55: nine prices from $1.15 to $1.95 in intervals of 10 cents. This simulated an uncertain market. At the opposite pole for the same expected price we could have a fixed resale price of $1.55. This would represent a market in which the buyers had perfect knowledge of the resale characteristics and the only uncertainty was on the buying side of the market.

We see that there are two kinds of uncertainties involved in the sealed bid auctions under discussion. There is the uncertainty inherent in the bidding for purchase and the uncertainty in the resale.[4] Manipulation of the resale mechanism allows for further study of uncertainty in the secondary market.

A third variable is what we will call "information" or "knowledge of expected value." All of the theory underlying the predictions is based upon utility maximization. Some predictions are made assuming liniarity of utility of money. It is not clear that the participants in the market necessarily behave that way, nor that they understand or calculate the expected values of the profits under the varying situations. A variation of the experiment then, is to replicate the original experiments with one change: the addition of a profit table describing the profit that could be expected if a participant entered a particular bid and if the lowest bid accepted was any other bid. These are the variables then that are systematically manipulated in the extensions of the original work of Smith.

The reward structure of the original experiments was as follows: Subjects were given a capital balance of $1.00 at the beginning of the experiment. The profits gained by a subject on each trial (or the losses incurred) were then algebraically summed for the entire experiment and added to the initial one dollar stipend. The profits on the trial period (zero-th period) were not included as this was merely a practice session to familiarize the subjects with the rules.

The profit structure is important. One does not want a subject to treat the experiment as a game. One does not want him to feel that he is playing "Monopoly" during his normal class period, but rather to see the situation as one in which he is acting as a real economic agent under the rules specified by the theoretical mechanism in question.

Extensions of Smith's Experimental Work

The original experimental work of Smith was extended in this study along the following dimensions: number of bidders, bids per bidder, resale price mechanism, and information.

The first set of variants on the original paradigm is indicated in Table 2 as the "few bidder" or "unlimited bid" experiments. There are three experiments in that series. DR(9, 4) had almost the same excess demand (18 vs. 16) as DR(17, 2) but there were nine bidders and four bids per bidder. Comparison of DR(9, 4) to DR (17, 2) allowed a test of the hypothesis that it was the excess demand and not the composition of the excess demand that was relevant. Effects of composition are discussed later.

Experiments DR(9, ∞) and CR (9, ∞) had discriminative and competitive rules, respectively. Each one had nine participants and each participant was allowed an unlimited number of bids. In all other respects these experiments were basically the same as those originally performed.

The "single bid" series was the same as the original experiments except in the "single bid" series the number of bidders in the original experiments was doubled and the number of bids per bidder halved. These experiments can then be compared to the experiments of the original series in order to test the effect of components of excess demand, all other factors having been held constant.

The "profit table" series were identical in all respects to the original experiments except that a profit table was supplied. These profit tables are shown in tables 3 and 4 for competitive and discriminative auctions, respectively. These profit tables were important because they emphasized and made clear the expected algebraic profit that a subject would gain if he were to bid a given number and the low accepted bid was any other specified bid. These profit tables can be viewed in a game-theoretic framework where the subject's bid is a strategy and the low accepted bid is a state of

Table 2. Experimental Conditions

Experiment Identification[a]	Rules[b]	Resale[c] Prices	Number of Bidders	Bids per Bidder	Prediction[d]	Profit Table[e]	Excess Demand[f]
Original							
DR(13,2)	D	R	13	2	No	No	8
CR(13,2)[g]	C	R	13	2	No	No	8
DR(15,2)	D	R	15	2	No	No	12
CR(15,2)	C	R	15	2	No	No	12
DR(17,2)	D	R	17	2	No	No	16
CR(17,2)	C	R	17	2	No	No	16
"Few Bidder" or "Unlimited Bid"							
DR(9,4)	D	R	9	4	No	No	18
DR(9,∞)	D	R	9	∞	No	No	∞
CR(9,∞)[h]	C	R	9	∞	No	No	∞
"Single Bid"							
DR(26,1)	D	R	26	1	No	No	8
CR(26,1)	C	R	26	1	No	No	8
DR(30,1)	D	R	30	1	No	No	12
CR(30,1)	C	R	30	1	No	No	12
DR(34,1)	D	R	34	1	No	No	16
CR(33,1)[i]	C	R	33	1	No	No	15
"Profit Table"							
$DR_t(13,2)$	D	R	13	2	No	Yes	8
$CR_t(13,2)$	C	R	13	2	No	Yes	8
$DR_t(15,2)$	D	R	15	2	No	Yes	12
$CR_t(15,2)$	C	R	15	2	No	Yes	12
$DR_t(17,2)$	D	R	17	2	No	Yes	16
$CR_t(17,2)$	C	R	17	2	No	Yes	16
"Fixed Price"							
DF(13,2)	D	F	13	2	No	No	8
CF(13,2)	C	F	13	2	No	No	8
DF(15,2)	D	F	15	2	No	No	12
CF(15,2)	C	F	15	2	No	No	12
DF(17,2)	D	F	17	2	No	No	16
CF(17,2)	C	F	17	2	No	No	16
CF*(15,2)[j]	C	F	15	2	No	No	12
"Fixed Price-Prediction"[k]							
$DF_p(17,2)$	D	F	17	2	Yes	No	16
$CF_p(13,2)$	C	F	13	2	Yes	No	8
"Experienced Subjects"							
$DR_p(15,2)$	D	R	15	2	Yes	No	12
$CR_p(15,2)$	C	R	15	2	Yes	No	12
Replication							
CR*(13,2)[l]	C	R	13	2	No	No	8

[a] This mnemonic device was described in footnote 3.
[b] C = Competitive; D = Discriminative.

Table 2 (*Contd.*)

^cR = Rectangular ($1.15–$1.95 at intervals of $.10) F = Fixed Price ($1.55).
^dYes if required to predict highest bid entered and lowest accepted bid. No if not.
^eYes if given expected profit Tables (Tables 3 or 4) as supplementary information. No if not.
^fNumber of bidders X bids per bidder minus 18.
^gContinuation of DR(13,2) using same subjects but prices for periods 9 to 16 from price series A.
^hSwitched to discriminative rules in 11th period.
ⁱExperimental design called for 34 persons. Class had only 33. Experiment run with 33.
^jCF*(15,2) replicates CF(15,2) with exception that subjects were *not* allowed to enter bids exceeding $1.55.
^kRandom price series B (Appendix B) used for those experiments.
^lReplication of CR(13,2) with exceptions that: (1) price series A entries 0–8 used, and (2) an independent subject group participated.

Table 3. Expected Profits for Competitive Rules

I Bid (in cents)	Lowest Accepted Bid (in cents)								
	115	125	135	145	155	165	175	185	195
115	40	0	0	0	0	0	0	0	0
125	40	30	0	0	0	0	0	0	0
135	40	30	20	0	0	0	0	0	0
145	40	30	20	10	0	0	0	0	0
155	40	30	20	10	0	0	0	0	0
165	40	30	20	10	0	−10	0	0	0
175	40	30	20	10	0	−10	−20	0	0
185	40	30	20	10	0	−10	−20	−30	0
195	40	30	20	10	0	−10	−20	−30	−40

Table 4. Expected Profits for Discriminative Rules

I Bid (in cents)	Lowest Accepted Bid (in cents)								
	115	125	135	145	155	165	175	185	195
115	40	0	0	0	0	0	0	0	0
125	30	30	0	0	0	0	0	0	0
135	20	20	20	0	0	0	0	0	0
145	10	10	10	10	0	0	0	0	0
155	0	0	0	0	0	0	0	0	0
165	−10	−10	−10	−10	−10	−0	0	0	0
175	−20	−20	−20	−20	−20	−20	−20	0	0
185	−30	−30	−30	−30	−30	−30	−30	−30	0
195	−40	−40	−40	−40	−40	−40	−40	−40	−40

nature. With this framework, one draws the same conclusions regarding the relative effects on the bidders as are drawn from the bidding theory (see Smith, 1967). In both cases the only assumptions that need to be made about the utility functions of individuals are that they are monotonically increasing. Therefore, profit tables were used in order to test the hypothesis that people would behave more like expected utility maximizers given that explicit information.

A second reason for the use of profit tables was to make clear to the subjects what profits they could expect, on the average, under varying conditions. There is little reason to believe that they have this information or are able to compute it. Various hypotheses can be formed to test the effect of this information and these experiments can be compared to the original set, as well as the "single bid" series.

The "fixed price" experiments were the last complete set of experiments performed and only one condition of the original experiments was varied, i.e. the resale price mechanism. In the original experiments a random resale price mechanism, representing uncertainty in the secondary or resale market, was used. In the "fixed price" experiments subjects were informed that any units purchased would automatically be resold at a fixed price of $1.55. This price was the mean of the prior rectangular distribution.

One additional experiment, CF* (Friedman, 1964; Aumann and Maschler, 1964), was performed in this set. This experiment was carried out with 15 bidders under competitive rules where the subjects were informed at the beginning of the experiment that they would not be allowed to enter any bid in excess of $1.55, the resale price. The reasons for this were not stated, it was simply one of the rules. This experiment was performed because participants in several competitive experiments entered bids that exceeded any possible resale price. This was also true in experiment CF(15,2), a fixed price experiment with 15 bidders and competitive rules. Replication of this experiment, with the one additional stipulation that no bid in excess of $1.55 would be accepted, made it possible to examine the effect of bids exceeding $1.55, if any, on the results. This was important because one could view these bids which were in excess of any possible resale price in several ways: (1) as conscious strategies designed to scare other subjects into lowering bids, (2) as a "game" which had no rational explanation, or (3) as reflections of high utility of successful bids. This replication allowed the experimenter to examine these possible explanations.

The "fixed price" experiments must be compared to the original experiments, to the "single bid" experiments, and to others, in order to test the effects of uncertainty or the removal of uncertainty in the secondary market. The premise that the results of the "fixed price" experiments were due to uncertainties only in the primary market allowed other analyses to be carried out. Comparisons allow one to study the existence or lack of existence of a risk premium.

Two additional "fixed price" experiments were performed, $DF_p(17,2)$ and $CF_p(13,2)$. They differed from those in the "fixed price" series in that subjects predicted what they thought the high and low accepted bid in each period would be at the same time as they entered their bids for that period. These experiments were performed for two reasons: (1) to obtain at least a partial replication of some experiments already performed and determine the stability of the results, and (2) to examine the relationship of the bids entered by subjects and predictions of low and high accepted bids made by those subjects.

$DR_p(15,2)$ and $CR_p(15,2)$ were identical to the original experiments $DR(15,2)$ and $CR(15,2)$ with the exception that (1) the subjects were required to predict the high and low bid in the period, (2) the subjects had all participated in prior experiments, and (3) the random resale prices were drawn from another series because the subjects had participated in prior experiments.

These experiments were carried out with several purposes in mind. One purpose was to study, as in $DF_p(17,2)$ and $CF_p(13,2)$, the relationship between the predicted bids and the actual bidding behavior. A second purpose was to study the effects of prior participation, or learning, on the behavior of subjects. The question raised here was whether the behavior which resulted would be substantially the same as the behavior of "naive" subjects.

The last "set" of experiments consisted of only one experiment, $CR*(13,2)$. This was considered to be a replication of one other experiment, $CR(13,2)$. Experiments $DR(13,2)$ and $CR(13,2)$ were run on a common subject group with $DR(13,2)$ performed during the first part of the experimental session and $CR(13,2)$ performed during the last part of the session. Thus, rules were changed from discriminative to competitive. $CR*(13,2)$ could be compared to $DR(13,2)$ on the same basis as $CR(17,2)$ could be compared to $DR(17,2)$, $CF(15,2)$ to $DF(15,2)$ and so on.

HYPOTHESES

Macro-Hypotheses

Two types of hypotheses are tested with respect to these experiments, (1) macro-hypotheses, and (2) micro-hypotheses. Macro-hypotheses involve individual *and* aggregate behavior elicited by these experiment while micro-hypotheses involve only individual behavior. Both types of hypotheses are of interest. The utility theory analysis of the sealed bid auctions, which can be found in Smith (1967), is not repeated here, but the macro-hypotheses that flow from it are reiterated.

Hypotheses developed from the game-theoretic analysis are further explicated in this section. The micro-, or individual hypotheses, are simply stated as behavioral in nature. That is to say that, rather than deriving from analytic frameworks, they are derivatives of behavioral assumptions. Some further micro-hypotheses are drawn from considerations of behavior under risk.

The original hypotheses derived by Smith are:

H_1: In the t-th auction period, the variance of bids tendered by subjects in a C (competitive) group $V(B_c^t)$ exceeds the variance of bids tendered by subjects in corresponding D (discriminative) group $V(B_D^t)$, i.e.

$$V(B_c^t) > V(B_D^t), \text{ for } t = 1,2,\ldots n.$$

H_2: In the t-th auction, the bids B_c^t, tendered by subjects in a C (competitive) group, exceed the bids B_D^t tendered by subjects in a corresponding D (discriminative) group, i.e.

$$B_c^t > B_D^t \text{ for } t = 1,2,\ldots n.$$

H_3: In the t-th auction, the total revenue to a seller in a C group R_c^t exceeds that of a corresponding D group R_d^t, i.e.

$$R_c^t > R_D^t, t = 1,2,\ldots n.$$

H_4: With a fixed offer quantity, in corresponding auction periods, bids tendered by the subjects in D groups, B_D^t, are higher the greater the excess demand, i.e.

$$B_D^t(NR_1) > B_D^t(NR_2) > B_D^t(NR_3) > B_D^t(NR_k); \text{ for } t = 1,2,\ldots n.$$

if

$$NR_1 > NR_2 > NR_3 \ldots > NR_k$$

H_5: Same as H_4 applied to C groups, i.e.

$$B_C^t(NR_1) > B_c^t(NR_2) > B_c^t(NR_3) \ldots > B_c^t(NR_n)$$

if

$$NR_1 > NR_2 > NR_3 > \ldots > NR_n \text{ for } t = 1,2,\ldots n.$$

Hypotheses H_1, H_2, and H_3 are labeled H_1^1, H_2^1, and H_3^1 respectively, when used for the same subjects subjected to both conditions, CR(13,2) and DR(13,2), in the same experiment.

One micro-hypothesis was derived by Smith. That is H_6.

H_6: Subjects whose utility is linear in money will submit equal bids, each less than $\bar{P}$ (average resale price, $1.55) in a discriminative auction and equal bids equal to $\bar{P}$ in a competitive auction.

Table 3 is the profit table under the competitive rules and Table 4 the profit table under the discriminative rules. The rows in Tables 3 and 4 represent "strategies" available to the subject and the columns represent "states of Nature." Looking first at Table 4 we see that all strategies of bids equal to or greater than $1.55 are dominated by all strategies of bids less than $1.45. It is clear that a participant, whose utility of money was monotonic, would never bid in excess of $1.45. That is, he would always bid below the expected mean. On the other hand, if we observe Table 3, the competitive rules expected profit table, we see that strategies "I bid $1.45" or "I bid $1.55" are equally good and dominate *all other strategies*.

Analysis of these expected profit tables must be carried out with several reservations. The same profit table applies as the uncertainty in the resale market can be represented by a symetric distribution with a finite variance and mean price of $1.55. Each entry in Tables 3 and 4 is the expected profit for *one successful bid only* at a given amount and under a given state of nature.

To completely analyze these profit tables one would have to make assumptions about the subjective density function a subject associated with the various states of nature. One of the major difficulties in deriving hypotheses is that the subject must take into account not only his own behavior but the interactions of his behavior and all others as it affects the final outcomes. We summarize his consideration of these interactions in the density function which he assigns to the low accepted bid. We hope to learn what assumptions we are justified in making from analysis of the experiments in which subjects predicted the low and high bids in each period at the same time as they entered their bids. The a priori assumption here is that in the absence of explicit cooperative or collusive behavior the subjects assume that the low accepted bid in period $t + 1$ will not vary much from the low accepted bid in period t.

We could expect the market under consideration to go through a dynamic process, during which the price would rise and then stabilize. While the price was rising the low accepted low bid in period $t + 1$ would be expected to exceed that in period t, and when equilibrium was reached the accepted low bid would be expected to be equal to that in the prior period.

Examining Table 4, the expected profit table for the discrimination auction, we observe that any bids equal to or greater than $1.55 are dominated by any bids equal to or less than $1.45. Assuming only that the subjects had monotonic utility functions, we would expect that no bid would exceed $1.45. We should observe no bids at the mean price (or greater) of the resale distribution in discrimination auctions.

On the other hand, we observe that under the competitive rules (Table 3), the expected profits for a single bid are such that strategies of bidding $1.45 or $1.55 are equally good and dominate all other strategies. Under the discriminative rules bids less than $1.55 represent strategies, none of which are dominated and none of which dominate others. These two facts, in conjunction, result in the same conclusion as Hypothesis H_2: the bids tendered in a competitive group exceed the bids tendered in a discriminative group, all other factors being equal.

Expecting bids to be $1.45 or less under the discriminative rules, and either $1.45 or $1.55 under the competitive rules, is not sufficient to imply Hypothesis H_1, i.e., from the profit table analysis alone we would not conclude that bids under the competitive rules would have a greater variance than bids under the discriminative rules. To draw that conclusion using the profit tables we would need some assumption about the subjective probability individuals place on the low accepted bid. Regardless of the subjective density function placed upon the accepted low bid by the subjects, there is no reason to exceed the mean resale price under the discriminative rules.

On the other hand, under the competitive rules, if a subject places zero probability (or a probability sufficiently low) on low accepted bids exceeding the mean price or equalling the mean resale price, then he could bid in excess of this price. We would then require, within this analysis of the profit tables, that subject's density functions for the low accepted bid be uniformly below, or equal to, P (mean resale price) for the variances under the competitive condition to be greater. This hypothesis can be tested using the data from the experiments in which subjects predicted the low accepted bid. The hypothesis is as follows:

Hypothesis: The density functions for the low accepted bid are at or near the prior low accepted bids and below the mean resale price for most of the subjects.

Confirmation of this hypothesis would lead us to formulate hypothesis H_1 from the game-theoretic analysis.

From the profit table, we can also conclude H_3, the hypothesis that the revenue to a seller under the competitive rules exceeds the revenue to a seller under the discriminative rules. Examination of the profit table indicates that under the discriminative rules we would expect the individual bids to be $1.45 or $1.55 or greater and, hence, the market clearing price to be in that range. It also follows that although revenue differences may exist in equilibrium (under this analysis) they do not necessarily exist in the dynamic approach to the static equilibrium. We shall state H_3 as a hypothesis without further support.

The hypothesis, H_4, that the greater the excess demand the greater will be the level of bids tendered by a discrimination group, is stated as a behavioral hypothesis. Hypothesis H_5, that H_4 applies to the competitive group, is also a behavioral hypothesis.

The final macro-hypotheses considered are those dealing with risk premium. We would expect uncertainty in the secondary market to require compensation to the buyers. Revenue under the fixed price resale condition should exceed the revenue under the random resale price condition, all other factors being equal. This is tested by comparison of revenue per period in the corresponding "fixed price" and original experiments.

The macro-hypotheses are tested by comparing results that are a function of the group behavior. These tests are a period-by-period analysis. The level of the bids and the variance of the bids under varying conditions is compared for corresponding periods. The macro-hypotheses are tested both in the dynamic state and under equilibrium conditions. The tests do not directly distinguish the dynamic and static states. It is implicitly assumed that the nth period in a given condition is equivalent to the nth period in the comparative condition.

Micro-Hypotheses

On the other hand, the individual analyses are comparisons of behavior across periods rather than within periods and within subjects rather than across subjects. The question here is: Can a person's bids be predicted or explained from the prior observations of other variables?

The individual micro-hypotheses were derived from behavioral asumptions regarding individual behavior. The first hypothesis is that subjects' bids are related to what they predict the low bid to be. This hypothesis states that people enter bids consistently related to predictions across periods. For example, an expected profit maximizer ought to enter bids equal to his expectation of the low bid rather than equal to the mean resale price. There will be persons who can be expected to consistently enter bids somewhat above the expected low bid because they have a greater utility for winning smaller amounts. If we hypothesize linear utility functions we should expect that in a linear regression, in which the bids are the dependent variables and the low accepted bid the independent variable, we should obtain an intercept of 0 and a slope of one. Naturally, there would be variation, but for large groups the distribution of a and b should approximate these assumptions. The data available allow this relationship to be tested for the four experiments in which subjects predicted the low accepted bid.

A second individual hypothesis is that subjects treat the low accepted bid in period t as an estimate of the low accepted bid in period $t + 1$. It would follow from the first micro-hypothesis that there should be a relationship between bids entered and the low accepted bid lagged one period. This hypothesis can be tested for all subjects. The test is the same as in the prior hypothesis.

The third individual hypothesis tested relates to the resale price lagged one period. The participants in the auction verbalize the belief that the resale price is not a random variable whose consecutive values are uncorrelated. Assuming gambler's fallacy (in some form) we should expect a significant relationship between the resale price lagged one and the bids. It would seem that when the resale price was close to an extreme the bids should move closer to the mean. We would expect that bids would be increased when the resale price is "unusually" low and that the bids should be decreased when the resale price is "unusually" high. We can test the hypothesis that bidding behavior is independent of the resale price when it is a random variable. This is important as this is an assumption that underlies much of the analysis and, consequently, should be tested prior to other analyses. This individual hypothesis is also related to the hypothesis of risk premium. The risk premium theory implies that the bidding behavior is independent of the particular resale price observed but is a function of the magnitude of the variance of the resale price. For individuals we should observe that the bids are independent of the lagged resale prices and should observe greater revenue in the fixed price experiments than in the random resale experiments. We can test the hypothesis about the individual behavior with respect to the resale prices only for those persons not in the fixed price experiments.

The last micro-hypothesis is that bidding behavior is influenced by recent profits. This is tested by examining an assumed linear relationship between bids and profits lagged one period.

Other Hypotheses

There are a number of experiments that can be considered as replications. Comparisons of the results (whether they relate to revenue, bid level, or variance of bids) obtained in the replicated experiments provides us with a measure of the variation between experiments when all conditions are held constant except for subject group. It is important to have estimates of the various kinds of errors that we can encounter in such situations so as to be able to estimate the effects of each variable.

We can measure equilibrium in several ways: (1) as a measure of revenue and its stability—when does the revenue settle down and keep a constant level: (2) by comparing the inter-period bids—when do the distributions of bids in adjacent periods appear similar? Equilibrium measures of both revenue and interperiod bidding, and experimental session replicability are reported.

A one-to-one correspondence does not necessarily exist between the measures of individual behavior and the measures of aggregate behavior for the pertinent macro-economic variables.[5] For example, revenues could be equal even though the "level" of bids in one situation exceeded the "level" of bids under another condition. We would then conclude that the macro-economic effects were relatively insensitive to the conditions. The relationships between the macro- and micro-variables are reported where this is possible.

Summary of Macro-Hypotheses

(1) Bids tendered under the competitive rules exceed bids tendered under discriminative rules, all other factors being equal.
(2) The variance of bids under competitive rules exceed the variance of bids under discriminative rules, all other factors being equal.
(3) In corresponding periods, revenue from competitive auctions exceeds revenue from discriminative auctions, all other factors being equal.
(4) The greater the excess demand (with a fixed offer quantity) the higher are the bids for discriminative auction.
(5) The greater the excess demand (with a fixed offer quantity) the higher are the bids for competitive auctions.
(6) Revenue from fixed price experiments exceeds revenue from uncertain resale experiments all other factors being equal.

Summary of Micro-Hypotheses

(1) Bids entered by each individual are related to their prediction of the low accepted bid.
(2) Bids entered by each individual are related to the low accepted bid lagged one period.
(3) Bids entered by each individual are *independent* of the resale price lagged one period.
(4) Bids entered by each individual are related to profits in the prior period.

RESULTS OF MACRO-ANALYSIS

In this section the results for each macro-hypothesis are presented and discussed. Where it seems particularly useful, the results of two or more hypotheses are discussed in relationship to each other. In general, however, a discussion of the interrelationships is reserved for the Summary and Discussion.

Test of H_1

Hypothesis H_1: The variance of the bids under the competitive condition will exceed the variance of the bids under the discriminative condition in the corresponding periods, all other factors being equal.

Homogeneity of variance was tested under the null hypotheses using the F statistic. Table 5 reports the results of the F test by period for the appropriate comparisons.

There were several competitive rule experiments in which extraordinarily high bids were entered. Bids in excess of maximum possible resale price, $1.95 in the case of the rectangular resale distribution, and $1.55 in the case of the fixed price experiments were set equal to $1.95 and $1.55, respectively. The explicit assumption here is that a person would not want their bid to win if, in fact, they had to enter a bid in excess of maximum resale price. This need not be true when one considers a longer time period or the existence of arguments in the utility function other than money. Other explanations could account for excessively high bids.

McDonald and Jacquillat (1974) provides an explanation of apparently unreasonably high bids in the French auction of common stock and Vickrey (1961) provides a sound rationale for eliminating the high bid in a sealed bid Dutch auction.

In the French common stock auctions "excessively" high bids are rejected. High but acceptable bids are filled 100 percent, bids in a mid-range are filled 50 percent, and bids between the offering price established by the committee controlling this auction and the mid-range are filled 30 percent. Bids below the offered price are rejected. A single market clearing price is charged all persons receiving part of the allocation. The "excessively" high bids are comparable to bids at market in the Treasury Bill auction and are assumed to be based on little information. They basically represent uniformed bidding. Since the purpose of the French auction *is to establish* a fair market, they are rejected. Bids in excess of $1.95 entered in our experiments may have similar motivation to the "excessively" high bids in the French common stock auction.

Vickrey demonstrates that in a sealed bid Dutch auction awarding the object to the top bidder at the second high bidder's price ("second-price method") increases aggregated profits of the buyers and sellers over the "top-price method" which is the award of the object to the top bidder at *his bid*. Allocative efficiency is improved. This is another reason for elimination of "excessive" bids.

Since the results of the comparison of variances were still significant where this change was made, it can be concluded that the variance under the competitive condition was greater than the variance under the discriminative condition.

The use of reduced maximum bids for the t-tests was justified because the alternative was a nonparametric statistic that assumed only the characteristic "greater than." If the maximum bid entered in one experiment is $1.55, any bid in excess of $1.55 in a second experiment has an equal effect in the computation of the nonparametric statistic. Thus, the extremely high bids entered in those competitive auctions would not increase the measures of the difference in the levels of the bids biasing toward acceptance of the hypothesis.

The data, in general, support the hypotheses H_1 and H'_1. In the original set of experiments all F's were significant with the exception of the first four trials of the low excess demand condition and the third trial of the

Table 5. F Ratio Test of H_1 and H_1': $V(B_c^l) > V(B_D^l)$[a]

Row No.	Paired Experiment	Degrees of Freedom f_c	f_d	Auction Period 0	1	2	3	4	5	6	7	8	9	10	11	12	13	14
1	CR(13,2)																	
2	DR(13,2) vs CR(15,2)	25	25	0	2.3°	1.5	1.0	11.7*	6.7*	5.7*	3.6*	3.0*						
3	DR(15,2) vs CR(17,2)	29	29	2.3°	3.2*	12.9*	.6	9.4*	20.8*									
4	DR(17,2) vs CR*(13,2)	33	33		13.5*	19.3*	20.5*	28.0*	3.5*	43.9*	21.5*	1105.5*	62.2*	124.5*				
5	DR(13,2) vs CR(9,∞)	25	a	1.2	1.4	1.6	1.2	4.4*	3.2*	3.3*	3.9*	3.9*						
6	DR(9,∞) vs CR(26,1)	60	60	1.8	1.0	1.8	2.5°	1.6	.6	1.3	.7	9.9*	21.4*	10.6*				
7	DR(26,1) vs CR(30,1)	25	25	2.0^x	4.9*	6.7*	4.8*	2.1^x	8.5*	1.1	1.3	1.6	2.5°	3.6*	3.5*	4.2*		
8	DR(30,1) vs CR(33,1)	29	29	.9	2.0^x	2.4°	3.1*	5.6*	5.5*	6.8*	.4	2.9°	.7	.2				
9	DR(34,1) vs CR$_1$(13,2)	32	32	1.1	9.0*	4.1*	6.7*	7.5*	4.6*	12.2*	47.7*	19.6*	.2					
	DR$_1$(13,2) vs	25	25	.6	2.2°	1.5	3.2*	3.9*	3.1*	3.8*	6.6*	8.0*	11.6*	6.5*	15.2*			

	Comparison																	
10	$CR_t(15,2)$ vs $DR_t(15,2)$	29	29	2.5°	3.6*	1.8	2.2°	7.1*	1.9^x	9.8*	7.7*	5.2*	.2	10.0*				
11	$CR_t(17,2)$ vs $DR_t(17,2)$	33	33	1.1	2.7°	2.5°	2.3°	6.7*	5.6*	6.2*	7.1*	13.2*	4.9*					
12	$CF(13,2)$ vs $DF(13,2)$	25	25	.4	3.1*	3.6*	6.0*	.9	15.9*	.9	2.4*	4.4*						
13	$CF(15,2)$ vs $DF(15,2)$	29	29	.7	2.0°	5.4*	1.1	4.0*	8.3*	.4	70.7*	.2	108.3*	43.6*	.9	.6	.2	1.6
14	$CF(17,2)$ vs $DF(17,2)$	33	33	1.4	3.2*	3.3*	3.7*	13.3*	.5	17.6*	11.8*	55.7*	2.6°					
15	$CR_p(15,2)$ vs $DR_p(15,2)$	29	29	14.2*	1.2	5.9*	21.0*	36.3*	33.2*	35.2*	53.7*	42.3*	12.9*	25.1*	62.3*	30.9*		

^x Significant at $p = .05$
° Significant at $p = .025$
* Significant at $p = .005$

$^a F = \dfrac{V(B_C^t)}{V(B_D^t)}$ where $V(B_C^t)$ = variance of bids in period t under competitive rules;
and $V(B_D^t)$ = variance of bids in period t under discriminative rules.

Table 6. T-Test of H_2 and H'_2: $B'_c > B^{t,a}_D$

Row No.	Paired Experiment	Excess Demand	0	1	2	3	4	5	6	7	8	9	10	11	12	13	14
1	CR(13,2) vs DR(13,2)	8	8.5*	4.5*	9.6*	8.0*	6.2*	6.4*	4.7*	7.7*	7.4*						
2	CR(15,2) vs DR(15,2)	12	2.2	4.3*	3.7*	4.4*	5.0*	3.5*									
3	CR(17,2) vs DR(17,2)	16		.7	.7	1.0	1.7	.6	.9	1.2	.1	.4	0				
4	CR*(13,2) vs DR(13,2)	8	2.3°	2.3°	3.1*	3.0*	3.1*	2.7°	2.0ˣ	1.7ˣ	1.8ˣ						
5	CR(9,∞) vs DR(9,∞)	8	.9	5.8*	5.0*	5.6*	9.3*	5.1*	6.1*	4.8*	5.5*	6.2*	1.0	.5			
6	CR(26,1) vs DR(26,1)	8	−.5	.2	−.1	.7	1.0	.6	1.3	1.9ˣ	1.5	2.6°	3.1*	2.7°	2.2*		
7	CR(30,1) vs DR(30,1)	12	.7	2.6°	3.0*	3.7*	3.5*	2.7°	1.1	2.9*	4.3*	1.6	1.9ˣ				
8	CR(33,1) vs DR(33,1)	16	0	1.7ˣ	1.7ˣ	2.8*	3.2*	2.4°	4.3*	.3	1.9ˣ	2.0ˣ					
9	CR$_f$(13,2) vs DR$_f$(13,2)	8	−.6	1.7	−.6	1.4	2.8*	5.4*	4.0*	3.7*	4.4*	6.2*	5.1*	4.4*			
10	CR$_f$(15,2) vs DR$_f$(15,2)	12	−.5	1.1	3.6*	2.7°	2.9°	4.3*	3.0*	3.4*	3.9*	9.5*	3.7*				

11	$CR_I(17,2)$ vs $DR_I(17,2)$	16	−.2	.8	.8	.4	−1.9	−.7	.5	.4	−.8	.2
12	$CF(13,2)$ vs $DF(13,2)$	8	1.9^x	1.2	.9	1.3	1.5	.8	$2.1°$	$2.7°$	−.7	
13	$CF(15,2)$ vs $DF(15,2)$	12	−.4	1.4	1.9^x	$2.3°$	1.2	.1	$3.0*$	−.1	$2.3°$	.1	−.7	.7	1.5	2.0^x	$3.5*$
14	$CF(17,2)$ vs $DF(17,2)$	16	−.1	1.0	1.3	1.1	1.2	1.3	1.4	−.1	0	.5	.2	1.6	1.0	$2.7°$
15	$CR_p(15,2)$ vs $DR_p(15,2)$	12	.5	.5	$3.3*$	$2.9*$	1.0	$2.5°$	$2.4°$	$2.0°$	.5	1.9^x	1.5

^{x}Significant at p = .05
$^°$Significant at p = .025
*Significant at p = .005.

$$a_t = \frac{\bar{B}^t_c - \bar{B}^t_D}{\sqrt{\frac{V(B^t_c) + V(B^t_D)}{m}}} \quad \text{where}$$

$\bar{B}^t_c$ = mean of competitive bids in t-th period;
$\bar{B}^t_D$ = mean of discriminative bids in t-th period;
$V(B^t_c)$ = variance of bids in period t under competitive rules;
$V(B^t_D)$ = variance of bids in period t under discriminative rules; and
m = number of paired observations.

intermediate excess demand condition (12 units). All but two of the significant values were at the .005 level. Those two were at the .025 level. The profit table experiments (lines 9–11) also strongly support the hypothesis. The few exceptions were the first several periods (having insignificant F's for the low excess demand condition) and the 9th period in the intermediate excess demand condition.

The fixed price experiments, in general, support the hypotheses, although this support is somewhat weaker being greatest in the high and low excess demand conditions.

With one exception the F's were significant at or about the .005 level under the condition using the experienced subjects.

One major exception should be noted, that is, the unlimited bidding experiments in which, with the exceptions of the 9th and 10th periods, only two of the variances were significantly greater under the competitive condition.

The general conclusion we would draw from this evidence is that under most of the conditions examined there is a significantly greater variance under the competitive rules than under the discriminative rules, but that convergence of the distributions takes place under the unlimited bid condition.

Comparison of CR(13,2) to DR(13,2) shows the same pattern as the tests of hypothesis H_1 for the comparison of CR*(13,2) and DR(13,2). In the initial periods variance was not significantly greater under the competitive condition when the same subjects were used and the rules were changed in mid-game, but variances were greater under the competitive condition in periods 4 through 8. The same results were obtained using two different subjects' populations. This can be interpreted as an encouraging result in that the same effects were obtained using the same subjects and using independent subject groups. This lends further support to the interpretation that it is the rules and not other factors that produce the effect.

Tests of H_2 and H'_2

Hypothesis H_2 asserts that for independent subject groups, all other factors being equal, the bids tendered in a competitive auction will "exceed" the bids tendered in a discriminative auction.

In the original study by Smith the hypotheses H_2 and H'_2 were tested using the Jonckheere test (order statistic). A paired-observation t-test was used in addition to the Jonckheere test.

Table 7 presents the results of the Jonckheere order this found in Smith (42 p. 68) and Table 6 presents the t-values obtained for the same data. Comparison of the results of the Jonckheere order statistic and the t-test for the original experiment allows generalization to the remaining tests.

Table 7. Jonckheere Test of H_2 and H_2': $B_c^t > B_D^t$

Paired Experiments[a]	Excess Demand	Auction Period									
		1	2	3	4	5	6	7	8	9	10
CR(13,2) vs DR(13,2)	8	3.3	6.0	6.1	4.5	4.6	2.8	4.5	3.8		
CR(15,2) vs DR(15,2)	12	3.6	3.9	4.3	4.1	4.0					
CR(17,2) vs DR(17,2)	16	−1.0	−.7	.5	1.4	1.4	.4	0	0	.1	.6

Note: Entries are z unit normal deviates. Table taken from Smith (1967, p. 68).
[a]In order of predicted increasing level of bids. Entries in first two rows significant in predicted direction at $\alpha = .001$. Entries in bottom row not significant in predicted direction.

Using the Jonckheere test, results of comparisons between corresponding periods for CR(13,2) and DR(13,2) (excess demand equaled 8) and CR(15,2) and DR(15,2) (excess demand equaled 12) were all significant at $\alpha = .001$. The comparison of CR(17,2) and DR(17,2) (excess demand equaled 16) indicated no significant entries. Lines 1, 2, and 3 of Table 6 correspond to lines 1, 2, and 3 of Table 8. In Table 6, lines 1 and 2, all t-values (period 1 on) are significant at the .005 level. In line 3 no values are significant.

The t-values using the paired observation t-test technique were greater than the corresponding z's using the Jonckheere order statistic. This follows reasonably from the fact that the Jonckheere order statistic is a non-parametric test making fewer assumptions about the form of the distribution. The Jonckheere test gives results consistent with those of the t-tests.

The t statistics reported here are based upon the paired observation technique where the F was significant. Where the F was not significant, the t was recomputed by the standard procedure if the t, based on the paired observation method, was not already significant. A t-value of 5, computed with the paired observation technique, would be equal to a t-value of 7 using the standard procedure. It was not felt necessary to recompute these when such recomputation would not change the conclusion.

The original experiments (lines 2–4) indicate that under the low and intermediate excess demand a significant difference in bid level existed between the competitive and discriminative auctions confirming H_2. Under high excess demand the null hypothesis was not rejected. H'_2, the comparisons of CR(13,2) and DR(13,2), was also accepted. This again is confirming evidence that rules, given uncertainty in the secondary market, affected the results.

The same conclusions are reached for the profit table experiments. With eight and twelve rejected bids there was a significant difference in the level of the bids, but not with 16 rejected bids. The results of the t-tests, and F-tests indicate greater similarity between the original experiments and the profit table modifications. This would suggest that the introduction of information in the form of the profit table did not affect the results.

The replication using experienced subjects gives confirming evidence to the hypothesis in only about half of the periods run. Under the single bid condition positive results with respect to this hypothesis were obtained under all excess demand conditions, but less consistently. Under the fixed price condition there were only a few confirmations of the hypothesis. There is no statistically significant difference between competitive and discriminative rules in corresponding periods under the fixed price condition. While it is tempting to attribute this to the lack of uncertainty in the secondary market, it is important to recognize that this is confounded with the fact that every agent had equal resale prices. The effect of having resale prices both certain and unequal could be tested. One conjecture is that certain but unequal resale prices would more closely parallel the differing perceptions given an uncertain secondary market and generate the difference between competitive and discriminative treatments. Under the unlimited bidding condition, with the exception of the final period, significant differences between the competitive and discriminative conditions were found throughout.

In the original experiment the conclusion was drawn that with high excess demand the differences between bids no longer existed (compared to 8 and 12 rejected bids). See Table 6, lines 2–4, and Table 7. We should expect to find the same thing true in the comparison of the rules in the unlimited bidding condition. The unlimited bidding condition had nine subjects, each of whom could enter as many bids as he desired. Nevertheless, for this condition bids were greater under the competitive rules than under the discriminative rules. It would appear that it is not simply the excess demand (or number of rejected bids) that causes differences in bid level when the rules are compared.

We found a significant difference in the level of bids for all excess demand conditions in the single bid experiments (which were all uncertain resale prices) and no significant differences for any excess demand conditions in the fixed price experiments. An explanation for the latter result would be convergence of the general level of bids due to the removal of the uncertainty in the secondary market, but this should be qualified because of the confounding of certainty in the secondary market with a common resale value for all agents.

In the original experiments and all of the following experiments the offer quantity was 18. When there were 16 rejected bids in the two bid case it was due to the fact that there were 17 subjects each of whom could enter two bids. Under this condition a skewness or bimodality would be produced if one bid was a "real" bid and one a "throwaway." If there was a tendency to operate in this manner, with a "real" and a "throwaway" bid, we might expect to find little difference between the two treatments.

On the other hand, in the single bid experiment there was no possibility of a "throwaway" bid and, in the fixed prices experiments, the removal of the uncertainty in the secondary market made a throwaway bid quite unnecessary when one was bidding in a range that guaranteed a profit if the bid were accepted.

Why do the unlimited bidding case and the original experiments differ? Both have approximately the same number of bidders while the unlimited has a much greater ratio of demand to supply. The conclusion to be drawn from this analysis is that the relevant variable is not rejected bids as a proportion of the total (i.e. 16 rejected out of 34 tendered, or approximately 50 percent) but rather is related to the number of bidders. If this is correct it would seem that (1) when the number of bidders was approximately equal to the number of units being offered and (2) when each bidder was allowed two bids, we would observe the same results as we did in the comparison of CR(17,2) and DR(17,2) and $CR_1(17,2)$ and $DR_1(17,2)$. Whether this would be true for other numbers of bidders is conjectural.

The results obtained here suggest that we need a different explanation than the ratio of rejected bids to total bids to explain the phenomenon. The following explanation is tentatively offered. In the case of the original experiments and profit table experiments (replications of the original experiments) with eight and twelve rejected bids we observe a difference in the means of the competitive and discriminative bid distributions but do not observe a difference with sixteen rejected bids. If, in fact, the ratio of rejected bids to total bids were the correct explanation, we should observe no difference under the unlimited bidding condition. We observe, however, significant differences (with one exception) under the unlimited bidding condition. Further, if excess demand as a ratio to total demand is used as an explanation, we should observe no difference in results when comparing single bid experiments with sixteen rejected bids. We observe, however, significant differences throughout the experiment.

The following is a testable hypothesis explaining the above data. We tentatively attribute the lack of difference between distribution means in the fixed price experiments to the elimination of uncertainty in the secondary market. This elimination of uncertainty allows a person to bid in a range which guarantees a profit and is not too different under the varying conditions. If we accept this, we can return to the problem of reconciling the significant differences observed under the single bid rectangular resale price with the fact that no differences are observed in the original experiments or the corresponding profit table experiments for the same excess demand. The tentative hypothesis or explanation tendered here is that it is not the excess demand per se, which is important, but the view of one bid as a "real" bid and the second as a "throwaway" bid, when the number of bidders is approximately equal to the number of units being offered for sale. This, in fact, did happen with some subjects. Under the single bid condition, the possibility of a "throwaway" did not exist. In the unlimited bid condition, there were only nine subjects and, hence, the nine persons could be considered to be competing for more than one unit. We must distinguish here between subjects competing for more than one unit and the subjects competing for one unit in the high excess demand two bid experiment.

This would offer us a consistent explanation of the observed data and would suggest a further line of experimentation. The explanation would be tested by varying the offer quantity. We would expect to observe no difference, regardless of the number of bids allowed per bidder, when the offer quantity was equal to, or approximately equal to, the number of bidders. If subjects react as if they have one effective bid this would occur. It may be that we would find this to be true only for the two bid case. We would then have to construe it as a very special case in the whole system. It may be, though, that this would be true over a more general range.

We would conclude, in general, that H_2 was supported over a broad range of circumstances. It was not supported when uncertainty was not present in the secondary market and in the special case where the number of bidders equalled the quantity offered.

Tests of H_4 and H_5

Hypothesis H_4: With a fixed offer quantity, in corresponding auction periods, bids tendered by subjects in D groups B_D^t are higher the greater the number of rejected bids, i.e.

$$B_D^t(NR_1) > B_D^t(NR_2) > \ldots B_D^t(NR_k)$$

where NR_1 is the number of rejected bids in the i th group for

$$NR_1 > NR_2 > \ldots NR_k.$$

Hypothesis H_5: Same as H_4 applied to C groups.

The results of the tests of these hypotheses are shown in Tables 8 through 11. The hypotheses assert that greater pressure in the form of a

Table 8. Jonckheere Test of H_4 and H_5 for Original Experiments

A. z's for H_4 DR(17,2) > DR(15,2) > DR(13,2)

	Auction Period					
	0	1	2	3	4	5
z max	4.9	6.5	7.9	9.2	8.2	9.3
z min	3.3	5.5	6.1	6.5	5.6	4.3
z̄	4.1	6.0	7.0	7.9	6.8	6.8

All z's significant at p = .005.

B. z's for H_5 CR(17,2) > CR(15,2)

	Auction Period					
	0	1	2	3	4	5
z max	−.7	−.5	0	.8	1.7*	1.5
z min	−1.5	−1.3	−.9	−.5	.5	−.1
z̄	−1.1	−.9	−.5	.2	1.1	.7

*Significant at p = .05. No other entries significant.

Table 9. Jonckheere Test of H_4 and H_5 for Profit Table Experiments

A. z's for H_4 $DR_1(17,2) > DR_1(15,2) > DR_1(13,2)$

	Auction Period										
	0	1	2	3	4	5	6	7	8	9	10
z max	NS .5	* 2.0	3.4	5.5	7.0	6.6	6.9	7.5	7.7	8.3	7.9
z min	NS −1.0	NS −.5	NS −.4	NS 1.2	2.8	2.5	* 2.4	2.8	3.0	3.7	2.8
z̄	NS −.3	NS .8	NS 1.5	3.4	4.9	4.6	4.7	5.2	5.4	6.0	5.4

NS = Not significant.
* Significant at p = .05.
All other entries significant at p = .005.

B. z's for H_5 $CR_1(17,2) > CR_1(15,2) > CR_1(13,2)$

	Auction Period									
	0	1	2	3	4	5	6	7	8	9
z max	* 2.1	.4	1.4	* 2.0	.5	−.5	.7	1.1	.4	−.6
z min	.7	−1.3	−.9	0	−1.7	−3.0	−2.1	−1.6	−2.8	−3.9
z̄	1.4	−.5	.3	1.0	−.6	−1.8	* −.7	−.3	−1.2	−2.3

*Significant at p = .05.
No other entries significant.

Table 10 Jonckheere Test of H_4 and H_5 for Single Bid Experiments

A. z's for H_4 $DR(34,1) > DR(30,1) > DR(26,1)$

	Auction Period										
	0	1	2	3	4	5	6	7	8	9	10
z max	* 1.8	5.7	5.3	3.7	4.2	3.7	4.7	7.0	7.0	6.2	6.9
z min	NS 0	NS −1.8	NS 0	NS −2.9	NS −1.6	NS −1.5	NS −1.4	* 2.5	NS 0	NS −.9	NS 0
z̄	NS .9	* 2.0	2.7	* .4	NS 1.3	NS 1.1	NS 1.7	4.8	3.5	2.7	3.5

NS = Not Significant.
*Significant at p = .05.
All others significant at p = .005.

Table 10 (*Contd.*)

B. z's for H_5 CR(33,1) > CR(30,1) > CR(26,1)

	Auction Period									
	0	1	2	3	4	5	6	7	8	9
z max	* 2.0	4.0	3.3	3.2	3.4	* 2.3	4.8	* 2.3	4.0	4.2
z min	NS .1	NS 1.6	NS 1.0	NS 0	NS .6	NS .7	* 1.7	NS −.6	NS .2	NS −.5
$\bar{z}$	NS 1.1	* 2.8	NS 2.2	* 1.6	NS 2.0	1.5	3.7	NS .9	* 2.1	* 1.9

NS = Not significant.
*Significant at p = .05.
All other entries significant at p = .005.

Table 11. Jonckheere Test of H_4 and H_5 for Fixed Price Experiments

A. z's for H_4 DF(17,2) > DF(15,2) > DF(13,2)

	Auction Period								
	0	1	2	3	4	5	6	7	8
z max	* 1.9	+ 3.5	+ 4.5	+ 4.8	+ 4.4	+ 5.7	+ 5.9	+ 5.3	+ 6.2
z min	.1	.9	.3	−1.7	−2.7	−5.2	−4.9	−5.9	−6.1
$\bar{z}$	1.0	* 2.7	* 2.4	1.6	.9	.3	.5	−.3	.1

*Significant at p = .05.
+Significant at p = .005.
All other entries not significant.

B. z's for H_5 CF(17,2) > CF(15,2) > CF(13,2)

	Auction Period										
	0	1	2	3	4	5	6	7	8	9	10
z max	.5	* 1.9	* 2.4	1.0	+ 2.7	+ 2.9	+ 3.9	* 2.3	+ 3.1	+ 3.2	* 2.5
z min	−.9	−.4	−.7	−3.6	−4.0	−4.4	−4.8	−6.3	−4.1	−4.9	−4.8
$\bar{z}$	−.2	.8	.9	−1.3	−.8	−.8	−.5	−2.0	−.5	−.9	−1.2

*Significant at p = .05.
+Significant at p = .005.
All other entries not significant.

greater number of rejected bids or excess demand leads to a higher bidding level for *all combinations of other factors* (held constant, of course, within the comparison). Three figures for the z scores are reported in Tables 8 through 11, z minimum, z maximum and $\bar{z}$. Z min is computed assuming ties in opposition to the hypothesis; z max assuming ties in favor of the hypothesis, $\bar{z}$ assumes half the ties in favor of and half the ties opposed to the hypothesis. The most meaningful statistic of the three is z bar since it is the only one which results in a zero z score for identical distributions. Interpretation of the other z values will be discussed later.

Let us first examine the data with respect H_4. Every observation for the original experiments was significant at or above a p value of .005. This is extremely strong confirmation of the hypothesis for this set of experiments. In the profit table experiments (replications of the original experiments with the addition of a profit table) all z min values were significant at the .005 level from the fourth period on (with the exception of the sixth period). For $\bar{z}$, all values from the third period on were significant at the .005 level. For z max, all values from the second period on were significant at the .05 level. This, again, is strong confirmation of the original hypothesis.

The fact that both the original experiments and the profit table experiments confirm hypotheses H_4 is interesting in that the profit table experiments were esentially a replication of the original experiments.

Table 10, single bid experiments, indicates confirmation of the hypothesis as measured by $\bar{z}$. If we observe z minimum we do not find confirmation. The z max implies strong confirmation, but, of course, cannot be interpreted as such. We would conclude, however, that the hypothesis is confirmed for the single bid experiments when we take fifty percent of the ties into account ($\bar{z}$).

It is worth pointing out at this time the appropriate interpretation of the negative z scores. Negative z scores, as shown in the z minimum, may have been erroneously interpreted as meaning that the lower the excess demand (or the lower the number of rejected bids) the greater the bids. If one observes both the z min and the z max, one sees that such an interpretation is fallacious due to the large number of ties. Considering $\bar{z}$ to be the appropriate statistic, we conclude that the hypotheses is confirmed.

The fixed price experiments show an interesting pattern. The z minimums are, from the third period on, negative and highly significant (a reversal of the hypothesis). Performing a one-sided test reversing the hypothesis, all z max would be significant at the .005 level from the first period on. With the exceptions of the first, second, and third periods, none of the $\bar{z}$ would be significant. This is what we would expect to observe if two distributions were very similar. This is what is observed for the fixed price experiments. The distributions do not differ significantly under the discrimination condition for the varying number of rejected bids when the resale price is fixed.

A tentative explanation of the finding (that the bidding distributions do not differ) is that the removal of the uncertainty in the secondary or the resale market is the causal factor. There will be further explication of this point.

Now let us examine the data with respect to hypothesis H_5. H_5 is the same as H_4, except that it is applied to the competitive rules.

Only one z value was significant for the original experiments. We do not, then, reject the null hypothesis of no difference. In the profit table experiments we find only two significant z values. There is weak evidence that if a difference is to be found, its direction would be opposite to that hypothesized. The conclusion drawn from the original experiments now has this additional support.

The similarity between the original experiments and the profit table experiments was great for both hypotheses H_4 and H_5. We observe only two significant z values for the single bid experiments and would not reject the null hypothesis on that basis. All but three z maximum values were significant at or above the .005 level. The $\bar{z}$ values were, with two exceptions, significant. Two were significant at the .005 level and the remaining six at the .05 or .10 level. This is weaker confirmation, but still suggests that the bids were greater given a greater excess demand when single bids, only, were allowed under the competitive rules. The phenomenon is not so strong, however, as under the discriminative rules.

The z minimum were, for the most part, negative in the fixed price experiments, and significant if we were to make a one-sided test of the reversed hypothesis: $CF(13,2) > CF(15,2) > CF(17,2)$. The z max values were significantly positive. With the exception of the seventh period, the $\bar{z}$ were not significant. What conclusions can we draw from this? Focusing upon the z bar statistic we could conclude no difference. We would not reject the null hypothesis. Observing z min and z max would give some weak evidence that the directionality was opposite to that hypothesized. The basic conclusions which we draw with respect to hypotheses H_4 and H_5 for the fixed price experiments are identical. There was no difference in the bidding distributions.

Test of Revenue Hypotheses

There are two kinds of revenue hypotheses tested here: (1) greater revenue is produced by a competitive auction than by a discriminative auction, and (2) the less uncertainty in the secondary market the greater the revenue of the auction.

The hypothesis with respect to the effect of the auction rules is H_3.

H_3 : in the t-th auction period the total revenue to a seller in a C group, R_c^t, will exceed that in a corresponding D group, R_D^t, i.e.

$$R_c^t > R_D^t \text{ for } t = 1, 2, \ldots n.$$

The hypotheses regarding revenue and risk premium were not among the original hypotheses to be tested. The design of the experiment included one set of experiments in which there was no uncertainty in the secondary market. No assumptions had been made regarding revenue and uncertainty in the resale market. In carrying out the study, however, it became apparent that this was an opportunity to test the hypothesis with respect to risk premium. We would assume that if a risk premium exists it would be a function of all risks. Removal of uncertainty in the secondary market would remove part of the need for a premium. We would then expect revenue to be greater for the seller when no uncertainty exists in the secondary market. This hypothesis was tested.

One methodological problem existed in testing the revenue hypothesis. Under the discriminative rules there was no problem of discreteness, that is, the revenue could be measured within intervals of 10 cents. On the other hand, under the competitive rules the revenue could be measured only to within intervals of $1.80.

The revenues that can be observed under the competitive rules are 10 times the low accepted bid because of the steps of $1.80. Revenue in a competitive auction must exceed revenue in a discriminative auction by 90

Table 12. Equilibrium Revenue

Experiment	Equilibrium Revenue	Comments	Support For H_3
DR(13,2)	23.70	Average of last four periods	
CR(13,2)	26.10		Yes
CR*(13,2)	26.10		
DR(15,2)	23.15	Average of last two periods	Yes
CR(15,2)	26.10		
DR(17,2)	26.31	Average of last seven periods	
CR(17,2)	26.10		No
DR(9,4)	26.16	Average of last eight periods	
DR(9,∞)	27.70	Average of last three periods	
	26.72	Average of last five periods	?

Sealed-Bid Auctions   313

Table 12 (*Contd.*)

Experiment	Equilibrium Revenue	Comments	Support For H_3
$CR(9,\infty)$	27.90 or 29.70		
$DR(34,1)$	25.35	Average of last nine periods	No
$CR(33,1)$	26.10	Low prob. of 26.10	
$DR(30,1)$	25.26	Average of last five periods	No
$CR(30,1)$	26.10		
$DR(26,1)$	26.57	Average of last ten periods	No
$CR(26,1)$	26.10		
$DR_1(13,2)$	23.45	Average of periods 5 through 8	
	23.94	Average of periods 9 through 11	Yes
$CR_1(13,2)$	24.30	Average of periods 5 through 8	
	26.10	Average of periods 9 through 11	
$DR_1(15,2)$	25.78	Average of Periods 6 through 10	No
$CR_1(15,2)$	26.10		
$DR_1(17,2)$	26.46	Average of last six periods	No
$CR_1(17,2)$	24.30		
	26.10	Last Trial	
$DF(13,2)$	26.25	Average of last four periods	
$CF(13,2)$	26.10	Low Prob. of 27.90	No
$CF_p(13,2)$	24.30		
$DF(15,2)$	25.91	Average of last eight periods	
$CF(15,2)$	27.90	Low Prob. of 26.10	?
$CF^*(15,2)$	26.10		
$DF(17,2)$	26.18	Average of last seven periods	
$CF(17,2)$	26.10		No
$DF_p(17,2)$	26.17	Average of last four periods	
$DR_p(15,2)$	25.16	Average of last five periods	No
$CR_p(15,2)$	26.10		

cents before we conclude a true difference. This follows from the assumption that the competitive auction's revenue will go to the most probable of two adjacent values.

Appendix C gives the revenue by period for each experiment. Table 12 gives the equilibrium revenue by experiment. The concept of equilibrium revenue here is the average, or more probable revenue, once an equilibrium has apparently been reached. Hence, if revenue rose in the first four periods

Table 13. Comparison of Equilibrium Revenue for Constant Excess Demand

| Competitive | | Discriminative | | |
Experiment	Revenue	Experiment	Revenue	
CR(13,2)	26.10	DR(13,2)	23.70	
CR*(13,2)	26.10			
CR(26,1)	24.30	DR(26,1)	25.35	Eight Rejected Bids
CR_1(13,2)	24.30 (26.10 low prob.)	DR_1(13,2)	23.58	
CF(13,2)	26.10	DF(13,2)	26.25	
CF_p(13,2)	24.30			
CR(15,2)	26.10	DR(15,2)	23.15	
CR(30,1)	26.10	DR(30,1)	25.26	
CR_1(15,2)	26.10	DR_1(15,2)	25.78	
CF(15,2)	27.90 (26.10 low prob.)	DF(15,2)	25.91	Twelve Rejected Bids
CF*(15,2)	26.10			
CR_p(15,2)	26.10	DR_p(15,2)	25.16	
CR(17,2)	26.10	DR(17,2)	26.31	
		DR(9,4)	26.16	
CR(33,1)	26.10	DR(34,1)	26.23	
CR_1(17,2)	24.30 (26.10 last period)	DR_1(17,2)	26.46	Sixteen Rejected Bids
CF(17,2)	26.10	DF(17,2)	26.18	
		DF_p(17,2)	26.17	
CR(9,∞)	27.90 or 29.70	DR(9,∞)	27.70 (last three) 26.72 (last five)	Unlimited Number of Rejected Bids.

Table 14. Comparison of Equilibrium Revenue Constant Excess Demand for Fixed vs. Uncertain Resale Price Auctions

Fixed Price		Rectangular Resale		
Experiment	Revenue	Experiment	Revenue	
CF(13,2)	26.10	CR(13,2)	26.10	
CE$_p$(13,2)	**24.30**	CR*(13,2)	26.10	Eight
DF(13,2)	26.25	CR(26,1)	**24.30**	Rejected
		CR$_1$(13,2)	**24.30** (26.10 low probability)	Bids
		DR(13,2)	**23.70**	
		DR(26,1)	25.35	
		DR$_1$(13,2)	**23.58**	
CF(15,2)	27.90 (26.10 low probability)	CR(15,2)	26.10	
		CR(30,1)	26.10	Twelve
CF*(15,2)	26.10			Rejected
		CR$_1$(15,2)	26.10	Bids
DF(15,2)	25.91			
		CR$_p$(15,2)	26.10	
		DR(15,2)	**23.15**	
		DR(30,1)	25.26	
		DR$_1$(15,2)	25.78	
		DR$_p$(15,2)	25.16	
CF(17,2)	26.10	CR(17,2)	26.10	
		CR(33,1)	26.10	
DF(17,2)	26.18	CR$_1$(17,2)	24.30	
DF$_p$(17,2)	26.17		(26.10 last period)	Sixteen
				Rejected
		DR(17,2)	26.31	
		DR(9,4)	26.16	Bids
		DR(34,1)	26.23	
		DR$_1$(17,2)	26.46	
		CR(9,∞)	27.90 or 29.70	Unlimited Number of Rejected
		DR(9,∞)	27.70 (last three) 26.72 (last five)	Bids

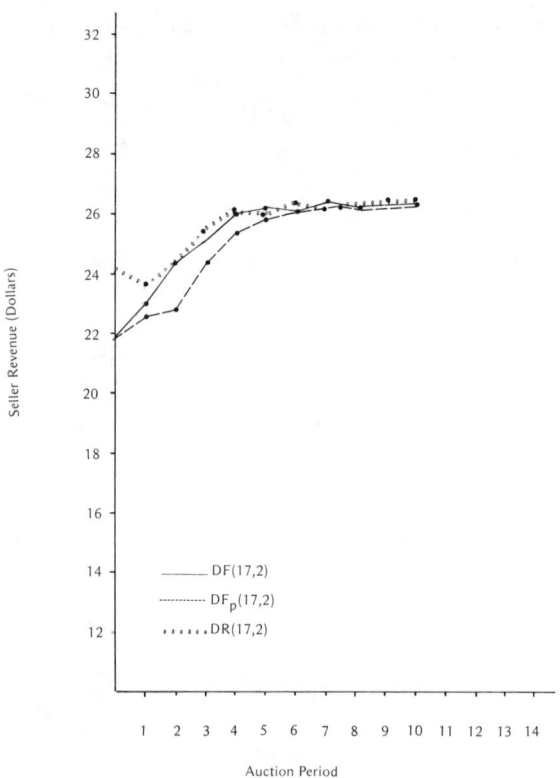

Figure 3. Seller Revenue by Auction Period: Test of $R_c^t > R_D^t$ for CR(17,2), DR(9,4) and DR (17,2).

of a given experiment and then remained constant (an ideal case) throughout the rest of the experiment, that constant value would represent the equilibrium revenue. The equilibrium revenue in the discriminative experiments was that average of the constant value (or what appeared to be the constant value) with some stochastic variation. If the stopout price is relatively constant, the revenue would be that associated with this steady figure. On the other hand, if the revenue under a competitive condition can fluctuate between two figures (say, $26.10 and $27.90), we would consider the equilibrium to be one of those values or a probabilistic combination of the two. Table 12 lists these equilibrium revenues with the information relevant to their determination.

Table 14 is a test of the risk premium hypothesis using the concept of the equilibrium revenue. There appears to be few differences due to bidding rules holding excess demand *and* resale conditions constant. The one circumstance where a lower level of revenue is evident is when there are both a low level of

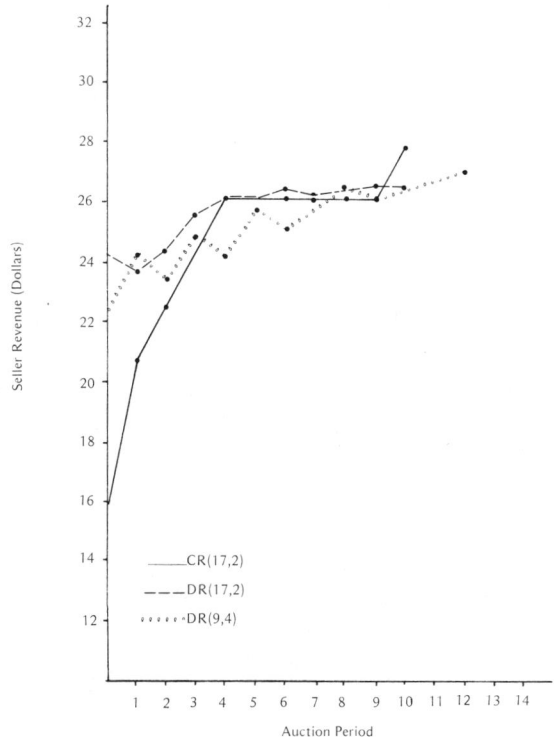

Figure 4. Seller Revenue by Auction Period: Test of $R_c^t > R_D^t$ for DF(17,2), CF(17,2) and $DF_p(17,2)$.

excess demand (8) and uncertain resale price. This would seem reasonable evidence of an interaction effect and suggestive of further lines of inquiry.

Data for testing hypothesis H_3 is shown in Table 13. Revenue appears to be somewhat greater under the competitive condition with an excess of eight rejected bids. Evidence favoring this hypothesis is restricted to the original experiments and the profit table experiments. For twelve rejected bids the only evidence favorable to H_3 is found in the original experiments. Where there are sixteen rejected bids the revenue is, if anything, greater or equal under the discriminative condition. Using the concept of equilibrium revenue we would then conclude that the revenue differences appear to slightly favor the competitive rules, but *only under* very limited conditions. These directions should be explored.

Figures 3, 4 and 5 are graphic comparisons of revenue by period for several different conditions. Twenty such comparisons were made but only these three presented. They are used here to indicate the sort of insights this approach can give us.

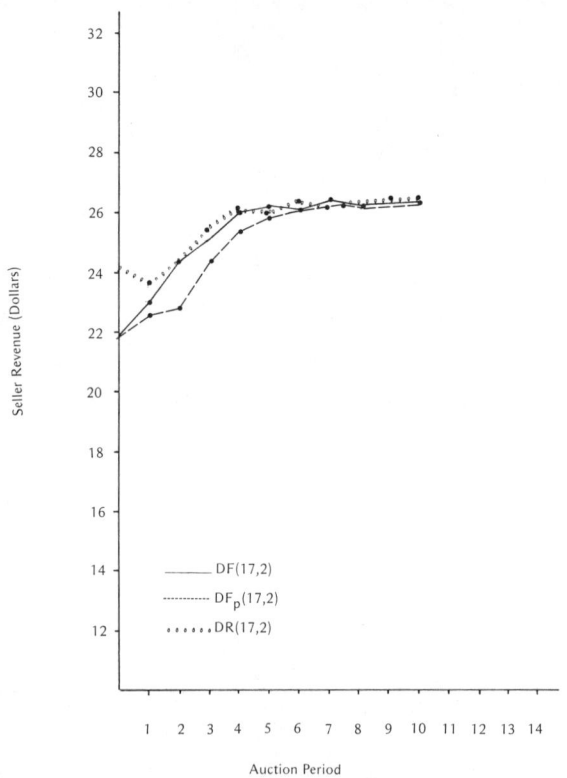

Figure 5. Seller Revenue by Auction Period: Test of Risk Premium Hypothesis for DF(17,2), $DF_p(17,2)$, and DR(17,2).

Figure 3 shows a comparison of revenue from competitive and discriminative auctions under the standard conditions for an excess demand of 16. It appears that the initial revenue is lower under the competitive conditions but reaches about the same equilibrium level as the discriminative auction quickly. Figure 4 (excess demand of 16 for the fixed price experiment) shows the same pattern. Figure 5 suggests that resale price conditions do not affect either the equilibrium level or adjustment process.

The other 17 graphic comparisons provide a similar picture. This data reinforces the conclusion based upon Tables 12, 13 and 14.

RESULTS OF MICRO-ANALYSIS

The purpose of the following analysis is to attempt to isolate those factors affecting individual behavior.

There are many implications for a utility analysis in this work. The original work of Smith did not support the assumption of linearity of utility. The prediction was that subjects linear in utility of money would enter both bids equal to the mean of the resale distribution for a competitive auction and both bids equal but lower than the mean for a discrimination auction. Modifications of these predictions have already been discussed. The consequences of these modifications are not worked out in detail and, in fact, no statistical test was made of the hypothesis of linearity of utility. There were several reasons for this.

A test of the utility behavior in a gambling situation performed with subjects who had participated in earlier bidding experiments indicated quite clearly that there were few subjects linear in utility over a range of − .50¢ to $2.50. These tests were essentially single gamble non-repetitive events. This range took in a substantial part of the earnings of subjects in the bidding experiments.

Subjects' behavior in the utility experiment did not clearly relate to their behavior in the bidding experiments. It became clear that in the bidding experiments such things as subjective beliefs regarding low bids and low accepted bids lagged one period influenced bidding behavior. The further analysis studies the relationship of the actual bids and other variables.

The analysis of the individuals was performed with linear regressions, with emphasis upon comparisons of the distributions of the correlation coefficients, or correlagrams. These correlagrams were compared for competitive and discriminative conditions within experiment groups. Some aggregation of experiment groups was made. The effect of the discriminative and competitive rules on the observed individual behavior was quite prevalent. As would be expected, participants in discriminative actions behaved more consistently than those in competitive auctions.

Relationship of Bids to Low Accepted Bids Lagged One Period

The hypothesis tested here is that subjects react to the prior low accepted bid as an indicator of the future low accepted bid. Figures 7, 8, 9, and 10 present the data.

Figure 7 indicates a clear difference between the discriminative and competitive auctions for the original set of experiments. This corresponds to the findings in the analysis of the relationship between bids entered and predicted low bids (Figure 6). The relationship shows up more clearly when the discriminative rules are applied than when the competitive rules are applied. The relationship exists in the latter case, but is not as strong. For the profit table experiments we see a weaker bias in favor of the discriminative rules. The profit table experiments were basically a replication of the original experiments.

The single bid experiment show almost identical correlagrams under

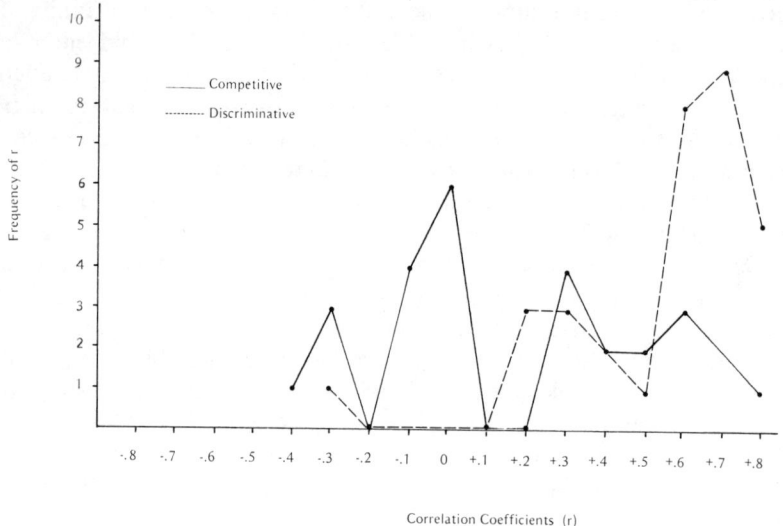

Figure 6. Correlagram for Relationship of Predicted Low Bid and Actual Bid for Prediction Experiments.

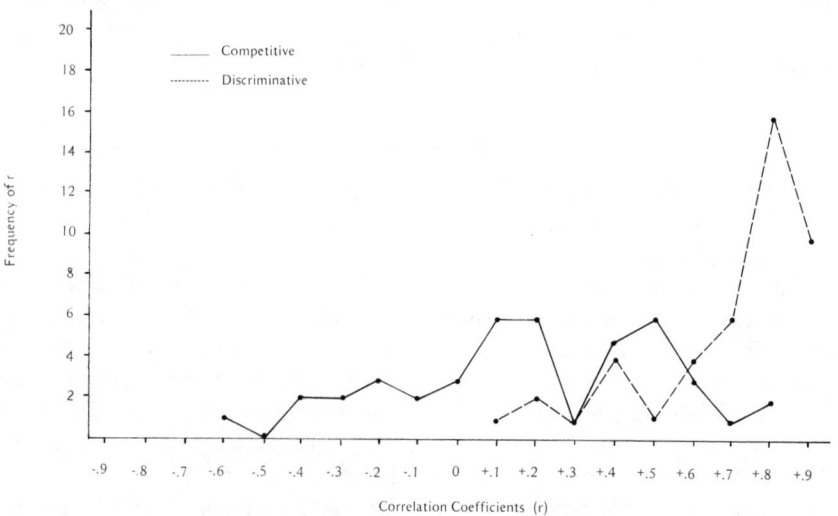

Figure 7. Correlagram for Relationship of Low Bid Lagged One and Actual Bid for Original Experiments.

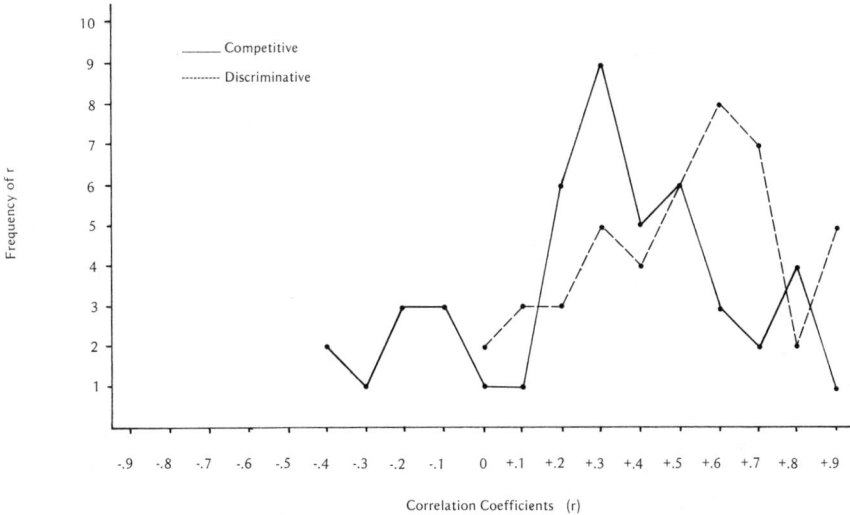

Figure 8. Correlagram for Relationship of Low Bid Lagged One and Actual Bid for Profit Table Experiments.

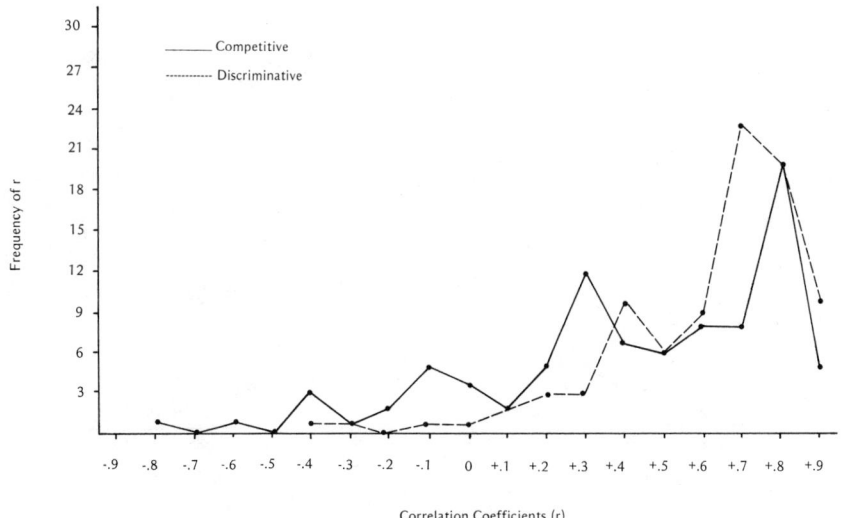

Figure 9. Correlagram for Relationship of Low Bid Lagged one and Actual Bid for Single Bid Experiments.

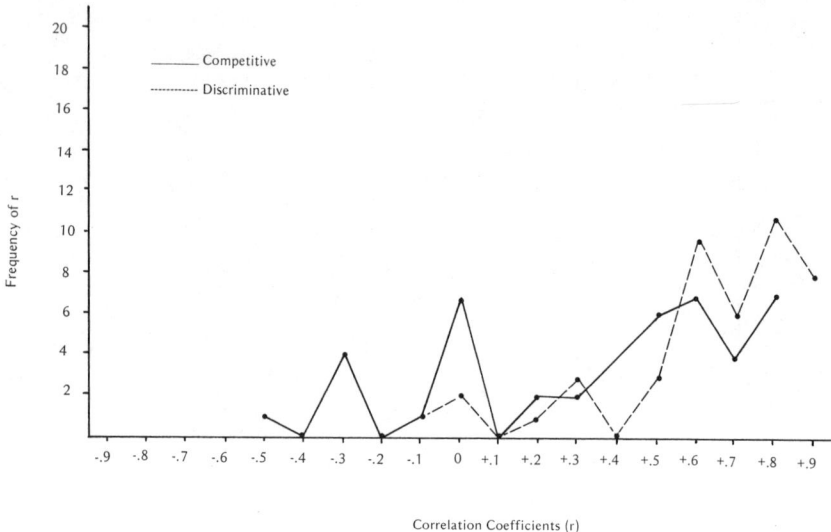

Figure 10. Correlagram for Relationship of Low Bid Lagged One and Actual Bid for Fixed Price Experiments.

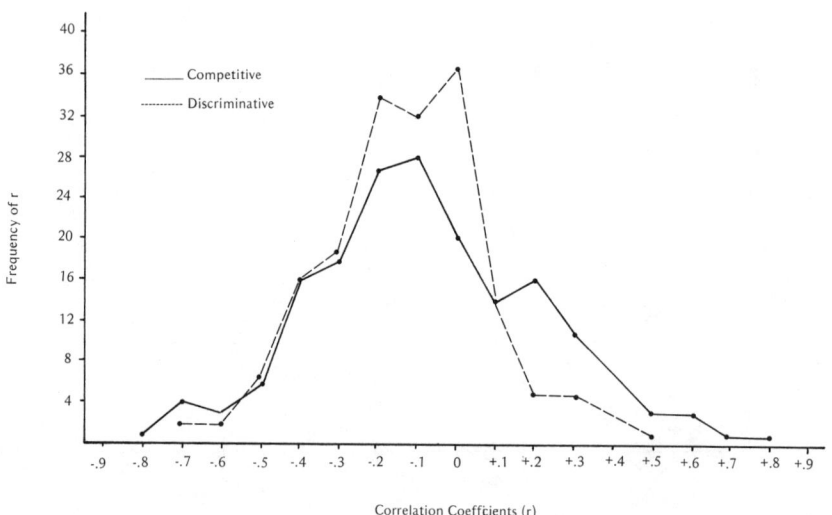

Figure 11. Correlagram for Relationship of Resale Price Lagged One and Actual Bid for Original, Profit Table, Experienced Subjects, and Single Bid Experiments.

both sets of rules and indicate that there is a strong relationship between the low accepted bid lagged one and bids in the following period. Note the difference when a person can enter only one bid rather than two bids. Had we done the analysis of the two bid experiment taking the highest bid (for each subject) as one series and the lowest bid as a second series, we might have obtained different results. This is an interesting approach that ought to be used.

Data for the fixed price experiments are shown in Figure 10. The results are substantially the same as for the original and profit table experiments.

The general conclusion we can draw is that there is a relationship, under all conditions, between bids entered and the low accepted bid lagged one period. Subjects utilize the prior information as an indicator of the probability of the next low bid. This relationship was strongest (and was independent of the auction rules) when only a single bid was allowed. The relationship was stronger under the two-bid condition when the discriminative rules were followed than when competitive rules were followed. This may be a function of the rules themselves or a function of the fact that there were two bids, which in other instances has been shown to be a peculiar case. The results would suggest that the interaction of the number of bids and the rules contributes to the difference.

Relationship of Bids to Resale Prices Lagged One

The hypothesis is that bids and resale price lagged one are uncorrelated. For this to be false, some form of "gambler's fallacy" would have to be operating since there is, in fact, no true relationship. In this context, a gambler's fallacy would be the belief that a high (higher?) price is more probable in the t-th period because a low price has been drawn in period t-1. This implies rejection of the independence of resale prices. Post experiment debriefing of subjects indicated that they held the belief that they had been influenced by the random resale prices. Statements like "I bid higher because the price was low last time" were common. The evidence, though, contradicts these verbal assertions.

The distribution of correlation coefficients was examined for each of the variables—number of bids, rules, resale price conditions, and excess demand. In no case did the distribution deviate significantly from what would be expected given the null hypothesis.

What does this mean? It means that no significant gambler's fallacy was operating. We can assume that the resale market was perceived as a random variable with interperiod independence.

Relationship Between Profits Lagged One Period and Bids

This section describes the results of the linear regressions between bids and profits lagged one period. The analysis was carried out to determine the effects, if any, which the winnings or losses had upon behavior. In other words, we ask whether subjects increased or decreased their bids when they had incurred a loss of profits in the prior period.

There is no real priori hypothesis to be stated here since so many equally good alternatives exist. For example, we could assert that rational behavior would dictate that a person ignore the prior events and do the best he can under the circumstances. This is the familiar notion of a "sunk cost." On the other hand, we know that firms operate not only to make a profit, but also to stay in business, and know that a firm may forego an investment that could result in a tremendous profit even if there is only a small probability of a substantial loss. Also, a firm will forego investment in preference to liquidity. Often this is at the option of the firm; sometimes it is forced by bank credit requirements.

This relationship was examined by an analysis of the distribution of the correlation coefficients. The results are equivocal and suggestive at best because of the extent to which there are confounding variables. No substantial differences exist between competitive and discriminative treatments. There tends to be some asymmetry with a negative skewness. Distributions vary widely in shape, being bimodal, unimodal, rectangular, and skewed with no apparent pattern.

What general conclusions can be drawn from this? The relationship tends to be negative, implying bid opposite in direction to the profit (loss) incurred in the prior period. This was observed for all but the experienced subjects. This finding is only suggestive.

SUMMARY AND CONCLUSIONS

A sealed bid auction is a mechanism for the sale of a commodity which makes unnecessary the prior setting of a price by the seller. The "price" is determined by the auction process. The auction can be either discriminative or competitive. A discriminative auction is one in which the highest bidders are awarded the commodity at their bid price. In a competitive auction a single "market clearing" price is determined and charged to all successful bidders. The sealed bid auction is especially important for commodities which must be sold by a specified time and for which failure to sell would be considered highly unfortunate and to be avoided.

The Treasury bill auction is probably the most important continuing market using this mechanism. The Treasury bill auction is run as a discriminative sealed bid auction. "Noncompetitive" bids, which are filled in full at the weighted average of the awarded competitive bids, are allowed.

The suggestion has been made that the Treasury bills be sold in a competitive auction. Advocates of this position claim that (a) revenue to the Treasury would increase, and (b) collusion, which they believe now exists because of the discriminative auction form, would be eliminated. Proponents of the present system argue that (a) the discriminative auction results in greater revenue, and (b) collusion, if it exists, would be independent of auction rules. There has been some empirical work which fails to support the argument that collusion exists. There has been no empirical study regarding revenue. Indeed, it is difficult to imagine how one might carry out such a study.

The importance of theory as a foundation upon which all economics rests is generally accepted. Much argument is generated in discussion of the implications of a theory for actual markets, empirical studies, and experimental studies. Measurement requires theory. Empirical studies require theory. Experimental studies require theory. One can improve his understanding of a theory by examining both its empirical and experimental implications. Experimental methods are used here to examine sealed bid auction theory.

The first systematic application of experimental tests to economic theory was carried out by Fouraker and Siegel (1963). Smith (1967) designed and carried out experiments based on the sealed bid auction paradigm. The present work builds on that of Smith.

In the present work systematic examination is made of the effect of: (1) rules—discriminative vs. competitive, (2) excess demand (ED = $N \times B - OQ$) where N = number of bidders, B = bids per bidder, and OQ = offer quantity, and (3) uncertainty in the secondary market. Study is made of the components of excess demand.

There are two types of hypotheses, macro and micro. The macro-hypotheses assert that: bids in competitive auctions will have greater variance and higher levels than bids in corresponding discriminative auctions; competitive auctions will produce greater revenue; reduction of uncertainty in the secondary market will increase revenue; and the greater the excess demand the higher will be the level of the bids. The macro-hypotheses assert that bids tendered will be related to predicted low accepted bid, low accepted bid lagged one period, and profits lagged one period, but not to resale price lagged one period. The relationship between micro- and macro-measures is discussed.

The major conclusions were as follows:
(1) The variance of bids under the competitive condition is greater than the variance under the discriminative condition.
(2) The "level" of bids is greater under (a) the competitive condition for the original and profit table two bid experiments with excess demand equal to 8 and 12 units, and (b) the unlimited bidding condition. No difference if found for the fixed price experiments and high excess demand, two-bid experiments. The results of the single bid experiments

are somewhat ambiguous, but suggest a higher level of bids under the competitive rules. A behavioral explanation is offered for the above findings.
(3) For discriminative auctions greater excess demand leads to higher bids when uncertainty exists in the secondary market but not when it is removed.
(4) For competitive rules greater excess demand leads to higher bids only under the single bid condition.
(5) Revenue is greater under the competitive rules *only for the low excess demand two-bid experiments* (original experiments and profit table experiments).
(6) Revenue is greater for the fixed price experiments at low levels of excess demand. Risk premium is dominated by excess demand and bidding rules.
(7) Bids are positively related to predicted low bids. The relationship is stronger for discriminative auctions than for competitive.
(8) Bids are positively related to low accepted bids lagged one period. The relationship is stronger for discriminative than for competitive rules.
(9) Bids are not related to the resale price lagged one period.
(10) The micro-measures show less stability than the macro measures. Stability of macro variables can exist in spite of the erratic individual behavior.
(11) When there is no uncertainty in the secondary market the importance of bidding rules is slight.
(12) Under discriminative rules there are stronger linear relationships between bids and expected resale prices and bids and expected low bids than under competitive rules.

APPENDIX A: INSTRUCTIONS

Original Experiments Competitive Rules

This is an experiment in the economics of market decision making. The National Science Foundation has provided funds for conducting this research. The instructions are simple, and if you follow them carefully and make good decisions you may earn a considerable amount of money.

1. You will be given a starting capital credit balance of $1.00. Any profit earned by you in the experiment will be *added* to this sum, and any losses incurred by you will be *subtracted* from this sum. Your net balance at the end of the experiment will be calculated and paid to you in real money.

2. This experiment will simulate a certain kind of market in which you will act as buyers in a sequence of trading periods. Each trading period begins with an announcement indicating the quantity of the fictitious commodity that is offered for sale.

3. In each period, your task is to attempt to buy units of the commodity by submitting written bids for it in competition with other buyers. Each unit that you are able to purchase is then resold by you at a price whose determination is explained below in paragraph 5. How it is determined whether a bid for a unit is accepted, and the purchase price of that bid, will be explained in paragraph 6.

4. If a bid is not accepted your profit is zero. If a bid is accepted, you make a profit equal to the difference between your selling price and your purchase price. If this difference is negative, it represents a loss. That is, your profit for each unit is:

$$\text{Profit} = (\text{Selling Price}) - (\text{Purchase Price})$$

5. For all bids that are accepted, the resale price of each unit is determined by a random drawing (using a random number table) from the following nine numbers: $1.15, $1.25, $1.35, $1.45, $1.55, $1.65, $1.75, $1.85, $1.95.

Each of these prices is *equally likely to be drawn in each market period*. Since there are nine prices, this means that there is a one-ninth chance that any one price will be drawn in any market period. For example: if $1.25 is drawn in one period, this has no effect on the one-ninth chance that $1.25 will be drawn in any later market period.

You know the range within which the selling price will fall, $1.15–$1.95, and you know that each price in this range has one-ninth chance of occurring. But you do not know in advance, at the time you enter your bids to buy, what the exact selling price will be.

6. Whether a bid is accepted, and at what price is determined as follows: Suppose x units are offered for sale at the beginning of a market period. Each bidder submits two written bids on cards supplied for this purpose. Each bid specified a price for a single unit of the commodity. The bid prices

must be in dollars and cents, and end in the digit 5, for example, $1.35, $.75, $.45. These bids will be collected, and arrayed in descending order from the highest to the lowest. With × units offered for sale, the first × of these bids (starting with the highest) will be accepted, and the remaining bids will be rejected. In the case of ties at the lowest accepted bid price, random numbers will be used to determine which bids are to be accepted. The highest and lowest bids will then be announced. Each accepted bid will represent the purchase of one unit of the commodity at a purchase price equal to the *lowest accepted bid price, not your bid price.* Therefore, your potential profit is not decreased if your bid is above the lowest accepted bid. The higher your bid the more likely will it be above the low bid and, thereby, accepted. But your cost and potential profit is determined by the lowest accepted bid, not your bid.

7. Consider a numerical example. Suppose Jones submits two bids— one at $1.45, and another at $.65. Suppose hypothetically that the array of bids, and quantity offered, is such that the highest accepted bid is $1.55, and the lowest is $.45. Since both Jones's bids were above $.45, they are accepted. He has purchased two units at $.45. Now assume that the results of the drawing to determine selling price yields a price of $1.35. Then Jones has made a profit of $1.35 − $.45 = $.90 on each unit, or a total of $1.80 on the two bids.

As another example, suppose Jones submits bids of $.85 and $.25. Assume the highest accepted bid is $1.25 and the lowest is $.55. Then Jones's high bid was accepted while his low bid was not. That is, he has purchased one unit at $.55. Now let the result of the random drawing be a selling price of $1.65. His profit on the single unit is $1.65 − $.55 = $1.10.

* * *

You are not to reveal your bids, or profits, nor are you to speak to any other subject while the experiment is in process.

Are there any questions?

Instructions were minimally modified for variations from the Original Experiment Competitive Rules for discriminative rules, fixed price experiment, etc. They all had the identical format and changes in only a few words in one paragraph to several sentences in two paragraphs.

Profit Table and Explanation Competitive Rules: Explanation of Expected Profit Table

In the Expected Profit Table the columns indicate the lowest accepted bid and the rows your bid. The number in the cell at the intersection of a row and column is the expected profit, or the amount you would win on the average, if you were to bid the amount indicated by the row and the lowest

Sealed-Bid Auctions

accepted bid was to be the amount indicated by the column. As an example suppose that you bid $1.25 and the lowest accepted bid was $1.45. The expected profit is zero since you did not purchase a unit and thus had none to resell. Assume now that you bid $1.25 and the lowest accepted bid was $1.25. You purchased a unit of the commodity at the lowest accepted bid. You know that the resale price will be 1.15 one-ninth of the time, $1.25 one-ninth of the time, etc., or that your expected profit is:

$$1/9 \times (\$1.15 - \$1.25) + 1/9 \times (\$1.25 - \$1.25) + 1/9 \times (\$1.35 - \$1.25)$$
$$+ 1/9 \times (\$1.45 - \$1.25) + 1/9 \times (\$1.55 - \$1.25) + 1/9 \times (\$1.65 - \$1.25)$$
$$+ 1/9 \times (\$1.75 - \$1.25) + 1/9 \times (\$1.85 - \$1.25) + 1/9 \times (\$1.95 - \$1.25)$$
$$= .30$$

All the expected profits shown were determined in the same manner.
Are there any questions?

Expected Profit Table

Your Bid	Lowest Accepted Bid (in cents)								
	1.15	1.25	1.35	1.45	1.55	1.65	1.75	1.85	1.95
1.15	40	0	0	0	0	0	0	0	0
1.25	40	30	0	0	0	0	0	0	0
1.35	40	30	20	0	0	0	0	0	0
1.45	40	30	20	10	0	0	0	0	0
1.55	40	30	20	10	0	0	0	0	0
1.65	40	30	20	10	0	−10	0	0	0
1.75	40	30	20	10	0	−10	−20	0	0
1.85	40	30	20	10	0	−10	−20	−30	0
1.95	40	30	20	10	0	−10	−20	−30	−40

Profit Table and Explanation Discriminative Rules: Explanation of Expected Profit Table

In the Expected Profit Table the columns indicate the lowest accepted bid and the rows your bid. The number in the cell at the intersection of a row and column is the expected profit, or the amount you would win on the average, if you were to bid the amount indicated by the row and the lowest accepted bid was to be the amount indicated by the column. As an example suppose that you bid $1.35 and the lowest accepted bid was $1.45. The expected profit is zero since you did not purchase a unit and thus had none to resell. Assume now that you bid $1.35 and the lowest accepted bid was $1.25. You purchased a unit of the commodity at your bid price. You know that the resale price will be $1.15 one-ninth of the time, $1.25 one-ninth of the time, etc., or that your expected profit is:

$$1/9 \times (\$1.15 - \$1.35) + 1/9 \times (\$1.25 - \$1.35) + 1/9 \times (\$1.35 - \$1.35)$$
$$+ 1/9 \times (\$1.45 - \$1.35) + 1/9 \times (\$1.55 - \$1.35) + 1/9 \times (\$1.65 - \$1.35)$$
$$+ 1/9 \times (\$1.75 - \$1.35) + 1/9 \times (\$1.85 - \$1.35) + 1/9 \times (\$1.95 - \$1.35)$$
$$= .20$$

All the expected profits shown were determined in the same manner. Are there any questions?

Expected Profit Table

Your bid	Lowest Accepted Bid (in cents)								
	1.15	1.25	1.35	1.45	1.55	1.65	1.75	1.85	1.95
1.15	40	0	0	0	0	0	0	0	0
1.25	30	30	0	0	0	0	0	0	0
1.35	20	20	20	0	0	0	0	0	0
1.45	10	10	10	10	0	0	0	0	0
1.55	0	0	0	0	0	0	0	0	0
1.65	−10	−10	−10	−10	−10	−10	0	0	0
1.75	−20	−20	−20	−20	−20	−20	−20	0	0
1.85	−30	−30	−30	−30	−30	−30	−30	−30	0
1.95	−40	−40	−40	−40	−40	−40	−40	−40	−40

Recording Sheet for Prediction Experiments
Predictions: *I think that the*

Period	Highest Bid Will be	Lowest Accepted Bid Will be	My Bids
1			
2			
3			
4			
5			
6			
7			
8			
9			
10			
11			
12			
13			
14			
15			
16			
17			
18			

APPENDIX B

Price Series

Period	A Resale Price (in cents)	B Resale Price (in cents)
Trial	175	115
1	115	155
2	195	185
3	135	194
4	195	155
5	145	155
6	115	155
7	135	175
8	185	135
9	135	135
10	145	115
11	135	165
12	175	165
13	195	185
14	125	175
15	175	195
16	135	145
17		155
18		135
19		125
20		195

APPENDIX C

Revenue (cents)

Experiment

Periods	DR(13,2)	CR(13,2)	DR(15,2)	CR(15,2)	DR(17,2)	CR(17,2)	DR(9,4)	DR(9,∞)	CR(9,∞)
0	1,660	2,320	1,990	1,890	2,420	1,570	2,210	2,055	2,070
1	1,880	2,250	1,980	2,250	2,370	2,070	2,420	2,350	2,610
2	1,920	2,430	2,080	2,430	2,440	2,250	2,340	2,280	2,610
3	2,050	2,610	2,015	2,610	2,560	2,430	2,490	2,410	2,790
4	2,210	2,430	2,290	2,610	2,610	2,610	2,420	2,450	2,790
5	2,310	2,610	2,340	2,610	2,610	2,610	2,580	2,520	2,790
6	2,450	2,610			2,640	2,610	2,520	2,580	2,790
7	2,400	2,610			2,620	2,610	2,580	2,610	2,970
8	2,320	2,610			2,640	2,610	2,640	2,640	2,790
9					2,650	2,610	2,610	2,710	2,970
10					2,650	2,790	2,630	2,810	2,790
11							2,670	2,790	2,970
12							2,700		2,910
13									2,970

Appendix C (Contd.)

					Experiments				
Periods	$DR(26,1)$	$CR(26,1)$	$DR(30,1)$	$CR(30,1)$	$DR(34,1)$	$CR(33,1)$	$DR_1(13,2)$	$CR_1(13,2)$	$DR_1(1,52)$
0	2,160	1,350	2,210	1,710	2,410	2,070	1,730	990	2,220
1	2,230	1,890	2,370	2,070	2,430	2,430	2,200	2,070	2,380
2	2,330	2,070	2,270	2,250	2,450	2,430	2,290	1,890	2,370
3	2,470	2,250	2,360	2,430	2,470	2,610	2,280	2,070	2,490
4	2,530	2,430	2,430	2,610	2,580	2,610	2,290	2,250	2,490
5	2,520	2,430	2,430	2,430	2,610	2,610	2,340	2,430	2,530
6	2,560	2,430	2,530	2,610	2,620	2,790	2,350	2,430	2,550
7	2,520	2,430	2,480	2,610	2,630	2,610	2,340	2,430	2,540
8	2,540	2,430	2,540	2,610	2,640	2,610	2,350	2,430	2,610
9	2,530	2,610	2,530	2,610	2,660	2,610	2,340	2,610	2,590
10	2,540	2,610	2,550	2,610	2,680		2,470	2,610	2,580
11	2,560	2,430			2,730		2,370	2,610	2,590
12	2,620	2,610			2,750		2,410		2,610
13					2,680				

Appendix C (Contd.)

Periods	$CR_1(15,2)$	$DR_1(17,2)$	$CR_1(17,2)$	$DF(13,2)$	Experiments $CF(13,2)$	$DF(15,2)$	$CF(15,2)$	$DF(17,2)$	$CF(17,2)$
0	1,350	2,200	1,710	1,785	1,450	2,370	1,890	2,190	1,710
1	2,070	2,340	2,070	2,020	1,710	2,380	2,250	2,300	2,250
2	2,430	2,370	2,250	2,250	2,070	2,450	2,610	2,440	2,430
3	2,610	2,500	2,430	2,410	2,430	2,520	2,790	2,510	2,610
4	2,610	2,610	2,250	2,610	2,610	2,610	2,790	2,600	2,610
5	2,610	2,650	2,430	2,610	2,610	2,590	2,610	2,620	2,610
6	2,610	2,640	2,430	2,620	2,610	2,570	2,790	2,610	2,610
7	2,610	2,660	2,430	2,640	2,790	2,610	2,790	2,630	2,430
8	2,790	2,660	2,430	2,630	2,610	2,620	2,790	2,620	2,430
9	2,610	2,660	2,610		2,610	2,610	2,790	2,620	2,610
10	2,610	2,640			2,610	2,640	2,610	2,630	2,610
11					2,790	2,640	2,790		
12					2,790	2,610	2,610		
13					2,610	2,620	2,610		
14					2,610	2,520			

Appendix C (Contd.)

Periods	$CF^*(15,2)$	$DF_p(17,2)$	$CF_p(13,2)$	$DR_p(15,2)$	$CR_p(15,2)$	$CR^*(13,2)$
0	1,530	2,190	1,450			1,890
1	2,070	2,260	1,530	2,300	1,710	2,070
2	2,250	2,280	1,530	2,290	2,430	2,250
3	2,430	2,440	1,710	2,430	2,610	2,430
4	2,610	2,540	1,890	2,460	2,610	2,430
5	2,610	2,580	2,070	2,400	2,610	2,610
6	2,610	2,610	2,250	2,390	2,610	2,610
7	2,610	2,620	2,430	2,430	2,610	2,430
8	2,610	2,620	2,610	2,480	2,610	2,610
9	2,610	2,620	2,430	2,510	2,610	
10	2,610		2,430	2,530	2,610	
11			2,430	2,480	2,610	
12				2,580	2,790	
13					2,610	

Experiments

FOOTNOTES

*The author would like to thank the conference participants and an anonymous referee whose comments on an earlier draft were extremely helpful.

1. The same model applies when there is one buyer, who offers to purchase a fixed quantity of some commodity, and more than one seller (supplier). Since there are no substantive differences between the two cases and since interest in this study is in the single seller case, the entire discussion will deal with that case.

2. This was not true in the original experiments since classes with 75 minute periods were available and the experiments were completed well before the end of the class period.

3. The experimental identification is a shorthand device to facilitate the exposition. The first letter indicates the rules (C or D, competitive or discriminative). The second letter indicates the resale conditions (R or F, rectangular or fixed price). The second resale condition is not used in Table 2; it will be used in Table 3. The bracketed order pair indicates first the number of bidders and second the number of bids per bidder. All experiments performed can be described in this way with the addition of the subscripts I (Profit table) and P (prediction) after the second letter and before the parentheses. These terms will be explained later. Therefore, $CF_p(n.B)$ would read "a competitive auction with a fixed resale price in which predictions of the bidding range were made and n persons participated, each being allowed B bids."

4. Ties at the low accepted bid introduce a third uncertainty. This "kind" of uncertainty is considered throughout the study to have no practical significance.

5. For a different view, see Estes (1954).

REFERENCES

Atkinson, R. C., Bowers, C. H., and Crothers, E. V. (1965), *An Introduction to Mathematical Learning Theory*, New York: John Wiley & Sons.

Aumann, R. J., and Maschler, M. (1964), The Bargaining Set for Cooperative Games," in M. Dresher, L. S. Shapley, and A. W. Tucker (eds.), *Advances in Game Theory*, Princeton, N. J.: Princeton University Press.

Becker, G. M., and McClintock, C. G. (1967), Value: Behavioral Decision Theory," *Annual Review of Psychology* 18: 239–286.

Belovicz, Meyer (1967), "The Sealed Bid Auction: Experimental Studies," Ph.D. thesis, Purdue University.

Berelson, B., and Steiner, G. A. (1964), *Human Behavior*, New York: Harcourt, Brace & World.

Brimmer, A. (1962), "Price Determination in the United States Treasury Bill Market," *Review of Economics and Statistics* 44: 178–183.

Carson, D. (1959), "Treasury Open Market Operations, *Review of Economics and Statistics* 41: 438–442.

Chamberlin, E. H. (1948), "An experimental Imperfect Market," *Journal of Political Economy* LVI: 95–108.

Coombs, C. H., and Beardslee, D. (1954), "On Decision Making Under Uncertainty," in R. M. Thrall, C. H. Combs, and R. L. Davis (eds.), *Decision Processes*, New York: John Wiley & Sons.

David, F. N. (1954), *Tables of the Correlation Coefficient*, Cambridge, Eng.: Cambridge University Press.

Edwards, W. (1961), "Behavioral Decision Theory, *Annual Review of Psychology* 12: 473–498.

Estes, W. K. (1954), "Individual Behavior in Uncertain Situations: An Interpretation in Terms of Statistical Association Theory," in R. M. Thrall, C. H. Combs, and R. L. Davis (eds.), *Decision Processes.* New York: John Wiley & Sons.
Feather, N. T. (1959), Subjective Probability and Decision Under Uncertainty, *Psychological Review* 66: 150–164.
Fouraker, L. E., and Siegel, S. (1963), *Bargaining Behavior,* New York: McGraw-Hill.
Friedman, M. (1964), Comment on "Collusion in the Auction Market for Treasury Bills," *Journal of Political Economy* 72: 513–514.
——— (1960), *A Program for Monetary Stability,* New York: Fordham University Press.
Goldstein, H. (1962), "The Friedman Proposal for Auctioning Treasury Bills," *Journal of Political Economy* 70: 386–392.
Halter, A. N. (1961), "Utility of Gains and Losses," in G. L. Johnson and A. N. Halter (eds.), *A Study of Managerial Processes of Midwestern Farmers,* Ames, Iowa: The Iowa State University Press.
Hotelling, H. (1961), "The Behavior of Some Standard Statistical Tests Under Nonstandard Conditions," *Proceedings Fourth Berkeley Symposium Mathematics Statistics and Problems* 1: 319–359.
Joint Economic Committee, Congress of the United States (October 1959), "Constructive Suggestions for Reconciling and Simultaneously Obtaining the Three Objectives of Maximum Employment and Adequate Rate of Growth and Substantial Stability of the Price Level," In *Hearings: Employment Growth, and Price Levels,* 86th Cong., 1st Session: 3023–3026.
Jonckheere, A. R. (1954), "A Distribution-Free k-Sample Test Against Ordered Alternatives," *Biometrika* 41: 133–145.
——— A Test of significance for the relation between m rankings and k ranked categories. *British Journal of Statistics and Psychology,* 1954, 7, 93–100.
Jones, L. V. (1959), "Prediction of Consumer Purchase and the Utility of Money," *Journal of Applied Psychology* 43: 334–337.
Kelly, H. H., Thibaut, J. W., Radloff, R., Munday, D. (1962), "The Development of Cooperation in the 'Minimal Social Situation,'" *Psychological Monographs,* 76, no. 538.
Marschak, J. (1951), "Why 'Should' Statisticians and Businessmen Maximize 'Moral expectation,'" *Proceedings of the Second Berkeley Symposium on Mathematics, Statistics and Problems*: 493–506.
McDonald, J. G., and Jacquillat, B. C. (1974), "Pricing of Initial Equity Issues: The French Sealed-Bid Auction," *Journal of Business*: 37–47.
Meltzer, A. H., and Kinde, von der G. (December 1960), *A Study of the Dealer Market for Federal Government Securities.* Materials prepared for the Joint Economic Commitee, 86th Cong., 2nd Session.
Messick, S., and Brayfield, A. H. (ed.) (1966), *Decision and Choice,* New York: McGraw-Hill.
Mosteller, F., and Nogee, P. (1951), "An Experimental Measurement of Utility," *Journal of Political Economy* LIX: 371–404.
Murphy, J. L. (1963), "Effects of the Theory of Losses on Duopoly Bargaining," Institute Paper No. 59, *Institute for Quant. Research in Economy and Management.*
Rieber, M. (1963), "The Primary Market for United States Treasury Bills," unpublished doctoral dissertation, MIT.
——— (1964a), "Collusion in the Auction Market for Treasury Bills," *Journal of Political Economy* 72: 509–512.
——— (1964b) "Collusion in the Auction market for Treasury Bills," rejoinder, *Journal of Political Economy* 72: 515.

——— (1965), "Some Characteristics of Treasury Bill Dealers in the Auction Market," *Journal of Finance*: 49–58.
Scott, I. O., Jr. (1965), *Government Securities Market*, New York: McGraw-Hill.
Shubik, M. (1959), *Strategy and Market Structure*, New York: John Wiley & Sons.
Siegel, S., and Fouraker, L. E. (1960), *Bargaining and Group Decision Making—Experiments in Bilateral Monopoly*, New York: McGraw-Hill.
Smith, V. L. (1964), "Effect of Market Organization on Competitive Equilibrium," *Quarterly Journal of Economics* 78: 181–210.
———(1965), "Experimental Auction Markets and the Walrasian Hypothesis," *Journal of Political Economy*, 73: 387–393.
——— (1966), "Bidding Theory and the Treasury Bill Auction: Does Price Discrimination Increase Bill Prices?" *Review of Economics and Statistics* 48: 141–146.
——— (1974), "Bidding and Auction Institutions: Experimental Results," Social Science Working Paper No. 71, California Institute of Technology.
——— (1967), "Experimental Studies of Discrimination vs. Competition in Sealed-Bid Auction Markets," *Journal of Business* 40: 56–84.
Thrall, R. M., Coombs, C. H., and Davis, R. L. (eds.) (1954), *Decision Processes*, New York: John Wiley & Sons.
Thurstone, L. L. (1931), "The Indifference Function," *Journal of Social Psychology* 2: 139–167.
Vickrey, W. (1961), "Counterspeculation, Auctions, and Competitive Sealed Tenders," *Journal of Finance*: 8–37.

ON THE NUMBER OF TYPES OF MARKETS WITH TRADE IN MONEY: THEORY AND POSSIBLE EXPERIMENTATION

Martin Shubik, YALE UNIVERSITY

I. INTRODUCTION

This paper explores the number of different market structures that are to be expected under certain reasonable restrictions on the nature of trade, when we construct models of closed exchange economies with trading using a money.[1] In particular we limit ourselves to markets without bargaining, haggling or recontracting mechanisms. A move by a trader will be construed as a bid or offer which is accepted or rejected. The main models presented here have been analyzed using noncooperative game theory (Shubik, 1972; Shapley and Shubik, 1977; Dubey and Shubik, 1976; Shubik, 1976; Shubik, 1977). They are fortunately sufficiently simple in structure that they afford an

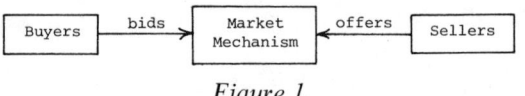

Figure 1.

opportunity for comparative examination by experimentation as well as theory.

2. BIDS, OFFERS AND MARKETS

Consider an economy with m commodities and a money (which may or may not be a commodity). We consider a market to consist of a set of buyers, a set of sellers and a mechanism which matches their bids and offers.

We assume that all buyers and sellers bid simultaneously and independently. Furthermore, no complex contingent bids or offers are considered.

It is assumed that markets are for single commodities and that the method and mechanism of exchange in each market is the same.

A buyer must use money to bid. He may specify a price or accept the market price and he may specify a specific quantity or buy what he can. Limiting ourselves to money payments and to specifications concerning price and quantity to be purchased we have:

2.1. Bids

(a) A Money Bid

A trader i bids an amount of money b_j^i for the jth commodity. He has no reserve price and takes what the market gives him. This provides an extremely simple quantity bid that enables us to construct a mechanism similar to that of Cournot.

The market clearing mechanism will give the trader an amount q_j^i which lies on the hyperbola $p_j q_j^i = b_j^i$ as is shown in Figure 2a (Bid Type 1.1).

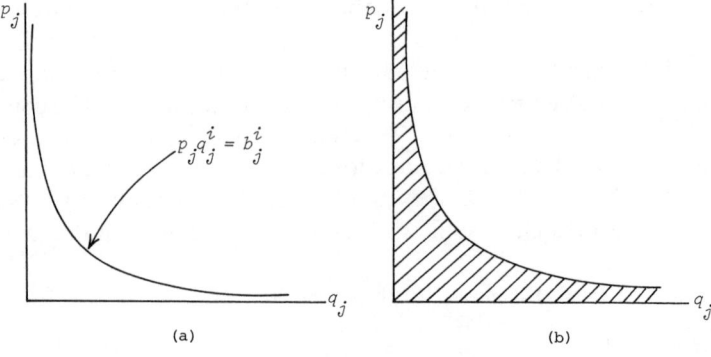

Figure 2.

Table 1

p_j	q_j^i	u.b.	l.b.	none
u.b.				
l.b.				
none				

Suppose that the trader bids b_j^i, but agrees to trade for less than all of the money bid. The feasible set of trades includes the shaded area in Figure 2b (B.T. 1.2).[3]

There are nine minor variations of these two models to take into account whether or not upper or lower bounds are imposed on prices or quantities which will be accepted by the bidder.

These variations truncate the range of the hyperbola.

(b) *The Price-Quantity Bid*

Suppose that a trader offers a price p_j for an amount q_j^i. It is reasonable to expect that he is willing to buy q_j^i for a price less than p_j^i hence the outcomes acceptable to him are indicated by the line AB in Figure 3a (B.T. 2.1).

There is an implicit limit in this bid inasmuch as q_j^i, p_j^i must be less than or equal to the credit line and cash of the individual.

It is possible that the trader will accept an amount less than q_j^i, if he is unable to fill his total order. If he is willing to take a partial fulfilment then any outcome in the shaded rectangle indicated in Figure 3b is feasible (B.T. 2.2).

If the bidder has to expose his bid to the seller (as, for example in an advertisement for purchase) the bid may be at a single price p_j^i for a specific quantity q_j^i (B.T. 2.3) this is shown by the point M in Figure 3b. A single price bid may be for any amount up to some limit. This is shown by the line AM in Figure 3b (B.T. 2.4).

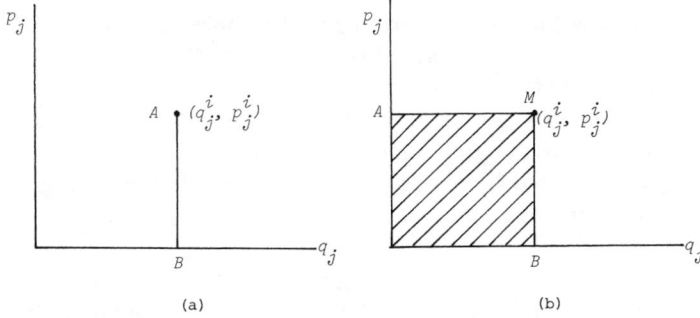

Figure 3.

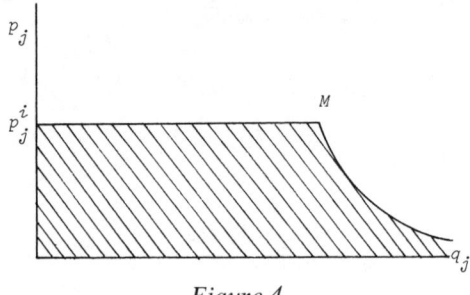

Figure 4.

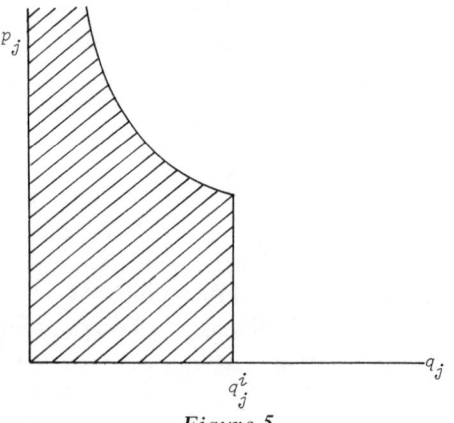

Figure 5.

(c) *The Price Bid*

The trader states a price p_j^i and stands willing to buy any amount he can obtain at p_j^i or less. This has an implicit bound in it as his expenditures cannot exceed his cash and credit. Any point in Figure 4 is feasible. The point M is where the credit constraint becomes relevant (B.T. 3.1).

We can modify this bid by introducing an upper or lower bound on the quantity to be accepted (or both a lower and upper bound).

(d) *The Quantity Bid*

The individual bids for a quantity q_j^i at any price. If credit constraints are introduced this gives the same model as B.T. 2.1.

The trader could bid for q_j^i or less. This gives as a feasible set of outcomes those shown in Figure 5 (B.T. 4.1).

2.2. Offers

The seller or offerer does not have quite the same possibilities as a buyer. It is theoretically possible that he could announce a willingness to sell any

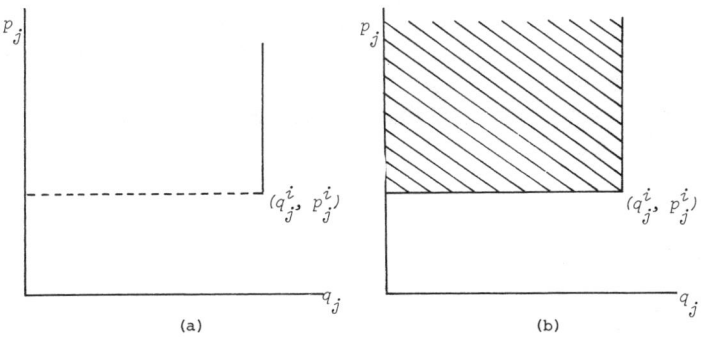

Figure 6.

amount q_j^i at any price p_j^i so long as $q_j^i p_j^i \geq M^i$ where M^i were his monetary requirement. However it appears more reasonable to restrict the seller to price and/or quantity offers of the commodity being sold, whereas the buyer more naturally has bids involving not only price and the quantity of the commodity but also or alternatively the quantity of money.

The seller may offer q_j^i at p_j^i or more. This is shown in Figure 6a (O.T. 1.1). Alternatively his offer could be for the sale of q_j^i or less at p_j^i or more as is shown in Figure 6b (O.T. 1.2).

(a) *The Price Offer*

A seller offers any amount at p_j^i or above. This offer must be modified by the limit imposed by the amount of the commodity he has available. When this limit i imposed we have essentially O.T. 1.2.

If the seller's offer is disclosed ahead of time to the buyer then we may wish to consider a simple statement of price p_j^i. This is shown in Figure 7. The outcomes are restricted to the line AM. Most retail sales involve offers of this variety[4] (O.T. 2.1).

(b) *The Quantity Offer*

A seller may offer q_j^i at any price. This case can be included in O.T. 1.1 by setting $p_j^i = 0$; similarly the sale of q_j^i or less is covered by O.T. 1.2.

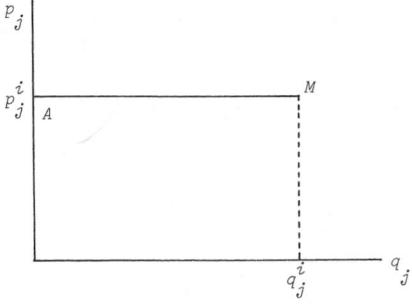

Figure 7.

We may also wish to include the possibility that the trader is required by the rules to offer all of his stock for sale—this leaves him no strategic freedom as a seller: $q_j^i = A_j^i$ (O.T. 3.1).

In a single market with simultaneous moves it appears as if at most the eight types of bids and four types of offers noted can reasonably be considered as inputs to a market clearing mechanism. These are considered further in 2.4 and 4.1.

2.3. Credit Constraints and Transactions Costs

Although eight types of bids and four types of offers have been suggested there are a host of minor variations which depend upon credit conditions and market technology. These conditions appear as ad hoc requirements in any attempt to completely specify "the rules of the game" for any market mechanism.

Several examples of the types of conditions and market details to be covered are given.

(a) *Credit:* An individual may wish to bid beyond his immediate cash resources. He may have to arrange bank credit and bid by certified cheque before his bid is considered valid. The seller in some instances might be willing to extend credit, hence no third party will be required.

(b) *Transactions Costs:* The transportation, storage, display, packing and unpacking of many commodities may be extremely expensive. Ripe tomatoes sent to market which are not sold are essentially confiscated, in the sense that the costs of retrieval may easily exceed worth.

Even a money bid which is not accepted involves costs. The money has been tied up during the market and there may be broker or specialist fees to pay.

2.4. Market Mechanisms and Clearing Devices

From one point of view a market is a function, a mechanism or a transformation which takes in bids and offers and transforms them into purchases and sales at a market price.

Different institutional conditions may be reflected in the sequencing of bids, information and communication. Here however we restrict our enquiry to the three simplest types of single move games. They are (1) where buyers and sellers bid and offer simultaneously and a market mechanism resolves trade; (2) sellers move simultaneously but their offers are disclosed to the buyers before they move, and (3) buyers bid simultaneously, but their bids are disclosed to the sellers before they move.

Let B^i be the set of bids available to buyer i and S^j be the set of offers available to seller j. A market mechanism is a mapping T which transforms the vector of bids and offers $(b_1^1, b_2^1, \ldots, b_m^{n_1}; s_1^1, s_2^1, \ldots s_m^{n_2})$, where n_1 is the number of bidders and n_2 the number of sellers, into a vector of trades and prices.

More precisely, let us consider n individuals where individual i has an endowment A_j^i of good j where $j = 1, \ldots, m$ and an endowment of money of M^i. Let there be m individual markets, one for each commodity j where that commodity is exchanged for money.

It might be a reasonable limitation to assume that individuals are not simultaneously buyers and sellers of the same commodity at the same time. However this rules out the oligopolistic stock market phenomenon of "wash sales" were an individual buys and sells in order to transmit a false signal of market activity. Although this assumption may be convenient for some analyses, in general, it would be preferable to *deduce* the conditions under which an individual is not simultaneously a buyer and seller of the same commodity.

If there are no overall credit constraints each market could be treated independently so that in each market j an individual i would have a set of moves in market j, $B_j^i \times S_j^i$ where a move could be described by a pair (b_j^i, s_j^i). If we wished to assume that an individual is at most a buyer or seller we could add the condition $b_j^i s_j^i = 0$.

In each market j there is a mechanism such that

$$(b_j^1, s_j^1, b_j^2, s_j^2, \ldots, b_j^n, s_j^n; A_j^1, A_j^2, \ldots, A_j^n) \xrightarrow{T_j} \quad (1)$$
$$(p_j^1, p_j^2, \ldots, p_j^n; A_j^1 + x_j^1 - z_j^1, \ldots, A_j^n + x_j^n - z_j^n).$$

This transformation takes all bids and offers and initial holdings in market j into prices, amounts bought (x_j^i) and amounts sold (z_j^i) of all commodities. This also enables us to calculate net changes in money holdings.

A reasonable restriction on the mechanism is that all trade is required to take place at the same price. This requires that $p_j^i = p_j$ for $i = 1, \ldots, n$.

In general we cannot assume that bids in one market are independent of bids in another. There is at least a credit interlinkage which may or may not be independent of the nature of the bids (for example different "margin" requirements may make an individual's credit line a function of his bids). Without credit constraints the set of all moves in all markets for i is:

$$\prod_{j=1}^{m} B_j^i \times S_j^i. \quad (2)$$

With a credit constraint, the size of the set of feasible moves must be appropriately restricted.

2.5. Moves, Strategies and Contingencies

Markets were characterized in 2.4 as devices which map market moves (bids and offers) and initial holdings of goods into prices, a new array of resources and a new set of net balances of money.

A move is *not* in general, the same as a strategy. A strategy is a plan which an individual uses to select his moves as a function of the information available when he is called upon to move.

Limiting ourselves to markets with simultaneous moves by the buyers and sellers and with symmetric knowledge by all about the states of nature, then even though the market clearing mechanism may be complicated and the bids complex, they cannot reflect knowledge of the moves of others. There is no recontracting.

If one set of individuals move first and these moves are announced before the others move then the strategies of the latter group will call for moves to be selected *contingent* on the behavior of the former.

2.6. Information and Search

There have been a considerable number of articles recently on search models of trade where individuals check on different employment opportunities sequentially, or go from gas station to gas station or check sequences of car dealers or house brokers. Rothschild has a survey of some of this literature (Rothschild, 1973).[5]

When these models are viewed from the perspective of markets with strategic traders they are clearly not ones with symmetric information conditions. The search processes are complicated strategies dependent upon what was found out by the potential buyer after having examined offers by some sellers.

For example consider one buyer, wanting to buy a unit of a single commodity facing two sellers. We may imagine that all sellers announce a price simultaneously. The buyer does not know these prices. At a cost of c per inspection he can check on a single price.[6] He then has the choice to buy or to sample again. Suppose the payoff to a seller j is p_j if he sells a unit at price p_j otherwise it is 0. The payoff to the buyer is as follows:

$$P_B = 0, -c, -2c \text{ if no purchase after 0, 1 or 2 searches}$$
$$= K - p_j - c \text{ or } K - p_j - 2c \text{ if purchase from j after}$$
1 or 2 searches (for j = 1, 2).

We may wish to assume that if both sellers have been inspected, then there either is or is not an extra cost to return from the second to buy at the first. In this example assume no extra cost. The game tree below is drawn as if the price bids were discrete.

The sellers simultaneously each set a price. The buyer can opt out with a score of 0 or pay c and decide to find out the price of seller 1, or the price of seller 2. These are represented by the branches 1, 2, 3 at his first move. He then moves again, he can opt out with a score of $-c$ or he can buy obtaining a score of $K - p_1 - c$ or $K - p_2 - c$ or he can obtain more information.

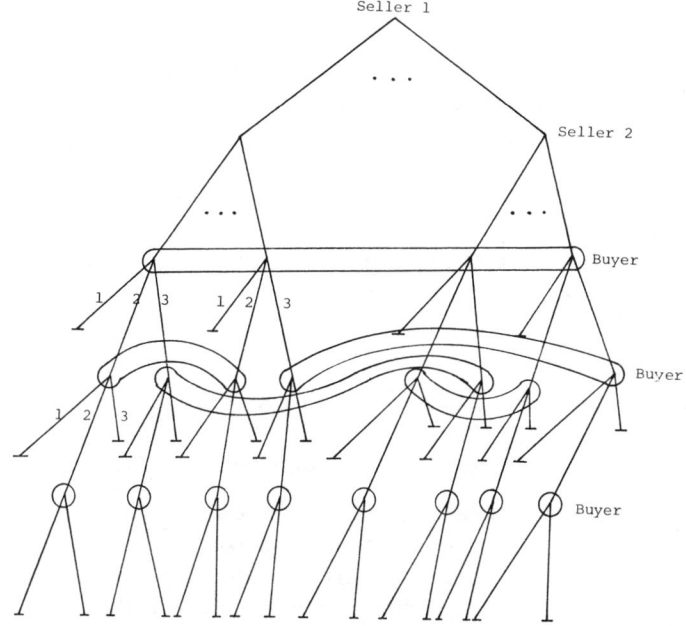

Figure 8.

These are indicated by branches 1, 3 and 2 in his second move. At this third move he has complete information and must abstain from buying which gives him a score of $-2c$ or he can buy and obtain a score of $K - \min[p_1, p_2] - 2c$, (where if $p_1 = p_2$ the buyer randomizes between the sellers).

Assume $K \geq 2c$. Let $\phi(p_j)$ be the probability that seller j charges p_j. The expected payoff to the buyer can be expressed as follows

$$P_B = \begin{cases} K - c - \int_0^\infty p_j \phi(p_j) & \text{if he buys after one sample} \\ -c & \text{if he quits after one sample} \end{cases}$$

$$P_B = \begin{cases} K - 2c - (1 - \Phi(p_j))p_j - \int_0^{p_j} p_i d\phi(p_i) & \text{if he buys after two samples} \\ -2c & \text{if he quits after two samples} \end{cases}$$

where Φ is the cumulative distribution of ϕ.

These type of games provide representations of many interesting problems in marketing. The stress in this paper is not on the solution of specific problems of this variety, but the example shows that on simultaneous strategy markets: the basic feature of markets with search is the nonsymmetry of information conditions, the possibility of the purchase of additional information and the recognition by all parties of the nonsymmetry in the information structure.

In an example such as the one above, when looked at as a game of strategy for all, or even given subjective probabilities for the price policies of the sellers, the buyer has a potentially complex sampling strategy.

In the context of a closed economic system there are some difficult modelling problems to be faced in accounting for the search costs. As the major concern of this paper is with bidding, offers and market mechanisms in general without search costs, these problems are not analyzed any further here.

3. ON DIFFERENT MARKETS

3.1. Stock and Commodity Double Auction Markets

In 2.1 and 2.2 it was suggested that when there is symmetry in strategic information (i.e. bidders and sellers must make their bids on offers in ignorance of each others' moves) there are eight types of bids and four types of offers[7] to consider. Leaving aside minor variants this would give us at most 32 possibilities in any market combining each bid type with an offer type.

The market mechanism must then take these bids and offers into prices and final goods and money distributions. Shubik (1972, 1976), Shapley (1976), Shapley and Shubik (1977) and Dubey and Shubik (1976) have already considered several bidding offering combinations where the mechanism produces one market price in each market.

We can observe that of the 32 combinations many will be extremely similar. In particular for the reason given below we could pick B.T. 1.2 over 1.1, 2.2 over 2.1, 2.3 or 2.4 and O.T. 1.2 over 1.1. This cuts down the combinations to $4 \times 3 = 12$.

The alternatives we may wish to eliminate are the ones in which "all or none" bids or offers are involved. When numbers of traders are few, such bids are difficult to handle by market clearing houses. The similar bids which also accept partial fulfilment of an order are easier to match. However, when numbers of traders are large the difference between the two becomes vanishingly small if the size of the bidders and sellers relative to the market becomes small.

The simplest way to generate a price is to sum the bids and offers and name the price at the intersection. The summation can always be done as the bids and offers are in commensurate units.

We may summarize the surviving bid and offer types and the number of markets as follows:

Bid Type
   Money Bid   B.T. 1.2
   Price-quantity B.T. 2.2 (p or less for q or less)
   Price   B.T. 3.1 (p or less)
   Quantity   B.T. 4.1 (p or less)

Offer Type
   Price-quantity O.T. 1.2 (q or less at p or more)
   Price   O.T. 2.1 (q or less at exactly p)
   Quantity   O.T. 3.1 (sell all)

A 4 × 3 table can be generated using the above to define 12 market structures which we consider below. For convenience we relebel the four types of bids B1,...,B4 and the three offer types O1, O2, O3. The models are numbered as indicated in Table 2. (The extra notation in some of the cells, such as F9 indicates the number of a figure showing a picture of market clearance.

Table 2

	O1	O2	O3
B1	1 F9	2	3 F10
B2	4 F11	5	6
B3	7 F12	8	9
B4	10	11	12 F14

Model 1

The bidders bid a sum of money (or less) and each seller i offers to sell an amount q_j^i or less for a price p_j^i or more. The market clearing house sums bids and offers together and obtains an aggregate supply and demand picture as is shown in Figure 9. Price is set at p_j^*, the volume of a trade at q_j^* and a device for rationing along the supply segment AB must be specified. There are several ways in which rationing can be done. For example, those suppliers whose offers are represented by the segment AB could be selected randomly AM is obtained, or their sales could be prorated.[8]

The model originally suggested by Shubik (1972) is Model 3 which can be regarded as a simplified version of Model 1 where a buyer i offers a sum of money B_j^i and all sellers offer all of their goods with a reserve price of $p_j = 0$. This gives clearance as shown in Figure 10.

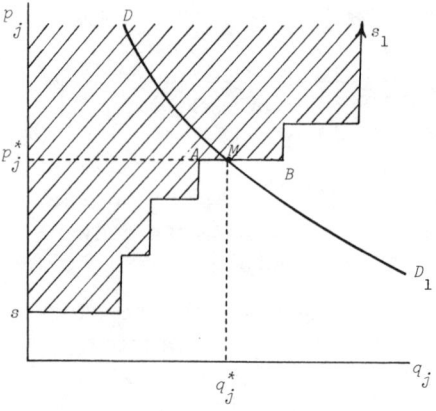

Figure 9.

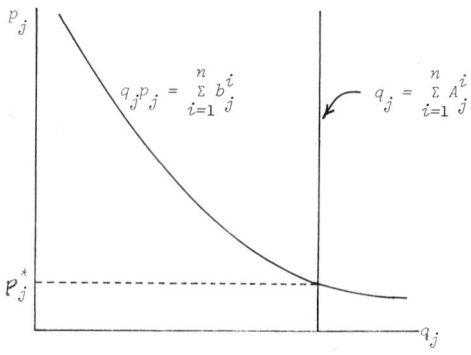

Figure 10.

This market mechanism helps to define a noncooperative bidding game which has a noncooperative equilibrium point arbitrarily close to the competitive equilibrium for a large enough group of traders (Shubik, 1972; Shapley, 1976; Shapley and Shubik, 1977).

Model 4

The bidder i demands an amount q_j^i or less for a price p_j^i or less. A seller k offers an amount q_j^k or less for a price p_j^k or more. The market lines up bids in descending order of price and offers in ascending order as is shown in Figure 11. This model has been discussed in detail in Shubik (1976; 1977) who showed that the competitive equilibria are always noncooperative equilibria. Furthermore for finite numbers a continuum of noncooperative equilibria may exist.

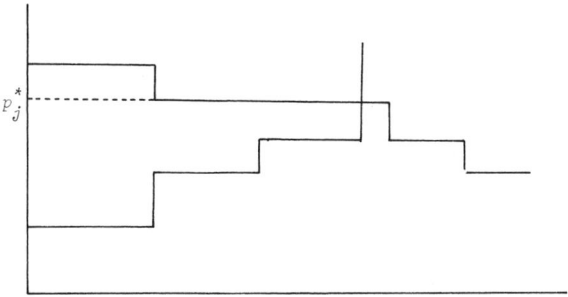

Figure 11.

In this model it is possible that the aggregate supply and bid curves do not intersect. A reasonable convention is to assume no trade during this period. The details of tie-breaking and the possible rationing of marginal bidders or offerers are discussed elsewhere (Shubik, 1976).

Model 7

The bidder i offers to take all he can get at a price p_j^i or less. This bid must be modified by a total amount of credit he has available. A seller k offers q_j^k or less for a price of p_j^k or more. The difference between this and Model 4 is that the aggregate bid curve will have some hyperbolic scallops in it. These are shown in Figure 12.

$Model 10

The bidder specifies the quantity q_j^i (or less) that he is willing to buy at any price. After $q_j^i p_j$ exceeds the money and credit of the bidder the quantity demanded must be scaled back. This is shown in Figure 13 where the location of D_1 is given by summing all of the q_j^i. As the price p_j increases gradually various bidders cannot pay for a full q_j^i demanded thus the hyperbolic scallops appear as demand falls off.

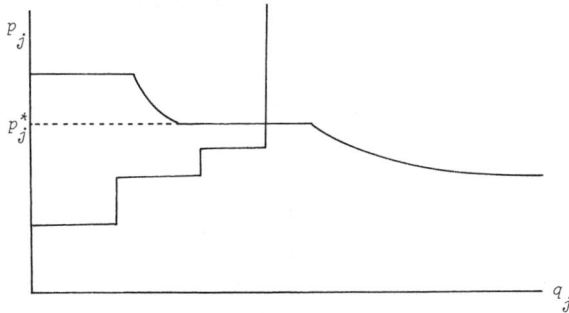

Figure 12

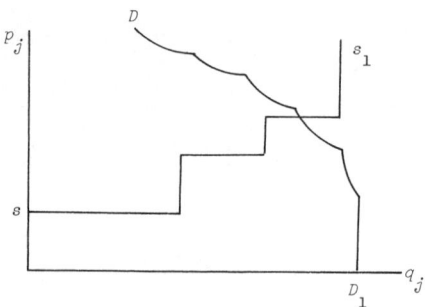

Figure 13.

Model 12

Model 12 is illustrated in Figure 14.

The remaining seven models are not illustrated.

In order to examine with complete rigor the existence of a noncooperative equilibrium and its behavior when the number of traders is large it is necessary to be precise in the definition of the rationing and credit mechanisms. Examples of the level of detail required are given elsewhere (Shapley and Shubik, 1977; Shubik, 1976). It is my belief that with many traders (in the sense of replication of a market) that all of these market models have noncooperative equilibria arbitrarily close to the competitive equilibria; i.e., there are many detailed marketing arrangements which when used as the basis for a noncooperative game with many traders of all types have noncooperative equilibria close to the competitive equilibria of the barter exchange or Walrasian system.

2. Retail Trade

For the most part the symmetry of information condition suggested for the market mechanisms in 3.1 does not hold for retail markets. For many items such as goods in department stores and supermarkets a price is displayed. The customer faces the type of problem noted in 2.6.

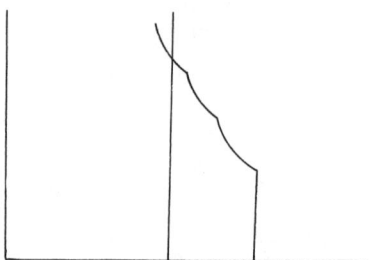

Figure 14.

The purchase of a house or automobile or even other major consumer durables tend to involve both nonsymmetric information and search and face-to-face communication and bargaining. Offers and counteroffers are made, and negotiations frequently break off while the buyer looks elsewhere and the seller deals with other buyers.

The simplest market model where information about the moves of players is not symmetric is where the buyer can see at no cost all of the prices named by the sellers before he has to act.

3. Auctions, Dutch Auctions and Sealed Bids

There is now an extensive literature on bidding and a comprehensive bibliography has been prepared by Stark and Rothkopf (1975). This literature is highly related to the problems discussed in Section 2. The major difference being that for the most part the markets being examined are essentially "open" or onesided. The seller or buyer is assumed as given. The competition is all on one side of the market as among bidders at an auction or contractors making sealed bids in order to gain a contract.

The condition calling for one price for each commodity is not even necessarily true for a simultaneous bid market. For example in bidding for Treasury issues once a market clearing price has been calculated, those whose bids were higher have their orders filled at the higher prices. In open auctions it is not uncommon to have a sequence of identical items auctioned sequentially with different sales prices being obtained for them.

4. MONEY GAMES

1. Market Models and Disequilibrium

The Walrasian auctioneer with his mysterious tatonnement process was not a completely useful simplification in general equilibrium theorizing. By avoiding the specification of exactly how price is to be formed the key element needed for the incorporation of markets, money and financial institutions was thrown away in general equilibrium theory. The possibility for fully appreciating this limitation imposed by the modelling was minimized by using the competitive equilibrium solution concept rather than the noncooperative equilibrium solution concept. The former is nonstrategic and in the search for an equilibrium which is essentially a static concept it is easy to avoid defining the state of the economic system for all positions of disequilibrium. Aggregate excess supply and demand conditions are only hypothetical—they do not serve to ration goods in disequilibrium.

Even though the noncooperative equilibrium solution concept is essentially static; the rigid requirements of game theoretic modelling force us to define a completely explicit model for all positions of disequilibrium. This entails being explicit about price formation in the markets; credit conditions; the sequencing of moves and about the information conditions. Thus although the noncooperative solution is static, the model of the economy is basically dynamic in the sense that it describes a mechanism for the explicit calculation of *all* feasible states of the system.

The mathematical economist approaching the problem of modeling an explicit market mechanism for a closed economic system might at first be horrified in contemplation of a morass of alternatives, each with different institutional overtones. The argument here is that if we require the conditions that bids are simultaneous and that the mechanism must generate only one price for each commodity, then there are only 12 somewhat different reasonable mechanisms[9] with other closely related ones with extra minor differences.

Regardless of which mechanism appears to be the best, the act of modelling with any one of them leads to the construction of closed economic models where the mathematical necessity of well defining the system creates the need for conditions which amount to markets, money, credit and a variety of financial institutions (Shubik, 1975; Shubik, 1978).

2. Dynamics, Adjustment and Institutions

When an economy is in equilibrium, the role of markets, financial institutions and money tends to disappear. The institutions such as organized markets, firms and banks are the carriers of process and a major part of the information and communication flow of an economy. In disequilibrium they appear clearly.

The first understanding of the role of money and financial institutions and where they fit into a general closed economic model, can be obtained with a static solution concept, but a dynamic model. A deeper understanding requires the development of dynamics. Thus, for example, it is likely that the disequilibrium paths of the market models in 3.1 are different even though they might have the noncooperative equilibria which approach the same limit. This can at least be checked experimentally as is noted in Section 5.

The design of financial and economic institutions is intimately related to the way in which we select adjustment processes in any economy. Many different institutions may have the same static efficiency properties, but it is possible that they manifest considerably different dynamic properties. The questions concerning the selection of optimal financial institutions in a fully dynamic context have hardly been asked in a precise form, let alone answered.

5. MODELS OF TWO SIDED MARKETS

1. A Potential for Experimentation

In the last twenty years there has been a small, but important growth in experimental economics as is illustrated by the work of Friedman (1967), Fouraker, Shubik and Siegel (1953), Hoggatt (1967), Siegel and Fouraker (1966), Shubik (1970), Smith (1962; 1965), and many others, as well experimentation devoted specifically to bidding (Stark and Rothkopf, 1975). Virtually all of this work has been devoted to essentially open or "partial equilibrium" models of the economy.

The models suggested in this paper appear to be simple enough to offer the possibility of running experiments with one or two consumer goods and a money in a full "general equilibrium" (or disequilibrium) context. In 5.2, three of the twelve models noted in Section 3 are specified in detail together with the results from the application of noncooperative game theory to them. It is suggested that versions of these models with few commodities are experimentally feasible.

There are several practical difficulties to be overcome, some of these are noted in 5.4.

Most market processes naturally involve money and credit mechanisms. In these models one item is distinguished from the others *strategically*. It is used as a means of payment for the rest. If it has positive worth as a consumer good it can be regarded as a commodity money. If it is merely symbolic, such as paper, then in order to prevent individuals from trying to create an unbounded amount of "paper promises" some form of bankruptcy or "punishment" rule must be introduced. The rules and their effect on the game have been discussed in detail elsewhere (Shubik and Wilson, 1976; Dubey and Shubik, 1977).

2. Three Market Models

In this section three models of trade are described formally and the results of analyzing each via a noncooperative equilibrium theory.

Let $I_n = \{1,\ldots,n\}$ be the set of traders. An initial allocation of trader i is a vector $a^i \in \Omega^{m+1}$ (where Ω^{m+1} is the non-negative orthant of an Euclidean space of dimension $m + 1$). There are $m + 1$ consumer goods, the last of which is used as a money.

A trader i's utility function is real values, concave, continuous and nondecreasing

$$u^i : \Omega^{m+1} \to \Omega^1, i \in I_n.$$

We say that i desires good j if $u^i(x^i)$ is an increasing function of the variable

x^i_j, for any fixed choice of the other variables. We assume that all traders desire money. A trader is "monied" if he has $a^i_{m+1} > 0$.

(a) The Sell All Model

All traders are required to deposit all holdings of their first m commodities at m trading points. Thus post j has:

$$a_j = \sum_{i=1}^{n} a^i_j$$

units for sale

A strategy of a trader is is a vector of m dimensions describing a bid.

$$\bar{s}^i = \bar{b}^i = (b^i_1, b^i_2, \ldots, b^i_m)$$

where

$$b^i = \sum_{j=1}^{m} b^i_j \leq a^i_{m+1}.$$

The payoff to trader i is given by:

$$\prod{}^i(\bar{b}^1, \bar{b}^2, \ldots, \bar{b}^n) = u^i(b^i_1/p_1, \ldots, b^i_m/p_m; a^i_{m+1} - b^i + \sum_{j=1}^{m} p_j a^i_j)$$

where

$$p_j = b_j/a_j.$$

This model is illustrated in Figure 10.

(b) The Holdback Model

A strategy of a trader i is a vector of 2m dimensions describing a bid and an offer:

$$s^i = (\bar{b}^i, \bar{q}^i) = (b^i_1, q^i_1, b^i_2, q^i_2, \ldots, b^i_m, q^i_m)$$

Each trader i, not only has to make a money bid, but he has to decide upon how much he wishes to send to market of his holdings a^i_j of good j

$$\bar{b}^i \leq a^i_{m+1}$$
$$0 \leq q^i_j \leq a^i_j \quad j = 1, \ldots, m.$$

The payoff to trader i is given by:

$$\prod{}^i(s^1, s^2, \ldots, s^n) = u^i(a^i_1 - q^i_1 + b^i_1/p_1, \ldots, a^i_m - q^i_m + b^i_m/q_m,$$
$$a^i_{m+1} - b^i + \sum_{j=1}^{m} p_j a^i_j)$$

where $p_j = b_j/q_j$ (if $q_j = 0$ a special definition of p_j is required (Dubey et al., 1976)).

(c) The Price-Quantity, Bid-Offer Model

The strategy of a trader i is a vector of 4m dimensions describing buying and selling prices and quantities.

For each commodity j a trader i states four numbers $p_j^i, q_j^i; r_j^i, v_j^i$. The first pair is the selling price he is asking and the amount he offers; and the second pair is the buying price he bids and the amount he wants.

$$0 \leq p_j^i, 0 \leq q_j^i \leq a_j^i, 0 \leq r_j^i \text{ and } \sum_{j=1}^{m} r_j^i v_j^i \leq a_{m+1}^i$$

The last condition states that the individual must not bid for more goods than he could pay for if his orders were filled (frequently this condition is not adhered to in actual bidding).

$$\prod^i(s^1, \ldots, s^n) = u^i(x_1^i, \ldots, x_m^i, a_{m+1}^i + \sum_{j=1}^{m} p_j(a_j^i - x_j^i)).$$

Where the p_j are determined by the method shown in Figure 11 and the $(a_j^i - x_j^i)$ represent net trades. The full details of the calculation of market price and allocation of goods are given elsewhere (Shubik, 1976; 1977).

5.3. Noncooperative Equilibria and the C.E.

The analysis of the noncooperative equilibria of the three games noted above has been carried out in a series of papers elsewhere (Shapley and Shubik, 1977; Dubey and Shubik, 1976; Shubik, 1976; 1977). The results are sketched here. For all of these models under replication the N.E.s (noncooperative equilibria) approach the C.E.s. However for few traders the N.E.s of each model differ. In particular the holdback N.E.s are not as efficient as the Sell All basically because the markets are thinner than in the sell all.

In contrast with the other two markets, even for the two traders of every type, the price-quantity, bid-offer model has the C.E.s as N.E.s. It also has a continuum of other N.E.s determined by the maximum excess supply or demand being no larger than the stock of a single individual for any commodity $j, j = 1, \ldots, m$.

5.4. Some Prospects and Problems

Limiting $m + 1$ to 3, i.e. $m = 2$ and using a utility function structure of the form

$$u^i = f(x_1, x_2) + x_3$$

or even simpler such as:
$$u^i = f_1(x_1) + f_2(x_2) + x_3,$$
the three models noted above yield games which are playable and are currently well within the range of experimental controls.

The type of questions which appear to be worth considering are:
(a) how these games are played for m = 1, then m = 2?
(b) how performance in the three games differs?
(c) how the C.E. and N.E. compare as predictors of average or mass behavior?
(d) what happens as the number of traders of different types are increased?

It is worth noting that even with two commodities and two types of traders; say for example
$$u^1 = f_1(x_1^1) + x_2^1$$
and
$$u^2 = x_1^2 + f_2(x_2^2)$$
it is possible to have multiple C.E.s. Shapley and Shubik (1977) have calculated an example of this in detail. As Vern Smith has suggested in a conversation, it would be of interest to consider how players would behave in such a market.

The three models in 5.2 have all been described for a money commodity which is linear and separable in the utility functions of the traders. A new host of models now appear to be within reach of experimentation. These are those noted in 5.1 where credit or paper money is borrowed before bidding and must be paid back after incomes have been received and trade has ceased.

It is my belief that the experimental modeling and analytical approach noted above offers a fruitful way to the development of a mathematical institutional economics blending theory, observation and experimentation.

FOOTNOTES

This work relates to Department of the Navy Contract N00014–76–C–0085 issued by the Office of Naval Research under Contract Authority NR 047–006. However, the content does not necessarily reflect the position or the policy of the Department of the Navy or the Government, and no official endorsement should be inferred.

The United States Government has at least a royalty-free, nonexclusive and irrevocable license throughout the world for government purposes to publish, translate, reproduce, deliver, perform, dispose of, and to authorize others so to do, all or any portion of this work.

The author wishes to thank Professors Schmeidler, Postlethwaite, and Okuno for several valuable conversations.

1. These can also include credit, but for simplicity credit is not discussed further here.

2. The meaning of this will be made clear in 2.5.
3. B. T. stands for bid type.
4. The point to be stressed here is that the information conditions make the more flexible bid (of p_j^i or above) essentially of no advantage over the bid p_j^i. Thus even minute communication or transmission costs rule out the more complicated bid in favor of the simple. Stores do not advertize a radio for sale at "$100 or more."
5. With little reference to marketing or bidding literature.
6. The cost may be a trip or a phone call to a store, for example.
7. Two bids and one offer naming a specific price, which were more natural to nonsymmetric information were also noted.
8. For a full definition of the market mechanism what happens when bids are 0 and/or offers are 0 must be given.
9. When production is modeled a new set of difficulties are encountered owing to the sequencing of moves and the information conditions required by the nature of the production cycle (Dubey and Shubik, 1976).

REFERENCES

Dubey, Pradeep, and Martin Shubik (1976), "Theory of Money and Financial Institutions, Part 28, The Noncooperative Equilibria of a Closed Trading Economy with Market Supply and Bidding Strategies,"

———, ———,(1977), "A Theory of Money and Financial Institutions, Part 35. Bankruptcy and Optimality in a Closed Trading Mass Economy Modelled as a Noncooperative Game," CFDP 448, 2/15/77.

———, ———(1976), "A Closed Economic System with Production and Exchange Modeled as a Game of Strategy,"

Fouraker, L. E., M. Shubik, and S. Siegel (1953), "Oligopoly Bargaining: The Quantity Adjuster Models," University Park, Pa., Pennsylvania State University, RB No. 20. Partially reported in Fouraker, L. E., and S. Siegel, *Bargaining Behavior*, New York: McGraw-Hill.

Friedman, J. W. (1967), "An Experimental Study of Cooperative Duopoly," *Econometrica* 35: 379–397.

Hoggatt, A. C. (1967), "Measuring Behavior in Quantity Variation Duopoly Games," *Behavioral Science* 12: 109–121.

Rothschild, M. (1973), "Models of Markets with Imperfect Information: A Survey," *Journal of Political Economy* 81: 213–225.

Shapley, L. S. (1976), "Noncooperative General Exchange," in S. A. Y. Lin (ed.), *Theory and Measurement of Economic Externalities*, New York: Academic Press.

———, and ———(1977), "An Example of a Trading Economy with Three Competitive Equilibria," *Journal of Political Economy*.

———, and Martin Shubik (October 1977), "Trade Using One Commodity as a Means of Payment," *Journal of Political Economy*.

———(1970), "A Note on a Simulated Stock Market," *Decision Sciences*, 1: 129–141.

———(December 1972), "Commodity Money, Oligopoly, Credit and Bankruptcy in a General Equilibrium Model," *Western Economic Journal* X, 4: 24–38.

———(1975), "The General Equilibrium Model Is Incomplete and Adequate for the Reconciliation of Micro and Macroeconomic Theory," *Kyklos* 28.

———(1976), "A Trading Model to Avoid Tantonnement Metaphysics," in Y. Amihud (ed.), *Studies in Game Theory and Mathematical Economics*, Bidding and Auctioning for Procurement and Allocation, New York: New York University Press, pp. 129–142.

———(May 1977), "A Price-Quantity Buy-Sell Market with and without Contingent Bids," TMFI, Part 22, CFDP.

———(1978), "Beyond General Equilibrium," *Economie Applique*.

———, and Charles Wilson (1976), "Theory of Money and Financial Institutions, Part 30. The Optimal Bankruptcy Rule in a Trading Economy Using Fiat Money," CFDP 424R, 2/9/76.

Siegel, S., and L. E. Fouraker (1960), *Bargaining and Group Decision Making: Experiments in Bilateral Monopoly*, New York: Macmillan.

Smith, V. L. (1962), "Experimental Studies of Competitive Market Behavior," *Journal of Political Economy* 70: 111–137.

———(1965), "Experimental Auction Markets and the Walrasian Hypothesis," *Journal of Political Economy* 73: 387–393.

Stark, R. M., and M. H. Rothkopf (October 1975), "Competitive Bidding: A Comprehensive Bibliography," Mimeographed, University of Delaware.

THE USE OF INDEPENDENTLY SCALED UTILITY FUNCTIONS IN THE EXPERIMENTAL APPLICATION OF GAME THEORY

Rudy V. Nydegger, UNION COLLEGE

The history of the development of the theory of games reveals two practically independent branches. One, dealing with two-person, zero-sum games, has generally approached the area by attempting to compute optimal strategies that offer some protection from an actively hostile opponent. The classical approaches offered by Harsanyi (1956), Isbell (1959), and Nash (1950) are representative of this area. The second branch, dealing with general-sum, two-person games, and with n-person games has been concerned principally with the bargaining among members of coalitions which may or may not form during the course of a game.

Technically speaking, the essential difference between these approaches is that the first is normative, and the second descriptive. Because of the difference in orientation and complexity, there has been, as one would suspect, some difference in the level of success these approaches have shared. The first branch has developed into a generally accepted theory (a few small objections notwithstanding) with principal emphasis upon the development of more efficient algorithms for the computation of optimal strategies. On the other hand, the second branch is beset by an embarrassment of riches—too many conflicting theories, each purporting to describe human behavior.

The general problem of n-person game theory is that there is a set of players $N = 1, 2, \ldots, n$ who can, by forming coalitions, improve their outcomes. That is, players can obtain greater utility by acting together in some fashion than by acting alone. The problem that faces the theorist is specifying which coalitions will form, and how much the members should gain as a result of their inclusion in the coalition. At this point in time a large number of solution concepts have been offered including the following:

1. Von Neumann and Morgenstern's stable sets
2. The Core
3. ψ stability
4. The Shapley Value
5. The Bargaining Set
6. The Kernal
7. The Nucleolus
8. Modifications of the above.

If, in fact, these theories pretend to describe human behavior, why are so many conflicting approaches still holding forth? There are several reasons for this confusing state of affairs. Unfortunately, these theories are both complex and underspecific; the distinctions among them are very subtle and difficult to tease out experimentally. Another problem is that there is a difference in background and approach between the theorists on the one hand, and the experimentalists on the other. The theorists are frequently mathematicians or economists who are concerned with the essential characteristics of the games, and often pay little attention to the content or implications of their models relative to human behavior *in vivo*. Further, these scientists are not ordinarily trained as experimentalists. Finally, the assumptions they make about human behavior are often at variance with those employed by more empirically oriented investigators. For example, in n-person game theory, von Neumann and Morgenstern (1947) assume that utility can be transferred, and that utility functions are linear and increasing. Since, however, they do not allow for interpersonal comparisons of utility, they assume no necessary equivalence of the slopes of the utility functions. Thus, interpersonal comparison of utility are impossible. Regarding two-person bargaining, Nash (1950) also included an axiom specifying invariance under linear transformations of utility, which also precludes interpersonal comparisons. Some theorists (e.g., Kalai, 1975) feel that the classical approaches are too strong on this issue, and suggest alternative ways of approaching the problem. Conversely, social scientists not only allow for and expect interpersonal comparisons to occur, but much of their research *depends* upon the fact that these comparisons are part of the bargaining process.

Furthermore, social scientists frequently use game-theoretic models (e.g., Prisoner's Dilemma) to simulate social situations, and often do not appreciate the formal and/or strategic implications of their research. It is also frequently true that the experimentalist makes the tacit assumption that the formal game theory models are, in fact, complete theories of behavior, and find that subjects rarely behave as the models suggest that they should.

In experimental settings predictions of behavior that are based on the optimization of payoffs, where utility functions are assumed to be linear for payoffs, are often not too successful. For example, in coalition formation studies it is frequently the result that emergent coalitions are more often based upon interpersonal considerations than upon strategic factors such as resources or payoff vectors (Sheers, 1967; Stryker and Psathas, 1960; Vinacke and Arkoff, 1957). There are several reasons for this lack of correspondence between approaches;

(1) subjects may knowingly or unknowingly violate one or more of the assumptions of the model being tested (e.g., attempting to effect interpersonal comparisons of utility);
(2) subjects may not respond to the payoff vectors in the expected way because they are including other aspects of the situation (e.g., being "fair") in their utility functions, which would result in a complex, multidimensional utility function that is not only idiosyncratic for each subject, but likely changes during the course of the game; and,
(3) finally, there are cognitve limits to rationality. That is, some games may be so complex that players cannot respond "rationally" because they cannot process all of the relevant data.

It should be clear that these differences in approach between the theorist on the one hand and the experimentalist on the other are not really "bad"; nor is one perspective superior to the other. However, the goals are often dissimilar, and thus misunderstanding occurs. Is a subject really "irrational" because he refuses to behave in a manner consistent with a particular model? It would seem equally likely that the model may simply not include enough parameters to accurately describe or predict. Furthermore, does the idiosyncratic behavior of a subject invalidate the logic and beauty of an optimal model?

It would seem that both approaches could stand to gain considerably from one another: the theorist by being more involved in experimentation could test and tune descriptive models to make them more powerful; the experimentalists could appreciate more of the formal characteristics and strategic implications of games, in order to add substance and theoretical richness to their work. What is lacking at present is work to develop reasonable correspondence between abstract theory and experimental approaches. This paper describes a series of four experiments that were carried out to begin to develop some correspondence between the two approaches to the study of games.

The first two studies describe work done on two-person, zero-sum games that were devised to test the Nash Axioms of two-person bargaining. The second two studies dealt with a three-person majority game.

SERIES I: EXPERIMENT I.1: AN EXPERIMENTAL TEST OF THE NASH AXIOMS

The first study of this series was based upon the collaboration of the present author (a social psychologist) and a mathematician, and is reported in Nydegger and Owen (1975). The authors felt that approaching game theory in a sound experimental manner must involve both formal and experimental soundness. Further, it was decided that early attempts should be very basic in order to provide a reasonable foundation upon which to grow. Thus, a series of three games was devised to test the Nash Axioms, and to evaluate an alternative model suggested by Smorodinsky and Kalai (1975).

It was assumed that in an abstract setting, each outcome could be represented by two numbers u and v (the respective utilities of Players I and II), yielding a set (S) of all outcomes in the uv plane. The numbers u_0 and v_0 (what Players I and II could obtain independent of any bargaining), and the set S, were the determining factors in the game.

Further, S was assumed to be compact (closed and bounded) or at least bounded above so that the subset S^+ of S which contains all (u, v) satisfying $u \geq u_0$, $v \geq v_0$, is bounded. Further, S is non-empty containing at least (u_0, v_0). Finally, S is assumed to be convex, and if necessary this convexity is to be obtained by joint randomization.

Under the above conditions, Nash (1950) says that a "reasonable" decision rule should assign each triple (S, u_0, v_0) a pair of numbers $F(S, u_0, v_0) = (u^*, v^*)$ which would satisfy the following axioms:

A1. $(u^*, v^*) \in S$ (Feasibility)
A2. $u^* \geq u_0; v^* \geq v_0$ (Individual Rationality)
A3. If there is $(u,v) \in S$, with $u \geq u^*, v \geq v^*$ then $(u,v) = (u^*, v^*)$ (Pareto Optimality)
A4. If S is such that $(u,v) \in S$ whenever $(v,u) \in S$, and $u_0 = v_0$, then $u^* = v^*$ (Symmetry)

A5. If $F(S, u, v) = (u^*, v^*)$, and T is a subset of S such that $(u^*, v^*) \in T$, then $F(T, u_0, v_0) = (u^*, v^*)$ (Independence of Irrelevant Alternatives)

A6. If (S, u_0, v_0) is transformed into (T, w_0, z_0) by linear transformations of the two players utility scales then the solution (w^*, z^*) is obtained from (u^*, v^*) under the same transformation (Invariance Under Linear Transformations of Utility)

Following from these axioms Nash (1950) would suggest a solution represented by a point in S^+ which maximizes the product $(u - u_0)(v - v_0)$ of the increments of utility. These axioms and their implications are discussed more fully in Nydegger and Owen (1975) and in Owen (1968).

A slightly different model has been proposed by Smorodinsky and Kalai (1975) which replaces A5 with a monotonicity axiom, and otherwise leaves the Nash Model intact. While Nash feels that alternatives that do not affect the optimal solution should not influence the outcome, Smorodinsky and Kalai (1975) suggest that if one player's best alternative is not improved, but the other's is not worsened, then the second player should not expect to do more poorly in the modified problem. This concept suggests a solution where the outcome is proportionate to the "best hopes" of both players. Thus, in a situation involving what Nash called "irrelevant alternatives", Smorodinsky and Kalai (1975) would suggest a solution involving the maximal point (u^*, v^*) of the form.

$$u^* = u_0 + t(u_m - u_0)$$
$$v^* = v_0 + t(v_m - v_0)$$

in the set S. Thus, given that $(u_m - u_0)$ and $(v_m - v_0)$ are the best hopes of Players I and II, then their actual gains $(u^* - u_0)$ and $(v^* - v_0)$ should be divided in the same ratio.

To experimentally investigate the Nash Model, and to test it against the alternative model suggested by Smorodinsky and Kalai, a series of three experiments was devised. In the first experiment, the players were simply told that if they could agree on how a small sum of money (two dollars) should be divided between them they could keep the money. While this game seems ridiculously simple, it did allow for the testing of Axioms A1, A2, A3, and A4 in the Nash Model. In this case all ten subject pairs (all of whom were college males) agreed on a 50–50 split, thus adding some experimental credence to the first four Nash Axioms.

The second study was devised to test Nash's Axiom on Independence of Irrelevant Alternatives against the Smorodinsky-Kalai Monotonicity Axiom. Subjects were told as before that if they could agree on how to divide some money they could keep it. The only difference was that they were told that Player A could not receive more than 60 percent of the payoff. Again, all ten subject pairs split the payoff 50–50 in conformance with the Nash Model predictions.

Finally, to test the Nash Axiom on Invariance Under Linear Transformations of Utility, subjects were given 60 poker chips, and were told that if they could decide on how to divide them, they could keep the money they represented. However, they were told that Player A's chips were worth two chips each, and Player B's were worth one chip each. Nash (1950) states that this transformation of utility scales should make no difference to the bargaining, since players have no real way to "know" the value of a given outcome to another player. Thus, the chips should be divided 30–30. However, all ten subject pairs in this experiment opted to split the chips 20–40 to equalize the eventual payoff. Obviously, they did this assuming that their utility functions were the same, and that the value of the money was the same for both of them. Thus, it was concluded that this result obtained because the players attempted to effect interpersonal comparisons of utility. In this particular game the players were faced with a problem because in their minds there were two ways to maximize their outcome: they could opt to maximize efficiency by maximizing the sum of u and v; or they could compare utility functions, assume them to be the same and maximize equity, or $u = v$. In the first two bargaining problems the efficient and equitable point coincided, but this was not true in the third case. If, as Nash suggests, they split the chips 30–30, then Player A would receive 60 cents and Player B 30 cents, which maximizes $u + v = 90$ cents. The subjects by choosing the "equitable" outcome, 20–40 received 40 cents each yielding $u + v = 80$ cents, which is clearly not efficient.

It was felt that when small sums of money are used, it is easier to be equitable, and this was probably a contributing factor in the outcome. However, it was also felt that money provides an easy metric for comparison, and almost "forces" players to effect interpersonal comparisons. This latter conclusion spurred the present author to develop a method for independent utility scaling that would minimize or at least control this problem.

EXPERIMENT 1.2: FURTHER TESTS OF NASH MODEL USING INDEPENDENTLY SCALED UTILITY FUNCTIONS

This study reported in Nydegger (1977) was an exact replication of the first experiment, even to the point of drawing subjects from the same pool (the same subjects were not used, however). The basic problem was to develop a method of utility scaling that would make payoffs dissimilar, but would also allow the construction of a utility scale for each subject that was meaningful, individual, and still allow for the transfer of utility.

The method involved several steps. First, allowing each subject to independently select and preferentially rank a number of payoffs that could be assumed to be of some value to him. Second, involved the assignment of arbitrary values to the items enabling a payoff vector to be constructed for each subject that allowed for the exchange of utility without assuming slope equivalence of players' utility functions. Finally, a bargaining situation had to be developed to allow for the method to be tested.

In this study, poker chips were used to represent single units of utility for each player, but care was taken to explain that the intrinsic worth of each chip was different for each player.

When the two subjects arrived for the experiment they were placed in two different rooms and given a list of 20 prizes ranging in value from 25 cents to $10. They were then asked to choose ten items from the list that they would like to have, and rank-order them preferentially. After having completed this task, they were then asked to value the "best" item at 100 units, and weight the others relative to this, the only requirement being to preserve the ordinality.

After all items were ranked and weighted, each subject had a list of valued items with an underlying scale indicative of their utility for the items. At this point, the subjects were given the instructions of the game, just as in the earlier study, but were also told that they would be bargaining for poker chips worth one unit of value on their scales. Thus, if they wanted an item worth 35 units, they must bargain for 35 chips, etc. They were also told that they had completely different lists, drawn from different prizes of different values, and it would be impossible to know what one chip would be worth to the other player. Further, they were instructed not to discuss or display their lists, nor to combine chips to get one highly preferable prize. At this point the bargaining began.

The results of the bargaining were compared with the first study to determine the effect of the use of the independently scaled utility functions. This was easily done since the players in Experiment 1 had behaved so consistently. Recall that in conditions 1 and 2 all players divided the money equally, effecting 50–50 splits, and substantiating Nash's Axioms A1-A5. In Condition 3 all subject pairs split the payoff 20–40, maximizing equity in terms of eventual payoff at the expense of efficiency, and in contrast to the Nash solution. These findings formed the basis for comparision for the second experiment.

In Condition 1 the payoffs were split between Players A and B at the average rate of 52.50–47.50 which does not differ significantly from the payoff splits in the first experiment ($t_{14} = 1.98$; not significant). This lack of significance obviously does not prove the samples equivalent, but does suggest that the payoffs did vary around the 50–50 point. In fact, five of eight subject pairs used a 50–50 division with the remainder using 45–55, 60–40 and 65–35 respectively.

In Condition 2 the Nash Axiom on Independence of Irrevant Alternatives was tested against the Smorodinsky-Kalai Monotonicity Axiom in the same manner as in the first experiment. Nash would predict a 50–50 split (substantiated by the first experiment) while Smorodinsky and Kalai would predict 37.50–62.50, which is proportionate to the players' best hopes. In the present study players divided the payoffs in the mean ratio if 43.25–56.75. To determine whether or not players in Experiment 1.2 behaved differently from players in Experiment 1.1, the linear distance between the Nash solution (50–50) and the Smorodinsky and Kalai solution (37.50–62.50) was divided in half, and the number of outcomes closest to the early solution was calculated. In Experiment 1.1 all players arrived at the Nash solution, while in Experiment 1.2 there were four outcomes close to the Nash point, and four close to the Smorodinsky-Kalai point. The results of Experiment 1.2 were significantly different from those in Experiment 1.1 (Fisher's exact probability test; $p = .023$), and this difference was due to a shift toward the Smorodinsky-Kalai solution on the part of at least half of the player pairs. Thus it can be concluded that Smorodinsky and Kalai's Monotonicity Axiom is at least as good as the Nash model in predicting subject behavior, and apparently some players do consider their "best hopes" when bargaining.

In Condition 3 the evaluation of Nash's Axiom on Invariance Under Linear Transformations of Utility was made and compared with the first experiment. Whereas all player pairs in Experiment 1.1 chose the 20–40 solution which maximized equity at the expense of efficiency, players in Experiment 1.2 split the chips in the mean ratio of 24.38–35.62. By using the method described above it was determined that four pairs arrived at a solution close to the Nash point, and four arrived at a solution close to the equity point. Thus, these results differed significantly from those in Experiment 1.1 (Fisher's exact probability test; $p = .023$), and were due to a shift toward the Nash solution. This finding not only lends some experimental credence to the Nash Model, but is fairly strong evidence that the method for utility scaling developed for this study does in fact minimize and allow some control over the interplayer value comparisons inherent in most bargaining settings.

There was one problem in comparing the results of these two studies that was not reported in the original research. Since the mean payoff/subject in Experiment 1.1 was about one dollar, and the mean payoff/subject in Experiment 1.2 was about five dollars in gifts, the differences might have simply been due to magnitude of payoff. To evaluate this possibility Experiment 1.2 was replicated with the values of the gifts ranging from five cents to two dollars. Fortunately for the original conclusions, these results were almost exactly the same as for Experiment 1.2. Thus, with even greater certainty it can be asserted that the method for independent utility scaling not only seems to work, but is relatively independent of the magnitude of payoffs.

What, then, do these results mean? It must be pointed out that no model is ever going to be 100 percent descriptive of subject behavior due to the complexity and inherent variability of most response systems. This does not, however, preclude the development of descriptive models that are reasonably powerful and meaningful. The fact that the subjects in the first experiment all behaved the same suggests that the solutions were obvious, and comparison processes so easy to invoke that there was little room for negotiation. The increased variability of responding in the second study is likely reflective of an increased importance placed on the negotiated outcome rather than having strong demand characteristics force a solution.

The conclusions of these two studies can be summarized as follow:
1. The method introduced in the second study apparently does minimize and give some control over interpersonal comparisons of utility;
2. when "irrelevant alternatives" are introduced into the bargaining the Smorodinsky-Kalai model is at least as good as the Nash model in predicting behavior;
3. when interpersonal comparisons of utility are minimized, then linear transformations of utility do not affect bargaining as much as when subjects bargain directly for money.

These findings suggest that further studies need to be carried out to try and determine what role comparison processes actually play in bargaining, and how they could be more fruitfully studied. This led to the second series of experiments.

SERIES II: N-PERSON GAMES

After having looked at the experimental evaluation of a normative model, and the subsequent employment of independently scaled utility functions on a two-person, zero-sum bargaining game, the next step was to begin looking at the n-person case. As mentioned above, n-person game theory, and theories of coalition formation, are replete with a variety of models and solution concepts suggesting many approaches to optimization. The difficulties in testing these approaches were enumerated above, and the current studies were a bit more humble in scope than attempting definitive theory testing. The next series of experiments was devised to lay the groundwork for developing a reasonable technology for approaching the area experimentally without some of the usual problems.

EXPERIMENT II.1: THE NORM OF EQUITY IN A THREE-PERSON MAJORITY GAME WITH SIDE PAYMENTS

This reasearch, reported in Nydegger and Owen (1977), investigated subject behavior in a standard three-person majority game with side payments. It was felt that by providing a setting where predictions from existing models could be made, but where there were no obvious solutions from the subjects' standpoint, a situation would exist that would maximize the likelihood that subjects would rely upon psycho-social rather than strategic considerations in arriving at a solution. This in and of itself is neither new nor surprising, but set the stage for subsequent work.

This game used three players, A, B, and C, and was based on a two-dollar total payoff. Solution only required two of the players to arrive at a decision as to how the money was to be divided. They were told that if A and B chose to split, then they would each get half of the payoff. However, if either A or B decided to split with C, then A or B would receive 40 percent and C would receive 60 percent. At this point the solution seemed obvious until the notion of side payments was introduced. Since there were no power weights or resources, and all subjects were bargaining for was eventual payoffs, then most formal models would predict that any two-way coalition was equally likely.

Due, however, to the confusing bargaining situation, it was predicted that the AB coalition would form first, and that C would attempt to lure A or B away with sidepayments, and then if C were so aggressive as to pit A and B against one another, then they would reject C's overtures and form a coalition that allowed for an easy and equitable split of payoffs. An additional prediction was that by looking at players' attitudes toward one another before and after bargaining there would be a greater change in attitude toward the excluded player than toward the others since there would be a need to justify excluding him after having violated the norm of equity.

This latter prediction derived from several lines of reasoning. Anyone placed in an ambiguous situation is quite likely to look outside himself for cues for appropriate behavior. What generally happens is that norms are generated or adopted to cover the behavior in question and provide an external reference point for determining appropriate courses of action. In American culture a widely held norm is equity, manifested in most aspects of life. Subjects placed in an ambiguous experimental setting would likely grab onto a norm like equity quickly, opt for an easy 50–50 split, and then provide a rationalization for excluding the odd man by changing their opinion of him.

The experimental procedure was quite simple. The subjects were seated around a table, randomly assigned a letter (A, B, or C), and asked to fill out a questionnaire regarding their initial impressions of the other two players. The attitude questionnaire was a 20-item Semantic Differential constructed from items described in Osgood (1952). Then, the players were given the instructions of the game, allowed to bargain, and were again given the Semantic Differential to determine if any change of attitude had occurred.

The results of the bargaining were quite surprising. It was true that the AB split was employed by 15 of 20 triads, while BC was used twice and AC three times, which differed significantly from the rectangular distribution expected by most models ($x^2 = 15.69$; $df = 19$; $p < .001$). However, 13 of the 20 groups opted to use their side payments to pay off the excluded member after the bargaining was completed to form fully inclusive and equitable three-way split. This was neither predicted nor foreseen, but provides even more support for the idea that psychological solutions are likely to be invoked when subjects are unsure of a correct response, and do not stand to either win or lose a great deal of money. In retrospect it was felt that the three-way splits resulted for three reasons. First, there was not much money at risk ($$2.00), and it is easy to be a "nice guy" for a few cents. Second, a three-way split avoided conflict. Finally, if equity was operating, then this was the most equitable payoff since it was equal to each individual player's expected value of return. In fact, two of the seven two-way split groups employed a coin toss to eliminate the third player, so they had the same expected payoff as the three-way groups.

It could be argued that the three-way split is the most logical solution, but there are others who think differently. For example, Gamson (1961) and Riker (1962) both concluded that smaller coalitions are more likely to form than large ones, and in fact suggests that the smallest winning coalition should be the one to form. By looking at power weights or resources one would expect that any two-way split was equally likely. This was not, however, substantiated.

The attitude change scores for included members was compared with excluded members in the two-way splits across all groups and no differences were found. Due to the unexpected finding involving the three-way splits, another analysis was performed. Since the odd man in a three-way group was eventually paid, even though he did have to be initially excluded, there was no motive for changing opinions of him. Thus, the change scores for the third man in the three-way groups were compared with the change scores for the excluded player in the two-way split groups. The finding was in line with the original predictions. There was greater attitude change toward the excluded player in the two-way split groups, than the subsequently included player in the three-way split groups ($t = 1.83$; $df = 19$; $p < .05$; one-tailed). This finding suggests that the norm of equity did in fact play a part in the bargaining, and that violation of that norm provided a motivational basis for attitude change among the players.

This study was interesting in terms of its unexpected results, but resulted in conclusions that were not particularly surprising. That is, when subjects are placed in an ambiguous game setting with unclear solutions, psychological factors are more likely to play a part than strategic ones. Second, when small payoffs are used solution concepts like equity are more likely to be used. Finally, notions like equity imply interpersonal comparison processes which are facilitated by the use of money in payoffs. That is, money is a convenient metric, and makes likely such assumptions as equality of utility functions.

These conclusions led to the next study.

EXPERIMENT II.2: THE USE OF INDEPENDENTLY SCALED UTILITY FUNCTIONS IN A THREE-PERSON MAJORITY GAME

On the basis of the previous study in this series it was safe to assume that there was a push for a "psychological" solution to the three-person bargaining problem, and that this solution implied the use of interpersonal comparisons of utility. In such a three-person game with side payments, and equal resources one would expect that any two-way coalition would be as likely as any other. The authors felt that comparison processes had made it difficult for any individual player to optimize his payoffs. To test this, the same three-person majority game with side payments was conducted with triads composed of subjects drawn from the same pool as those in the previous studies. In this game, however, rather than using monetary payoffs, the subjects each constructed a utility scale as described in Experiment 2 of Series I. Thus, they were bargaining for chips which were worth one unit of utility for each player, and which could be used to buy items from their lists. The range of prices for these items was 25 cents to $7.00.

Unlike the first experiment in this series, only 20 percent (two of ten) of the triads opted to use side payments to effect a three-way division of payoffs, as compared with 65 percent (13 of 20) of the triads in the first study. The remaining two-way splits were as follows: AB four times; AC three times; and BC once. This distribution of coalitions differed significantly from the earlier study ($x^2 = 5.40$; df = 29; $p < .05$), and was much closer to the predictions of many coalition formation models. The mean price for the prizes won for each subject was a little over $3.00.

DISCUSSION

It would appear that several conclusions can be drawn from this series of experiments. First, this method of independent utility scaling apparently minimizes and allows some degree of control over the interpersonal comparison of utilities. Second, when comparison processes are minimized subjects tend to behave more in accordance with the formal models and less in accordance with psycho-social considerations. Third, in an ambiguous bargaining game with low payoffs, subjects are more apt to invoke norms (e.g., equity) to govern their behavior than strategic considerations, and this seems to hold for two-person, zero-sum games, and for n-person games as well. Finally, with respect to the Nash Axioms, it appears that when irrelevant alternatives are introduced into a bargaining situation, the Smorodinsky-Kalai Monotonicity Axiom is at least as good a predictor of subject behavior as the Nash Model.

This latter point raises an important issue. Of what relevance is real behavior to a normative model? Many game theorists are quick to judge human behavior as irrational just because it does not fit an optimal model. Now while idiosyncratic subject behavior does not invalidate the logic of a mathematically derived model for optimizing utilities, the variability of human behavior does not necessarily imply capriciousness. Optimal models can only be generalized to actual behavior insofar as their assumptions meet those under which subjects are operating, and to the degree to which they include the parameters of functional relevance to the behavior in question.

As pointed out above, most normative models assume that utility can be transferred, but that utility scales cannot be compared because they are subjective. In actuality, when people transfer utility they make assumptions about the worth of the transfer to the other party. They may not assume scale equivalence but they behave as if they "know" what the other person's underlying the scale is. Given this state of the world, it would seem logical to devise methods for studying this process so that formal models would have more descriptive and predictive power, and thus possibly greater prescriptive validity.

Simply developing independent utility scales is not enough to accomplish full correspondence between theory, experimentation and application, but it is a start. What was interesting in the above series of experiments, was that by merely minimizing comparison processes, people behaved more like the formal models say that they should. This encouraging result suggests that further work on the transfer of utility can result not only in better methods of testing formal models, but more importantly, in improved correspondence that will result in more applicable and generalizable theories, more substantive and important research, and better prospects for applying these ideas to "real world" problems.

REFERENCES

Gamson, W. A. (1961), "A Theory of Coalition Formation," *American Sociological Review* 26: 373–382.
Harsanyi, J. C. (1956), "Approaches to the Bargaining Problem Before and After the Theory of Games: A Critical Discussion of Zeuthen's, Hick's and Nash's theories," *Econometrica* 24: 144–157.
Isbell, J. R. (1959), "Absolute games," *Annals of Mathematical Studies*: 357–396.
Kalai, E. (1975), "Propositional Solutions to Bargaining Problems," Tech. Rep. No. 179, Northwestern University.
Nash, J. F. (1950), "The Bargaining Problem," *Econometrica* 18: 155–162.

Nydegger, R. V. (1977), "Independent Utility Scaling and the Nash Bargaining Model," *Behavioral Science* 22: 283–289.
———, and Owen, G. (1975), "Two-Person Bargaining: An Experimental Test of the Nash Axioms," *International Journal of Game Theory* 3: 239–249.
———, and ———(1977), "The Norm of Equity in a Three-Person Majority Game," *Behavioral Science* 22: 32–37.
Osgood, C. E. (1952), "The Nature and Measurement of Meaning," *Psychological Bulletin* 49: 197–237.
Owen, G. (1968), *Game Theory*, Philadelphia: Saunders.
Riker, W. H. (1962), *The Theory of Political Coalitions*, New Haven: Yale University Press.
Shears, L. (1967), "Patterns of Coalition Formation in Two Games Played by Male Tetrands," *Behavioral Science* 12: 130–137.
Smorodinsky, M., and Kalai, E. (1973), "Other Solutions to Nash's Bargaining Problems," Tech. Rep. No. 11, University of Tel Aviv.
Stryker, S., and Psathas, G. (1960), "Research in Coalitions in the Triad," *Sociometry* 23: 217–230.
Vinacke, V., and Arkoff, A. (1957), "An experimental Study of Coalitions in the Triad, *American Sociological Review* 22: 406–414.
von Neumann, J., and Morgenstern, O. (1947) *Theory of Games and Economic Behavior*, Princeton, N. J.: Princeton University Press.

Research in Experimental Economics

A Research Annual

Series Editor: **Vernon L. Smith, College of Business & Public Administration, University of Arizona.**

Supplement 1 to Research in Experimental Economics

An Experiment in Non-cooperative Oligopoly

James W. Friedman, University of Rochester and Austin C. Hoggatt, University of California — Berkeley.

                      August 1979   Cloth   225 pages   Institutions: $ 21.50
ISBN 0-89232-122-9   Individuals: $ 12.50

CONTENTS: Preface. An Overview of the Experiment. The Market Model and Experimental Design. The Experimental Designs. Experimental Procedures. Some Global Aspects of Price Choice. The Timing of Price Quantity Changes. The Characteristics of Production Policy. Price Choosing Behavior. A Summary of the Main Results and Comparison with Earlier Experiments. References. Index.

A 10 percent discount will be granted on all institutional standing orders placed directly with the publisher. Standing orders will be filled automatically upon publication and will continue until cancelled. Please indicate which volume Standing Order is to begin with.

JAI PRESS INC., P.O. Box 1285, 165 West Putnam Avenue Greenwich, Connecticut 06830.

Telephone: 203-661-7602   Cable Address: JAIPUBL

OTHER ANNUAL SERIES OF INTEREST FROM JAI PRESS INC.

Consulting Editor for Economics: Paul Uselding, University of Illinois

ADVANCES IN APPLIED MICRO-ECONOMICS
Series Editor: V. Kerry Smith, Resources for the Future, Washington, D.C.

ADVANCES IN ECONOMETRICS
Series Editors: R. L. Basmann, Texas A & M University, and George F. Rhodes, Colorado State University

ADVANCES IN ECONOMIC THEORY
Series Editor: David Levhari, The Hebrew University

ADVANCES IN THE ECONOMICS OF ENERGY AND RESOURCES
Series Editor: Robert S. Pindyck, Sloan School of Management, Massachusetts Institute of Technology

APPLICATIONS OF MANAGEMENT SCIENCE
Series Editor: Randall L. Schultz, Krannert Graduate School of Management, Purdue University

RESEARCH IN AGRICULTURAL ECONOMICS
Series Editor: Earl O. Heady, Director, The Center for Agricultural and Rural Development, Iowa State University

RESEARCH IN CORPORATE SOCIAL PERFORMANCE AND POLICY
Series Editor: Lee E. Preston, School of Management and Center for Policy Studies, State University of New York, Buffalo

RESEARCH IN ECONOMIC ANTHROPOLOGY
Series Editor: George Dalton, Northwestern University

RESEARCH IN ECONOMIC HISTORY
Series Editor: Paul Uselding, University of Illinois

RESEARCH IN EXPERIMENTAL ECONOMICS
Series Editor: Vernon L. Smith, College of Business and Public Administration, University of Arizona

RESEARCH IN FINANCE
Series Editor: Haim Levy, School of Business, The Hebrew University

RESEARCH IN HEALTH ECONOMICS
Series Editor: Richard M. Scheffler, University of North Carolina, Chapel Hill and the Institute of Medicine, National Academy of Sciences

RESEARCH IN HUMAN CAPITAL AND DEVELOPMENT
Series Editor: Ismail Sirageldin, The Johns Hopkins University

RESEARCH IN INTERNATIONAL BUSINESS AND FINANCE
Series Editor: Robert G. Hawkins, Graduate School of Business Administration, New York University

RESEARCH IN LABOR ECONOMICS
Series Editor: Ronald G. Ehrenberg, School of Industrial and Labor Relations, Cornell University

RESEARCH IN LAW AND ECONOMICS
Series Editor: Richard O. Zerbe, Jr., SMT Program, University of Washington

RESEARCH IN MARKETING
Series Editor: Jagdish N. Sheth, University of Illinois

RESEARCH IN ORGANIZATIONAL BEHAVIOR
Series Editors: Barry M. Staw, Graduate School of Management, Northwestern University, and Larry L. Cummings, Graduate School of Business, University of Wisconsin

RESEARCH IN PHILOSOPHY AND TECHNOLOGY
Series Editor: Paul T. Durbin, Center for the Culture of Biomedicine and Science, University of Delaware

RESEARCH IN POLITICAL ECONOMY
Series Editor: Paul Zarembka, State University of New York, Buffalo

RESEARCH IN POPULATION ECONOMICS
Series Editors: Julian L. Simon, University of Illinois, and Julie DaVanzo, The Rand Corporation

RESEARCH IN PUBLIC POLICY AND MANAGEMENT
Series Editors: Colin C. Blaydon, Institute of Policy Studies and Public Affairs, Duke University, and Steven Gilford, Chicago

ALL VOLUMES IN THESE ANNUAL SERIES ARE AVAILABLE AT INSTITUTIONAL AND INDIVIDUAL SUBSCRIPTION RATES. PLEASE WRITE FOR DETAILED BROCHURES ON EACH SERIES

A 10 percent discount will be granted on all institutional standing orders placed directly with the publisher. Standing orders will be filled automatically upon publication and will continue until cancelled. Please indicate which volume Standing Order is to begin with.

 **JAI PRESS INC.**
P.O. Box 1285
165 West Putnam Avenue
Greenwich, Connecticut 06830

(203) 661-7602   Cable Address: JAIPUBL.

Applications of Management Science
A Research Annual

Series Editor: **Randall L. Schultz,** Krannert Graduate School of Management, Purdue University.

The aim of this series is to present original research dealing with the application of management science. The utilization of operations research, management science, decision science and management information system technology in organizations for the improvement of decision making is stressed. The series is essentially a research anthology of original papers that are substantive and may exceed the length limitations of traditional journal articles. The overall editorial mission is to bring management science closer to the arena of business and organizational decision making without sacrificing the quality of models or research results.

Volume 1. December 1979 Cloth Ca. 350 pages Institutions: $ 27.50
ISBN 0-89232-023-0   Individuals: $ 14.00

TENTATIVE CONTENTS: Application of Management Science Techniques to Dental Practice Management, Arnold Reisman, Susumo Morito, Juan Rivand, Hamilton Emmonds, Case Western Reserve University and Edward J. Green, Dental School, Case Western Reserve University. **Stakeholder Management: Case Study of U.S. Brewers and the Container Issue,** Edward Freeman, The Wharton School, University of Pennsylvania. **Towards Formalization of Strategic Planning: A Conceptual Approach,** Arnold C. Hax and Nicolas S. Majluf, Massachusetts Institute of Technology. **Consumer Oriented Transportation Service Planning: Consumer Analysis and Strategies,** John R. Hauser, Alice M. Tybout, and Frank S. Koppelman, Northwestern University. **Forward Algorithms for Forward Thinking Managers,** Thomas Morton, Carnegie-Mellon University. **Acquisition of an Interactive Computing System: Theory and Practice,** Richard E. Nance and John F. Heafner, Virginia Polytechnic Institute and State University. **Managing a Forecasting System,** Robert Leone and Steven C. Wheelwright, Harvard University. **Application of a General Decision Support System to Project Management,** Robert H. Bonczek, Purdue University. **Descriptive Decision Making and Its Application,** Milan Zeleny, Columbia University. **A Stochastic Programming Algorithm for Portfolio Revision: Theory, Computational Implementation and Empirical Results,** J.G. Kallberg and W.T. Ziemba, The University of British Columbia.

A 10 percent discount will be granted on all institutional standing orders placed directly with the publisher. Standing orders will be filled automatically upon publication and will continue until cancelled. Please indicate which volume Standing Order is to begin with.

JAI JAI PRESS INC., P.O. Box 1285, 165 West Putnam Avenue, Greenwich, Connecticut 06830.

Telephone: 203-661-7602   Cable Address: JAIPUBL